French is a syntactically interesting language, and various aspects of its word order and clause structure have triggered a number of important developments in syntactic theory over recent decades. *The Syntax of French* is a concise and accessible guide to the syntax of the modern language, providing a clear overview of those aspects of French that are of particular interest to linguists with cross-linguistic and theoretical interests. A broad variety of topics are covered, including the development and spread of French; the evolution of its syntax; syntactic variation; lexical categories; noun, verb and adjective phrases; clause structure; movement; and agreement. Developing the work of a wide range of scholars, it highlights the important role of French in the development of syntactic theory and shows how French challenges some fundamental assumptions about syntactic structure. An engaging and in-depth guide to all that is interesting about French, it will be invaluable to students and scholars of syntactic theory and comparative linguistics.

PAUL ROWLETT is Head of the School of Languages at Salford University, UK. He is author of *Sentential negation in French* (1998) and *The French language today: a linguistic introduction* (2000).

D1547414

CAMBRIDGE SYNTAX GUIDES

General editors:
P. Austin, B. Comrie, J. Bresnan, D. Lightfoot, I. Roberts, N. V. Smith

Responding to the increasing interest in comparative syntax, the goal of the Cambridge Syntax Guides is to make available to all linguists major findings, both descriptive and theoretical, which have emerged from the study of particular languages. The series is not committed to working in any particular framework, but rather seeks to make language-specific research available to theoreticians and practitioners of all persuasions.

Written by leading figures in the field, these guides will each include an overview of the grammatical structures of the language concerned. For the descriptivist, the books will provide an accessible introduction to the methods and results of the theoretical literature; for the theoretician, they will show how constructions that have achieved theoretical notoriety fit into the structure of the language as a whole; for everyone, they will promote cross-theoretical and cross-linguistic comparison with respect to a well-defined body of data.

Other books available in this series:

O. Fischer *et al.*: *The Syntax of Early English*
K. Zagona: *The Syntax of Spanish*
K. Kiss: *The Syntax of Hungarian*
S. Mchombo: *The Syntax of Chichewa*

The Syntax of French

PAUL ROWLETT

CAMBRIDGE
UNIVERSITY PRESS

CAMBRIDGE UNIVERSITY PRESS

Cambridge, New York, Melbourne, Madrid, Cape Town, Singapore, São Paulo

Cambridge University Press
The Edinburgh Building, Cambridge CB2 8RU, UK

Published in the United States of America by Cambridge University Press, New York

www.cambridge.org
Information on this title: www.cambridge.org/9780521542999

First published 2007

Printed in the United Kingdom at the University Press, Cambridge

A catalogue record for this publication is available from the British Library

ISBN   978-0-521-83532-9 hardback

ISBN   978-0-521-54299-9 paperback

For Danny and Jason

Contents

Preface

This book has two distinct but related goals: broad description and selected theoretical depth. On the one hand, it provides a concise, empirical overview of the syntax of Modern French for the benefit of linguists unfamiliar with the language. While it doesn't rely on readers having any particular theoretical background, it does assume familiarity with traditional grammatical terminology.

On the other hand, it offers in-depth discussion of selected syntactic features of the language which are of particular interest, from either a theoretical or a cross-linguistic perspective. This is of relevance to syntacticians generally, irrespective of their degree of familiarity with, or specific interest in, French: my intention is to show how aspects of French syntax are relevant to syntacticians, whatever their theoretical or language-specific interests. Thus, unlike other English-language books on French syntax, or French linguistics generally, this book isn't specifically aimed at students or researchers with a particular focus on French. If anything, it aspires to take (the syntax of) French beyond its traditional constituency, showing a wider audience how it relates to their concerns.

For the benefit of readers in need of 'raw' data, the discussion is based on an uncontroversial empirical presentation of the facts relating to the syntax of French. For the benefit of theoreticians, the discussion goes on to show how the analytical tools of contemporary syntax have been able to shed light on those facts. Bearing in mind the interests of readers with comparative interests, I concentrate on syntactic aspects of French of cross-linguistic interest. Without making claims of comprehensiveness (this would be unreasonable given length constraints), the book thus has both breadth and depth. The theoretical discussion is couched within contemporary Chomskyan syntactic theory. This is for reasons having to do with my own background, rather than a desire to bang any particular theoretical drum. The purpose of the book is to make clear what's interesting about French syntax and what syntactic theory possibly has to say about it.

The book is structured as follows. Chapter 1 provides the context for the book, charting the development of French generally, and its syntax in particular. The chapter also provides a brief overview of the syntactic framework adopted throughout. Chapter 2 looks at the thematic and morphosyntactic properties of lexical categories. Chapters 3 and 4 discuss the extended functional structure above noun phrases and verb phrases, respectively. Chapter 5 looks at left-clause-peripheral phenomena. Although this book focuses on syntactic issues, reference is regularly (and unavoidably) made to semantics. Readers interested in pursuing semantic matters are referred to the excellent collection of papers in Corblin and de Swart (eds.) (2004).

Book projects like this are rarely to be credited to the author alone, and I'm pleased to be able to record my thanks to a number of individuals and bodies. I would like publicly to express my gratitude for the award of two grants, one from the Arts and Humanities Research Council under the Research Leave Scheme, and another from the University of Salford's Research Investment Fund, without which I wouldn't have been able to take two semesters' study leave from February 2004 to January 2005 to write this book. At Cambridge University Press I would like to thank three of the series' general editors, Ian Roberts, Neil Smith and Nigel Vincent, for their initial encouragement to contribute a volume. I am also aware of my indebtedness to my commissioning editor, Andrew Winnard, whose patience in waiting for me to submit the original proposal, and whose enthusiastic support ever since, have been much appreciated. I would like to extend particularly heartfelt thanks to Adam Ledgeway, who was kind enough to read through an entire first draft of the manuscript and to provide me with very detailed and useful comment. Many improvements were made to the text thanks to his feedback.

Closer to home I am grateful to my colleagues in the School of Languages at Salford for their flexibility and forbearance in covering for me during my 2004–5 absence on study leave. Janet Lloyd deserves special thanks for looking after my administrative responsibilities during this time. I would also like to thank those native-French-speaking friends and colleagues who kindly agreed to remain on my email distribution list and to receive – and respond helpfully to – regular requests for grammaticality/acceptability judgements.

On a personal level, I would like to thank Danny and Jason who, between them, have kept an eye on me at home over the last six years. I can't even begin to imagine how empty life would have been without them, and gladly dedicate the book to them.

Manchester   P. R.
December 2006

Abbreviations and symbols

1/2/3	first/second/third person		NOM	nominative
A	adjective		Num	number
ADV	adverb(ial)		O	object
Agr	agreement		OBL	oblique
APPLIC	applicative		OF	Old French
BCE	before the christian era		P	preposition
C, COMP	complementiser, conso-nant		PERF	perfective
			PI	pronominal inversion
CE	christian era		PL	plural
CI	complex inversion		PRS	present
CL	Classical Latin		PRSPRT	present participle
CL	clitic		PST	past
COND	conditional		PSTPRT	past participle
ConF	Contemporary French		RD	right dislocation
DO	direct object		S	subject
EModF	Early Modern French		SG	singular
F	feminine		SI	stylistic inversion
FP	functional projection		SUB	subject
FUT	future		SUBJ	subjunctive
Gen	gender		T	tense
I, INFL	inflection		UG	Universal Grammar
IMP	imperative		V	verb, vowel
IMPF	imperfect(ive)		VL	Vulgar Latin
IND	indicative		θ	theta role
INF	infinitive		φ	phi feature
IO	indirect object			
IRR	irrealis			
K	case			
LD	left dislocation			
M	masculine			
MidF	Middle French			
ModF	Modern French			
N	noun			
N	neuter			
NEG	negative marker			

1

Introduction

I start by looking at the external history of French (§1.1), the distribution of the language around the world today (§1.2), the internal syntactic history of the language and the major typological features of the modern language (§1.3). In §1.4 I give a taste of what's syntactically interesting about French, both theoretically and cross-linguistically. Finally, I provide a brief overview of the syntactic framework in which the rest of the book is couched (§1.5).

1.1   Development and spread of French

Like all Romance languages, French has its roots in Latin, more particularly the vernacular spoken by the Romans who, in the first and second centuries BCE, colonised Gaul, at the time a predominantly Celtic-speaking area. Over the next five hundred years Celtic gradually gave way to Latin, the language of power, which therefore survived the demise of the Roman Empire towards the end of the fifth century CE. However, as was the case with varieties spoken in other regions of the Empire, the variety of Latin spoken in Gaul had begun to diverge from the Latin of Rome, and this process of divergence accelerated following the loss of the centralising influence of the Empire. Thus, while written Latin remained stable, the vernacular did not.

One major factor determining how the Latin of Gaul developed after the fall of Rome was the invasion of Germanic speakers, who by the end of the sixth century CE controlled most of Gaul. In contrast to the Romans, though, these Visigoths, Burgundians and Franks didn't impose their language on the indigenous peoples. On the contrary, they were willing to adopt much of what they found in their conquered lands, language and religion alike. The period of Germanic–Latin bilingualism which preceded the adoption of the local Romance variety played a significant role in the way the Latin of Gaul developed. A number of features of the invaders' Germanic tongues rubbed off on the local varieties of Latin.

This was most noticeable in the north, which was peripheral to the Empire and occupied by the Germanic hordes first. The social disruption caused by occupation was therefore greatest, while the influence of Rome had been weakest. Conversely, the influence of the Germanic tongues on the local varieties of Latin was least noticeable in the south, where the impact of Roman civilisation had been greatest and lasted longest. It's for this reason that the development of Latin in Gaul formed two distinct dialect areas, a linguistically innovative (that is, more Germanic-influenced) one in the north (the Langue d'Oïl) and a conservative (that is, less Germanic-influenced) one in the south (the Langue d'Oc). And the contrast in terms of innovation and conservation continued into the second millennium CE: the changes which have taken place as the Langue d'Oc has developed from Old Occitan into Modern Occitan aren't as great as those which have taken place as the Langue d'Oïl has developed from Old French (OF) into Modern French (ModF).

The history of Gallo-Romance and French is usually divided in four/five stages. The OF period stretches from 842 (the oldest extant 'French' text, the Serments de Strasbourg, being dated then) to around 1300, Middle French (MidF), from around 1300 to around 1500. Early Modern French (EModF) covers the sixteenth century, only, while ModF stretches from around 1600 to the present day. To capture some of the more recent developments in the language, some linguists recognise a further stage of Contemporary French (ConF). I suggest in §1.4 that ModF and ConF are in fact two contemporary varieties spoken in a diglossic situation.

There was much variation, both dialectally and diachronically within the 450-year-long OF period. The unifying influence of Francian – the variety of the Langue d'Oïl spoken in the Ile-de-France that ultimately developed into what we know today as French – didn't come until the late OF period, around the turn of the thirteenth century. The significant turning point in the history of the language, and the one which arguably led to ModF being as lacking in characteristically Romance features as it is, came at the beginning of the MidF period, as Francian spread throughout Gaul. By the Renaissance, this spread was complete. The EModF period saw the beginning of political unity and a centralised monarchy, and is the time when French was first felt to be a national language and a reflection of national unity. It was also when French was first exported to North America and parts of Africa. Interest in, and concern for, the state of the national language continued and became more systematic in the ModF period. During the twentieth century, the development of a common French, independent of sociolects and dialects can be attributed to the social and geographical mobility which followed World Wars 1 and 2, as well as the development of (tele)communications, especially television.[1]

1.2   French in the world today

Counting the number of French speakers in the world today isn't easy. There are two reasons for this, and neither is specific to French. First, in most places around the planet, people aren't actually asked which language they speak; few countries – not even France! (see Rowlett 2006a) – include questions on language use and proficiency in their censuses. Second, even when people *are* asked which language(s) they speak, their answers aren't always straightforward. Certainly, it's

---

[1] For a sketch of the external history of French see Battye *et al.* (2000: 9–50) and Marchello-Nizia (2003).

difficult to define the notion 'a French speaker' in any meaningful way. In France it's true that 82% of the population are monolingual French speakers with native-speaker competence. Elsewhere in the Francophone world, however, this is the exception rather than the rule. Often speakers don't have native-speaker competence, and might more usefully be called French users rather than French speakers. Significantly, the status and function of French vary widely from one place to another: it may be an official language, vehicular language or vernacular language. So while French may well be used in numerous countries, it's often one of many languages within a multilingual setting, and often not even the dominant language. Thus, the notion 'Francophone country' is doubly problematic. On the one hand, what on the surface might look like a French speaker might in truth have a rudimentary competence in the language, only. On the other hand, it's not even the case that everyone living in a 'Francophone country' has any competence in French at all: there are some 500 million people living in the fifty or so member states (and six observers) of the *Organisation internationale de la Francophonie* (OIF), some three times the size of the world's French-speaking population. The use of the notion 'Francophone country' in estimating the size of the world's French-speaking population isn't therefore as straightforward as it might seem.

Despite the difficulty inherent in the enterprise, estimates of the number of French speakers in the world have been produced. The most recent edition of the report *La francophonie dans le monde* (Haut conseil de la francophonie 2005) speaks of 175 million *francophones* worldwide of whom sixty million are *francophones partiels*. Gadet (2003: 146–8, using sources dating from 1997) catalogues 142 million *francophones réels* and a further sixty-three million *francophones partiels*. Between 100 and 110 million people are learning French as a foreign language. French is thus the tenth or eleventh most widely spoken language in the world. Within international organisations like the United Nations (14% of speeches delivered to the General Assembly in 2001) and the European Union (30% of original documents produced by the European Commission), French is second only to English.

Nevertheless, official circles are clearly concerned at the potential international decline of the language, and the OIF has launched a *Plan d'urgence pour la relance du français dans les organisations internationales* 'Emergency plan to re-establish French within international organisations' and a *Plan pluriannuel d'action pour le français en préparation de l'élargissement de l'Union européenne* 'Multiyear plan of action in support of French in preparation for the enlargement of the European Union'. The OIF is also endeavouring to work closely with organisations promoting the use of Spanish and Portuguese, in order to defend multilingualism within international organisations, and cultural diversity more generally (Rowlett 2006a).[2]

---

[2] For details of the geographical distribution of French around the world see, for example, Battye *et al.* (2000: 2–9), Rossillon (1995) and Walter (1988). For recent trends see Haut conseil de la francophonie (2005). On the linguistic situation of French within France see

1.3   Evolution of French syntax

Classical Latin (CL) was, like Proto-Indo-European, overwhelmingly (S)OV. While CL had long been thought to have free word order, non-(S)OV orders were in fact marked and used for pragmatic effect. As expected from a typological perspective, CL used (synthetic, morphological) postdetermination: it had three noun classes (M, F, N), five nominal declensions, six nominal cases, but no prenominal articles; in verb syntax CL had four verbal inflection classes (plus one mixed class), fifteen simple verb paradigms (giving non-defective verbs up to eighty-five distinct finite forms and at least another nine non-finite forms), but was pro drop. Synthetic future, perfect and passive verb paradigms were available; comparative and superlative adjectives bore synthetic suffixes. However, even within CL, there were indications of typological changes to come: the adverbial sentential negative marker NON was preverbal rather than occupying its typologically expected postverbal position.

In Vulgar Latin (VL) innovation was widespread, with shifting patterns of basic word order and a move from postdetermination to (analytic, syntactic) predetermination. The three-way noun-class system was simplified into a two-way distinction, with the loss of the neuter; two of the five nominal declensions were also lost; the case distinctions were weakened by phonetic erosion, leading to an increased reliance on prepositions, especially DE and AD, to mark case distinctions. VL also developed prenominal articles, derived from the demonstratives and the numerals. CL's synthetic future/perfect/passive verbal paradigms and comparative/superlative adjectives were replaced by analytic ones. The verbs had a postposed auxiliary; the adjectives, a preceding adverbial.

VL and early Romance shifted away from CL in terms of basic word order, too. First, (S)OV moved to a TVX pattern of sentence-initial topics (rather than subjects), and verb-second (in the case of Gallo-Romance possibly a Frankish influence). Clause-initial phrasal constituents of various classes could provide the pragmatic link to the preceding discourse. Unless it was a topic, the object formed part of a pragmatically ordered postverbal sequence of constituents. However, TVX was vulnerable because the kind of evidence required by children to ensure its acquisition wasn't readily available. For a child unambiguously to arrive at a TVX model of clause structure, clauses need to be available with (a) overt subjects and (b) non-subject topics (Roberts 1993). Yet OF was still optionally pro drop, and topics and subjects often coincided. Thus, the TVX status of early Romance was far from robust and ultimately doomed. Consequently, the preverbal topic position regrammaticalised as the subject position: TVX → SVX (see Li and Thompson's 1976 notion of the subject as the grammaticalised topic). By the fifth century CE, SVO was widespread (particularly in subordinate contexts). Thus, verb-final had become verb-medial and SVO provided the unmarked word order for early

Rowlett (2006a).

Romance. Much of the broad picture of the evolution of late Latin into early Romance and modern Romance – the functional load shifting from morphology to syntax, from synthesis to analysis – can be attributed more or less directly to the typological OV → VO shift in basic word order (Marchello-Nizia 2003).

By the MidF period, the typological shift from postdetermination to predetermination had taken firm hold. The preverbal position had become increasingly regrammaticalised as the position of the subject. The spoken language had lost several person/number markers on finite verb forms, meaning that preverbal subject proforms were now an essential marker of subject φ features (a later resurgence in pro drop was due to Italian or Latin influence). Topicalised constituents could still precede the preverbal subject, but this was via the innovative device of left dislocation, which meant that they had a separate intonational contour and often co-occurred with a core-clause-internal resumptive proform. Crucially, there was no longer any systematic inversion, so the finite verb no longer occupied its characteristic second position (except residually in clauses introduced by such adverbials as *peut-être* 'maybe' and *sans doute* 'doubtless') (Kroch 2001). Unmarked TVX word order was thus lost, replaced by SVO core-clause word order, with a pragmatically activated left periphery. Small levels of residual verb-final structures are attributed to Latin influence.

As for nominal structure, the ongoing development within Latin and into Gallo-Romance saw the decline of the nominal case system (Vincent 1997). OF had just a two-way NOM–OBL distinction (*li chevaliers* NOM ~ *le chevalier* OBL 'the knight'; *li chevalier* NOM ~ *les chevaliers* OBL 'the knights'). The loss of case distinctions was accompanied by the rise of articles: definite *le* and *la* developed from demonstrative ILLUM and ILLAM and indefinite *un* and *une* from the numerals UNUM and UNAM during the fourth and fifth centuries.

Apart from in the pronominal system, the NOM–OBL distinction showed up on M nouns and adjectives, only, and later (around 1200 onwards) even this was lost, with the NOM being discarded in favour of the now multi-purpose OBL. Concomitantly, basic word order became increasingly fixed, and the use of determiners spread further. Determinerless nouns had been possible in generic or vague contexts, but definite and, later, indefinite articles were used here, too. From the fourteenth century onwards the articles were grammaticalised as default nominal markers rather than semantic markers of (in)definiteness. The spoken language lost the PL -*s* and F -*e* suffixes; prenominal articles were thus important markers of number and gender.

The loss of case distinctions also led to changes in the expression of dependency relations. Within nominals, the morphological genitive gave way to preposed dependants (*l'autrui joie* 'the joy of others'), as well as various strategies involving postposed dependants (*la fille le duc* 'the duke's daughter', *la fille a un roi* 'the daughter of a king', *la mort de Rollant* 'R.'s death').

The general OV → VO shift, together with the loss of word stress and its replacement with phrase stress, had a significant consequence for pronominal structures, specifically object proforms (Boucher 2003). Previously preverbal, the stressed object proforms became postverbal, as expected. However, the fact that object proforms don't need to be stressed (typically, they encode old rather than new information) meant that the preverbal position didn't lose its object proforms altogether. Rather, a separate, *un*stressed set of object proforms survived preverbally, forming a phonological unit with the verb. Thus, the Latin object proforms survive as two distinct sets in Romance. This was particularly strong in French (for example, ME > unstressed preverbal *me*, stressed postverbal *moi*), as opposed to the other Romance languages (cf. Spanish and Italian where unstressed object proforms are sometimes postverbal), because French also lost pro drop: the preverbal position of unstressed *object* proforms allowed them to cluster with the increasingly compulsory unstressed *subject* proforms.

The development of sentential negation within French correlates nicely with the OV → VO shift, too. As we have seen, CL marked sentential negation using the negative adverbial NON, but in the unexpected preverbal position, a fact which suggests that a typological shift was already underway; certainly, there was no new shift in the behaviour of NON in VL. Rather, NON suffered the same morphosyntactic fate as the object proforms. Like the proforms, NON split into stressed and unstressed forms (*non* and *ne*, respectively); and as with the object proforms, unstressed *ne* was restricted to preverbal position (where it, too, formed a phonological unit with the verb), while its stressed counterpart (*non*) enjoyed considerable syntactic freedom. In OF *ne* was sufficient to mark sentential negation on its own. Increasingly, though, there was a problem: unlike the object proforms which, as replacements for discourse-familiar constituents, typically encode old as opposed to new information, the negative marker is very high in information content. This was problematic in that the division of labour between *ne* and *non* meant that sentential negation was marked by *ne*, the very negative marker which was incompatible with stress, and was squeezed in between a preceding (pro)nominal subject and a following object-proform(s)-plus-verb cluster. In order to highlight sentential negation, therefore, *ne* came increasingly systematically to be reinforced by postverbal elements, which could be stressed. This trend has now gone so far that *ne* is no longer capable of marking sentential negation on its own, and one particular postverbal negative reinforcer, *pas*, preferred in Francian, has become the default negative marker. Indeed, the weakening of *ne* is now such that its very presence in preverbal position is under threat, arguably since it prevents subject and object proforms from forming a single preverbal pronominal cluster.

Turning to the syntax of interrogatives, OF had no specific morpheme marking yes–no questions, although a marked verb-initial word order was available, involving inversion of the verb around a (pro)nominal subject. ('Inversion' is still possible with pronominal subjects, but was lost in the context of nominal subjects in the sixteenth century.) As for wh questions, fronting of the wh phrase, with the verb again inverted (but now in second position), was also possible early on. The interrogative marker *est-ce que* was available from the twelfth century in wh questions as an alternative to verb-second. Initially, *est-ce que* was perceived as a pragmatically marked, syntactically complex sequence, involving inversion (*c'est que → est-ce que*). Uninverted wh + *c'est que* + SVO was also possible, as was wh + *que* + SVO. From the fourteenth century, however, *est-ce que* was seen as an atomic unit, and it expanded into yes–no questions around the fifteenth and sixteenth centuries. Significantly, atomic *est-ce que* has the attraction of allowing interrogation to be marked without disturbing SVO word order in the core clause. The French pattern known as complex inversion arose, not surprisingly, in parallel with the loss of simple inversion around a nominal subject, from the phenomenon dating from the fifteenth to seventeenth centuries of left dislocating the inverted pronominal subject (*Jean, est-il parti?* 'Has J. left?'). Reanalysis as a core-clause-internal phenomenon, and the loss of the comma intonation, resulted in the modern construction (*Jean est-il parti?*).

The EModF and ModF periods, because of the growing symbolic role of French as a reflection of national unity, saw growing concern about the state of the language spill over into interference with it. The official guardian of the language (within France, at least), the *Académie française*, was set up in 1635 and coincided with something of an obsession with *le bon Usage*. Of relevance here is the fact that some of the syntactic features of the modern standard language can, at least in part, be attributed to rulings by this artificial linguistic authority, rather than being the result of a natural evolution. For example, while concessive conjunctions previously happily introduced either IND or SUBJ subordinate clauses, the *Académie* decided that they should select the subjunctive, only. Conversely, while bridge verbs (of saying or thinking) originally also selected either IND or SUBJ dependent clauses, they were later ruled by the *Académie* to take the indicative, only (unless they appeared in negative or interrogative clauses). Theoretical syntacticians therefore need to be wary of how much relevance they attach to mood distinctions.

The orthographic representation of morphology hasn't gone untouched, either. The phenomenon of present-participle agreement, for example, was the subject of interference in 1679, when the *Académie* decided (by ten votes to six!) that present participles like *aimant* 'loving' should agree with their subject in structures like *une femme aimante* 'a loving woman', but not in structures like *une femme aimant ses enfants* 'a woman loving her children' (Klare 1998: 136). Section 2.3.2 shows how the artificial (irrelevant) orthographic rules relating to adverbial *tout* mask an underlying (relevant) phonological simplicity. And §2.2.1.4 suggests that orthographic norms imposed on imperative verb forms introduce a red herring of a complication. With past-participle agreement, too, care is needed. The (mostly but not entirely exclusively orthographic) phenomenon was introduced during the EModF period, in line with the pattern found in Italian. Now, given the structural similarities between the two languages, it's plausible that the phenomenon of past-participle agreement introduced in French reflects a valid underlying syntactic feature. Indeed, theoretical syntacticians have used the (im)possibility of past-participle agreement to support analyses of syntactic structure. However, if we aren't careful, we can be led astray by spelling conventions: recent orthographic reform of the 'rules' governing past-participle agreement might otherwise be taken to indicate a change in the syntax of structures involving the causative verb *laisser* and subnominal *en₂* 'of it'. Such a conclusion would clearly be implausible. Thus, to the extent that, in a language like French, syntacticians look to the orthographic representation of otherwise phonologically non-overt morphological agreement for clues to syntactic structure, they need to be cautious.[3]

1.4   Syntactic interest of French

Should linguists be particularly interested in French? One reason for concluding that they should comes from the fact that, over the last half-century, the language has provided much of the empirical base which has triggered developments within theoretical syntax, particularly among researchers with comparative interests:

- the phenomenon of rightward quantifier float inspired Sportiche's (1988) work on the VP-internal subject hypothesis, an approach now extended to all thematic lexical items;
- auxiliary selection in Italian and French was at the heart of Perlmutter's seminal work on unaccusativity in the late 1970s;
- the contrast between verb–adverbial order in French and adverbial–verb order in English, as well as the syntactic differences between finite and non-finite verb forms in French, led to Emonds' (1978) analysis of V movement and Pollock's seminal (1989) work on the split-INFL hypothesis, approaches to clause structure which led directly to Cinque's (1999) massively exploded and hierarchical analysis of core-clause structure;
- contrasting noun–adjective orders in various Germanic and Romance varieties, including French and English, led to the parallel approach to nominal structure in terms of a strictly ordered hierarchy of functional categories and cross-linguistically varied degrees of N movement (Bernstein 2001);
- broader issues having to do with nominal-internal architecture and the distribution of formal features have usefully been investigated on the basis of the behaviour of French determiners;
- Pollock's (1989) idea that polarity is associated with a dedicated functional head/projection, Neg(P), was based largely on French bipartite negation;
- Kayne's (1975) seminal work on French clitics, including his classic tests for clitichood, led to much subsequent work within generative syntax on clitics;
- finally, our understanding of clause-initial phenomena such as wh fronting and subject–verb inversion has benefited greatly from consideration of some very recalcitrant facts from French, first because French doesn't fit neatly within the traditional distinction between wh-movement and non-wh-movement languages, and second because French patterns of inversion appear very different to those found in modern Germanic.

---

[3] For more detailed overviews of the development of French syntax see Harris (1978), Posner (1997: 198–214, 344–418) and Rickard (1989: 8–17).

Thus, the syntax of French has much to offer linguists, even those not crucially interested in the language per se.

Quite apart from factors like those set out above, there's another reason to be interested in the syntax of French: the phenomenon of syntactic variation. Relevant here isn't so much the use of *on* instead of *nous* for 1PL subjects, the omission of negative *ne* in the expression of sentential negation or the omission of impersonal *il*.[4] Rather, of relevance is the idea that there's something much more significant and syntactically interesting going on. It's sometimes claimed that there's been no significant syntactic change in French since the end of the seventeenth century, and that the label ModF reflects a three-century-long period of grammatical stability. However, as the book progresses, we'll see evidence that to talk of stability is to massively oversimplify the situation with a convenient sociopolitical fiction hiding a degree of variation which suggests that two distinct grammatical systems co-exist, each with its own properties, in a situation of diglossia. Thus, ModF (Massot's 2003 *français classique tardif*, Bernstein's 1991 *literary French*), the conservative variety taught in schools, is distinguished from ConF (Frei's 1929 and Zribi-Hertz's 1994 *français avancé*, Raymond Queneau's *néo-français*, Massot's 2003 *français démotique contemporain*, Bernstein's *colloquial French*), the more innovative vernacular learnt in the home. Gadet (1997) characterises ConF in terms of a *séquence progressive*, fixed word order, analyticity, invariability, but *not* simplification. Some linguists have gone so far as to suggest that the degree of innovation which has occurred in the vernacular is such that ModF is no longer a coherent or psychologically real variety (Bauche 1926; Côté 1999). For others, the variation found within French is to be explained by concluding that speakers switch, on the basis of sociosituational factors, between two grammars, which differ from each other in a number of quite specific ways, for example:

- the status of number marking within nominals (§3);
- the pragmatic status of the canonical subject position (§5.3);
- the locus of the feature marking yes–no interrogatives (§5.7).

From such a perspective, what looks superficially like sociolinguistic variation along a continuum is code-switching between the two grammars, and possibly amounts to an extended period of change in progress.

1.5   Theoretical framework

I round off this introductory chapter with an overview of the theoretical framework assumed in the book. The formal discussion throughout is couched within contemporary Chomskyan syntactic theory (Chomsky 1991; 1993; 1995a, b; 2000; 2001; 2005).

---

[4] For an accessible discussion of variation within French see Battye *et al.* (2000: 257–310) and Walter (1998). Particularly useful in this context is Gadet (1997: part three, syntax).

Lexical items are drawn from the (lexicogrammatical) lexicon as (more or less complex) bundles of phonological, semantic and formal (morphosyntactic) features. The grammar builds structures which allow the morphosyntactic requirements expressed by the formal features of lexical items to be satisfied. The grammar does this with two generalised, iterable, structure-building mechanisms, Merge and Move. Each combines two syntactic objects into one, allowing a feature of one (the dependant, or argument) to satisfy a requirement expressed by a feature of the other (the head, or functor). They differ with respect to the relationship between the functor and the argument: with Merge the functor and the argument are two independently existing syntactic objects; with Move the argument is (the copy of) a subpart of the functor. The formal mechanism relating a functor with an argument is Checking.

Thus, in (1) X is a predicate (a noun, a verb or an adjective[5]) associated with a lexical argument structure, that is, a number of θ roles each of which needs to project in syntax. This is possible by the intermediary of a θ head. X therefore needs a θ head, and this need is satisfied by merging with $\theta°$. Since $\theta°$ is underspecified for any particular θ role, it needs access to a lexical argument structure. This need is satisfied by X moving to $\theta°$. The [X $\theta°$] complex can now assign a θ role, and does so by merging a dependant as a left-branching specifier. [X $\theta°$] then checks its θ role against SpecθP. θP is an extended projection of X, in the sense of Grimshaw (1993). Phrases generated by Merge are thus binary branching, endo-centric and antisymmetric (Kayne 1994).

(1)

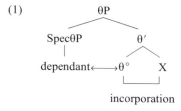

incorporation

Merge and Move are driven by (and therefore dependent on) the existence of a functor, that is, a syntactic object whose feature composition expresses a need (for an argument). If the inherent semantic structure of X includes no thematic grid, then no θ head is merged and no dependant either. More generally, a syntactic object whose formal-feature composition doesn't encode the need for an argument is, by definition, not a functor, and won't merge with an argument. The only way such a syntactic object is able to merge at all is as an argument (of some other functor). If the thematic grid of X contains more than one argument, then the structure in (1) is augmented by as many θP shells as are needed to provide a specifier position for

---

[5] There's an ongoing debate as to whether lexical items already bear categorial features when they are drawn from the lexicon, or whether categorisation is a by-product of the derivation (Borer 2005a, b). For ease of exposition, I assume that lexical items are marked for category from the outset.

each required dependant. The relationship between X and its multiple dependants is articulated by successive incorporation of X into a hierarchy of θ heads, whereby each θ head in turn merges a unique dependant as specifier. The order in which the θ heads (and the dependants) merge is determined by a thematic hierarchy encoded in Universal Grammar (UG), as in (2):[6]

(2)   Thematic hierarchy:
       Agent>Beneficiary>Recipient/Experiencer>Instrument>Theme/Patient>Location

Thus, the way a predicate's arguments are projected in syntax is predictable from the predicate's lexical semantics; there's a transparent mapping from (lexical) semantics to (underlying) syntax (Fillmore 1968; Larson 1988), and argument-realisational verb classes are epiphenomenal, the result of the combination of more basic elements of meaning (Levin and Rappaport Hovav 2005: 16, 18).

This approach to the relationship between a lexical predicate and its thematic dependants means that the familiar categories of noun phrase, verb phrase and adjective phrase are over-simplistic. The minimal domain containing X and X's thematic dependants isn't XP, but rather X augmented by one or more θPs. To avoid confusion, I shall use the notation NP*/VP*/AP* to refer to this lexico-thematic complex. This approach to θ-role assignment also means that thematic dependants only ever merge as specifiers;[7] they can't be complements. Thus, direct objects and dependent clauses are merged as specifiers rather than complements. The complement position is restricted to a grammatical (rather than a thematic) dependency.

Clausal architecture is divided into three broad domains. The lowest is the thematic VP*. The middle domain, traditionally labelled inflection phrase (IP, headed by INFL), encodes the inflectional properties of verbs (such as tense, mood, aspect and polarity) and the semantic relationship of predication. The highest domain of the clause, traditionally labelled complementiser phrase (CP, headed by COMP), articulates the relationship between IP and its broader context, both the pragmatics of the discourse and the syntax of any matrix clause. It's here that the information structure of the clause is encoded in terms of topic–comment and focus–presupposition. Much work over the last two decades suggests that, like the thematic VP* shell, IP and CP are actually much more complex than the single projections they were once thought to be. They are intricately articulated hierarchical structures, each containing a number of projections whose order is determined by UG. Consequently, as with VP* (and NP* and AP*), the labels IP* and CP* are

---

[6] Different versions of the thematic hierarchy have been proposed, and this has prompted Newmeyer (2002: 65) to comment as follows: 'There is reason for strong doubt that there exists a thematic hierarchy provided by UG. That seems to be the best explanation for the fact that after over three decades of investigation, nobody has proposed a hierarchy of θ roles that comes close to working.' See Levin and Rappaport Hovav (2005: ch. 6).
[7] This means that Mark Baker's (1985; 1988) Universality of Theta-role Assignment Hypothesis (UTAH) is trivially true.

convenient shorthand for *domains* within clause structure rather than *individual* projections:

(3) $[_{CP*} \ldots [_{IP*} \ldots [_{VP*} \ldots$

The detailed internal structure of IP* has been the focus of attention since Pollock's (1989) proposal to split I°, previously seen as the host of all inflection features, into distinct T(ense) and Agr(eement) heads, augmented by an intervening Neg(ation) head. The potential of the split-INFL hypothesis is most fully realised in Cinque's (1999) massively exploded INFL, comprising an extensive hierarchy of tense, mood and aspect heads, all UG ordered in the same way as the thematic heads in (2). The value of Cinque's approach to IP* is explored in §4.

The idea of an exploded COMP is exploited in most detail in Rizzi (1997): the once monolithic C° is recast as a number of functionally specific heads, each potentially projecting a full phrasal structure, which express the pragmatic force of the clause (declarative, interrogative, imperative, exclamative) and its morpho-syntactic status (finite, non-finite) as well as providing the locus for such discourse information-structure notions as focus–presupposition and topic–comment. Rizzi's CP* structure is exploited in the discussion of dislocation and focus fronting in §§5.3, 5.4.

The same approach as that sketched above for clause structure has also been applied to nominals: a thematic NP* shell is augmented, in turn, by two hierarchi-cally organised grammatical domains articulating, first, morphosyntactic features such as number and gender, and, second, discourse notions such definiteness, reference and case. The labels Cl(assi)f(ier)P(hrase)* and D(eterminer)P(hrase)* are used to indicate that these are domains above NP* rather than individual phrases:

(4) $[_{DP*} \ldots [_{ClfP*} \ldots [_{NP*} \ldots$

The parallel approach to clausal and nominal structure has been exploited in analyses of the syntax of adverbials and V movement on the one hand, and adjectives and N movement on the other. Work going back to the late 1970s has shed light on hierarchical clause structure, and a picture has emerged of the assumption that clause-internal phrasal elements like adverbials occupy essentially functionally determined fixed specifier positions, while verbs undergo more or fewer instances of movement into/through functional heads (Emonds 1978; Pollock 1989; Cinque 1999):

(5)   a. Principle: Adv_F (an adverbial with function F) occupies SpecFP (the specifier of a functional projection whose head bears formal feature F) within a univer-sal hierarchy of functional projections above VP*.
       b. Parameter: a verb raises overtly through more or fewer functional heads.

Such an approach neatly accounts for Cinque's (1999) conjecture that adverbials of various classes are subject to universal ordering constraints with respect to one another, but that verb placement within an ordered array of adverbials is subject to parametric variation. The N-movement approach to the relative order of nouns and nominal-internal phrasal elements like attributive adjectives transfers this assumption about adverbials in extended VP* structure to adjectives in extended NP* structure (Scott 2002):

(6)   a.   Principle: A_F (an adjective with function F) occupies SpecFP (the specifier of a functional projection whose head bears formal feature F) within a universal hierarchy of functional projections above NP*.

       b.   Parameter: a noun raises overtly through more or fewer functional heads.

Assuming this approach is justified, (5) and (6) can be seen as two trivial variants of a single pattern:

(7)   a.   Principle: $A(dv)_F$ occupies SpecFP above NP*/VP*.

       b.   Parameter: a lexical head raises overtly through more or fewer functional heads.

In the remaining chapters of the book, I discuss the morphosyntax of lexical categories, the extended structure of nominal and clausal constituents, and the (essentially pragmatic) properties of the left periphery. Further relevant details of the theoretical framework adopted are provided as necessary.

2

___

Lexical categories

In this chapter I outline the morphosyntactic and thematic properties of nouns (§2.1), verbs (§2.2), adjectives/adverbials (§2.3) and prepositions (§2.4). In each case, I begin by considering syntactically conditioned inflectional morphology. With nouns and verbs, this prepares the ground for the discussion of extended noun phrases and verb phrases in §3 and §4, respectively. I turn then to the syntactic projection of thematic structure. I show how empirical details can be elegantly captured on the basis of the kind of UG-determined thematic shells proposed in §1.5.

2.1   Nouns and noun phrases

Nouns are simple (*maison* 'house') or complex. The internal structure of complex nouns is discussed in §2.1.1. Nouns bear abstract gender and number features, which are sometimes overtly marked (§2.1.2). The syntactic realisation of nominal argument structure is discussed in §2.1.3. Discussion of extended nominals is postponed until §3.

2.1.1   Complex nouns

Complex nouns are head initial. They can be:

– N1–N2 compounds:

(1)   a.   centre-ville   b.   porte-fenêtre
             centre-town   door-window
             'town centre'   'French window'

The compound noun *centre-ville* is relational (*centre* bears a relation (part–whole) to *ville*); the compound noun *porte-fenêtre* is equative (*porte* is being equated with *fenêtre*).[1] In both cases, N2 functions like an intersective attributive adjective

___

[1] Equative N1–N2 compounds like (1b) are firmly established in the language, and clearly motivated. According to Goosse (2000: 119) the examples in (i), in which N2 is equated with N1 metaphorically rather than literally, illustrate an innovative kind of equative N1–N2 compounding which emerged in the late twentieth century:

(§2.3.1), necessarily having a distinguishing role.[2]

– N1-*de* ('of')-N2 compounds:

(2)   chemin de fer
       path of iron
       'railway'

N1-*de*-N2 compounds behave differently from non-compound N1-*de*-N2 structures (for example, *preuves d'innocence* 'proof of innocence'). The various differences set out in (a)–(e) below show that compounds form tighter syntactic units than non-compounds:

(a) post-N attributive AP*s (§3.7) necessarily follow N1-*de*-N2 in compounds, but can follow N1 in non-compounds:

(3)   a. [chemins de fer] <u>français</u>   b. [preuves] <u>totales</u> d'innocence
          paths of iron French   proofs total of-innocence
          'French railways'   'conclusive proof of innocence'

(b) similarly, the locative reinforcers -*là*/-*ci* '(t)here' used with demonstratives (§3.2.2) follow N1-*de*-N2 in compounds, but can follow N1 in non-compounds:

(4)   a. ces [chemins de fer] <u>là</u>   b. ces [preuves]-<u>là</u> d'innocence
          these paths of iron there   these proofs there of-innocence
          'those railways'   'that proof of innocence'

(c) clefting (§5.5) of *de*-N2 is possible in non-compounds but not in compounds:

(5)   a. C'est <u>d'innocence</u> [que je cherche des preuves –].
          it-is of-innocence that I seek of.the proofs
          'It's innocence that I'm searching for proof of.'

        b. *C'est <u>de fer</u> [que je cherche le chemin –].
          it-is of iron that I seek the path

(d) N1 can be ellipsed in non-compounds, but not in compounds:

(i)   a. poste-clé   b. solution-miracle
          post key   solution miracle
          'key position'   'miracle cure'

[2] The necessarily distinguishing role of N2 underlies the contrasting grammaticality of (ia) and (ib):

(i)   a. son grand-père ingénieur   b. *son père ingénieur
          his great-father engineer   his father engineer
          'his engineer grandfather'   'his engineer father'

Since an individual has two grandfathers, N2 can serve to distinguish one from the other in (ia); in contrast, an individual has just one father, so N2 in (ib) has no distinguishing role (Bouchard 2003: 68–9).

(6)   a.   Je veux des preuves, et non seulement [– d'innocence].
           I want of.the proofs and not only of-innocence
           'I want proof, and not just (proof) of innocence.'

      b.   *Je veux des chemins, et non seulement [– de fer].
           I want of.the paths and not only of iron

(e) *de* N2 can be pronominalised as *en*$_1$ 'of it/them' (§4.4.3) in non-compounds, but not in compounds:

(7)   a.   J'en cherche des preuves.   b.   *J'en cherche des chemins.
           I-of.it seek of.the proofs   I-of.it seek of.the paths
           'I'm looking for proof (of innocence).'   (Jones 1996: 206)

There are also morphological differences. For example, the irregular PL *yeux* 'eyes' of *œil* 'eye' (§2.1.2.2) is found with non-compound *œil de N* forms but not with compound *œil de N* forms:

(8)   a.   des <u>yeux</u> de séducteur   (non-compound)
           of.the eyes of seducer
           'seducer's eyes'

      b.   des <u>œils</u>-de-bœuf/chat/perdrix/pie/tigre   (compound)
           of.the eyes of beef/cat/partridge/magpie/tiger
           'bull's eye windows/cat's eyes/soft corns/eyelets/tiger's-eyes'

For further discussion of nominal-internal *de* see §3.6.

– N1-*à* ('to, at')-N2 compounds:

(9)   verre à vin
      glass to wine
      'wineglass'

– V–N compounds:

(10) a.   ouvre-boîte   b.   grippe-sou   c.   taille-crayon
           open-can   grab-penny   trim-pencil
           'can opener'   'penny pincher'   'pencil sharpener'

– P–N compounds:

(11) a.   après-midi   b.   avant-bras
           after-midday   before-arm
           'afternoon'   'forearm'

– A–N compounds:

(12) a.   haut(-)fourneau   b.   petit-ami
           high-oven   little-friend
           'blast furnace'   'boyfriend'

– N-*à* 'at'-V$_{inf}$ compounds:

(13) a. machine à laver   b. fer à repasser   c. machine à tisser
machine to wash   iron to iron   machine to weave
'washing machine'   'iron'   'loom'

Compounds differ from syntactic N-à-V$_{inf}$ sequences like (14) in terms of the argumental relationship between N and V$_{inf}$:

(14) chemise à laver
shirt to wash
'shirt to be washed'

In compounds N is understood as the subject of V; in non-compounds N is understood as the object.

The varying degrees of closeness between the component parts of complex nouns can be reflected in the orthographic representation. The least close relationship is reflected by writing the compound as unhyphenated separate words: *haut fourneau*. A closer relationship is represented with hyphenation: *centre-ville*. A particularly close relationship can be reflected by writing the compound as a single word: *autoradio* 'car radio'.[3] Orthography is, however, merely indicative, and there's some variation: *mange-tout* vs. *mangetout*; *haut fourneau* vs. *haut-fourneau*. If the varying degrees of closeness in the relationship between the parts of a compound represent a cline of lexicalisation, and if orthography is an (imperfect) reflection of that closeness, then such variation is expected to exist, and to move in a specific direction over time, namely, from separation, to hyphenation, to fusion.

2.1.2 Nominal inflection

Common count nouns bear gender (§2.1.2.1) and number (§2.1.2.2) features; common mass nouns bear gender, too (on number in common mass nominals see §2.1.2.3). Some proper nouns bear gender and number features (*Le Limousin* M.SG, *Les Pyrénées* F.PL), especially those which are derived from common nouns (*Le Pays* M.SG *de Galles* 'Wales', *Les Landes* F.PL), while others bear neither (*Paris*, *Adidas*). Where gender and number are both marked and distinct, gender marking appears closer to the stem than number marking: *étudiant-e-s* [student.F.PL] 'female students' (§3).

2.1.2.1 Gender

Nouns are assigned one of two genders, unmarked M and marked F. With animate nouns, gender is typically semantically motivated (*taureau* M 'bull', *vache* F 'cow'; *enfant* 'child' M or F depending on the sex of the referent), yet *sentinelle* 'sentry' is F and *mannequin* 'model' is M, despite the sex of the individuals to whom

---

[3] While such forms will in time likely be reanalysed as simple nouns, they are presumably still compounds while PL marking (§2.1.2.2) appears on both parts of the compound: *les autosradios* 'car radios'.

these labels typically refer. Where animate (and some non-animate) nouns come in morphologically related M–F pairs, M is typically unmarked while F bears the suffix -e: *étudiant* [etydjɑ̃] ~ *étudiante* [etydjɑ̃t] 'male/female student'.[4]

With non-animate nouns, gender is typically arbitrary, often simply inherited from Latin and acquired as a lexical feature. There's variation, though: some nouns have changed gender over time (*horloge* M→F 'clock', *ombrelle* M→F 'parasol', *enzyme* M→F 'enzyme', *synopsis* F→M 'synopsis'[5]); others have either gender (*après-midi* M/F 'afternoon', *emmerde* M/F 'problem'); with others there's dialectal variation (*pli* M 'trick (in card games)', *acétate* M 'acetate' and *pétale* M 'petal' are sometimes used as F, while *abscisse* F 'abscissa' is sometimes used as M).[6] Finally, a small number of ambigenous nouns are M in the SG, F in the PL: *l'amour* M.SG 'love' ~ *les amours* F.PL 'love affairs', *le délice* M.SG 'delight' ~ *les délices* F.PL 'delights'.[7]

The gender of non-animate nouns is sometimes predictable on the basis of (orthographic or morphological) ending. For example, all nouns ending in orthographic *-um* or *-reau* are M (*rhum* 'rum', *bureau* 'office, desk'), as are those ending in the suffix *-age* (*mariage* 'marriage'). The F nouns *plage* 'beach', *cage* 'cage' and *image* 'image' aren't exceptions because *age* here is part of the stem rather than a suffix.

Since complex nouns (§2.1.1) are head initial, *centre-ville* 'town centre', for example, is M because *centre* 'centre' is M, even though *ville* 'town' is F. V–N compounds are typically M by default (§2.1.2.3) since their head, a verb, doesn't bear an inherent gender feature (*ouvre-boîte* M 'can opener'). However, some erstwhile V–N (and N–V) compounds have been fully lexicalised as simple F nouns (*garde-robe* M → *garderobe* F 'wardrobe'; cf. *garde-boue* M 'mudguard'; *sangsue* F 'leech, blood sucker' lit. 'blood-suck'). (See footnote 3.)

2.1.2.2 Number

Count nouns bear a two-valued number feature, unmarked SG or marked PL. Mostly, the value of number is motivated, although some discrete SG objects have PL number (pluralia tanta) (*les lunettes* F.PL '(pair of) spectacles'), and a number of abstract mass concepts have PL number (*les arrhes* F.PL 'deposit').

PL is typically marked orthographically by *-s* (*plage* ~ *plages* 'beach(es)') or,

[4] For details of the orthography and phonology of gender marking on French nouns see Battye *et al.* (2000: 146ff.).
[5] On the basis of some very idiosyncratic agreement rules, Judge and Healey (1983: 269) conclude that the erstwhile F non-count PL *gens* 'people' 'has become nearly entirely masculine, but not quite'!
[6] Queffélec (2000a: 786) gives examples of speakers from the Maghreb using French nouns with their Arabic genders.
[7] This is problematic and many speakers treat such nouns as M. The standard pattern poses problems for structures like *un(e?) de mes plus grand(e?)s amours* 'one of my greatest loves'.

more rarely, -x (*bijou* ~ *bijoux* 'jewel(s)'). Exceptionally, nouns whose SG form is *s*, *x* or *z* final have zero PL marking (*vis* 'screw(s)', *noix* 'walnut(s)', *nez* 'nose(s)'). The numeral *mille* 'thousand' is invariable (*deux mille ans* 'two thousand years'), while *cent* 'hundred' takes orthographic PL -*s* provided it's numeral final (*deux cents ans* 'two hundred years' ~ *deux cent_ dix ans* 'two hundred and ten years'). More radically, some -*ail*- and -*al*-final nouns mark PL with -*aux* (*travail* ~ *travaux* 'work(s)', *cheval* ~ *chevaux* 'horse(s)'). The PL of *œil* 'eye' is *yeux* (but see examples (8b) on page 16); the word *ail* 'garlic' has two plurals, *ails* and *aulx*, as does *aïeul*: *aïeuls* 'grandfathers' and *aïeux* 'ancestors'.

PL isn't usually marked orally on nouns themselves (*plage* [plaʒ] ~ *plages* [plaʒ] 'beach(es)'). Rather, it's marked on the nominal as a whole, which usually means it surfaces on the determiner (§§3.2, 3.4). However, with the -*ail*/-*al*~-*aux* pairs ([tʁavaj]~[tʁavo]), as well as with the two pairs *bœuf* [bœf] ~ *bœufs* [bø] 'bull(s)' and *œuf* [œf] ~ *œufs* [ø] 'egg(s)', number is marked on the noun itself. Similarly, SG *os* 'bone' [ɔs] is distinguished from the homograph PL *os* 'bones' [o]. And even where PL isn't overtly marked on a noun's citation form, it can reappear in some phonological contexts, for example, through liaison (Battye *et al.* 2000: 109–12):

(15) a. une plage intéressante
[ynplaʒɛ̃teʁesɑ̃t]
'an interesting beach'

b. des plages intéressantes
[deplaʒɛ̃teʁesɑ̃t]
'interesting beaches'

Number marking in complex nouns varies. With N1–N2 compounds a clear logic underlies usage: with relational N1–N2 compounds PL marking usually appears on N1 (*timbres-poste* 'postage stamps'), while with equative N1–N2 compounds it typically appears on both N1 and N2 (*canapés-lits* 'sofabeds'). Apparent N1–N2 compounds in which PL is marked on N2 alone (*auto-écoles* 'driving schools') are rare, and arguably aren't N1–N2 compounds at all.[8] Despite the logical pattern of (orthographic) PL marking, given the absence of oral marking, there's considerable room for variation, and official bodies have sometimes felt the need to meddle with usage. Orthographic PL marking in V–N compounds (§2.1.2.2) is similarly variable: *porte-savon(s)* (lit. 'carry-soap(s)') 'soapholder(s)', *chauffe-eau* (lit. 'heat-water') 'boiler(s)'.

The status of [NUMBER] on nominals is the first point at which the grammars of ModF and ConF (§1.4) might be thought to diverge. Much evidence suggests that PL marking on nominals is unstable. First, and perhaps most significantly and as already noted, most nouns aren't phonologically marked for number. Second, even where there are morphologically regular subpatterns of overt number marking, not all candidate nouns follow the pattern. For example, not all -*ail*/-*al*-final SG nouns have -*aux*-final plurals: *bal* ~ *bals*/*baux* 'ball(s)'. (The form *baux* [bo] is in fact

---

[8] For example, the head of *auto-école* is *école*, which is unexpected in a compound. Under an analysis in which *auto*- is, instead, a prefix, PL marking and right-headedness are both expected. A similar analysis might be appropriate for *autoradio* 'car radio'. (See footnote 3.)

the irregular PL of *bail* 'lease'.) Third, in common with other languages, speakers are sometimes uncertain as to the PL of infrequently occurring irregular nouns. With *yeux*, the PL of *œil* 'eye', speakers hesitate when using PL in non-liaison contexts: *les yeux* [lezjø] 'the eyes' ~ *quatre yeux* [katʁ(?z)jø] 'four eyes', and intrusive liaison is sometimes found. (And again, see examples (8b) on page 16.) Given that *ail* 'garlic' is usually either treated as a mass noun (*de l'ail* 'some garlic') or counted in terms of heads or cloves (*deux têtes/gousses d'ail* 'two heads/cloves of garlic'), the two plurals of *ail* 'garlic' (*ails/aulx*) are so rare as arguably not to be part of the active language. Uncertainty can lead to overregularisation (Pinker 1995) which, in French, means no overt number marking at all, for example, *chacal* ~ *chacaux/%chacals* 'jackal(s)'. The irregular PL *vaux* of *val* 'valley' is poetic or archaic in comparison with the overregularised *vals*; it appears in the fixed expression *par monts et par vaux* 'on the move' but is otherwise rare. Furthermore, even the pattern illustrated in (15), whereby the latent PL marker on nouns (and adjectives; §2.3.1) surfaces in liaison contexts, is absent in ConF (Massot 2004):

(16) a. soldats̲ italien̲s̲ et américain̲s̲   b. [sɔldaz̲italjɛ̃z̲eameʁikɛ̃]   (ModF)
          soldier.PL Italian.PL and American.PL   c. [sɔldaitaljɛ̃eameʁikɛ̃]   (ConF)
          'Italian and American soldiers'

The theoretical significance of the contrast in (16b, c) is taken up in §3.

2.1.2.3 Default gender and number

Default gender is M; default number is SG. The unmarked nature of M gender is evidenced by its use with mixed M–F combinations:

(17) [Jean et Marie], il̲s̲ sont content̲s̲.
      J. M and M. F they.M.PL are happy.M.PL
      'J. and M. are happy.'

M is also used for constituents with no inherent gender feature: (a) nouns created from infinitives (18a); (b) V–N compounds (18b); (c) clausal constituents (19):

(18) a. manger 'to eat' →   le manger   b. le tire-bouchon
          eat.INF   the.M.SG eat.INF   the.M.SG pull-cork
          'to eat'   'foodstuff'   'the corkscrew'

(19) [Qu'il t'aie appelé] est intéressant.
      that-he you-have called is interesting.M
      '[That he called you] is interesting.'

Quite apart from the unstable status of PL number marking discussed in §2.1.2.2, the unmarked nature of SG number is further evidenced by its use with nouns which have no inherent number feature, for example, nouns created from infinitives (see

(18a)) and mass/non-count nouns (20):[9]

(20)   a.   du beurre   b.   de la jalousie
          of.the.M.SG butter   of the.F.SG jealousy
          '(some) butter'   'jealousy'

On the default usage of the M.SG clitic *le* (*l'*) for direct objects with no φ features see §4.4.1; on the default usage of the M.SG subject clitic *il* in impersonal contexts see §4.4.4.

2.1.3   *Thematic structure of nominals*

In §3 I discuss the richly articulated functional structure above NP*, which is largely independent of a noun's thematic properties. As a prelude to that discussion, here I provide empirical evidence from thematic nominals to support the hierarchical NP* structure proposed in §1.5.

There are two phenomena usually believed to be subject to hierarchical constraints, namely, extraction and binding, which suggest the existence of a thematic hierarchy whereby a noun's thematic dependants – Possessor (P), subject/ Agent (S), object/Theme/Patient (O), typically realised as *de*-marked nominals (§3.3) – are hierarchically ordered underlyingly: P>S>O (Giorgi and Longobardi 1991).[10] Consider first the data in (21), from Valois (1991), cited in Coene and D'Hulst (2003a: 23):

(21)   a.   le portrait <u>de [chaque collectionneur,] de son, artiste favori</u>
          the portrait of each collector of his artist favourite
          'each collector's (P) portrait of/by his favourite artist (S/O)'

     b.   *le portrait <u>de son, mécène de [chaque artiste favori,]</u>
          the portrait of his benefactor (P) of each artist favourite (S)

Note that the position of neither the definite article nor the head noun itself is relevant to the grammaticality judgements: the definite article is merged within functional structure above NP*, while the head noun undergoes N movement out of NP* (see §3 for details). The examples in (22) show that linearisation of the inherent-case-marked dependants isn't relevant, either: the order can be reversed, without affecting grammaticality:

---

[9] Mass nouns pluralise where they mean 'kinds of . . . ', as in (ia), or where they mean 'pragmatically relevant units of . . . ', as in (ib):

(i)   a.   trois vin<u>s</u>   b.   trois bière<u>s</u>
          three wine.PL   three beer.PL
          'three kinds of wine'   'three glasses/bottles of beer'

[10] The Possessor θ role doesn't appear in the thematic hierarchy in (2) in §1.5 since verbal predicates don't have a Possessor.

(22) a. le portrait de son$_i$ artiste favori de [chaque collectionneur$_i$]
          the portrait of his artist favourite of each collector
          = (21a)

      b. *le portrait de [chaque artiste favori$_i$] de son$_i$ mécène
          the portraint of each artist favourite of his benefactor
          = (21b)

What is relevant in (21) is the relationship between the two inherent-case-marked thematic dependants of the head noun. The possessive determiner *son* (§3.2.3) within one can be bound by the bracketed quantified expression within the other in (21a/22a), as indicated by the co-indexation, but not in (21b/22b). The relevant difference between the grammatical and the ungrammatical examples relates to the thematic hierarchy: a quantified P can bind a possessive S/O, but a quantified S/O *can't* bind a possessive P. This suggests that, rather than being simply adjoined in line with their linear order (an approach which would incorrectly predict (21a)/(22b) to be grammatical and (21b)/(22a) to be ungrammatical), these thematic dependants are in fact merged in a fixed hierarchical order which is determined by their thematic relation to the head noun, as in (23), and then reordered (NP* externally) for pragmatic reasons. Crucially, the binding configurations relevant to the judgements in (21) and (22) are those in (23). Thus, the reason why the quantified expression can bind the possessive in (21a)/(22a), but not (21b)/(22b), is that θ_pP is above $\theta_{S/O}P$ and therefore the merge position of P (Specθ_pP) c-commands the merge position of S/O (Spec$\theta_{S/O}P$), rather than the other way round: the c-command condition on binding is therefore satisfied in (21a)/(22a) (P binds S/O), but not in (21b)/(22b) (S/O fails to bind P).

(23) θ_pP = NP*

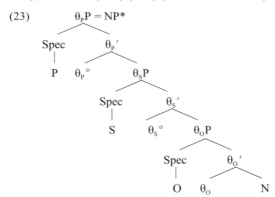

Second, consider the data in (24), cited in Coene and D'Hulst (2003a: 23), which show that the thematic hierarchy also explains constraints on extraction:

(24) a. le collectionneur dont$_i$ je connais la photo t$_i$ de ce photographe
          the collector of-whom I know the photo of this photographer
          'the collector (P) whose photo of/by this photographer (S/O) I know'

b. *le photographe dont$_i$ je connais la photo de ce collectionneur t$_i$
   the photographer (S/O) of-whom I know the photo of this collector (P)

In the grammatical (24a) the higher thematic dependant, the P merged in Specθ_PP, undergoes wh fronting in the relative clause (§5.6.1); in the ungrammatical (24b) in contrast, a lower thematic dependant, the S merged in Specθ_SP, undergoes fronting. The two (simplified) configurations are illustrated in (25):

(25) a. [dont$_i$ . . . [$_{NP*}$ . . . t$_i$ . . . de ce photographe . . .]]

b. *[dont$_i$ . . . [$_{NP*}$ . . . de ce collectionneur . . . t$_i$ . . .]]
   ✗

The ungrammaticality can thus be attributed to a minimality violation (Rizzi 1990; 2001), but only if NP* is assumed to have the articulated hierarchical structure in (23).[11]

Finally, the possibility of realising a θ-marked dependant as a possessive determiner (§3.2.3) is also subject to the thematic hierarchy. In principle, P, S and O can all be realised as a possessive determiner. The nominals in (26a, b) are both three ways ambiguous: *Jean/sa* can denote the *subject* of the photo (O), the *taker* of the photo (S) or the *owner* of the photo (P):

(26) a. la photo de Jean   b. sa photo
          the photo of J.   his photo
          'J.'s photo'   'his photo'

However, the possibility of realising one of these dependants as a possessive determiner is sensitive to the presence of other dependants, and the generalisation is that the realised dependant most highly ranked on the thematic hierarchy alone can appear as a possessive determiner. Thus, in (27a) either *ma* denotes P, in which case *Jean* denotes either S or O, or else *ma* denotes S, in which case *Jean* denotes O; *ma* cannot denote O and neither can *Jean* denote P. In (27b) the restrictions are even tighter; since all three dependants are represented, *ma* necessarily denotes P:

(27) a. ma photo de Jean   b. ma photo de Jean de Marie
          my photo of J.   my photo of J. of M.

The ungrammaticality of all the other a priori possible interpretations is due to the interaction between the derivation of the possessive determiner and the thematic hierarchy: derivation of the possessive determiner involves raising the relevant dependant out of NP* into the higher nominal structure (§3.2.3). If the raised dependant is no higher on the thematic hierarchy than any other realised dependant, raising creates a minimality violation along the lines of (25).

In conclusion, P, S and O respect a thematic hierarchy: P>S>O. This suggests

---

[11] See Keenan and Comrie (1977)'s 'NP-accessibility hierarchy' in the context of relativisation.

that they aren't merely adjoined PPs, but that, rather, they occupy hierarchically distinguished thematic positions made available by assuming the kind of NP* structure in (23).

2.2   Verbs and verb phrases

In §2.2.1 I consider the morphosyntactic properties of verbs, and in §2.2.2 and §2.2.3, respectively, thematically and pragmatically determined VP* structure. Functional structure above VP* is discussed in §4.

2.2.1   Verbs

French verbs can (almost entirely uncontroversially) be divided into finite and non-finite forms. Finite forms show morphosyntactic agreement with a grammatical subject (§2.2.1.1) and are taken from one of a number of inflectional paradigms, expressing such notions as tense, mood and aspect (§2.2.1.2). The inflectional morphology of non-finite forms is much more restricted (§2.2.1.3), although participles can show agreement in some contexts (§5.8.2). Slightly problematic for the finite–non-finite distinction are imperatives (§2.2.1.4).

2.2.1.1   Agreement

Morphological subject–verb agreement is most evident with the most common (and most highly irregular) verb *être* 'to be', with six fully distinct forms in the PRES.IND, as in (28a–f).[12] With regular verbs, in contrast, phonetic erosion has removed most of the morphological exponence of subject–verb agreement from the spoken language, leaving a three-way rather than a six-way distinction, as in (28a'–f'):

(28) a. je suis [sɥi(z)] 'I am'   a'. je parle [paʁl] 'I talk'
      b. tu es [e(z)] 'you SG are'   b'. tu parles [paʁl] 'you SG talk'
      c. il est [ɛ(t)] 'he is'   c'. il parle [paʁl] 'he talks'
      d. nous sommes [sɔm(z)] 'we are'   d'. nous parlons [paʁlɔ̃] 'we talk'
      e. vous êtes [ɛt(z)] 'you PL are'   e'. vous parlez [paʁle] 'you PL talk'
      f. ils sont [sɔ̃(t)] 'they are'   f'. ils parlent [paʁl] 'they talk'

Further, given the increasingly common use of *on* instead of *nous* (§4.4.4) as 1PL personal proform, and the fact that *on* triggers 3SG subject–verb agreement, there's effectively just a two-way distinction. Note also that, with the largest inflectional class of verb, the 2PL -*ez* [-e] suffix is homophonous with that found on past participles -*é* and infinitives -*er*. Thus, not even [-e] unambiguously marks an agreeing finite verb form.

---

[12] The segments in regular brackets are absent from the citation forms and only surface in liaison contexts (Battye *et al.* 2000: 109–12). For speakers who have neutralised the [ɛ]~[e] distinction, the contrast between *(tu) es* and *(il) est* is lost outside such contexts.

2.2.1.2 Verbal paradigms

French has retained many of the inflectional paradigms of Latin to encode various semantic features associated with verbs (Battye *et al.* 2000: 244–54). There are seven simple and seven compound paradigms; in each set, five are IND, two, SUBJ (§5.1.2). The 3PL simple forms are illustrated in Table 2.1.

3PL	present	imperfect	future	conditional	past-historic	present subjunctive	imperfect subjunctive
faire 'to do'	font [fõ]	faisaient [fəzɛ]	feront [fəʁõ]	feraient [fəʁɛ]	firent [fiʁ]	fassent [fas]	fissent [fis]
aller 'to go'	vont [võ]	allaient [alɛ]	iront [iʁõ]	iraient [iʁɛ]	allèrent [alɛʁ]	aillent [aj]	allassent [alas]

Table 2.1. Simple verb paradigms.

Pre-empting some of the theoretical discussion in §4, the transparent nature of the morphology of simple verb forms in French has been taken since Pollock (1989) to point to a model of clause structure in which inflectional morphemes correspond, one-to-one, to functional heads (see also Baker 1988). Pollock originally posited splitting the single I(nflection)P(hrase) into two inflectional FPs in clause structure, namely, T(ense)P and Agr(eement)P, an idea supported by the match such an idea offered between syntactic structure and inflectional morphology:

(29)   Nous part-i-ons.
       we leave.PST.1PL
       'We were leaving.'

If such a one-to-one relationship is deemed potentially to hold between syntax and inflectional morphology, then the future and, especially, the conditional paradigms suggest that a third inflectional FP should be posited, MoodP, the locus of a [±REALIS] feature, with the marked [–REALIS] value realised as the *r* affix of infinitives, futures and conditionals (Pollock 1997):

(30)   Nous part-ir-(i-)ons.
       we leave.IRR.PST.1PL
       'We will leave.'/'We would leave.'

The table in (31) shows how the verbal stem *part-* 'leave' can combine with 1PL agreement and all four logically possible combinations of marked and unmarked mood and tense:

(31)

Paradigm	Word	Root	Mood	Tense	Agreement
PRS	*partons*	part-	–	–	-ons
FUT	*partirons*	part-	-ir-	–	-ons
IMPF	*partions*	part-	–	-i-	-ons
COND	*partirions*	part-	-ir-	-i-	-ons

Returning to more strictly morphological issues, distinctions aren't made as consistently reliably as Table 2.1 suggests. For example, while common verbs like *être* 'to be', *avoir* 'to have' and *faire* 'to do' each have six PRS.SUBJ forms distinct from six PRS.IND forms, in the case of *avoir* one of the distinctions (1SG) relies on the [ɛ]~[e] distinction being maintained (*j'ai* [ʒe] 'have.1SG.IND' ~ *j'aie* [ʒɛ] 'have.1SG.SUBJ'), which doesn't happen for many speakers. And with verbs in the largest inflectional class (for example, *parler* 'to speak'), PRS.IND forms are largely formally identical to PRS.SUBJ forms, as shown in Table 2.2. Only 1/2PL are distinct. And even there, the SUBJ forms are actually identical to the IMPF.IND, so not even these are unambiguously SUBJ.

The compound paradigms are derived from the simple paradigms by a straightforward function: precede the simple form with a perfective auxiliary, *être* 'to be' or *avoir* 'to have' (§2.2.2.6), in the same paradigm; replace the original simple verb form with the PSTPRT (§2.2.1.3). Table 2.3 shows the 3PL compound paradigms of *avoir*-taking *faire* 'to do' and *être*-taking *aller* 'to go'.[13]

	1SG	2SG	3SG	1PL	2PL	3PL
PRS.IND	parle [paʁl]	parles [paʁl]	parle [paʁl]	parlons [paʁlɔ̃]	parlez [paʁle]	parlent [paʁl]
PRS.SUBJ				parlions [paʁliɔ̃]	parliez [paʁlie]	

Table 2.2. IND–SUBJ distinctions.

3PL	perfect	pluperfect	future perfect	conditional perfect	past anterior	perfect subjunctive	pluperfect subjunctive
avoir fait	ont fait	avaient fait	auront fait	auraient fait	eurent fait	aient fait	eussent fait
être allé(e)s	sont allé(e)s	étaient allé(e)s	seront allé(e)s	seraient allé(e)s	furent allé(e)s	soient allé(e)s	fussent allé(e)s

Table 2.3. Compound verb paradigms.

These paradigms typically mark tense, mood and/or aspect distinctions, but often only vaguely, and changes have taken place as recently as over the last one hundred years. In the spoken language the perfect (*ont fait*) has effectively replaced the past-historic (*firent*) as a marker of past tense; in doing so its role as a marker of perfectivity has diminished.[14] The past anterior has been replaced in matrix clauses

---

[13] Where the perfective auxiliary *être* is selected, the PSTPRT agrees in gender and number with the subject; where the perfective auxiliary *avoir* is selected, PSTPRT agreement is triggered in certain syntactic contexts, only (§5.8.2).

[14] Perfectivity can be emphasised using what's known as the *passé surcomposé* 'double compound past' (Carruthers 1993; Engel 1990; 1994; 1996; Paesani 2001), which goes back to the OF period and is found in particular in temporal clauses (Charaud 2000: 647). It's

by the pluperfect. Furthermore, the status of some of these paradigms is very unstable; the past-historic and IMPF.SUBJ forms are extremely rare in the spoken language.[15]

Aspect isn't the exclusive reserve of inflectional morphology. For example, the quasi-aspectual distinction between states, activities and events (Vendler 1967) is often simply a lexical property. Further, French has developed a number of periphrastic devices to fill in the aspectual inadequacies of the morphology: *commencer à* 'to begin (doing something)', *finir de* 'to finish (doing something)', *cesser de* 'to cease (doing something)', *continuer à/de* 'to continue (doing something)', *ne cesser de* 'to persist in (doing something)', *aller* 'to be going (to do something)', *venir de* 'to have just (done something)',[16] *être en train de* 'to be in the process of (doing something)', *être sur le point de* 'to be about to (do something)'.

SUBJ mood is marked, and typically associated with subordinate contexts (§5), where it's triggered by a syntactico-semantic feature of either the matrix predicate or the complementiser itself (§5.1.2).

---

formed by reapplying the function which derives the compound paradigms from the simple ones; the perfective auxiliary is thereby itself turned into a compound:

(i) Je l'ai eu fait, mais je le fais plus depuis longtemps.   (Gadet 2003)
     I it-have had done, but I it do no.more since long.time
     'I did once do it, but I haven't done it for ages.'

[15] Some regions are holding on to these forms longer than others, and the past-historic was still common in Western and Southern France in the second half of the twentieth century (Charaud 2000: 646). Jones (2000) discusses a very robust PRS.SUBJ and IMPF.SUBJ in Guernsey Norman French. Also, the use of a marked inflectional paradigm can be used for stylistic effect, and Goosse (2000: 114) mentions three French public figures well known for their taste for the IMPF.SUBJ. Elsewhere, sequence-of-tense 'rules' which, in (ia, b), for example, in principle require the 'tense' of the subordinate SUBJ to match that of the matrix IND are followed only rarely and inconsistently, with PRS.SUBJ forms typically being used across the board, as in (ic):

(i) a. Il faut qu'ils fassent leurs devoirs.
         it is.necessary.PRS that-they do.PRS.SUBJ their duties
         'They have to do their homework.'
     b. Il fallait qu'ils fissent leurs devoirs.
         it is.necessary.IMPF that-they do.IMPF.SUBJ their duties
     c. Il fallait qu'ils fassent leurs devoirs.
         it is.necessary.IMPF that-they do.PRS.SUBJ their duties
         b, c: 'They had to do their homework.'

[16] Non-standard varieties allow the combination of *venir de* with a PERF dependent clause, as in (ia) (cf. standard (ib)):

(i) a. %Je viens de t'avoir appelé.   b. Je viens de t'appeler.
         I come of you-have called   I come of you-call
         a, b: 'I just called you.'

2.2.1.3 Non-finite forms

Unlike finite verb forms, non-finite forms don't have an overt subject and don't show morphological agreement with one. In addition to the INF (*regarder* 'to watch', *partir* 'to leave', *répondre* 'to answer'), which is found in non-finite clauses of various kinds (§5.2), verbs have two other unambiguously non-finite forms, namely, the PRSPRT (*regardant* 'watching', *partant* 'leaving', *répondant* 'answering') and the PSTPRT (*regardé* 'watched', *parti* 'left', *répondu* 'answered'). The interaction between the participles and inflectional structure within the clause is taken up in §4.2. The PSTPRT occurs in compound paradigms expressing perfective aspect (§2.2.1.2). The PRSPRT is often introduced by *(tout) en* 'by, while' and used in small-clause contexts expressing imperfective aspect:

(32)   Gagnez de l'argent en <u>lisant</u> des mails!
       earn of the-money in reading of.the mails
       'Earn money by/while reading email!'

While French doesn't have agreeing infinitives (cf. European Portuguese), in certain syntactic contexts, both PRSPRT and PSTPRT agree with a nominal. Agreement is in gender/number and is realised the same way gender/number agreement is realised on adjectives (§2.3.1): *pris(e)(s)* 'take.PSTPRT.F.PL', *aimant(e)(s)* 'love.PRSPRT.F.PL'.

2.2.1.4 Imperatives

Imperatives are mentioned separately here since their status with respect to the finite–non-finite distinction is unclear. In §2.2.1.3 non-finite verb forms were distinguished from finite ones in not agreeing with a subject, and in not co-occurring with an overt subject. The status of imperatives is unclear because, while they don't co-occur with an overt subject (unless it's dislocated[17]), as shown in (33), they do show morphological agreement with an implicit subject, as shown in (34):

(33)   a. Pars!   b. *Tu/Toi pars!   c. *Pars-tu/toi!
           leave.IMP.2SG   you leave.IMP.2SG   leave.IMP.2SG you
           'Leave!'

(34)   a. Pars!   b. Partez!   c. Partons!
           leave.IMP.2SG   leave.IMP.2PL   leave.IMP.1PL
           'Leave (SG)!'   'Leave (PL)!'   'Let's leave!'

The forms of the imperative in (34) allow the distinction between 2SG, 2PL and 1PL (implied) subjects. While in the largest inflectional class of verb the written morphology of 2SG imperatives typically lacks the characteristic final -*s* of finite 2SG verb forms (*Va!* 'Go!'; cf. *Tu vas* 'You're going'), there are at least two reasons

---

[17] When imperatives are accompanied by a subject (*Arrête, toi!* 'Stop it, you!' ~ *Toi, arrête!* 'You, stop it!'), the prosody characteristic of dislocation is found (§5.3.1). The core clause containing the imperative therefore contains no overt subject.

to doubt this is anything more than an artificiality of the orthography, and that the 2SG imperatives are truly agreeing forms. First, the 2SG imperatives of *-ir*/*-re* verbs have final orthographic *-s* (as in *Pars!* in (34a)). Second, the written language is an imperfect reflection of the spoken language and has been tampered with at various points (§1.3). Third, there's phonological evidence to suggest that the inflectional suffix *-s* is underlyingly present on 2SG imperatives, even if it's typically absent from the orthography: where a 2SG imperative is followed by the proform *y* or *en*₁ (§4.4.3),[18] the latent *-s* is pronounced, and indeed re-appears in the orthography, too:

(35) a. Vas̲-y! [vazi̲] 'Go (there)!'
      b. Profites̲-en! [pʁɔfit(ə)za̅] 'Make the most of it!'
      c. Commences̲-en [kɔma̅s(ə)za̅] un autre! 'Start another one!'

It looks, therefore, as though the missing final orthographic *-s* in 2SG imperatives of *-er* verbs is merely an artificial convention, and that imperatives really do agree with an implicit subject. Thus, the status of imperatives with respect to the finite–non-finite distinction remains unclear.[19]

2.2.2   *Thematic VP* structure*

In this section, I consider lexical subcategories of verb and how these are reflected in VP* structure. In terms of 'verbiness' verbs range from highly thematic verbs (*donner* 'to give': three-place predicate), via raising verbs (*sembler* 'to seem'), defective verbs of various kinds (*falloir* 'to be necessary': only ever impersonal), to non-thematic modals and auxiliaries (*être* 'to be': copula, perfective auxiliary, passive auxiliary; *avoir* 'to have': perfective auxiliary). In §2.1.3 we saw empirical evidence that NP* is a layered structure determined by the thematic hierarchy in §1.5; here, we see similar evidence for VP*.

2.2.2.1 Thematic verbs

Thematic verbs are associated with one or more thematic dependant(s). They can be realised as intransitive (36a), direct monotransitive (36b), indirect

---

[18] For orthographic *-s* and phonological [z] to appear, the proforms *y*/*en* must be a *post*posed dependant of the *imperative*, rather than a *pre*posed dependant of a following *infinitive*, as shown in (i):
(i)   Va(*s) [va(*z)] en prendre deux!
      go.IMP of.them take two
      'Go take two of them!'
[19] Independently of the inflectional morphology of imperatives, a number of strictly syntactic issues remain. These are dealt with in the discussion of non-subject clitic proforms in §4.4.1 and the negative marker *ne* in §4.5.1.

monotransitive (36c), ditransitive (36d), 'prepositional'[20] (36e, f) or pronominal verbs (§4.4.2):

(36) a. Jean rit.   b. Jean aime [$_{DO}$ Marie].
          J. laughs   J. loves M.
          'J.'s laughing.'   'J. loves M.'

      c. Jean parle [$_{IO}$ à Marie].   d. Jean envoie [$_{DO}$ ses livres] [$_{IO}$ à Marie].
          J. speaks to M.   J. sends his books to M.
          'J.'s speaking to M.'   'J. send his books to M.'[21]

      e. Jean dépend [de Marie].   f. Jean pense [à Marie].
          J. depend of M.   J. thinks to M.
          'J.'s depending on M.'   'J.'s thinking about M.'

Dyadic verbs like those in (36b, c) have two θ roles to assign, illustrated in (37):

(37) a.   b.

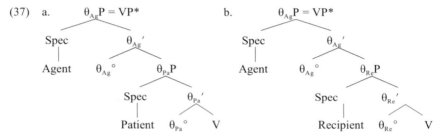

Typically, this results in a direct monotransitive structure like (36b), more rarely, an indirect monotransitive structure like (36c) (Van Peteghem 2006). The ditransitive verb *envoyer* 'to send' in (36d) has three θ roles to assign. In fact, the semantic structure of the verb allows the inherent movement to be towards a person (bearing the θ role Recipient) or towards a place (bearing the θ role Location). This flexibility has consequences for the order in which arguments are projected in syntax, in line with the thematic hierarchy (§1.5), as illustrated in (38) and (39):

---

[20] The term 'prepositional' is in inverted commas since it's inappropriate to think of *de* and *à* in (36e, f) as prepositions, or the bracketed constituents – which are clearly thematic dependants of the verb – as PPs. See §§2.4.2, 3.3 for discussion.

[21] Direct objects typically precede indirect objects, unless the former is 'heavy':

(i)   Jean a donné [$_{IO}$ à Marie] [$_{DO}$ tous les détails de son prochain voyage en Inde].
       J.has given to M. all the details of his next trip to India
       'Jean gave M. all the details of his next trip to India.'

Due to Germanic influence the French spoken in Alsace allows even 'light' direct objects to follow indirect objects (Wolf 2000: 698):

(ii)   Je donne [$_{IO}$ aux vaches] [$_{DO}$ du foin].
       I give to.the cows of.the hay
       'I give some hay to the cows.'

(38)

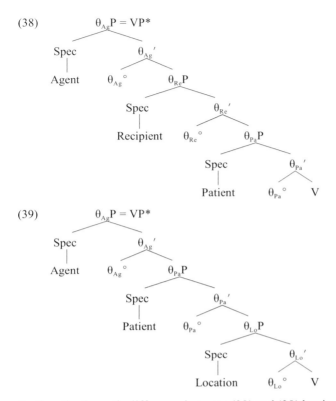

(39)

Further, the thematic difference between (38) and (39) has implications for how the Recipient/Location is realised in syntax. Since Recipient is higher than Patient in the thematic hierarchy, it's realised as an indirect object, as in (36d); since Location is lower, it isn't realised as an indirect object. Instead, it's realised as an inherent-case-marked dependant. While the difference isn't apparent with nominals (they're both marked with *à*; cf. (36d) and (40)), it shows up with pronominals, as in (41a, b): the indirect object is pronominalised using an indirect-object clitic (§4.4.1); the inherent-case-marked dependant is pronominalised as *y* (§4.4.3):

(40)   Jean envoie [$_{DO}$ ses livres] [à Paris].
        J. sends his books to Paris
        'J. sends his books to Paris.'

(41)   a. Jean lui envoie ses livres.   b. Jean y envoie ses livres.
            J. to.her sends his books   J. there sends his books
            'J. sends his books to her (= to M.).'   'J. sends his books there (= to Paris).

A parallel contrast to the one between (36d) and (40) is found in (36c) and (36f). The bracketed constituent in (36c) is an indirect object, the one in (36f), an inherent-case-marked dependant. The contrast is illustrated in (42) and (43). Indirect objects are pronominalisable using indirect-object clitics, as in (42b), and feed reflexivisation (§4.4.1), as in (42c); inherent-case-marked dependants do neither, as in (43b, c) (cf. (43b', c')):

(42) a. Jean parle [à Marie].
          J. speaks to M.
          'J.'s talking to M.'

      b. Jean <u>lui</u> parle.   c. Jean <u>se</u> parle.
          J. to.her speaks   J. self speaks
          'J.'s talking to her.'   'J.'s talking to himself.'

(43) a. Jean pense [à Marie].
          J. thinks to M.
          'J.'s thinking about M.'

      b. *Jean <u>lui</u> pense.   b'. Jean pense à <u>lui</u>.
          J. to.her thinks   J. thinks to her
                                                'J.'s thinking about him.'

      c. *Jean <u>se</u> pense.   c'. Jean pense à <u>soi-même</u>.
          J. self thinks   J. thinks to self
                                                'J.'s thinking about himself.'

The inherent-case-marked dependant in (43a) pronominalises as the clitic *y*, as in (44):

(44) Jean y pense.
      J. there thinks
      'J. is thinking about it.'

However, as we see in §4.4.3, *y* pronominalises [à cela] 'to that', and isn't therefore appropriate for a human referent (see the translation in (44), with *it* rather than *her*).

2.2.2.2 Variation and multiple argument realisation

In this section I discuss two kinds of variation in the way the inherent semantic structure of verbs is projected in syntax. The first is dialectal variation. For example, the verb *aider* 'to help', direct monotransitive in the standard language, is – unusually given the observation in §2.2.2.1 – *in*direct monotransitive in a number of eastern varieties, probably due to Germanic influence (Goosse 2000: 108):

(45) a. Jean aide Marie.   b. %Jean aide à Marie.
          J. helps M.   J. helps to M.
          a, b: 'J. helps M.'

Conversely, with the verb *enseigner* 'to teach', the entity benefiting from the teaching is realised as an indirect object in the standard language, but as a direct object in some sub-Saharan Africa varieties (Queffélec 2000b: 827):[22]

(46) a. J'enseigne <u>aux</u> enfants.   b. %J'enseigne <u>les</u> enfants.
         I-teach to.the children   I-teach the children
         a, b: 'I teach the children.'

And with the verb *jouer* 'to play (a musical instrument)' the instrument played is
marked with *de* in the standard language, but in Belgium is treated as a direct
object:

(47) a. Je joue du piano.   b. %Je joue le piano.
         I play of.the piano   I play the piano
         a, b: 'I play the piano.'

   There are in principle two ways of dealing with such variation. First, the contrast
between (45a) and (45b), between (46a) and (46b) and between (47a) and (47b)
might reflect a *grammatical* difference whereby one and the same thematic
dependant is realised as different kinds of object. Second, the contrast might reflect
a lexical semantic difference whereby speakers conceptualise the meaning of the
verbs *aider*, *enseigner* and *jouer* in subtly different ways. Given that such variation
is lexical-item specific, the second approach is arguably preferable.
   An interesting case study of reconceptualised lexical semantic structure is
provided by the verb *rappeler* 'to recall' and its reflexive counterpart *se rappeler*
'to remember'. In the standard language *rappeler* is ditransitive, as in (48):

(48) Jeanne a rappelé [$_{DO}$ les dates de ses vacances] [$_{IO}$ à sa mère].
        J. has recalled the dates of her holiday to her mother
        'J. reminded her mother of the dates of her holiday.'

The entity recalled is realised as a direct object, the person reminded, as an indirect
object. Used reflexively to mean 'to remember', the reflexive clitic (§4.4.1) is
therefore an indirect object:[23]

(49) Jeanne s'est rappelé [$_{DO}$ les dates de ses vacances].
        J. self.IO-is reminded the dates of her holiday
        'J. reminded herself of the dates of her holidays.'
        'J. remembered the dates of her holidays.'

For many speakers, however, the syntactic structure which *se rappeler* projects is

---

[22] This is in line with the general rarity of indirect monotransitive verbs (§2.2.2.1). A further
example of transitivisation is blamed by Goosse (2000: 139) on English influence. In
standard French, the dependant of the verb *jouer* 'to play (a competitive game)' which
indicates the person against whom one plays is marked with the preposition *contre* 'against',
as in (ia). Increasingly, though, this dependant can be realised as a direct object, as in (ib):
(i)   a. Federer joue contre Roddick.   b. %Federer joue Roddick.
          F. plays against R.   F. plays R.
          a, b: 'Federer is playing (against) Roddick.'
[23] As an indirect object, the reflexive clitic doesn't trigger PSTPRT agreement (§5.8.2).

different, and follows the pattern of the near synonym *se souvenir. Se souvenir* is a pronominal verb (§4.4.2). This means: (a) that it can *only* be used reflexively; and (b) that the reflexive clitic is a direct rather than an indirect object. Two consequences follow from this. First, the reflexive clitic triggers PSTPRT agreement (§5.8.2). Second, the entity recalled can't be realised as a direct object; instead, it surfaces as a *de*-marked nominal:

(50)   %Jeanne s'est rappelée [des dates de ses vacances].
        J. self.DO-is reminded of.the dates of her holiday
        ≈ (49)

Again, rather than claiming that the contrast between (49) and (50) reflects an underlying grammatical difference between different varieties, we might assume, instead, that the relevant speakers conceive of the inherent lexical semantic structure of *(se) rappeler* differently. For speakers using (50) *se rappeler* has the same semantic structure as *se souvenir*; for speakers using (49) the two verbs have subtly different semantic structures.[24]

There's a second kind of variation of interest here and which also relates to differing conceptions of inherent lexical semantic structure. A number of verbs allow what Levin and Rappaport Hovav (2005) call multiple argument realisations. That is, they appear to be flexible in how their thematic structure is projected in syntax. A well known example of this is the causative–inchoative alternation, illustrated in (51):

(51)   a. Le ballon roule.   b. Marie roule le ballon.
            the ball rolls   M. rolls the ball
            'The ball rolls.'   'M. rolls the ball.'

The argument *le ballon* 'the ball' is realised as the subject in (51a) and the direct object in (51b). Yet it's the Theme in both cases, and presumably merges as $Spec\theta_{Th}P$. The difference in syntactic realisation isn't therefore due to subtly different conceptualisations of semantic structure per se. Rather, it's due to the

---

[24] Leeman-Bouix (1994: 27) suggests that co-occurrence restrictions on clitics (§4.4.1) partly explain why speakers reanalyse *se rappeler* along the lines of *se souvenir*. Since *me* and *la* appear in *different* columns in Table 4.1 on page 127, the example in (i) is grammatical:
(i)   Je me la rappelle.
        I me her recall
        'I remember her.'
However, since *me* and *te* appear in the *same* column, there's no way of expressing the notion 'I remember you' on the basis of the standard ditransitive structure of *rappeler*:
(ii)   a. *Je me te rappelle.   b. *Je te me rappelle.
            I me you recall   I you me recall
However, structural analogy with *se souvenir* opens the door to (iii):
(iii)   %Je me rappelle de toi.
        I me recall of you
        'I remember you.'

flexibility of the lexical semantic structure of *rouler* 'to roll', which allows, but doesn't require, the realisation of an Agent.[25] In (51b) the option of realising an Agent is taken up, via merger of a θ_{Ag} head above $\theta_{Th}P$, in line with the thematic hierarchy, as in (52b); in (51a) it's not, as in (52a):

(52) a. $\theta_{Th}P = VP^*$ b. $\theta_{Ag}P = VP^*$

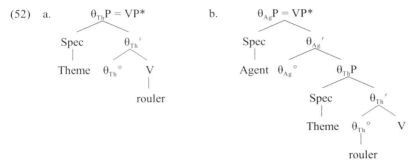

The divergent VP* structures in (52) mean that the Theme is realised as subject in (52a), but not in (52b), where the Agent is realised as subject, the Theme, as direct object. This is a further example of the context dependence of argument realisation: the way one argument is realised syntactically depends on the presence/absence of (an)other argument(s) (Levin and Rappaport Hovav 2005: ch. 6).

A different kind of flexible inherent semantic structure is illustrated in the examples in (53) and (54):

(53)   a. Des fourmis grouillent dans le jardin.   b. Le jardin grouille de fourmis.
          of.the ants teem in the garden   the garden teems of ants
          'Ants are teeming in the garden.'   'The garden is teeming with ants.'

(54)   a. Jean charge les verres sur le plateau.   b. Jean charge le plateau de verres.
          J. loads the glasses on the tray   J. loads the tray of glasses
          'J. loads the glasses onto the tray.'   'J. loads the tray with glasses.'

Taking the example of (54) for illustration, the alternating argument structures of *charger* 'to load' can't be accounted for along the lines of (51) and (52): the difference between (54a) and (54b) isn't a matter of the projection/non-projection of an optional thematic dependant. Rather, the alternation suggests that the inherent semantic structure of the verb *charger* is flexible in terms of which internal argument is cognitively salient, whereby cognitive salience is related to the Patient θ role. If 'the glasses' is cognitively salient and bears the θ role Patient, then 'the tray' is a locative; if 'the tray' is cognitively salient and the Patient, then 'the glasses' is conceived of as some kind of Instrument. The different VP* structures

---

[25] The alternation in (51a, b) differs from passivisation (§2.2.3.1) in two ways. First, there's no passive morphology. Second, there's no reconceptualisation of the inherent semantic structure of the verbal predicate from an activity to a (change of) state and, therefore, no suppression of the Agent θ role (non-realisation isn't the same as suppression).

then fall out directly from the thematic hierarchy.

2.2.2.3 Multiple argument realisation and middle voice

The multiple argument realisation illustrated in (55a, b) is familiar from §2.2.2.2:

(55) a. Jean ouvre la porte.   b. La porte ouvre.   c. La porte s'ouvre.
          J. opens the door   the door opens   the door self opens
          'J. opens the door.'   'The door opens.'   ≈ (55b)

In (55a) the subject is the Agent, while the direct object is the Theme; in (55b) the flexibility of the inherent semantic structure of *ouvrir* 'to open' allows a non-agentive interpretation, where no Agent is projected and the subject is therefore the Theme. More common (but see below) than the alternation in (55a, b) is the alternation in (55a, c). The structure in (55c) is known as middle voice, and contains a direct-object reflexive clitic, 'middle *se*'. As in (55b), no Agent is projected. That the subject isn't the Agent is suggested by the unavailability of agentive adjuncts. Compare (56a) (a true transitive reflexive with an agentive subject) and (56b) (containing middle *se*) (data from Cornips and Hulk 1996: 5):

(56) a. Jean se lave <u>pour ennuyer les gens/délibérément</u>.
          J. self washes for annoy the people/deliberately
          'J. washes (himself) to annoy the people/deliberately.'

      b. *Le verre se casse <u>pour ennuyer les gens/délibérément</u>.
          the glass self breaks for annoy the people/deliberately

The similarity between middle *se* and regular reflexive *se* is therefore more apparent than real. Middle *se* doesn't 'stand for' an object, and doesn't alternate with a DP* object, such as proforms suffixed with *-même(s)*. Compare (57) with (58), taken from Cornips and Hulk (1996: 4):

(57) a. Marie se lave.   b. Marie ne lave qu'elle-même.
          M. self washes   M. NEG washes but-her-self
          'M. washes herself.'   'M. washes only herself.'

(58) a. La branche se casse.   b. *La branche ne casse qu'elle-même.
          the branch self breaks   the branch NEG breaks but-her-self
          'The branch breaks.'

In fact, with middle voice, no Agent *can* be projected. The reason for this is that middle *se* itself realises the agentivity of the verb. Unlike what we find in passives (§2.2.3.1), therefore, no Agent can optionally surface within an Agent phrase with middle voice:

(59) a. La porte a été ouverte (par Jean).   b. La porte s'ouvre (*par Jean).
          the door has been opened by J.   the door self-opens by J.
          'The door was opened by J.'

Very few verbs allow all three of the patterns in (55), and *ouvrir* 'to open' contrasts with both *briser* 'to break' in (60), which allows the pattern in (55c) but not the one in (55b), and *fondre* 'to melt' in (61), which allows the pattern in (55b) but not the one in (55c) (Cornips and Hulk 1996: 1–2 fn. 2), a consequence of the different inherent semantic structure of the two lexical verbs: while *briser* 'to break' is an agentive verb, *fondre* 'to melt' is not.

(60) a. Jean brise le vase.   b. *Le vase brise.   c. Le vase se brise.
          J. breaks the vase   the vase breaks   the vase self breaks
          'J. breaks the vase.'   'The vase breaks.'

(61) a. Le soleil fond la neige.   b. La neige fond.   c. *La neige se fond.[26]
          the sun melts the snow   the snow melts   the snow self melts
          'The sun melts the snow.'   'The snow melts.'

However, according to Goosse (2000: 124) a change is in progress, whereby the middle-voice pattern in (55c) and (60c) is giving way to the intransitive pattern in (55b) and (61b). Goosse gives the examples in (62), in which middle *se* is claimed to be increasingly absent:

(62) a. Le corsage (se) boutonne par derrière. b. Le vêtement (se) rétrécit au lavage.
          the bodice self buttons by behind   the garment self shrinks to.the wash
          'The bodice buttons up from behind.'   'The garment shrinks in the wash.'

Given the semantic characterisation above, this means that these verbs are being reconceptualised as non-agentive.[27]

Despite containing the same lexical verb (with a unique transitional semantic structure involving a process followed by an endpoint), the sentences in (55b, c) differ in terms of their presentational aspect (Zribi-Hertz 1987). In (55c) the endpoint of the transition is highlighted;[28] in (55b) there's no such highlighting, and

---

[26] The judgement in (61c) relates to the literal sense of *fondre*. Where the verb is used figuratively, middle *se* is found, as in (i):
(i)   Le jaune se fond au vert.
       the yellow self melts to.the green
       'Yellow fades into green.'

[27] For a broader discussion of the distribution of the patterns illustrated in (55)–(61) see Zribi-Hertz (1987) and Lagae (1990).

[28] With some verbs, support for endpoint highlighting is needed from elsewhere in the structure, for example, the verbal paradigm (i) or the presence of an adverbial (ii):
(i)   a. Son état s'est empiré.   b. *Son état s'empire.
           his state self is worsened   his state self worsens
           'His state has got worse.'
(ii)   a. La cire se coule dans le moule. b. *La cire se coule.
           the wax self runs in the mould   the wax self runs
           'The wax runs into the mould.'
(Not all speakers agree on the ungrammaticality of (ib).) See Cornips and Hulk (1996: 19), Labelle (1990; 1992), Zribi-Hertz (1987).
The endpoint is also highlighted in the non-standard use of the reflexive in (iii):

both process and endpoint are accessible, for example, to adverbial modification, as shown by the contrast in (63a, b):

(63) a. L'écluse s'est ouverte *pendant trois heures/en très exactement trente minutes.
          the lock self is opened during three hours/in very exactly thirty minutes
          ≈ 'It took precisely thirty minutes for the lock to (fully) open.'

      b. L'écluse a ouvert <u>pendant trois heures/en très exactement trente minutes</u>.
          the lock has opened during three hours/in very exactly thirty minutes
          Either: ≈ (63a)
          or: ≈ 'The lock was in the process of opening for three hours.'

Middle voice is therefore appropriate where the Agent is irrelevant, for example, when describing the generic features of activities; it can't be used in specific contexts, as shown in (64c):

(64) a. L'apéritif se boit avant le repas en France.
          the aperitif self drinks before the meal in France
          'In France, an aperitif is drunk before meals.'

      b. *L'apéritif se boit avant le repas <u>par les Français</u>.
          the-aperitif self drinks before the meal by the French

      c. *<u>Hier soir</u>, l'apéritif <u>s'est bu</u> après le repas.
          yesterday evening the-aperitif self-is drunk after the meal

2.2.2.4 Impersonal verbs

Impersonal verbs lack a thematic dependant realised as a subject. When an impersonal verb appears in a finite clause, it therefore has impersonal *il* 'it' (§4.4.4) as its grammatical subject, for example, weather verbs (65a), *être* 'to be' used to tell the time (65b), *s'agir* 'to be a matter of' (65c), *falloir* 'to be necessary' (65d) and the presentative *y avoir* (65e):

(65) a. Il pleut.   b. Il est [sept heures].
          it rains   it is seven hours
          'It's raining.'   'It's seven o'clock.'

      c. Il s'agit [dans cet article] [des problèmes économiques de la France].
          it self-act in this article of.the problems economic of the France
          'This article is about France's economic problems.'

      d. Il [me] faut [partir].   e. Il [y] avait [du vin].
          it me is.necessary leave   it there has of.the wine
          'I have to leave.'   'There was wine.'

(iii) Je <u>me</u> prends une orange et je <u>me</u> la mange.
       I me take an orange and I me it eat
       'I take an orange and eat it up.'
The *up* in the translation indicates that the activity of eating reaches its endpoint.

While the weather verb in (65a) lacks any dependant at all, none of the dependants (in square brackets) of the other verbs in (65b–e) can be realised as the subject. This is because these dependants bear inherent case by virtue of their θ role and don't need to become grammatical subject in order to be assigned structural case.[29]

2.2.2.5 Pseudo-modals

In this section I discuss the syntax of verbs like *pouvoir* 'to be able to', *devoir* 'to have to' and *vouloir* 'to want to', which are followed by a bare infinitive, as in (66):[30]

(66) Nous pouvons/devons/voulons partir.
      we are.able.to/have.to/want.to leave
      'We are able/have/want to leave.'

I shall call them pseudo-modals. They warrant discussion together because of three features. One has to do with their infinitival V-movement properties (§4.2.2). Another relates to clitic climbing (§5.2.3). The final relevant feature is that these verbs have an unclear status with respect to the raising/control distinction. *Pouvoir* and *devoir* are arguably raising verbs (in their epistemic readings), while *vouloir* looks more like a control verb. However, things aren't that straightforward. First, *pouvoir* and *devoir*, for which a prima facie case for raising status can be made, can appear with a thematic subject and a pronominal direct object, as in (67):[31]

(67) Puisque nous le pouvons, alors nous le devons.
      since we it are.able.to so we it have.to
      'Since we can, we must.'

The example in (67) is unexpected if these are raising verbs since *le* would then be a pronominalised form of a constituent containing the trace of the raised subject. Second, in some Northern and Eastern varieties, *vouloir* is used as an alternative to *aller* to mark an imminent and likely future event (§2.2.1.2), as in (68):

---

[29] There's doubtless more to be said about these impersonal verbs. See §2.2.3.1 for discussion of flexibility with respect to the syntax of impersonal verbs.

[30] For further discussion of verbs which are followed by bare infinitives see §5.2.3.

[31] This is the case at least with epistemic modals as in (ia), for which it makes sense to assume an underlying structure along the lines of (ib) whereby impersonal *il* raises to become the matrix subject:

(i)   a. Il pourrait pleuvoir demain.   b. [e pouvoir [il pleuvoir demain]]
          it may rain tomorrow
          'It may rain tomorrow.'

With deontic modals the situation is less clear cut. Under a deontic interpretation of *Paul doit partir* 'Paul must leave', there's clearly a privileged relationship between the modality and Paul which may well reflect a distinct underlying structure.

(68)   %Il veut pleuvoir.
        it wants rain
        'It's (probably) going to rain (soon).'

Presumably, *vouloir* is a raising verb here.

As with the pseudo-modals, verbs like *promettre* 'promise' and *risquer* 'to risk' are ambiguous between control verbs and raising verbs:

(69)   a. Je promets de venir.   b. Le film promet d'être un grand succès.
            I promise of come   the film promises of-be a big success
            'I promise to come.'   'The film promises to be a great success.'

(70)   a. Je risque de rater mon avion. b. Le mur risque de tomber.
            I risk of miss my plane   the wall risks of fall
            'I'm risking missing my plane.'   'The wall may well fall down.'

2.2.2.6 Perfective-auxiliary selection

We saw in Table 2.3 on page 26 in §2.2.1.2 that, like a number of Romance and Germanic languages, French has a perfect verb paradigm combining a PSTPRT and a preceding *be* or *have* auxiliary. In the unmarked case *avoir* 'to have' is used. A small set of just over a dozen simple (intransitive) verbs – some 0.3% of the 10,000 verbs listed in the Bescherelle conjugation guide (Leeman-Bouix 1994: 88) – take *être* 'to be', instead, namely: *aller* 'to go', *venir* 'to come', *devenir* 'to become', *passer* 'to pass', *arriver* 'to arrive', *partir* 'to leave', *entrer* 'to go in', *sortir* 'to go out', *rester* 'to stay', *retourner* 'to return', *tomber* 'to fall', *naître* 'to be born', *mourir, décéder* 'to die', *descendre* 'to descend', as well as some, but not all, morphological derivatives. Around twice as many again are compatible with either *être* or *avoir* (with subtle semantic contrasts – see below). The auxiliary *être* is also used with all reflexive verbs. Auxiliaries are non-thematic; they don't assign a θ role. As expected, they are clause mate with the PSTPRT whose clitic dependants are realised on the auxiliary, as in (71) (§4.4):

(71)   a. J'y ai pensé.   b. J'y suis allé.
            I-there have thought   I-there am gone
            'I have thought about it.'   'I have been there.'

There are two broad approaches to perfective-auxiliary selection, syntactic and semantic. The syntactic account tries to exploit the fact that (non-reflexive) *être*-taking verbs are necessarily intransitive, as in (72a). Where these verbs are used transitively (non-reflexively), they necessarily take *avoir*, as in (72b):

(72)   a. Je suis sorti.   b. J'ai sorti l'argent.
            I am gone.out   I-have taken.out the-money
            'I went out.'   'I took the money out.'

Such accounts suggest that, while the subject of an *avoir*-taking transitive verb like *dire* 'to say' is merged in the same configuration as the subject of an *avoir*-taking intransitive verb like *rire* 'to laugh', the subject of an *être*-taking intransitive verb like *arriver* is in fact merged in the configuration of an underlying direct object. In other words, *avoir*-taking intransitive verbs are unergative, while *être*-taking ones are unaccusative. However, under the approach to lexical thematic structure set out in §1.5, such an analysis is meaningless: in the kind of VP* structure illustrated in §2.2.2, subjects and direct objects appear in the same kind of configuration (in a SpecθP position), and a VP* headed by a monadic verb has the same structure, irrespective of whether it takes *avoir* or *être* as perfective auxiliary. There's no sense in which a thematic dependant can be a direct object underlyingly and become a subject on the surface. A dependant doesn't 'become' a direct object until it leaves VP* and is marked with accusative case, and if a dependant does 'become' a direct object in this way, it remains a direct object. The sole argument of a verb like *arriver* 'to arrive' certainly doesn't do this.

Quite independently of this theoretical problem, the analysis of perfective-auxiliary selection in terms of underlying configurations is ill suited to deal with the attested variation (Charaud 2000: 637): *avoir*-taking verbs sometimes take *être*, as in (73b), while *être*-taking verbs are used widely with *avoir* in the Maghreb (Queffélec 2000a: 786).

(73) a. J'ai été malade.   b. %Je suis été malade.   (Gadet 2003)
          I-have been ill   I am been ill
          a, b: 'I have been ill.'

It's hard to believe that speakers vary in their underlying syntactic representation of a verb like *être*. Thus, it's likely that factors other than underlying configuration are at play in perfective-auxiliary selection.

An alternative approach appeals to semantics rather than syntax (Sorace 2000). The idea that, for example, what's relevant is whether or not a change of state is expressed is offered some support by the contrasting behaviour of the copulas in (74):

(74) a. Il a été malade.   b. Il est devenu malade.
          he has been ill   he is become ill
          'He was ill.'   'He became ill.'

The non-change-of-state copula *être* 'to be' selects *avoir* as its perfective auxiliary, while the change-of-state copula *devenir* 'to become' selects *être*. Standard reference grammars suggest a general tendency whereby *être*-taking verbs indicate motion or change of state, and that the subject of these verbs is therefore a Theme rather than an Agent. Recourse to the semantic notion of change of state can also shed light on some common patterns of both standard and non-standard usage. Leeman-Bouix (1994: 90–1) uses those verbs mentioned above which, depending on semantic nuance, even in the standard language are compatible with both *être* and *avoir* to illuminate the underlying contrast between the two, and to explain why some speakers extend the use of *être*. The examples in (75) are both standard and unambiguous: (75a), with *avoir*, describes an activity, (75b), with *être*, the change of state resulting from the activity:

(75) a. Pierre a changé.   b. Pierre est changé.
P. has changed   P. is changed
a, b: 'P. has changed.'

The same contrast is apparent in the examples in (76), although the correspondence between auxiliary selection and the semantic nuance is less clear cut:

(76) a. Emmanuel a disparu le 16 février 1996 à la gare SNCF de Rennes.
E. has disappeared the 16 February 1996 at the station SNCF of Rennes
'E. went missing 16 February 1996 at Rennes railway station.'

  b. Liu Yufeng est disparu depuis six ans.
L. Y. is disappeared since six years
'L. Y. has been missing for six years.'

Similarly, while intransitive *descendre* appears in the list of *être*-taking verbs, it can take *avoir* when what's relevant is the activity, rather than the change of state resulting from the activity. Leeman-Bouix suggests that it's the inherent ambiguity of, for example, *Elle est sortie* between the activity 'She went out' and the resultant (change of) state 'She's gone out' that underlies the non-standard contrasting use of the two auxiliaries, thus removing the ambiguity:

(77) a. %Elle a sorti.   b. Elle est sortie.
she has left   she is left
'She went out.'   'She has gone out.'

Sorace (2000; 2004) proposes a semantically motivated hierarchical (that is, implicational) approach to auxiliary selection with generalised *have* selection at the top and *be* selection at the bottom, and cross-linguistic variation determining: (a) how far down *have* selection extends; (b) how far up *be* selection extends; and (c) the location and breadth of any intermediate zones where auxiliary selection is subject to variation.[32]

The above discussion of perfective-auxiliary selection ignores the use of *être* with reflexive verbs. Compare (78a) with (78b), with a direct-object reflexive, and (79a) with (79b), with an indirect-object reflexive:

(78) a. Je l'ai lavé.   b. Je me suis lavé.
I it-have washed   I me be washed
'I washed him.'   'I washed myself.'

(79) a. Elle vous a fait mal.   b. Elle s'est fait mal.
she you has done bad   she self-is done bad
'She hurt you.'   'She hurt herself.'

If the semantic approach to perfective-auxiliary selection in terms of Sorace's hierarchy is going to work, then we need to identify a relevant contrast between the

---

[32] Sorace's hierarchy is: change of location > change of state > continuation of pre-existing state > existence of state > uncontrolled process > controlled process (motional) > controlled process (non-motional) (2004: 256, ex (9)).

reflexive and non-reflexive use of predicates like *laver* 'to wash' and *faire mal* 'to hurt'. Given the hierarchical nature of Sorace's approach, we would expect to find that reflexivity has the effect, in the standard language, of raising the verbal predicate sufficiently high up the hierarchy to trigger *être* selection. In those varieties[33] in which reflexives retain the *avoir* auxiliary, as illustrated in (81) (cf. the standard examples in (80)), the threshold for *être* selection is presumably higher.

(80) a. Je me suis appelé.   b. Je me suis téléphoné.
          I me am called   I to.me am phoned
          'I called myself.'   'I phoned myself.'

(81) a. %Je m'ai appelé.   b. %Je m'ai téléphoné.
          I me-have called   I to.me-have phoned

Under such an approach, the reason for the *absence* of variation the other way – for example, direct and indirect transitive non-reflexives never select *être* instead of standard *avoir*, as shown in (83) (cf. the standard examples in (82)) – would be that in no variety of French does the threshold fall sufficiently low:

(82) a. Je l'ai appelé.   b. Je lui ai téléphoné.
          I him-have called   I to.him have phoned
          'I called him.'   'I phoned him.'

(83) a. *Je le suis appelé.   b. *Je lui suis téléphoné.
          I him am called   I to.him am phoned

2.2.3   *Pragmatically determined VP* structure*

In addition to being determined by the inherent semantics of the verb, VP* structure can be determined by pragmatic factors. The grammaticalisation of SVO word order, as well as the prosodic inflexibility of fixed word-group-final stress, has consequences for information structure in that, by default, the core clause allows nothing other than the subject to be the topic. While this may be appropriate with agentive verbs in many contexts – and its overwhelming appropriateness doubtless played a role in SVO becoming grammaticalised in the first place – it's not appropriate everywhere, and there are a number of devices which allow pragmatic congruity to be maintained where the Agent isn't the topic, or indeed isn't expressed at all. In fact, one such device is illustrated by the alternation in (51) in §2.2.2.2, and another is middle voice (§2.2.2.3). Further, use of the [+HUMAN] proform *on* allows an agentive subject to be dethematised (§4.4.4). French grammar offers a number of other VP*-internal thematising/focalising devices which allow, for example, non-Agents to be topical or Agents to be focal. Some of these are set out in the following pages. IP*-*external* syntactic devices for modifying pragmatic information structure – dislocation, clefting and pseudo-clefting, inversion – are

---

[33] *Have* is found with reflexive verbs in the speech of children and also in some dialects, for example, Québécois.

discussed in §5.

2.2.3.1   Passives, impersonal passives and other impersonal structures

French passives resemble English passives. Formally, the passive verb in (84b) differs from the active in (84a) in being the combination of auxiliary *être* 'to be' and the past participle of the transitive verb:[34]

(84) a. Jean a copié le tableau.   b. Le tableau a été copié (par Jean).
      J. has copied the painting   the painting has been copied by J.
      'J. copied the painting.'   'The painting was copied (by J.).'

Semantically, passivisation modifies aspectual structure, turning an activity into a (change-of-)state, whereby the Agent θ role is dethematised, to use Baker *et al.*'s (1989) term. Consequently, the Agent doesn't merge in SpecθP and isn't realised as subject. Instead, the Theme/Patient is cognitively salient as the highest VP*-internal dependant and realised as subject (§4.3). Pragmatically, this prevents the Agent from being topical (§5). If the Agent isn't expressed at all, it has no pragmatic status; if it appears within an optional adjunct Agent phrase (*par Jean* in (84b)[35]), it's focal rather than topical. What's topical instead is the Theme/Patient, which, as the highest VP*-internal dependant, is realised as syntactic subject: the active sentence in (84a) tells us something about *Jean*, the passive in (84b), something about *le tableau* 'the painting'.

---

[34] Transitive verbs aren't all equally passivisable. For example, *concerner* 'to concern' has been ruled by the *Académie française* not to have a passive form (Goosse 2000: 109). See also Cinque (1999: 102). The absence in French (unlike English) of passives based on the output of dative shift is discussed in §2.2.3.2. Measure phrases can't be realised as syntactic subject following passivisation (§2.2.3.1):

(i)   a. Je pèse 80 kilos.   b. *80 kilos sont pesés par moi.
          I weigh 80 kg   80 kg are weighed by me
          'I weigh 80 kg.'

An apparently exceptional passivisation pattern is found in the alternation in (iia, b):

(ii)   a. On n'obéit plus au chef.   b. Le chef n'est plus obéi.
          one NEG-obeys no.more to.the boss   the boss NEG is no.more obeyed
          'People no longer obey the boss.'   'The boss is no longer obeyed.'

The subject of the passive in (iib) corresponds not to the *di*rect object of the active in (iia) but to the *in*direct object. The exceptional nature of the alternation is only apparent: the passive structure in (iib) is a vestige of an earlier stage in the language, when *obéir* 'to obey' was direct monotransitive.

[35] Passives with an Agent phrase are more common in writing than in the spoken language. Where the active verb denotes a state rather than an activity, the dethematised argument isn't an Agent. Where it resurfaces as an optional adjunct, it's introduced by *de* 'of' rather than *par* 'by':

(i)   a. Les élèves adorent la prof.   b. La prof est adorée des élèves.
          the pupils adore the teacher   the teacher is adored of.the pupils
          'The pupils adore the teacher.'   'The teacher is adored by the pupils.'

The pattern illustrated in (84b) isn't the only possible result of the dethematisation effected by passivisation. In a construction known as impersonal passive, illustrated in (85b), while the Agent is dethematised, the Theme/Patient fails to be realised as the grammatical subject (cf. the regular passive in (85a)):

(85)   a.   <u>Un four à micro-ondes</u> a été acheté.
            an oven to microwaves has been bought

       b.   Il a été acheté <u>un four à micro-ondes</u>.
            it has been bought an oven to microwaves.
            a, b: ≈ 'A microwave oven was bought.'

Instead, the Theme/Patient remains VP* internal syntactically and part of the focus pragmatically. This is possible because, by virtue of the θ role assigned to it, the Theme/Patient can be licensed by inherent case, and so remain in situ.[36] Given that the passive morphology dethematises the Agent, the fact that the Theme/Patient remains in VP* means that the syntactic subject position isn't filled by a nominal dependant of the verb, and is instead occupied by impersonal *il*.[37]

The motivation for the impersonal passive in (85b) (as opposed to the regular passive in (85a)) is pragmatic: it allows the Theme/Patient to remain focal. The motivation for those in (86) is slightly different: unlike (85b), (86a) doesn't have a regular passive alternative because the underlying verb isn't transitive; the impersonal passive in (86b) is preferred because of the heaviness of the clausal direct object:[38]

---

[36] Case licensing via inherent case has consequences for nominal determination, and definite nominals are typically excluded from postverbal position in impersonal constructions, as in (i):
(i)   *Il a été acheté <u>le</u> four à micro-ondes.
         it has been bought the oven to microwaves
Belletti (1988) suggests that the relevant inherent case here is partitive case. However, Goosse (2000: 125) comments that authors increasingly use definite nominals in this position, especially if the nominal is heavy, as in (ii):
(ii)   Il en est résulté <u>la</u> parution de l'Atlas linguistique de la France.
         it of.it is resulted that appearance of the-atlas linguistic of the France
         'This resulted in the appearance of the linguistic atlas of France.'
[37] As with middle voice (§2.2.2.3) (but unlike regular passives), the dethematised Agent in impersonal passives can't resurface within an Agent phrase:
(i)   *Il a été acheté un four à micro ondes <u>par plusieurs clients</u>.
         it has been bought an oven to micowaves by several customers
See Bouvier (2000) for an account in terms of the semantics of the impersonal construction.
[38] Complex 'verb–noun' verbs like *mettre fin à quelquechose* 'to put a stop to something' offer flexible passivisation patterns. Consider (i):
(i)   Le gouvernement a mis fin à ces pratiques illégales.
         the government has put end to these practices illegal
         'The government has put a stop to these illegal practices.'
The passive in (ii) is ungrammatical because *fin* doesn't head a regular nominal:

(86) a. Il a été procédé au décompte des votes.
          it has been proceeded to.the counting of.the votes
          'The votes were counted.'
          (cf. *Au décompte des votes a été procédé.)

      b. Il a été décidé que la prochaine réunion se tiendra demain.
          it has been decided that the next meeting self will.take.place tomorrow
          'It has been decided that the next meeting will take place tomorrow.'

What these examples suggest is that passivisation crucially is an operation of dethematisation. The realisation of the Theme/Patient as syntactic subject in (84b) and (85a) is a (common but not universal) secondary property of (regular) passives rather than an essential property of passivisation per se. This conclusion is further supported by the existence of impersonal passives based on intransitives, as in (87):[39]

(87) Il a été dansé.
      it has been danced
      'People danced.'

   Similar to (86b) above is the use of impersonal *il* in (88a, c):[40]

(ii)   *[Fin à ces pratiques illégales] a été mis(e) (par le gouvernement).
       end to these practices illegal has been put by the government
However, the bare nominal on its own can be realised as the subject of the passivised verb (even triggering past-participle agreement; §5.8.2):
(iii) Fin a été mise à ces pratiques illégales (par le gouvernement).
       end has been put to these practices illegal by the government
       'A stop has been put to these illegal practices (by the government).'
Alternatively, the impersonal passive is possible (but not with an Agent phrase):
(iv)   Il a été mis fin à ces pratiques illégales (*par le gouvernement).
       it has been put end to these practices illegal by the government
       'A stop has been put to these illegal practices (*by the government).'
[39] Impersonal passives based on monadic verbs are possible provided the verb can select a Theme cognate object (Cornips and Hulk 1996: 7 fn. 6), hence the ungrammaticality of the impersonal passives in (i):
(i)   a. *Il a été brillé.   b. *Il a été parti.
           it has been shone   it has been left
[40] The examples in (i) are similar to those discussed in footnote 38:
(i)   a. Il vaut mieux que tu partes.   b. Il importe peu qu'il pleuve.
           it is.worth better that you leave   it matters little that-it rains
           'You'd better leave.'   'It matters little that it's raining.'
While the postverbal subordinate clause can't replace impersonal *il* in preverbal position, as shown in (ii), the bare adverbials *mieux* and *peu* can, as in (iii):
(ii)   a. *Que tu partes vaut mieux.   b. *Qu'il pleuve importe peu.
           that you leave is.worth better   that-it rains matters little
(iii) a. Mieux vaut que tu partes.   b. Peu importe qu'il pleuve.
           better is.worth that you leave   little matters that-it rains
           = (ia)   = (ib)

(88) a. Il me plaît <u>qu'elle soit venue</u>.   →   b. <u>Qu'elle soit venue</u> me plaît.
         it to.me pleases that-she be come   that-she be come to.me pleases
         a, b: 'I'm pleased she came.'

      c. Il est possible aussi <u>de rester</u>   →   d. <u>(De) rester</u> est possible aussi.
         it is possible also to stay   of stay is possible also
         c, d: 'It's also possible to stay.'

Here, an (underlined) thematic finite/infinitival clause, which would normally be expected to appear in subject position, appears postverbally, while the subject position is occupied by impersonal *il*.[41] Examples (88a, c) differ from (88b, d) pragmatically: in (88a, c) the subordinate clause is focal, in (88b, d), topical. Syntactically, as we see in §5.1.1, finite clauses aren't nominal and don't need case, and so there's no case-licensing motivation for realisation as subject (or indeed any case-licensing problem with remaining VP* internal). In contrast, infinitives are nominal (§5.2.2), and the inherent-case marker *de* is needed when the infinitive remains VP* internal, but is optional when the infinitive is realised as syntactic subject, since structural case is available in this position.

    Finally, a number of intransitive verbs allow alternation of a similar kind:

(89) a. Une fille est arrivée.   b. Il est arrivé une fille.
         a girl is arrived   it is arrived a girl
         a, b: 'A girl has arrived.'

      c. Deux hommes sont morts hier   d. Il est mort deux hommes hier.
         two men are died yesterday   it is died two men yesterday
         c, d: 'Two men died yesterday.'

This pattern of alternation is possible with intransitive verbs which typically (but not exclusively) use the perfective auxiliary *être* (rather than *avoir*) (§2.2.1.2). Again, the difference between the two members of each alternation is pragmatic. And as we saw in footnote 36 the VP*-internal position of the postverbal nominal means that it bears inherent case.

2.2.3.2 Dative shift

    From a comparative perspective, one striking syntactico-pragmatic flexibility *not* afforded in French is the applicative construction (Tallerman 2005: 201–4), more commonly known in the context of English as dative shift, and illustrated in (90b):

(90) a. John gave [the book] [to Mark].   b. John gave [Mark] [the book].

In contrast to what's found in English, in some languages, for example, Indonesian, Chichewa and Dyirbal, the applicative construction is marked by a specific

---

[41] In ConF impersonal *il* can be replaced by *ce* (where the verb is *être* 'to be') (§4.4.4) or *cela/ça* (where the verb isn't *être*) (§3.8):
(i)   a. Ça/Cela me plaît qu'elle soit venue.   b. C'est possible aussi de rester.

applicative suffix on the verb. The Indonesian examples below are taken from Tallerman (2005: 6):

(91)   a.   Ali meng-kirim [surat itu] [kepada Hasan].   (Indonesian)
            A. send letter the to H.
            'A. sent the letter to H.'

       b.   Ali meng-kirim-<u>kan</u> [Hasan] [surat itu].
            A. send-APPLIC H. letter the
            'A. sent H. the letter.'

The existence (in some languages, at least) of an overt applicative morpheme suggests that the examples in (90b) and (91b) are characterised by the presence of a VP*-internal head into which the lexical verb incorporates; what varies is whether this head is overt (as in Indonesian) or covert (as in English). We might propose that the applicative morpheme effects a subtle modification in the semantic/aspectual structure of the verb, whereby the Recipient of the transfer (*Mark* in (90b); *Hasan* in (91b)) is (re-)conceptualised as the Patient, while the entity transferred (*the book* in (90b); *surat itu* 'the letter' in (91b)) is (re-)conceptualised as some sort of measure. In other words, the meaning of the verb in (90a) and (91a) is slightly different from the meaning of the verb in (90b) and (91b), as a consequence of the presence of an applicative morpheme. Such an approach to the applicative means that nothing further needs to be said about the syntactic realisation of the verb's arguments.

A further possibility opened up by the existence of the (c)overt applicative morpheme relates to passivisation (§2.2.3.1): since the applicative morpheme turns the Recipient into a Patient, causing it to be realised as direct object in active sentences, as in (90b) and (91b), this entity can be realised as syntactic subject in passive sentences, as in (92):

(92)   a.   <u>Mark</u> was given the book (by John).
       b.   <u>Hasan</u> di-kirim-kan [surat itu] (oleh Ali).   (Indonesian)
            H. be.sent-APPLIC letter the by A.
            'H. was sent the letter (by A.).'

Structures parallel to the English and Indonesian examples in (90b), (91b) and (92a, b) aren't available in French, as shown in (93):

(93)   a.   Jean a donné [le livre] [à Marc].   b.   *Jean a donné [Marc] [le livre].
            J. has given the book to M.   J. has given M. the book
            = (90a)   = (90b)

       c.   *Marc a été donné le livre (par Jean).
            M. has been given the book by J.
            = (92a)

This suggests that, unlike Indonesian, which has an overt applicative morpheme, and unlike English, which has a covert applicative morpheme, French has no applicative morpheme at all, neither overt nor covert. The absence of this morpheme directly rules out (93b), as required, and, indirectly, (93c), again as required.

2.3   Adjectives/adverbials and adjective/adverbial phrases

I consider the morphosyntactic properties of adjectives (§2.3.1) and adverbials (§2.3.2) and the lexical properties of AP*s and AdvP*s (§2.3.3). The specific issues surrounding attributive-AP* placement within nominals are discussed in §3.7, and those concerning AdvP* placement within clauses are set out in §4.1.

2.3.1   Adjectives

In terms of their agreement morphology, adjectives pattern much like nouns (§§2.1.2.1–2.1.2.3). First, they are compatible with (primarily orthographic) gender and number marking, in both attributive and predicative uses (cf. Walloon, for example, where marking occurs in attributive uses, only; Bernstein 1991).[42] Second, the regular patterns of gender marking (∅ M ~ -e F: *grand ~ grande* 'big M/F') and number marking (∅ SG ~ -s PL: *grand(e) ~ grand(e)s* 'big (F.)SG/PL') are the same as those found with nouns. Third, the kinds of irregularity found with adjectives match those found with nouns, for example, *social ~ sociaux* 'social SG/PL', *canadien(ne)* 'Canadian M/F'.[43]

A phenomenon widespread across Romance through the centuries, yet condemned by Etiemble (1964) as being the result of influence from English, involves the use of adjectives as manner adverbials:

---

[42] Simple colour adjectives typically agree, as in (ia); some simple colour adjectives which have been recruited from nominal uses don't agree, as in (ib):

(i)   a. des chemises vert-<u>e-s</u>   b. des chemises marron_
          of.the shirts green-F-PL   of.the shirts brown
          'green shirts'   'brown shirts' (*le marron* 'chestnut')

There is some hesitation in usage, with true adjectives sometimes failing to show agreement marking, and some noun-cum-adjectives showing agreement marking.

The adjective at the heart of a complex colour adjective doesn't agree, as in (ii):

(ii)   a. des chemises vert(*es) émeraude   b. des chemises vert(*es) clair
          of.the shirts green-F-PL emerald   of.the shirts green-F-PL clear
          'emerald-green shirts'   'light green shirts'

Received wisdom is that structures like (iia, b) are elliptical forms of those in (iiia, b), in which *vert* is in fact a noun:

(iii) a. des chemises <u>d'un</u> vert d'émeraude   b. des chemises <u>d'un</u> vert clair
          of.the shirts of-a green of-emerald   of.the shirts of-a green clear
          = (iia)   = (iib)

[43] A number of M/F alternations are found uniquely with adjectives. See Battye *et al.* (2000: 127ff.) for examples.

(94) a. conduire <u>mou</u>   b. <u>frais</u> peint   c. écrire <u>économique</u>
          drive soft   fresh painted   write economical
          'to drive sloppily'   'freshly painted'   'to write economically'
                                         (= 'wet paint')

2.3.2   Adverbials

The small set of morphologically simple adverbs (*bien* 'well', *mal* 'badly', *tôt* 'early', *tard* 'late') is augmented via a derivational adjective-to-adverb conversion process, namely, *-ment* suffixation, analogous to *-ly* suffixation in English:[44]

(95) a. ferme → fermement   b. patient → patiemment
          'firm'   'firmly'   'patient' 'patiently'

This process is not, however, as productive as *-ly* suffixation in English, and some adjectives are incompatible with it, as in (96a), where an inherent-case-marked nominal structure is found instead, as in (96b):

(96) a. intéressant → *intéressamment   b. de/d'une façon/manière intéressante
          'interesting' 'interestingly'   of/of-a fashion/manner interesting
                                                'interestingly'

A syntactically interesting category of adverbial comprises elements which also appear within complex determiners (§3.6), for example, *beaucoup* 'lots', *trop* 'too much', *peu* 'a little', *pas* 'no(t)', *combien* 'how much/many':

(97) a. Je t'aime <u>beaucoup</u>.   b. J'ai [beaucoup d'amis].
          I you-love lots   I-have lots of-friends
          'I love you lots.'   'I have lots of friends.'

The syntactic interest in these adverbials relates to their mobility (see §4.3.2).

French adverbials are almost exceptionlessly morphologically invariant. The exception is the adverbial *tout* 'all' which, like predeterminer *tout* (§3.2.4), shows some agreement.[45] Within attributive and predicative AP*s, *tout* is an adverbial 'intensifier'. In (98) *tout* agrees with the lexical head of the nominal:

---

[44] Suffixation typically adds *-ment* to the F or base form of the adjective. Where the adjective is *-ant(e)* or *-ent(e)* final, the derivation is more complex. See Battye *et al.* (2000: 152).

[45] The collocation *tout de son long* 'along its entire length', in which adverbial *tout* modifies [de son long], has been reanalysed as *de tout son long*, whereby *tout* has been absorbed into the nominal constituent as a predeterminer. The expression *tout au début* 'right at the beginning', in which the adverbial *tout* modifies [au début], has also been reanalysed, as *au tout début* (Goosse 2000: 121–2). Here, the new position/function of *tout* after the article (*au* = *à* + *le*) is neither straightforwardly that of adverbial *tout* (nouns don't take adverbial modification) nor that of predeterminer *tout* (predeterminer *tout* precedes the definite article); rather it looks like an adjective. Whatever the structure, it's been stable enough to allow backformation of *le tout début* 'the very beginning'. This use of *tout* is reminiscent of what is found in *le tout Paris* 'all Paris' (that is, 'everyone in Paris').

(98) a. cette [$_{AP*}$ <u>toute</u> petite] pièce   b. Cette pièce est [$_{AP*}$ <u>toute</u> petite].[46]
          this all small room   this room is all small
          'this very small room'   'This room is very small.'

The agreement waters are muddied somewhat by phonological linking phenomena and orthographic conventions which are artificial, unstable and counterintuitive. However, Miller *et al.* (1997) show that the relevant facts can be accounted for straightforwardly by ignoring spelling and looking exclusively at the all important spoken language, where judgements are very clear: pre-AP* *tout* is pronounced [tu] in M contexts before a consonant, as in (99a), [tut] in M contexts before a vowel, as in (99b), and [tut] in F contexts, irrespective of whether the adjective is consonant (99c) or vowel initial (99d):

(99) a. tout petit(s) M.SG/PL [tup(ə)ti] 'very small'
      b. tout étroit(s) M.SG/PL [tutetʁwa] 'very narrow'
      c. toute petite(s) F.SG/PL [tutp(ə)tit] 'very small'
      d. tout étroite(s) F.SG/PL [tutetʁwat] 'very narrow'

The pronunciations [tus] and [tuts], found with PL predeterminer *tous/toutes* in some quantifier-float environments (100a, b),[47] are never found with pre-AP* *tout*, even if the adjective is PL (101a, b) (and neither does *tout* bear the orthographic -s PL marker):[48]

---

[46] Example (98b) possibly illustrates quantifier float (§4.3.1), as analysed in (i):
(i)   [cette pièce]$_i$ est [$_{SC}$ [$_{PreDetP}$ toute t$_i$] [$_{AP}$ petite]]
However, the interpretation of (98b), as well as the existence of (98a), which can't be analysed as quantifier float, militate against an analysis of (98b) as (i).
[47] On quantifier float see §4.3.1.
[48] Note the contrast between (ia) and (ib):
(i)   a. Ils sont tous [tus] petits.   b. Ils sont tout [tu] petits.
           they are all.M.PL small   they are all.M.SG small
           'All of them are small.'   'They are very small.'
In (ia) *tous* is a quantifier which has floated off the subject and agrees in number and gender with the subject proform; in (ib) *tout* is an adverbial intensifier associated with the adjectival predicate and agrees in gender but not number.
    Miller *et al.* (1997: §3) extend their analysis to predicative nominals and concessive constructions. What is clear is that there's no agreement in number; however, agreement in gender is somewhat unstable, too.
    A different case is illustrated in (i):
(i)   Il a les yeux grand<u>s</u> ouvert<u>s</u>.
       he has the eyes big.M-PL open.M-PL
       'His eyes are wide open.'
Unlike adverbial *tout*, which agrees in gender but not number, the adjectival intensifier *grand* agrees in both number and gender. Where adverbial *tout* and adjectival *grand* co-occur, these agreement patterns are maintained, as in (ii):
(ii)   Il laisse les portes tout-e grand-e-s ouvert-e-s.
       he leaves the doors all-F big-F-PL open-F-PL
       'He leaves the doors wide open.'

(100) a. Ils sont tous [tus] partis.   b. Elles veulent toutes [tuts] entrer.
         they.M.PL are all left   they.F.PL want all enter
         'They M all left.'   'They F all want to come in.'

(101) a. tout étroits M.PL   b. tout étroites F.PL
         [tutetʁwa] ~ *[tusetʁwa]   [tutetʁwat] ~ *[tutsetʁwat]

This suggests that pre-AP* adverbial *tout* agrees in gender, but not in number.

2.3.2.1 Negative adverbials

Sentential negation is typically marked by a preverbal negative particle *ne* (§4.5.1) together with some other negative XP which can be a nominal (§3.5) or an adverbial. The unmarked adverbial is *pas* 'not'; other, more specific adverbials are *plus* 'no more', *jamais* 'never' and *guère* 'not much':

(102) Je ne fume pas/plus/jamais/guère.
     I neg smoke not/no.more/never/not.much
     'I don't smoke.'/'I don't smoke any more.'/'I never smoke.'/'I don't smoke much.'

The syntax of these adverbials is considered in the context of clause structure in §4.

2.3.3 *Adjective phrases and adverbial phrases*

2.3.3.1 Adjectives phrases

AP*s can be used predicatively, as in (103), or attributively, as in (104) (§3.7):

(103) a. Cette idée est <u>très bonne</u>.   b. Je trouve [cette idée <u>très bonne</u>].
         this idea is very good-F.SG   I find this idea very good-F.SG
         'This idea is <u>very good</u>.'   'I find this idea very good.'

(104) une <u>très bonne</u> idée.
      a very good-F.SG idea
      'a <u>very good</u> idea'

In each case, the adjective agrees in gender and number with the relevant noun. Agreement isn't always straightforward, and sometimes appears to follow common sense over structure, as in (105):

(105) a. le roi et premier ministre espagnol-s
       the king.SG and first.SG minister.SG Spanish-PL
       'the Spanish king and prime minister'

     b. les premier-s ministre-s espagnol et italien
       the first-PL minister-PL Spanish.SG and Italian.SG
       'the Spanish and Italian prime ministers'

In other contexts, it appears to follow structure over common sense (see the discussion of adjective agreement with *ce* (*c'*) 'this' in §4.4.4).

2.3.3.2 Dependants of adjectives

An adjective can select a nominal dependant. Like the nominal dependant of a noun (§2.1.3), the nominal dependant of an adjective is marked with inherent case (§3.3):

(106) a. content [de son travail]   b. semblable [à une rose]
        happy of her work   similar to a rose
        'happy with her work'   'similar to a rose'

An adjective can select a clausal dependant, too, either finite or infinitival. For a finite clause to appear with an overt inherent case marker *de* or *à*, it must first be 'nominalised' within a free relative headed by *ce*:[49]

(107) a. être content [(de ce) que tu sois là]
        to.be happy of this that you be there
        'to be happy that you're here'

      b. être attentif [(à ce) que les bâteaux soient conformes]
        to.be attentive to this that the boats be compliant
        'to make sure that the boats are in order'

Infinitives are nominal (§5.2) and so can be case marked:

(108) a. content [de partir]   b. prêt [à partir]
        happy of leave   ready to leave
        'happy to leave'   'ready to leave'

For further discussion of the syntax of subordinate clauses, see §5.

2.3.3.3 Modified adjectives and adverbials

In line with the typological shift within Romance from (S)OV to SVO (§1.3), the modification of adjectives/adverbials is predominantly analytic rather than synthetic. That is, an adjective/adverbial is preceded by an independent adverbial such as *très* 'very', *trop* 'too', *peu* 'not very', *un peu* 'a little' and *tout* 'all'.[50] The formation of comparatives and superlatives follows this basic pattern, too. A comparative is an adjective/adverbial preceded by the adverbial *plus* 'more', *moins* 'less' or *(tout) aussi* '(just) as'; the standard of comparison follows, optionally, and is introduced by *que* 'than, as':

(109) a. Il est plus/moins beau (que Marc).   b. Il parle (tout) aussi vite (que moi).
        he is more/less beautiful that M.   he speaks (all) also quickly that me
        'He is more/less handsome than M.'   'He speaks (just) as quickly as me.'

A small number of comparatives retain an inherited synthetic form: *bon* 'good'

---

[49] On the simplification of *de/à ce que* as *que* see §5.1.1.
[50] Synthetic forms like *rarissime* 'very rare', *chiquissime* (also *chic'issime*) 'very chic' and *grandissime* 'very large' (cf. Italian *grandissimo*) are informal and very rare.

→ *meilleur* 'better (A)', *bien* 'well' → *mieux* 'better (ADV)',[51] *mauvais* 'bad' → *pire* 'worse (A)', *mal* 'badly' → *pis* 'worse (ADV)', *petit* 'small' → *moindre* 'smaller':

(110) a. Le vin est <u>meilleur (que</u> la bière).   b. Il l'a fait <u>pis (que</u> moi).
      the wine is better that the beer   he it-has done worse that me
      'The wine is better than the beer.'   'He did it worse than me.'

Both *pire* and *pis* compete with the analytic *moins bon* and *moins bien*, respectively, especially when issues of politeness are involved: describing someone's efforts as *moins bons* 'less good' is less harsh than describing them as *pires* 'worse'.

Superlatives are formally a comparative preceded by an agreeing definite article (§3.2); given that adverbials are invariable, the 'agreeing' definite article is the default M.SG *le* (§2.1.2.3):[52]

(111) a. Mon idée est <u>la moins intéressante</u>.   b. Ses résultats étaient <u>les meilleurs</u>.
      my idea is the less interesting   his results were the better
      'My idea is the least interesting.'   'His results were best.'

     c. Tu as parlé <u>le plus franchement</u>.   d. Elle a chanté <u>le mieux</u>.
      you have spoken the more frankly   she has sung the better
      'You spoke most frankly.'   'She sang best.'

     e. la dame de la société <u>la plus belle</u> et <u>la mieux tournée</u>
      the lady of the society the more beautiful and the better turned
      'the most beautiful and best turned out lady in society'

Turning to distribution, comparative AP*s appear readily in predicative contexts:

(112) a. Mes livres sont <u>plus intéressants</u>.   b. Je trouve ses idées <u>plus convaincantes</u>.
      my books are more interesting   I find his ideas more convincing
      'My books are more interesting.'   'I find his ideas more convincing.'

In attributive contexts the picture is more complex, and discussion is postponed

---

[51] While etymologically an adverb, *bien* 'well' (together with its comparative form *mieux* 'better') is also used as an adjective to mean good. However, it differs semantically and syntactically from *bon* 'good'. First, while *bon* describes essential quality, *bien* describes superficial quality, as illustrated in (i):

(i)   a. L'homme est <u>bon</u>.   b. Cet homme est <u>bien</u>.
      the-man is *bon*   this man is *bien*
      'Mankind is good.'   'This man is good-looking.'

Second, while *bon* is prenominal when used attributively, *bien* is postnominal (§3.7):

(ii)   a. Je cherche un <u>bon</u> mec.   b. Je cherche un mec <u>bien</u>.
      I seek a *bon* bloke   I seek a bloke *bien*
      'I'm looking for a good bloke.'   'I'm looking for a good-looking bloke.'

[52] In some varieties, for example, Québécois, 'double' comparative/superlative marking is found, with synthetic and analytic forms co-occurring:

(i)   a. %moins pire que   b. %les plus pires
      less worse (A) than   the more worse (A)
      'less bad than'   'the worst'

until §3.7, where other issues having to do with nominal structure are considered.

2.4   Prepositions and prepositional phrases

In this section I consider the syntax of prepositions (§2.4.1) and PP*s (§2.4.3). Particular attention is paid to the items *de* 'of, from' and *à* 'to, at' (§2.4.2). In terms of the traditional analysis of the four major lexical categories as bundles of the two features [±N] and [±V], prepositions are [−N, −V] (Jackendoff 1977). Baker's (2003) approach to lexical categories excludes prepositions entirely, which are deemed to be functional, instead. In many languages, (some) prepositions are clearly the analytical equivalents of synthetic case markers, and an analysis of them as functional heads is thus attractive. In the history of French (and Romance more generally) the loss of case-marking morphology coincided with increased use of prepositions (§1.3). Prepositions were also recruited to fulfil the clearly grammatical function of non-finite complementiser (§5). Thus, the grounds for an analysis of prepositions, particularly *de* and *à*, as functional heads is very compelling.

2.4.1   Prepositions

Like many languages French has a small set of simple locative/directional prepositions, for example, *sur* 'on', *sous* 'under', *vers* 'toward', *derrière* 'behind'. The simple prepositions are supplemented by a set of complex prepositions, which exist either to fill genuine lexical gaps (*face à* 'opposite') or to make subtle semantic distinctions (*dans* 'in' ~ *au sein de* 'within' ~ *à l'intérieur de* 'inside') and to express more abstract relational notions (*par rapport à* 'with respect to').

The use of prepositions is unstable in various ways. First, it's subject to speaker variation. The usage in (113) is non-standard (cf. the standard counterparts in (114)), its spread to the standard language having been impeded by purists (Goosse 2000: 111):

(113) a. %Je suis allé <u>au</u> pharmacien.   b. %Je l'ai lu <u>sur</u> le journal.
          I am gone to.the chemist   I it-have read on the newspaper
          'I went to the chemist's.'   'I read it in the newspaper.'

(114) a. Je suis allé <u>chez</u> le pharmacien.   b. Je l'ai lu <u>dans</u> le journal.
          I am gone to the chemist   I it-have read in the newspaper
          = (113a)   = (113b)

Second, the language has welcomed 'new' prepositions, for example, *because/bicause* and *versus*, both directly calqued from English, and *circa* 'approximately', apparently borrowed from German (Goosse 2000: 131). Finally, complex prepositions are subject to innovative clipping, for example, *du côté de* 'concerning' (lit. 'of the side of') and *au niveau de* 'regarding' (lit. 'at the level of') are sometimes shortened to bare *côté* 'side' and *niveau* 'level':

(115) a. Pas de souci <u>côté argent</u>.   b. <u>Niveau mecs</u>, on a les mêmes goûts.
       not of worry side money   level blokes we have the same tastes
       'No worries regarding money.'   'We have the same taste in men.'

2.4.2 De *and* à

The idea that prepositions are functional rather than lexical can most clearly be articulated in the context of *de* 'of, from' and *à* 'to, at'. That they are functional rather than lexical in *some* contexts is indisputable. The most important of these contexts are merely listed here, then discussed in detail in the indicated sections. First, in the context of ditransitive and indirect monotransitive verbs (§2.2.2.1), as well as certain perception, movement and causative (PMC) constructions (§5.2.3), *à* marks indirect objects, which can be pronominalised using indirect-object clitics (§4.4.1). Second, *de/à* are inherent-case markers (§3.3), formally licensing nominals in contexts where structural case is unavailable, for example, the dependants of nouns (§2.1.3) and adjectives (§2.3.3.2). Third, *de/à* appear in complex nouns (§2.1.1). Fourth, *de* appears in various DP*-internal positions, for example complex determiners (§3.6). Finally, and related to their use as inherent-case markers, *de/à* introduce subordinate infinitival clauses which wouldn't otherwise be case licensed, as well as subordinate finite clauses which have been nominalised by *ce* (§5.1).

The case for analysing *de/à* as functional items isn't restricted, however, to their grammatical uses; it's equally valid where they have locative/directional content, as in (116) and (117). Here, the content can be thought of as mere grammatical case (elative/ablative and illative/allative); thus, these items have no lexical content whatsoever and are inherent-case markers on nominals. (See Luraghi 2003: §1.2.1.) In what follows I assume that, even in their locative/directional uses, *de/à* aren't prepositions. This follows the conclusion arrived at in Miller (1992) that locative/directional *de/à* are case-marking affixes (unlike the regular prepositions).

The items *de/à* demonstrate various unique properties. First, they exhibit morphological variation, undergoing obligatory fusion with the definite articles *le/les* (§3.2) as the portmanteau forms *au* (= *à* + *le*), *aux* (= *à* + *les*), *du* (= *de* + *le*) and *des* (= *de* + *les*):[53]

---

[53] The obligatory nature of this fusion is in line with a supposedly universal morphosyntactic blocking principle whereby an opaque (or suppletive) form precludes any transparent (or regular) form, or indeed a general economy principle requiring minimal overt means to be used (see Bresnan 2001: 15 and Collins 2001: 60).

Fusion into a portmanteau doesn't occur between *de/à* when introducing an infinitival subordinate clause (§5.2.2) and the direct-object clitic proforms *le* and *les* (§4.4.1):

(i)   a. Elle continue <u>à/de le</u> faire.   b. *Elle continue <u>au/du</u> faire.
        she continues to/from it do   she continues to.it/from.it do
        'She continues doing it.'

(116) a. Je vais au(x) marché(s).   b. Je viens du/des marché(s).
      I go to.the market(s)   I come from.the market(s)
      'I'm going to the market(s).'   'I'm coming from the market(s).'

Second, *de/à*-initial locative/directional nominals alternate with the clitics *en*$_1$ and *y* (§4.4.3), respectively:

(117) a. Je vais à Paris → J'y vais.   b. Je viens de Paris → J'en$_1$ viens.
      I go to P.   I-to.there go   I come from P.   I-from.there come
      'I'm going to Paris/there.'   'I'm coming from Paris/there.'

That this set of properties isn't shared by other prepositions suggests that *de/à* aren't in fact prepositions.[54]

Locative/directive *de/à* are also unique in participating in the two kinds of alternation discussed by Miller *et al.* (1997). In both cases they introduce a definite nominal referring to a country or region. First, when introducing locative/directional nominals, the unmarked sequence of *à* + the definite article (§3.2.1) alternates with the marked use of *en* without the definite article; second, and in parallel, when introducing elative/ablative nominals, the unmarked sequence of *de* + the definite article alternates with the marked used of *de* without the definite article, as illustrated in (118):[55]

(118)   le séjour/voyage . . .   le courrier/retour . . .
     a. F.SG.C   en France/*à la France   de France/*de la France

---

[54] The items *de/à* are also unlike prepositions in not allowing null topical dependants. Compare (ia) with (ib, c):
(i)   a. J'ai voté pour ⌀.
      I-have voted for
      'I voted for <some contextually relevant person/proposal>.'
     b. *J'ai pensé à ⌀.   c. *J'ai dépendu de ⌀.
      I-have thought to   I-have depended of
If this contrast follows from the availability of *en/y*, illustrated in text example (117), then encoding the necessarily overt nature of the 'dependant' of *de/à* in their lexical entry (as in Abeillé *et al.* 2004) is redundant.

[55] These alternations occur in locative/ablative contexts with geographical proper nouns, only. They don't occur in *non*-locative/ablative contexts, as shown in (i) and (ii), and neither do they occur with common nouns indicating a Location, as shown in (iii) and (iv). Here, the non-portmanteau sequences *à/de la* are both grammatical (as are the sequences *à/de l'* in the context of vowel-initial nouns):
(i)   a. une lettre à la France   b. *une lettre en France
      'a letter to (the people of) France.'
(ii)   a. la dépendance de la France   b. *la dépendance de France
      'the dependency of/on France'
(iii)   a. un séjour à la plage   b. *un séjour en plage
      'a stay at the beach'
(iv)   a. du sable de la plage   b. *du sable de plage
      'sand from the beach'

b.	F.SG.V	en Amérique/*à l'Amérique	d'Amérique/*de l'Amérique
c.	F.PL.C	*en Philippines/aux Philippines	*de Philippines/des Philippines
d.	F.PL.V	*en Indes/aux Indes	*d'Indes/des Indes
e.	M.SG.C	*en Canada/au Canada	*de Canada/du Canada
f.	M.SG.V	en Iran/*à l'Iran	d'Iran/*de l'Iran
g.	M.PL.C	*en Pays-Bas/aux Pays-Bas	*de Pays-Bas/des Pays-Bas
h.	M.PL.V	*en Etats-Unis/aux Etats-Unis	*d'Etats-Uni/des Etats-Unis
		'the stay/trip in/to . . .	'the mail/return from . . .

. . . France, the United States, the Philippines, India, Canada, Iran,
the Netherlands, the United States'

The marked use of bare *en*/*de* occurs when the head noun is either F.SG or a vowel-initial M.SG:[56] the presence versus absence of the definite article (as well as the choice between *à* and *en*) thus appears to depend, in part, on phonological factors, in violation of the Principle of Phonology-Free Syntax.

Of course, appearances can be deceptive. As noted by Cornulier (1972) and reported in Miller *et al.* (1997: 82), the marked option in (118) of bare *en*/*de* is found if and only if there's no portmanteau form corresponding to *à*/*de* + the definite article: *en* is used instead of *à la*/*l'* (but not instead of the portmanteau *au(x)*);[57] *de* is used instead of *de la*/*l'* (but not instead of the portmanteau *du*/*des*). Thus, the alternation illustrated in (118) isn't directly sensitive to *phonology*; rather, it's sensitive to *morphology* (which is in turn sensitive to phonology). Of course, such a pattern of sensitivity doesn't violate the Principle of Phonology-Free Syntax.

A final reason for doubting the lexical nature of *de* is its bleached semantics expressing the vague notion of association:[58]

[56] The pattern isn't watertight: the consonant-initial masculines *Danemark* 'Denmark', *Portugal* 'Portugal' and *Luxembourg* 'Luxembourg', as well as the French provinces *Limousin* and *Berry*, allow both *en*/*de* and *au*/*du*.

[57] The same pattern is found with the names of the four seasons: *au printemps* 'in spring', *en été* 'in summer', *en automne* 'in autumn' and *en hiver* 'in winter'. A portmanteau form combining *à* and the definite article is available and used with *printemps*, namely, *au*. No portmanteau form is available to replace *à l'*, which would be expected with *été*/*automne*/ *hiver*, and the marked *en* is used instead.

[58] Some varieties of French allow possession (rather than vague association) by an animate to be marked by *à* instead of *de*, as in (i) (Leeman-Bouix 1994: 129):

(i)   %la mère à David
       the mother to D.
       'D.'s mother'

The German Baader–Meinhof gang of terrorists active in the 1970s were called *la Bande à Baader* rather than *la Bande de Baader* (Goosse 2000: 118). This usage of *à*-marked nominals isn't new (see p. 5), and is doubtless reinforced by their standard use in (ii):

(ii)   Cet argent est à/*de David.
        this money is to/of D.
        'This money is D.'s.'

The use of *de* here could only have the literal meaning 'from', as in (iii):

(119) a. l'argent <u>de</u> Pierre
       the-money of P.
       'P.'s money'

b. le train <u>de</u> dix heures
   the train of ten hours
   'the ten o'clock train'

The low semantic content of *de/à* opens the door to the practice of omitting them altogether, as in (120), and explains the *de/à* variation illustrated in (121):

(120) a. pull (<u>de</u>) laine
       pullover of wool
       'woollen pullover'

b. d'une génération (<u>à</u>) l'autre
   of-one generation to the-other
   'from one generation to the next'

(121) a. une robe <u>de/à</u> €50
       a dress to/at €50
       'a €50 dress'

b. la confiture <u>de/à</u> fraises
   the jam to/at strawberries
   'strawberry jam'

With deverbal nouns, such *de*-marked nominals correspond to an argument of the related verb, as in (122), where *mon père* corresponds to the subject of the verb *partir* 'to leave' and *ce livre* corresponds to the direct object of the verb *lire* 'to read':

(122) a. le départ <u>de</u> mon père
       the departure of my father
       'my father's departure'

b. la lecture <u>de</u> ce livre
   the reading of this book
   'the reading of this book'

If the entire nominal is definite and the Possessor is a definite animate, the Possessor can be replaced by a possessive determiner (Table 3.1 on page 70), as in (123):[59]

(123) le départ de <u>mon père</u>   →   <u>son</u> départ
      the departure of my father   his departure

2.4.3   Preposition phrases

Prepositions select a (pro)nominal dependant which can be definite or indefinite, as in (124):

(iii) Cette lettre est <u>de</u> David.
       this letter is from D.
       'This letter is <u>from</u> D.'

Associates marked with *de* differ from those marked with *à* in being able to undergo wh fronting (§5.6.1) (Leeman-Bouix 1994: 132):

(iv) a. Il est l'ami [<u>de</u> qui]? → [<u>De</u> qui] est-il l'ami – ?
         he is the-friend of who
      b. Il est l'ami [<u>à</u> qui]? → *[<u>A</u> qui] est-il l'ami – ?
         he is the-friend to who
         'Whose friend is he?'

[59] *Le vol de ce soir* 'this evening's flight' can't be recast as *son vol* 'its flight' because 'this evening' isn't animate. The use of possessive determiners on menu items, as in *saumon fumé avec <u>ses</u> blinis* 'smoked salmon with its blinis' is a poetic device attributing animacy to the Possessor. See Godard (1986).

(124) a. avec l'argent   b. avec de l'argent   c. avec cela
          with the-money   with of the-money   with that
          'with the money'   'with (some) money'   'with that'

As we saw in footnote 54, where the dependant is topical, it can be non-overt. The prepositions *dans* 'in', *sur* 'on' and *sous* 'under' have special forms which are used in these 'absolute' contexts, namely, *dedans*, *dessus* and *dessous*:

(125) a. Je le mets dans/sur/sous le carton.   b. Je le mets dedans/dessus/dessous.
          I it put in/on/under the box   I it put in.it/on.it/under.it
          'I put it in/on/under the box.'   'I put it inside/on top/underneath.'

The 'absolute' use of prepositions like *avec* 'with', which don't have such special forms, has sometimes been condemned, or only begrudgingly recognised (Goosse 2000: 112) (examples from Porquier 2001: 124):

(126) a. Il a joué avec ⊘.   b. Il est venu sans ⊘.   c. On a couru après ⊘.
          he has played with   he is come without   we have run after
          'He played with.'   'He came without.'   'We ran after him, etc.'

2.4.3.1 Preposition stranding and pied piping

Like other Romance languages French doesn't allow preposition stranding, requiring fronted wh XPs which are dependants of a preposition to 'pied pipe' the preposition with them (§5.6), for example, in interrogatives and relatives:[60]

(127) a. *Qui tu votes pour – ?   b. [Pour qui] tu votes – ?
          who you vote for   for who you vote
                                                        'Who are you voting for?'

(128) a. *le candidat ⊘ que j'ai voté pour –   b. le candidat [pour qui] j'ai voté –
          the candidate that I-have voted for   the candidate for who I-have voted
                                                        'the candidate I voted for'[61]

(129) a. *[Quel arbre] il était caché [derrière –]?
      b. [Derrière quel arbre] il était caché – ?
          behind which tree he was hidden behind
          'Which tree was he hiding behind?'

(130) a. *Jean ne sait pas [quel arbre] il était caché derrière – .
      b. Jean ne sait pas [derrière quel arbre] il était caché – .
          J. NEG knows not behind which tree he was hidden behind
          'J. doesn't know which tree he was hiding behind.'

---

[60] On the formal difference between preposition-stranding and non-preposition-stranding languages see Pollock (1997: 97).

[61] In ConF preposition stranding is found, at least in relative clauses:
(i)   le mec ⊘ que je t'ai vu avec
        the bloke that I you-have seen with
        'the bloke I saw you with'

2.4.4 Il m'a sauté dessus, Je lui ai couru après

The examples in (131) illustrate a common but poorly understood phenomenon discussed recently by Porquier (2001):

(131) a. Il m'a sauté dessus.   b. Je lui ai couru après.
       he me-has jumped on   I him have run after
       'He jumped on top of me.'   'I ran after him.'

These examples are pragmatic and stylistic alternatives to those in (132):

(132) a. Il a sauté sur moi.   b. J'ai couru après lui.
       he has jumped on me   I-have run after him
       ≈ (131a)   ≈ (131b)

In (132) a dependant of the verb is expressed as a PP* in which the thematic dependant of P° is an animate pronominal. In (131) the preposition is used absolutely, that is, without a dependant, and the corresponding animate pronominal is realised as an indirect-object clitic (§4.4.1) instead. The alternation illustrated here is only possible with animate pronominals since indirect objects are necessarily animate. Other prepositions which appear in this alternation are: *autour (de)* 'around', *(par) derrière* 'behind', *à côté (de)* 'beside', *à droite (de)* 'to the right', *à gauche (de)* 'to the left', *au travers (de)* 'through', *avant* 'before', *(contre* 'against'[62]), *(au/par/en) dessous/dessus (de)* 'underneath/on top', *devant* 'in front of', *entre* 'between', *(pas) loin (de)* 'not far from', *(tout) près (de)* 'nearby'. The element *de* is in brackets here because it disappears in the course of the derivation:

(133) a. Il me tournait autour.   b. Il tournait autour d̲e̲ moi.
       he to.me turned around   he turned around of me
       'He was turning around me.'   ≈ (133a)

Prepositions which don't appear in this alternation include *sans* 'without', *avec* 'with', *pour* 'for', *chez* 'at the home of', *jusqu'à* 'until'.

---

[62] Porquier (2001) puts brackets around *contre* in this list because he found just a single example, in (ia), taken from the writings of San Antonio, who's well known for his creative use of language:

(i)   a. Il me meurt contre.   b. Il meurt contre moi.
           he to.me dies against   he dies against me
           'He's dying against me.'   ≈ (ia)

3

The extended noun phrase: DP*

In §2.1 we discussed the inflectional morphosyntax of nouns and the syntactic projection of thematic dependants within NP*. Binding and extraction facts (§2.1.3) suggest that a noun's thematic dependants – Possessor, Agent and Theme – are merged, not as adjuncts within a monolithic NP, but rather as a hierarchy of specifiers, as in (1):

(1) $[_{\theta PoP = NP*}$ Possessor $[_{\theta Po'}$ $\theta_{Po}{}^{\circ}$ $[_{\theta AgP}$ Agent $[_{\theta Ag'}$ $\theta_{Ag}{}^{\circ}$ $[_{\theta ThP}$ Theme $[_{\theta Th'}$ $\theta_{Th}{}^{\circ}$ N $]]]]]]$

Noun–dependant word order within nominals suggests that the noun incorporates into successive θ heads and then moves out of NP*. Thus, the *thematic* NP* is actually only part of a larger *grammatical* nominal structure. In this chapter, I consider this structure. This approach has become known as the (exploded) definiteness-phrase (DP) hypothesis. According to the DP hypothesis, NP* is augmented by a hierarchy of functional projections encoding various grammatical features of nominals, such as definiteness.

The chapter is organised as follows. In §3.1 I introduce the DP hypothesis and show how the functional structure above NP* provides head and specifier positions hosting the kinds of category and feature associated with nominals, as well as head positions into which the noun can raise. Following the practice in §2, the notation DP* is used to refer to the entire domain of functional nominal structure, comprising NP*, but also attributive adjectives and relative clauses, and determiners. In §3.2 I adopt the DP hypothesis to consider 'definite' determiners and the predeterminer *tout*, whose distribution is (mostly) restricted to definite contexts. In §3.3 I return to the issue held over from §2.4.2, namely, the role of nominal-initial *à/de* as inherent-case markers. Indefinite and negative nominals are considered in §3.4 and §3.5, bare nominals in §3.6. A number of what might be termed 'complex determiners' are also analysed in §3.6. Nominal-internal attributive adjectives are incorporated in §3.7 and pronominal DP*s are catalogued in §3.8. The distribution of DP*s within clause structure is postponed until §4.3, the syntax of clitic proforms, until §4.4.

3.1   Nominals as extended NP*s

An influential approach to the kind of syntactic interaction found cross-linguistically within a nominal between a noun and its various dependants (Brame

1982) assumes that a nominal isn't a mere lexical NP, or even the NP* in (1), but rather a thematic projection of the noun augmented by layers of functional structure, that is, a number of extended projections of N which encode various grammatical (as opposed to thematic) properties of the nominal. An early application of this approach (Abney 1987) posits a single grammatical determiner phrase (DP), as in (2):

(2)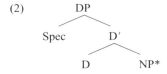

With its head and specifier positions, DP offers a template with(in) which to account for the cross-linguistic pattern whereby nominals are typically introduced by one (and often only one) head-like or phrasal determiner.

Abney's original DP hypothesis has been developed in many directions over the last two decades. First, just as the traditional lexical NP has been exploded as in (1), so it's been suggested that DP needs to be exploded into a *number* of hierarchically ordered projections, each encoding a distinct and unique grammatical property of the nominal. Some host a noun-related inflectional feature, for example, gender (or noun class), number, case. Others host attributive adjectives (§3.7).

Second, questions have been raised, for example, by Giusti (2002: 56), about whether determiner phrase is an appropriate label for the topmost functional phrase within nominals, and indeed whether the term 'determiner' means anything at all (see also Giusti 1997). Since referential nominals require case (see Chomsky's 1981 case filter), and since, when unmarked by inherent case in situ (§3.3), a nominal is required to move to a case-checking position, the topmost head of a nominal may be a case marker rather than a determiner. Following such lines of thinking, the model in (2) is doubly inappropriate: first, there's more than one functional projection above NP*; second, the topmost projection isn't a projection of a determiner. However, since the term DP is so familiar, I shall use the label DP* as shorthand for the complete nominal constituent (rather than Giusti's FP^{max}).

3.2   Definite determiners and predeterminer *tout*

This section deals with what might be termed definite determiners, that is, definite articles (§3.2.1), demonstrative determiners (§3.2.2) and possessive determiners (§3.2.3). These determiners agree in number and gender with the head noun, and thus make overt features which are often covert on the noun itself (§§2.1.2.1, 2.1.2.2), and distinguish between homonyms: *le poêle* 'stove M' ~ *la poêle* 'frying-pan F'. We'll see that definite articles, which often appear in generics, too, aren't unambiguous markers of semantic definiteness and neither are 'demonstrative' determiners unambiguously demonstrative, often looking more like mere definiteness markers.[1] Predeterminer *tout* (§3.2.4) is included in this section since it (typically) occurs in definite DP*s.

3.2.1 Definite articles

The definite articles are *le* (*l'*) M.SG, *la* (*l'*) F.SG and *les* M/F.PL.[2] They agree with the head noun:

(3) a. le garçon
         the.M.SG boy.M.SG
         'the boy'

     b. la fille
         the.F.SG girl.F.SG
         'the girl'

     c. les enfants
         the.M/F.PL children.M/F.PL
         'the children'

The definite article is ambiguous between a marker of semantic definiteness and a marker of mere nounhood, compatible with abstract and generic nouns:[3]

(4) a. l'homme
         the-man
         'the man', 'mankind'

     b. la cuisine
         the kitchen
         'the kitchen', 'cookery'

     c. les femmes
         the women
         'the women', 'women'

The extension to generics of the use of the definite article developed between the twelfth and fourteenth centuries (§1.3), and is usually related to the loss of overt gender and number marking on nouns (§2.1.2.2).[4]

How, then, to relate the role of the definite article as a marker of mere nounhood and its role as a marker of semantic definiteness? Rather than following Vergnaud and Zubizarretta's (1992) proposal to treat the definite article in French as an expletive determiner under a determiner head (see also De Cat 2002: 148), Guéron (2003: 201ff.) suggests that the definite article across Romance is a classifier, Clf°, associated with the φ features of number, gender and case, as well as the semantic mass–count distinction. For Guéron, the distinction between the definite and generic uses of the definite article hinges, not on the inherent properties of Clf°, but rather on the immediately higher structure. She suggests that, in definite nominals, ClfP is the complement of a [+DEFINITE] head, which she labels D°, but which we might usefully relabel Def(initeness)° (as proposed in Lyons 1994), and which triggers

[1] The development of demonstratives into definiteness markers isn't unusual, and happened earlier in Romance (§1.3). The ambiguity of the definite article between a definite and a generic interpretation is a further motivation for the innovative use of the demonstrative determiners as markers of definiteness. Consideration of any possible causal relationship between the non-definite use of the definite article and the non-demonstrative use of the demonstrative determiner is outside the scope of this book. For brief diachronic discussion of DP in French see Boucher (2005).

[2] On the fusion of *le/les* and *de/à* into the portmanteau forms *du/des/au(x)* see §§2.4.2, 3.3.

[3] Lyons (1999) proposes an incremental hierarchy of definite articles: English definite articles mark definiteness, only; in French they additionally mark genericity; Italian definite articles further mark possession; and in Greek they appear with proper nouns.

[4] This is in line with Giusti's (2002: 65) suggestion that the role of the definite article is to realise nominal φ features.

Clf°-to-Def° raising, as in (5a). In generic nominals, Def° isn't projected, as in (5b):

(5) a. [$_{DefP}$ [$_{Def°}$ les$_i$] [$_{ClfP}$ [$_{Clf°}$ t$_i$] femmes]]   b. [$_{ClfP}$ [$_{Clf°}$ les] femmes]
     the women   the women
     definite: 'the women'   generic: 'women'

Thus, while (5a, b) are both headed by the 'definite' determiner (and can therefore undergo fusion with de/à as des/aux), only (5a) is [+DEFINITE]. This explains how the definite/generic contrast can determine how otherwise formally identical DP*s containing a definite article can be pronominalised. The underlined DP* in (6a) is ambiguous, just like those in (4):

(6) a. J'aime le vin.   b. Le vin, je l'aime.   c. Le vin, j'aime (ça).
        I-like the wine   the wine I it-like   the wine I-like that
        'I like (the) wine'   'I like the wine.'   'I like wine.'

In (6b, c) the DP* is left dislocated (§5.3.1). Unlike (6a), the examples in (6b, c) are unambiguous: resumed with the direct-object clitic le, the dislocated DP* is definite, as in (6b); resumed with ça, or not resumed at all, it's generic, as in (6c). Where a DP* introduced by a definite article is incompatible with a definite reading, such as le jardinage 'gardening', the kind of dislocation illustrated in (6b) is ungrammatical, as shown in (7a) (De Cat 2002: 148):

(7) a. *Le jardinage, je l'aime.   b. Le jardinage, j'aime (ça).
        the gardening I it-like   the gardening I-like
                                          'I like gardening.'

Assuming the structures in (5), definite and generic DP*s of the form [definite article + noun] actually belong to two distinct categories, a DefP on the one hand, a ClfP on the other. The differing patterns of pronominal resumption are therefore not surprising. A direct-object proform is associated with a DefP, while ça and ⊘ are associated with a ClfP.

The structural contrast in (5) sheds light on how DP*s like those in (4) are interpreted in various contexts. For example, where the verb is punctual (§2.2.1.2), as in (8b), the generic use is impossible (cf. (8a)):

(8) a. J'aimais le vin.   b. J'ai aimé le vin.
        I-liked the wine   I-have liked the wine
        'I used to like (the) wine.' 'I liked the wine.'/*'I liked wine.'

The non-punctual aspect of the verb in (8a) can license Clf°, so the generic interpretation is available; in contrast, the punctual verb in (8b) can't, so the generic interpretation isn't available.

In summary, definite articles are phonologically weak functional heads, merged under Clf°, possibly raising to Def°. According to Giusti (2002: 56) articles are the *only* determiners which are functional heads. For her, the other determiners are specifiers. Such an approach to demonstratives and possessives is explored in the following sections.

3.2.2   *Demonstrative determiners*

The demonstrative determiners are *ce* (*cet*) M.SG, *cette* F.SG and *ces* M/F.PL:

(9)   a. ce garçon   b. cette fille   c. ces enfants
           DEM.M.SG boy   DEM.F.SG girl   DEM.M/F.PL children
           'the/this/that boy'   'the/this/that girl'   'the/these/those children'

Used on their own, demonstrative determiners have weak deictic force, only, and sometimes function as mere definiteness markers (see the translations of the examples in (9)). Note that they fail to distinguish degrees of proximity to any participant in the discourse (again, see the translations in (9)). Also, unlike true deictic determiners, they can introduce discourse-novel referents, as in (10):

(10)   Il y a ce type qui me harcèle.
        it there has this bloke who me bothers
        'There's a bloke hassling me.'

Finally, unlike deictic determiners, demonstrative determiners in French are compatible with restrictive relatives. Compare (11a, b):

(11)   a. *Je n'ai lu que ce livre-là que tu m'as donné hier.[5]   (deictic reading)
            I NEG-have read but this book-there that you me-have given yesterday

        b. Je n'ai lu que ce livre que tu m'as donné hier.   (non-deictic reading only)
            I NEG-have read but this book that you me-have given yesterday
            'I only read the book you gave me yesterday.'

Thus, the term demonstrative is misleading. I retain it, though, since it's the standard term for these determiners in the traditional and the generative syntactic literature.[6]

In order to capture the parallel between the non-deictic interpretation of the demonstrative determiner and the definite interpretation of the definite article, I propose to adopt a similar analysis: the non-deictic demonstrative determiner occupies Def°, the position to which the definite article raises from Clf°, if interpreted non-generically. This analysis is motivated below.

While the example in (12a) is ambiguous between a demonstrative and a definite reading, (12b) is unambiguously demonstrative:

(12)   a. J'aime ce vin.   b. J'aime ce vin-là.
            I-like this wine   I-like this wine-there
            'I like this/the wine.'   'I like *that* wine.'

In (12b) the demonstrative determiner is reinforced with a postnominal deictic

---

[5] Example (11a) is grammatical if there's a pause (comma intonation) after -*là*, in which case the relative clause is non-restrictive.

[6] In fact, the force of demonstrative determiners is so weak that Gary-Prieur (2001) claims that they can even introduce generic DP*s, provided the generic referent is being contrasted with some other generic referent(s).

locative, distinguishing between distal/proximal, as in (13):[7]

(13) a. ces jours-<u>ci</u>   b. ces jours-<u>là</u>
          these days-here   these days-there
          'these days'   'those days'

In recent work on demonstratives, Brugè (2002) and Giusti (2002) propose that: (a) (true) demonstratives in all languages are phrasal constituents merged as the specifier of a functional projection (which I shall label demonstrative phrase, DemP) low down in DP* (but above NP*); (b) demonstratives raise from SpecDemP to the topmost specifier in DP* to check a referentiality feature against the highest head in DP*; (c) raising from SpecDemP to SpecDefP is overt or covert, depending on the strength of the referentiality feature: assuming that the head noun raises to a head higher than Dem°, this means that, if demonstrative raising is covert, the demonstrative is postnominal, and if it's overt, the demonstrative is prenominal.

There's little in the syntax of the demonstrative determiners themselves in French to suggest such a movement-based approach; demonstrative determiners are always prenominal. However, this could simply be because the referentiality feature is strong in French and raising of the demonstrative determiner from SpecDemP to SpecDefP is therefore overt. Furthermore, we find clear support for the Brugè/ Giusti approach to demonstratives if we consider the syntax of the reinforcers -là/-ci, whose postnominal position is accounted for if they occupy SpecDemP. If, further, the surface position of -là/-ci, SpecDemP, is the underlying position of ce/ cet/cette/ces, then, in a nominal like ce livre-ci 'this book', for example, the sequence ce-ci is merged as a constituent in SpecDemP.[8] While -ci stays put,

---

[7] The reinforcers -là/-ci are weak forms of the distal/proximal locative adverbials ici 'here' and là 'there'. The full forms occur in ici/là-bas 'down (t)here' and ici/là-dedans 'in (t)here'. The weak forms occur within the demonstrative mass and count proforms cela/ceci 'that/ this' and celui/celle(s)/ceux-là/ci 'that/this/those/these one(s)' and the presentative voilà/ voici. Speakers in sub-Saharan Africa and Southern France use -là even with the definite article: l'autre-là 'the other one', le Boeing-là 'the Boeing' (Queffélec 2000b: 827). Distal -là is encroaching on proximal -ci (Goosse 2000: 130). Leeman-Bouix (1994: 140–3) attributes the loss of the -là/-ci contrast, at least in part, to the processing load associated with centre embedding (Dean Fodor 1995). In (i) the hearer has to associate celui-ci with Marc and celui-là with Jean, which disrespects linear order:

(i)   J'ai vu Jean et Marc; celui-ci a aimé mon projet, celui-là le trouvait mauvais.
       I-have seen J. and M.; this-one has liked my plan, that-one it found bad
       'I saw Jean and Marc; the latter liked my idea, the former thought it was bad.'

She concludes, '-ci n'est pas très clair dans la langue' ('-ci isn't very clear in the language') (p. 143).

[8] The idea that the demonstrative determiner and the locative reinforcer form a single constituent underlyingly is particularly appealing in Spanish where, unlike what's found in French, the two must be compatible in terms of a feature corresponding to proximity to the speaker (Brugè 2002: 27).

ce raises to SpecDefP. Thus, unlike non-deictic demonstrative determiners, which are functional heads merged in Def°, their deictic counterparts (together with the locative reinforcer, if present) are merged (as single constituents) in SpecDemP, following Brugè's (2002) proposal for Spanish. The surface order is derived, first, by raising the demonstrative determiner from its underlying position in SpecDemP to SpecDefP (leaving *-ci/-là* in situ), and, second, by raising the noun past *-ci/-là*:[9]

(14)

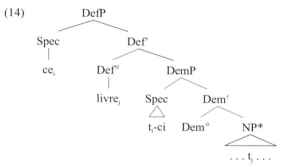

This analysis raises a number of questions regarding the linear placement of *-ci/ -là*. It's not just bare nouns that can intervene between the demonstrative determiner and the locative reinforcer in a structure like (14). Examples are given in (15):

(15) a. cette <u>robe jaune</u>-ci
          this dress yellow-here
          'this yellow dress'

      b. ce <u>projet de loi</u>-là
          this project of law-there
          'that bill'

      c. ces <u>3% de croissance</u>-ci
          these 3% of growth-here
          'this growth of 3%'

      d. ce <u>livre que tu m'as donné</u>-là
          this book that you me-have given-there
          'that book you gave me'

The example in (15a) is unproblematic if attributive AP*s merge higher than Dem°; the examples in (15b–d), in contrast, are very problematic. While we might argue that *projet de loi* in (15b) is a lexicalised complex noun which is merged under N and able to undergo N movement, such an approach isn't without its problems, and, in any case, certainly can't be adopted for *3% de croissance* and *livre que tu m'as donné* in (15c, d). If *-ci/-là* are merged outside NP*, then what these latter examples suggest is that the movement which takes the noun and its dependants out of NP* is phrasal movement rather than head movement. Phrasal movement out of NP* into DP* is explored further in §3.7 in the context of attributive-AP* placement. If such movement is needed independently, then it makes sense to assume that that's what

[9] In (14) the functional structure between Def° and DemP is omitted for expository purposes. The important point is that the noun raises over SpecDemP. For a slightly different movement analysis of the demonstrative determiners and their optional locative reinforcers see Bernstein (1997; 2001: 545–6).

underlies the word order in (15), too.[10]

In the above analysis, non-deictic demonstrative determiners (heads merged in Def°, the position to which truly definite articles raise) are distinguished from their truly deictic counterparts (phrases merged in SpecDemP which raise to SpecDefP). One might suppose, instead, that the demonstrative determiner is identical in both cases, and merged in Def°. The interpretative difference between the deictic and non-deictic interpretations would then hinge on -ci/-là. There is, however, hard semantic and syntactic evidence to support the dual analysis. First, *ce* can be interpreted deictically (albeit weakly), even without -ci/-là reinforcement. The second piece of evidence has to do with the extractability of a wh genitive. One of the parallels between DP* and CP* (§1.5) is that the highest specifier position is an escape hatch for wh fronting in both (§§5.6.1ff.), possibly because of the notion of phase edge (Chomsky 2001): SpecCP* is an intermediate landing site for wh fronting out of a clause, as in (16a); SpecDP* is an intermediate landing site for wh fronting out of a nominal, as in (16b):

(16) a. [$_{CP*}$ Quand$_i$ as-tu dit [$_{CP*}$ t$_i$ que Jean est parti t$_i$]]?
          when have-you said that J. is left
          'When did you say J. left?'

      b. [$_{CP*}$ [De quels étudiants]$_i$ as-tu corrigé [$_{DP*}$ t$_i$ les copies t$_i$]]?
          of which students have-you corrected the copies
          'Which students' scripts did you mark?'

In support of her analysis of Spanish demonstratives raising from SpecDemP to SpecD(ef)P, Brugè (2002: 22) notes that they block wh extraction. Compare (17a) with (17b):

(17) a. ¿De quién han publicado la foto?
          of who have.3PL published the photo
          'Whose photo did they publish?'

      b. *¿De quién han publicado esta foto?
          of who have.3PL published this photo

The dual analysis of the demonstrative determiner in French – non-deictic merged in Def°, deictic raised to SpecDefP – allows us to make a prediction about the extractability of a wh phrase from a 'demonstrative' DP*: while wh fronting should be impossible with truly deictic demonstrative determiners (because the demonstrative determiner occupies SpecDefP, the all-important escape hatch), it should be

---

[10] The data are clearly more complex than suggested by Brugè (2002: 38) who considers the data in (i):

(i)   a. ce livre-ci de Jean   b. *ce livre de Jean-ci
          this book-here of J.   this book of J.-here
          'this book of J.'s'

The examples in (15b, c) show that it's not enough to say that *de*-marked nominal dependants remain in their thematic SpecθP positions within NP* (§2.1.3).

fine with non-deictic demonstrative determiners (since SpecDefP is free). The facts relating to deictic demonstrative determiners can be readily observed, since the deictic reading can be forced using a locative reinforcer. In contrast, those relating to the non-deictic reading are less accessible, since the absence of deixis isn't formally marked. Nevertheless, the data suggest that the prediction is borne out. In (18a) the demonstrative determiner is clearly deictic (it's reinforced with -*là*), and wh fronting is ungrammatical, as expected. In (18b), provided the demonstrative is non-deictic, wh fronting is possible, exactly as in (18c), where the definite article replaces the demonstrative determiner:[11]

(18) a. *De quel livre as-tu lu ce chapitre-là?   (deictic reading)
          of which book have-you read this chapter-there

      b. De quel livre as-tu lu ce chapitre?   (non-deictic reading)
          of which book have-you read this chapter
          'Which book did you read the chapter from?'

      c. De quel livre as-tu lu le chapitre?
          of which book have-you read this chapter
          ≈ (18b)

Thus, I conclude that while the deictic demonstrative determiner raises to SpecDefP, the non-deictic demonstrative determiner occupies Def°.

3.2.3   Possessive determiners

The possessive determiners are set out in Table 3.1:

Possessor Possessum	1SG	2SG	3SG	1PL	2PL	3PL
M.SG	mon	ton	son			
				notre	votre	leur
F.SG	ma (mon)	ta (ton)	sa (son)			
M/F.PL	mes	tes	ses	nos	vos	leurs

Table 3.1. Possessive determiners.

There are six lexically distinct forms, one for each combination of the three person

---

[11] The example in (i) is fine:
(i)   Dans quel livre as-tu lu ce chapitre-là?
       in which book have-you read this chapter-there
       'In which book did you read that chapter?'
Example (i) differs from text example (18a) in the preposition *dans* 'in'. The difference crucially entails a different structural analysis, however. The PP *dans quel livre* 'in which book' is a VP* circumstantial of place rather than a thematic dependant of *chapitre*. As such, wh fronting doesn't involve extraction from DP*. The presence of the demonstrative isn't therefore expected to lead to ungrammaticality.

and two number features of the Possessor. No lexical distinction is made on the basis of the gender of the Possessor; *sa mère* corresponds to *his mother, her mother* as well as *its mother*. However, like the definite articles (§3.2.1) and the demonstrative determiners (§3.2.2), the possessive determiners agree with the number feature of the possessum: PL *mes/tes/ses/nos/vos/leurs* are distinct from the SG forms:

(19) a. mon/ton/son/notre/votre/leur livre   b. mes/tes/ses/nos/vos/leurs livres
          'my/your/his/our/your/their book'   'my/your/his/our/your/their books'

Again like the definite articles and the demonstrative determiners, the SG (but not PL) possessive determiners agree with the gender of the possessum: *mon/ton/son* are used with masculines (and vowel-initial feminines), *ma/ta/sa*, with consonant-initial feminines:

(20) a. mon père   b. mon école   c. ma mère
          my.M father   my.F school   my.F mother
          'my father'   'my school'   'my mother'

As with (deictic) demonstrative determiners (§3.2.2), Brugè (2002: 28) and Giusti (2002: 56) argue that, rather than being heads merged in Def°, possessive determiners are phrases. They are merged in the same NP*-internal SpecθP position as the semantically equivalent phrasal dependants, and then raise to SpecDefP.[12] They cite two pieces of evidence in support of this claim. First, like demonstratives, possessives can (in many languages, although not ModF) appear pre- or postnominally, as in the Spanish example in (21):

(21) a. la casa mía   b. mi casa   (Spanish)
          the house my   my house
          'my house'   = (21a)

Second, and again like deictic demonstrative determiners, possessive determiners prevent wh fronting, as shown in (22) (cf. (18a)):

(22) *$[_{CP*}$ [De quel roi] as-tu lu [son histoire t]] ?
       of which king have-you read his story

3.2.4 *Predeterminer* tout

The element *toutes* in (23) is referred to as predeterminer *tout* 'all':[13]

(23) tout-e-s les/ces/mes idées
      all-F-PL the/these/those/my ideas
      'all the/these/my ideas'

Predeterminer *tout* precedes one of the determiners discussed in §§3.2.1–3.2.3, and agrees in number and gender with the head noun, giving four forms:

[12] See the discussion of examples (26) and (27) on p. 23.
[13] On adverbial *tout* see §2.3.2.

(24)   a. tout   b. toute   c. tous   d. toutes
          all.M.SG   all.F.SG   all.M.PL   all.F.PL

Predeterminer *tout* is however incompatible with the generic use of the definite article. Thus, while the direct object in (25a) is ambiguous between a definite and generic interpretation, as shown in the translation, the one in (25b) containing predeterminer *tout* can only be interpreted as definite:

(25)   a. J'aime la musique.   b. J'aime toute la musique.
          I-like the music   I-like all the music
          'I like (the) music.'   'I like all the music.' *'I like all music.'

In the light of the analysis of the determiners in §§3.2.1–3.2.3, this suggests that predeterminer *tout* is sensitive to the presence of [+DEFINITE] Def°. However, this leaves open the issue of the position occupied by predeterminer *tout*. One possibility is SpecDefP. However, this can be ruled out given the analysis of deictic demonstrative and possessive determiners as occupying this position. Thus, predeterminer *tout* must occupy a position outside DefP. Note that wh fronting is possible from inside a DP* containing predeterminer *tout* and the definite article:

(26)   l'auteur [$_{CP*}$ dont j'ai lu [t tous les livres t]]
          the-author of.whom I-have read all the books
          'the author all of whose books I read'

It was suggested in §§3.2.2, 3.2.3 that a fronted wh phrase transits through the highest specifier position within DP*, and that the reason why wh fronting is impossible from within a DP* containing a deictic demonstrative or possessive determiner is that the determiner occupies SpecDefP and prevents the wh phrase from using this position as an escape hatch. The fact that wh fronting is possible from within DP* in (26) suggests that predeterminer *tout* doesn't occupy the topmost specifier position within DP*. Rather, it suggests that predeterminer *tout* occupies a head position, say PreDet°, selecting the [+DEFINITE] DefP as its complement, as in (27):

(27)   [$_{PreDetP}$ [$_{PreDet°}$ tout] [$_{DefP}$ Def°$_{[+DEFINITE]}$ . . .]]

Thus, in (26), the fronted wh phrase transits through both SpecDefP and Spec-PreDetP on its way out of DP*.[14]

3.3   *A* and *de* as DP*-internal inherent-case markers

The elements *à/de* were discussed in §2.4.2. In light of (a) the obligatory morphological fusion of *à/de* and *le/les* and (b) the existence of clitic counterparts (*y* and *en*), I followed Miller (1992) in concluding that these items aren't prepositions, but rather DP*-internal inherent-case markers, even when used to

---

[14] See the discussion of leftward quantifier float in §4.3.1 for further evidence that predeterminer *tout* is a head (rather than a specifier).

introduce locative/directional nominals. The reasons why these two factors suggest such a conclusion are as follows: (a) under the approach to the projection of syntactic structure driven by formal features (§1.5), morphological fusion affects functional heads; if *à/de* are DP*-*external* prepositions, then the morphological fusion which produces *au(x)/du/des* affects a *lexical* head; if *à/de* are DP*-*internal* case heads, the presence of morphological fusion is unsurprising; (b) pronominalisation as a clitic affects DP*s; if *à/de* are prepositions, the cliticisation which produces *y* and *en*$_1$ targets a PP* (§4.4.3); if *à/de* are DP*-internal case heads, cliticisation targets a DP*.[15]

In §1.5 we saw that case is a feature of the topmost head within nominal structure, but that there's morphosyntactic variation as to how this happens. Because of the general economy principle that structure is only merged if required, a separate case-marking head, K°, won't be merged if the morphology allows the case feature to be checked on some other head. Specifically, if the existence of a portmanteau form allows [CASE] and [DEFINITE] to be checked on one and the same functional head, then no separate case head is needed, as in (28), where [CASE] and [DEFINITE] are checked on the composite head K°/Def°:

(28)   [$_{KP/DefP}$ [$_{K°/Def°}$ au(x)/du/des] . . .]

If no portmanteau form is available, and [CASE] and [DEFINITE] can't be checked on a single head, they're associated with separate heads: [DEFINITE] on Def°, [CASE] on K°, merged above DefP, as in (29):

(29)   a.   [$_{KP}$ [$_{K°}$ à/de] [$_{DefP}$ [$_{Def°}$ la] . . .]]
       b.   [$_{KP}$ [$_{K°}$ à/de] [$_{PreDetP}$ [$_{PreDet°}$ tous] [$_{DefP}$ [$_{Def°}$ les] . . .]]]

The 'problem' with (29a), in comparison with (28), is that no portmanteau form exists which allows the case associated with *à* and the definiteness associated with *la* to be checked on the same head; with (29b) the issue is that the feature with which the predeterminer is associated has to be checked between [CASE] and [DEFINITE], thereby preventing these two features from being checked on the same head. The structures in (28) and (29) have the same distribution because they have the same (relevant) feature composition and therefore belong to the same category: they bear the same case feature and the same definiteness feature; they differ only in where those features are checked DP* internally.

3.4   Indefinite determiners

Indefinite determiners include indefinite articles for count and mass nouns, partitive articles and various quantifiers. The indefinite articles for SG count nouns are *un* M.SG and *une* F.SG:

---

[15] The use of *à* as an indirect-object marker is discussed in §4.3.

(30) a. un homme   b. une femme
          one man   one woman
          'a/one man'   'a/one woman'

The etymology of *un(e)* (<UNUM/UNAM 'one'; §1.3), as well as their use as cardinal numerals, suggests that they head a number phrase, NumP, distinct from ClfP/DefP, as in (31):

(31)   [$_{DefP}$ Def° [$_{ClfP}$ Clf° [$_{NumP}$ [$_{Num°}$ un(e)] . . .]]]

By distinguishing Def°/Clf° from Num° (rather, say, than treating *un(e)* as a realisation of a [–DEFINITE] Def°), we can account of the co-occurrence of a definite article and *un(e)*, as in (32):

(32) a. l'une après l'autre   b. l'un d'entre eux
          the-one after the-other   the-one of-between them
          'one after the other'   'one of them'

Turning to PL count nouns, no PL forms of *un(e)* exist in the modern language (cf. Spanish *unos, unas*).[16] Instead, the indefinite article for PL count nouns is *des* (= *de* + *les*) M/F.PL, that is, a combination of the inherent-case marker *de* and the definite article:

(33)   J'ai vu des étudiants dans le couloir.
       I-have seen of.the students in the corridor
       'I saw some students in the corridor.'

The same structure (*de* + definite article) is used for non-count nouns, too: *du* (= *de* + *le*) (*de l'*) M and *de la* (*de l'*) F:

(34) a. du beurre   b. de l'argent   c. de la confiture   d. de l'huile
          of.the butter   of the-money   of the jam   of the-oil
          '(some) butter'   '(some) money'   '(some) jam'   '(some) oil'

The *de*-initial *indefinite* articles illustrated in (33) and (34) can be contrasted with the paradigm of *de*-initial *partitive* articles which are formally identical – *du* (= *de* + *le*) (*de l'*) M.SG, *de la* (*de l'*) F.SG, *des* (= *de* + *les*) M/F.PL – but subtly semantically different. Consider the ambiguous string in (35):

(35)   J'ai mangé des cacahuètes.
       I-have eaten of.the peanuts

This can mean either 'I ate some (unspecified) peanuts' or 'I ate some of the peanuts (that is, some of those which are relevant in the discourse)'. In the first

---

[16] PL forms of *un(e)* are available in pronominal structures parallel to those in (32), as in (i):
(i)   a. les unes après les autres   b. Aidez-vous les uns les autres!
           the ones after the others   help-self the ones the others
           'one after another'   'Help one another!'
    In OF *un(e)s* was used as an indefinite determiner for entities conceived of as forming a pair or a set: *uns esperons* 'a pair of spurs', *uns ganz* 'a pair of gloves', *unes levres* 'lips'.

interpretation, the article is an indefinite, in the second, a partitive.[17]

In §3.3 I concluded that *de* is an inherent-case marker occupying the topmost head position, K°, within DP*, and that the portmanteau forms *du/des* occupy a composite K°/Def° head. *De/du/des* are therefore DP* internal, rather than heading a prepositional structure. Such an analysis is immediately attractive in the context of the *de*-initial indefinite/partitive articles. The alternative analysis of *de*, as a preposition, has unwelcome consequences for the analysis of indefinite nominals. If *de* were a preposition, then *de*-initial nominals would be PPs. Such a conclusion is implausible given that no other preposition can introduce a nominal. Further, PPs in French can't function as subjects and can't bear number or gender features (Abeillé *et al.* 2004), yet *de*-initial nominals can do both, as in (36):

(36)   Des étudiant-e-s sont arrivé-e-s.
       of.the students-F-PL are arrived-F-PL
       'Some (of the) (female) students arrived.'

Moreover, *de*-initial nominals can be co-ordinated with determiner-initial nominals, as in (37), and this again suggests that the former are, like the latter, nominal rather than prepositional:

(37)   J'ai acheté [des légumes] et [la pintade pour ce soir].
       I-have bought of.the vegetables and the guinea.fowl for this evening
       'I bought some vegetables and the guinea fowl for this evening.'

The ambiguity of the subject nominal in (36) between a partitive and an indefinite is reminiscent of the ambiguity of the definite article between a true marker of definiteness and a mere generic marker of nounhood (§3.2.1). Given that *de*-initial partitive/indefinite articles formally contain a definite article, we can deal with the partitive–indefinite ambiguity in (36) by exploiting the definite–generic ambiguity already covered: the indefinite interpretation of the subject in (36) is the combination of the inherent-case marker *de* and the generic version of the definite article, as in (38a); the partitive interpretation is the combination of the inherent-case marker *de* with the definite article, as in (38b):[18]

(38)   a. $[_{KP}$ de $[_{ClfP}$ la confiture]]]   b. $[_{KP}$ de $[_{DefP}$ la$_i$ $[_{ClfP}$ t$_i$ confiture]]]
           of the jam   of the jam
           'some jam' (indefinite)   'some of the jam' (partitive)

---

[17] The ambiguity is also found when the indefinite DP*s introduced by *de*-initial determiners are pronominalised with *en$_2$* (§4.4.3): *J'en ai mangé* means either 'I've eaten some' or 'I've eaten some of them/it'.

[18] The idea that partitive *des* effectively 'contains' a regular definite article is supported by the data in (i), where partitive nominals 'contain' demonstrative and possessive determiners, which are also semantically definite:

(i)   Je prendrai de ces/vos belles fraises.
       I will.take of those/your beautiful strawberries
       'I'll have some of those/your beautiful strawberries.'

Note that *de*-initial partitive/indefinite DP*s allow wh fronting, suggesting that SpecKP is available as an escape hatch (Abeillé *et al.* 2004):

(39)   les fruits dont$_i$ j'ai fait [$_{DP* = KP}$ t$_i$ de la confiture t$_i$]
        the fruits of.which I-have made of the jam
        'the fruits I made some (of the) jam out of'

Much ink has been spilled over what rules out (40c) below:

(40)   a. J'ai besoin de [ce livre].   b. J'ai besoin d'[un livre].
            I-have need of this book   I-have need of-a book
            'I need this book.'   'I need a book.'

        c. *J'ai besoin de [de l'aide].   d. J'ai besoin d'[aide].
            I-have need of of the-help   I-have need of-help
                                                    'I need (some) help.'

The element *de* can precede a definite and indefinite count DP*, as in (40a, b), but not a *de*-initial nominal, as shown in (40c) (cf. the grammatical (40d)). The 'problem' is usually seen from the perspective of an analysis of *de* as a preposition. If *de* is a preposition, the pattern looks odd since a preposition like *avec* 'with' can be followed by all three kinds of DP*, as in (41):

(41)   a. avec [ce livre]   b. avec [un livre]   c. avec [de l'aide]
            with this book   with a book   with of the-help
            'with this book'   'with a book'   'with (some) help'

However, if *de* isn't a preposition at all, but rather an inherent-case marker, as suggested in §3.3, then the issue can't be posed in the same terms: *de* isn't *expected* to behave like, say, *avec* 'with' because *de* is an inherent-case marker, while *avec* isn't. The reason why (40c) is ungrammatical is that it represents double case marking.[19]

Other indefinite determiners include the wh forms *quel* M.SG, *quelle* F.SG, *quels* M.PL, *quelles* F.PL (§5.6), as well as *quelque(s)* 'some, a few', *plusieurs* 'several' and *certains* 'some'. On the role of superlative APs as determiners see §2.3.3.3. On negative determiners see §3.5. Pseudo-partitive *de*, illustrated in (42), is discussed in the broader context of complex determiners in §3.6.

---

[19] Such apparent double case marking is common with *d'autres* 'other', as in (i):
(i)   a. des disques de d'autres catégories musicales
            of.the records of of-others categories musical
            'records from other musical categories'
        b. C'est par la propagande que les esprits de d'autres sont commandés.
            it-is by the propaganda that the spirits of of-others are commanded
            'It's via propaganda that the minds of others are controlled.'
This maybe suggests that the determiner *d'autres* is being grammaticalised to such an extent that its internal structure is no longer accessible.

(42)   J'ai beaucoup lu [de livres].
       I-have lots read of books
       'I've read lots of books.'

3.5   Negative DP*s

Negative DP*s can be simple negative proforms: *personne* 'nobody', *rien* 'nothing', *aucun(e)* 'none', *nul(le)* 'nobody':[20]

(43)   a.   Je ne vois personne/rien.   b.   Aucun n'était prêt.
            I NEG see nobody/nothing   none NEG-was ready
            'I can't see anyone/anything.'   'None was ready.'

       c.   Nul ne peut ignorer la loi.
            nobody NEG can ignore the law
            'Nobody is allowed to be ignorant of the law.'

Aucun(e) and *nul(le)* also function as negative determiners:

(44)   a.   Aucune femme ne veut me marier.   b.   Tu ne vas nulle part.
            no woman NEG wants me marry   you NEG go no place
            'No woman wants to marry me'   'You're going nowhere.'

Apart from *rien*, negative DP*s have the distribution of regular DP*s, discussed in §4.3. *Rien* follows the same pattern as the other universal quantifier, bare *tout* 'everything, all', discussed in §4.3.1 (see footnote 25 on page 113).

3.6   DP* structure and bare DP*s

In this section I discuss determinerless DP*s, that is, bare nominals, and various more complex nominal determiners. There's cross-linguistic variation in the acceptability of bare nominals, and Bernstein (1991) talks of a hierarchy from languages which are more, to those which are less permissive. Longobardi (2001: 582) notes that bare nominals in French can be predicates, idioms, exclamatives, vocatives and dependants of some prepositions, but not regular arguments. They can also occur in V–N compounds, where they are intensional rather than extensional (Bouchard 2003: 70). In French, only full DP*s can be arguments. Bare DP*s are thus more restricted in French than, say, English.

Bouchard (2003; see also Bouchard 2002) attributes the French–English contrast to the internal featural makeup of DP*s. He argues that the feature [NUMBER] is associated with N° in English but, as a result of morphophonological erosion, a functional head within ClfP* in French, with only secondary realisation on N°.[21]

---

[20] On *ne* (*n'*) see §4.5.1.
[21] Massot (2004) suggests that, in ConF, there isn't even secondary realisation of [NUMBER] on nouns. Similarly, Bernstein (1991) argues that Walloon nouns don't bear a [NUMBER] feature.

Bouchard claims this contrast is a factor in a number of empirical observations. First, number is rarely overt on French nouns (§§2.1.2.2, 2.1.2.3) and usually overt on determiners (§3.2); in English it's rarely overt on determiners and usually overt on nouns, instead (p. 56):

(45) a. [lə ʃa]   ~   [le ʃa]   b. the cat_ ~ the cats
          the.SG cat   the.PL cat
          'the cat'   'the cats'

Second, SG/PL uncertainty is reflected within the same DP* via co-ordinated SG/PL determiners in French, but via co-ordinated SG/PL nouns in English (p. 58):

(46) a. [tõ u te livʁ]   b. your book or books
          your.SG or your.PL book(s)
          'your book or books'

Third, French nouns are more readily ellipsed than English nouns in the presence of an attributive AP* (p. 59):

(47) a. la – verte   b. the green *(one)
          the green
          'the green one'

Fourth, various kinds of complex nouns (§2.1.1) which lack a nominal head are productive in French but not in English (p. 57), for example, V–N compounding and nominalised clauses.

(48) a. le tire-bouchon   b. le je-m'en-foutisme   c. les m'as-tu-vu
          the pull-cork   the I-me-of.it-do-ism   the me-have-you-seen
          'corkscrew'   'couldn't-care-less attitude'   'showoffs'

   Assuming that in order to refer, and in order to function as a grammatical argument (Bouchard 2003: 56), a DP* needs minimally to be marked for cardinality via the feature [NUMBER], then, given the locus of the feature [NUMBER] within the French DP*, French nouns are intensional (predicative) rather than extensional (referential) (Bouchard 2003: 60). Thus, French bare nouns can only be used intensionally, and resist functioning as arguments.
   However, bare DP*s headed by a common noun do occur, for example, in frozen V–N expressions, as in (49):

(49) a. avoir besoin   b. poser problème   c. faire peur
          have need   pose problem   make fear
          'to need'   'to be problematic'   'to scare'

There are restrictions on how N in such expressions can be modified. While pre-N attributive AP*s are possible, post-N ones aren't (§3.7). Compare (50a) with (50b), and (51a) with (51b):

(50) a. poser grand/petit problème   b. *poser problème énorme
          pose big/little problem   pose problem enormous
          'to be very/slightly problematic'

(51) a. faire grand'peur   b. *faire peur énorme
          make big fear   make fear enormous
          'to really scare'

With post-N AP* modification, a full DP* structure is required, as in (52):

(52) a. poser un problème énorme   b. faire une peur bleue
          pose a problem enornous   make a fear blue
          'to be enormously problematic'   'to scare the life out of'

In contrast, adverbial modification intervening between V and N is possible, as in (53):

(53) a. faire vraiment peur   b. poser souvent problème
          make really fear   post often problem
          'really to scare'   'often to be problematic'

These adverbials are merged VP* externally (§4.1); their medial position is a result of V movement out of VP* to a position above the adverbial (§4.2.2).

Bare nouns are also found in co-ordinate structures, as in (54):

(54) quand tu auras femme puis enfants
      when you will.have wife then children
      'once you've got a wife and children'

appositive contexts, as in (55):

(55) Paris, capitale de la France
      Paris capital of the France
      'Paris, the capital of France'

and profession titles used predicatively, as in (56):[22]

(56) Ma sœur est médecin.
      my sister is doctor
      'My sister is a doctor.'

The predicative use of a bare noun as a profession title resists certain kinds of modification, for example, relativisation, as shown in (57), where the relative clause necessarily co-occurs with a determiner:

---

[22] The examples in (ia, b) are subtly different:
(i)   a. Ma femme est actrice.   b. Ma femme est une actrice.
          my wife is actress   my wife is an actress
          'My wife is an actress.'   ≈ 'My wife behaves like an actress.'
The sentence in (ia) is an objective statement about a woman's profession; (ib) – the title of a film from 2001 – is a subjective evaluation of a woman's character, namely, that she behaves like an actress. Unlike (ia), the proposition expressed by (ib) can be true of a woman whose profession isn't acting. Thanks to Nancy Pallares-Pickles for discussion of this contrast.

(57)   Jean est *(un) médecin qui travaille beaucoup.
       J. is a doctor who works lots
       'J. is a doctor who works lots.'

Bouchard's analysis of some of the above contrasts in terms of the head with which the number feature is associated is also relevant to patterns of DP*-external agreement. Mostly, the French patterns match those in English. However, there are some contrasts. For example, unlike what's found in English, collective nominals like *la police* 'the police', *le gouvernement* 'the government' and *le monde* 'people' trigger 3SG agreement in line with their formal singularity despite referring to a plurality of individuals.[23]

Less straightforward are external agreement patterns of nominals which contain *de*, for example, those introduced by determiners comprising a member of the class of adverbial illustrated in (97) in §2.3.2 followed by *de*. Unlike the determiners seen so far, these fail to agree in gender and number with the head noun. And despite their syntactic complexity, it's still the head lexical noun that determines external agreement:

(58)   a.   [Combien d'argent] a été dépensé?   b.   [Beaucoup de femmes] sont venues.
            how.many of-money has been spent   lots of women are come
            'How much money was spent?'   'Lots of women came.'

Much attention has been paid over recent years to the syntax of DP*s introduced by such determiners. For (58b), den Dikken and Singhapreecha (2004: 19) propose an analysis in terms of an FP headed by what Hulk (1996) calls 'quantifier' *de*, with the adverbial merged as specifier, and the ClfP* as complement, as in (59):[24]

(59)   [$_{FP}$ beaucoup [$_{F'}$ de [$_{Clf P*}$ femmes]]]   = (58b)

The examples in (58) contrast with those in (60), with the structure in (61):

(60)   a.   combien des hommes   b.   beaucoup des femmes
            how.many of.the men   lots of.the women
            'how many of the men'   'lots of the women'

(61)   [$_{FP}$ combien [$_{F'}$ de [$_{DP*}$ les hommes]]]   = (60a) (*de* + *les* = *des*)

The examples in (60) differ from those in (58) in terms of the status of the quantified set of men/women, as indicated in the translations: in (58) no particular set of men/women is being quantified over; in (60), in contrast, it's the cardinality from within a pre-established set which is at stake. This difference is reflected in the

---

[23] In Québécois, *le monde* 'people' triggers 3PL agreement:
(i)   a.   Le monde vont pas te croire.   b.   Le monde me prennent pour une valise.
            the world go.3PL not you believe   the world me take.3PL for a suitcase
            'People won't believe you.'   'People treat me like a suitcase.'
[24] This analysis of these adverbials-cum-quantifiers as specifiers contrasts minimally with that of predeterminer *tout* in (§3.2.4) as a functional head. This difference is, however, motivated on the basis of the phenomenon of remote quantification, discussed in §4.3.2.

structure: in (59) the quantifier *de* selects an intensional ClfP*; in (61) it selects an extensional DP*. I return to the nature of *de* in these structures in §4.3.2.

The external agreement patterns of nominals containing *de* are discussed further in Doetjes and Rooryck (2003) (henceforth, D&R), who address the divergent agreement patterns triggered by quantitative and qualitative [(D) N1 de NP2] structures illustrated in (62) and (63), where the element determining the φ features of the entire DP* (and, therefore, external agreement) is underlined, as is the agreeing finite verb:

(62)   Quantitative (D&R, p. 278, ex. (2)):
    a. [Beaucoup de <u>livres</u>] <u>sont</u> tombés. b. [Une <u>montagne</u> de livres] <u>est</u> tombée.
       lot of books are fallen.M.PL   a mountain of books is fallen.F.SG
       'Lots of books fell.'   'A pile of books fell.'

(63)   Qualitative (D&R, p. 278, ex. (3)):
    a. [Ton phénomène de <u>fille</u>] <u>est</u> distraite.
       your phenomenon of daughter is distracted.F.SG
       'Your strange daughter is distracted.'

    b. [Ce <u>bijou</u> d'église romane] <u>a</u> été reconstruit.
       this jewel of-church Roman has been rebuilt.M.SG
       'This jewel of a Roman church has been rebuilt.'

D&R suggest the relevant difference between (62a)/(63a), where NP2 determines external agreement, and (62b)/(63b), where it's N1 that's relevant, stems from whether or not the quantifier/qualifier (that is, N1) retains its lexical semantics. In (62b)/(63b) *montagne* 'mountain' and *bijou* 'jewel' retain their lexical meaning (the books are being likened to a mountain; the church is being compared to a jewel), while in (62a)/(63a) *beaucoup* 'lots' and *phénomène* 'phenomenon' do not: they are semantically bleached expressions of (quantitative or qualitative) degree. D&R claim that this fundamental semantic difference ('comparative' versus 'pure degree' reading) results in divergent DP*-internal φ-feature percolation and DP*-external agreement patterns because there are two distinct underlying syntactic configurations.[25]

The 'comparative' reading in (62b)/(63b) is derived by inverting an underlying small-clause predicate structure within a functional projection headed by *de* (Kayne 1994), as in (64):

(64)   a. [$_{FP}$ [ce bijou]$_i$ [$_{F'}$ d' [$_{SC}$ [église romane] t$_i$]]]
    b. [$_{FP}$ [une montagne]$_i$ [$_{F'}$ de [$_{SC}$ [livres] t$_i$]]]

[25] The patterns illustrated are subject to change over time. Thus, while (ia) typically triggers SG agreement, (ib) has been grammaticalised and triggers PL agreement, even if the lexical noun is ellipsed; (ic) seems to be in a transitional stage: if DP* is PL, the entire nominal can trigger SG or PL agreement:

(i)   a. une bande de voyous   b. la plupart (des étudiants)   c. la moitié de . . .
        a gang of thugs   the most of.the students   the half of
        'a gang of thugs'   'most (of the students)'   'half of . . . '

Given that the nominal predicate which inverts to SpecFP retains its lexical semantics, it retains its φ features, too. By spec–head agreement, these are shared with F°, and by feature percolation, the entire FP, ensuring that SpecFP determines DP*-external agreement, as desired.

In contrast, in the 'pure degree' readings in (62a)/(63a), the semantically bleached quantifiers/qualifiers can't be predicated of a subject within a small clause. Instead, they're merged directly as the specifier of a functional projection, as in (65):

(65)   a. [$_{FP}$ [ce phénomène] [$_{F'}$ de [$_{ClfP}$ fille]]]   b. [$_{FP}$ [beaucoup] [$_{F'}$ de [$_{ClfP}$ livres]]]

Given their bleached semantics, these 'pure degree' quantifiers/qualifiers have no inherent φ features, and can't therefore determine the φ features of the DP*. Instead, F° inherits its features from N2.

There are reasons to doubt D&R's (p. 281) claim that, with the 'comparative' readings, D and N1 form a constituent. D&R explicitly reject Kayne's (1994) and den Dikken's (1995, 1998) analysis whereby the determiner is merged subsequent to inversion:

(66)   a. D&R: [[D N1]$_i$ [de [$_{SC}$ NP2 t$_i$]]]   b. K, dD: [D [N1$_i$ [de [$_{SC}$ NP2 t$_i$]]]]

D&R use co-ordination facts to support their analysis. Two [de NP2] sequences can be co-ordinated under a single D N1, as in (67a), while two [N1 de NP2] sequences can't be co-ordinated under a single D, as in (67b):

(67)   a. quelques merveilles [de robes] et [de souliers rouges]
           some marvels of dresses and of shoes red
           'one or two marvellous dresses and red shoes'

       b. *quelques [merveilles de robes] et [splendeurs de souliers rouges]
           some marvels of dresses and splendours of shoes red

According to D&R, these facts suggest that D forms a constituent with N1, as in (66a). Yet the relevance of the contrast in (67a, b) is unclear: independently of the structures under discussion here, it's well known that French determiners have to be repeated in co-ordinate structures (unlike English):

(68)   a. *les garçons et filles   b. les garçons et les filles   c. the boys and girls
           the boys and girls   the boys and the girls
                                          'the boys and the girls'

The ungrammaticality of (67b) isn't therefore instructive as to the constituency of superficial [D N1 de NP2] sequences.

In fact, there's good reason to take (66b) as the appropriate structure rather than (66a). First, in (64a) it's semantically implausible to claim that the demonstrative *ce* is part of the small-clause-internal underlying comparison/predicate:

(69)   [$_{SC}$ [église romane] [ce bijou]]

The Roman church isn't being compared with *this* jewel; rather, the property *bijou* is being predicated of *this* Roman church. Thus, the church is first compared to a jewel (*bijou d'église romane*) and only then merged with the demonstrative.

The semantic oddness of D&R's constituency is especially clear in the examples in (70), where the analysis in (66a) would mean that the bizarre properties *aucun bijou* 'no jewel' and *le ou les bijoux* 'the jewel or jewels' were being predicated of *église(s) romane(s)*:

(70) a. [Aucun bijou d'église romane] n'a été détruit.
         no jewel of-church Roman NEG-has been destroyed
         'No jewel of a Roman church has been destroyed.'

      b. [Le ou les bijoux d'églises romanes] auront été détruits.
         the.SG or the.PL jewels of-churches Roman will.have been destroyed
         'The jewel or jewels of Roman churches will have been destroyed.'

More plausibly, (70a) says that *no* Roman church that *does* have the property of being comparable to a jewel has been destroyed, while (70b) is about one or more Roman churches which are being compared with a jewel rather than Roman churches which are comparable with one or more jewels. In other words, the interpretation of these DP*s suggests the structure in (66b).

Note that the 'pure degree' data in (71), again taken from D&R (p. 284), also militate against the constituency in (66a):

(71) a. <u>cette grande diable</u> de fille   b. <u>ces sacré nom</u> de Prussiens
         this.F big.F devil of girl   this.PL sacred.SG name of Prussians
         'this big devil of a girl'   'these blasted Prussians'

According to D&R's (66a), the underlined sequences in (71) form a predicate-DP* constituent throughout. If this is right, the DP*-internal agreement patterns would be difficult to explain. The underlined sequence in (71a) comprises an M noun preceded by an F adjective and determiner; (71b) comprises an M.SG noun preceded by an M.SG adjective and a PL determiner. If, instead, the constituency in (66b) is assumed, the facts in (71) can be approached in an enlightening way. In (71a), first, assume that the underlying small-clause predication is between *fille* and *diable*. Predicate inversion then moves *diable* to the left of *fille*, into the specifier of the FP headed by *de*. Given the bleached semantics of *diable*, the (F.SG) φ features of FP are derived from *fille* rather than *diable*. When the adjective and demonstrative are subsequently merged, they have appropriate F forms. In (71b), second, the underlying small-clause predication is between *Prussiens* and *sacré nom*. Predicate inversion moves *sacré nom* to SpecFP. The determiner agrees with the φ features of *Prussiens* because of the bleached semantics of *sacré nom*. The subsequently merged demonstrative is therefore PL.

(72) a. $[_{DP^*}$ cette [grande $[_{FP}$ diable$_i$ $[_{F'}$ de $[_{SC}$ <u>fille</u> t$_i$]]]]]
      b. $[_{DP^*}$ ces $[_{FP}$ [sacré nom]$_i$ $[_{F'}$ de $[_{SC}$ <u>Prussiens</u> t$_i$]]]]]

In conclusion, then, (66b) is preferable to (66a) as an informal analysis of [D N1 de NP2] sequences with a 'comparative' reading:

(73) a. $[_{DP*}$ ce $[_{FP}$ [bijou]$_i$ $[_{F'}$ de $[_{SC}$ [église romane] t$_i$]]]]
      b. $[_{DP*}$ une $[_{FP}$ [montagne]$_i$ $[_{F'}$ de $[_{SC}$ [livres] t$_i$]]]]

3.7   DP*-internal attributive-AP* placement

Attributive AP*s in French are found DP* internally both pre- and post-N, as in (74):

(74)   un <u>bon</u> vin <u>blanc</u>
        a good wine white
        'a good white wine'

Attributive-AP* placement is subject to regional variation. Thus, while *gros* 'large' is usually pre-N, as in (75a), Queffélec (2000a: 786) gives the Maghreb French example in (75b), where it's post-N:

(75) a. un <u>gros</u> chat   b. un salaire <u>gros</u>
          a fat cat   a salary fat
          'a fat cat'   'a large salary'

Conversely, while *court* 'short' is usually post-N, as in (76a), Gadet (2003) gives the example in (76b), in which it's pre-N:

(76) a. une robe <u>courte</u>   b. une <u>courte</u> jupe[26]
          a dress short   a short skirt
          'a short dress'   'a short skirt'

Despite the variation, attributive-AP* placement is far from random, and is sensitive to various grammatical factors. A number of facts suggest that the post-N position is unmarked, and that pre-N attributive AP*s are in some sense specifically triggered.[27] First, while the vast majority of attributive AP*s appear post-N, only a subset appear pre-N. Second, while the interpretation of post-N attributive AP*s corresponds to their predicative use (where they have one), that of pre-N AP*s can differ.[28] In (77a)/(78a) *triste/seul* are used predicatively and mean 'sad'/'alone'; the

---

[26] Etiemble (1964) attributes the pre-N use of typically post-N attributive AP*s to the influence of English. See Rowlett (2006b). Gadet (2003) comments on the phenomenon in commercial/advertising/marketing contexts.

[27] Bouchard (2002: 147–53) catalogues semantic, phonological, syntactic, morphological as well as non-grammatical triggering factors.

[28] This works for the contrasting use of *grand* in (i), but not for *petit* in (ii), which underlies the non-contradictory nature of (iii) (Ricalens-Pourchot 2005: 67–8):

(i)   a. un homme grand   b. un grand homme
           a man big   a big man
           'a tall man'   'a great man'
(ii)   a. un homme petit   b. un petit homme
           a man little   a little man
           'a mediocre man'   'a short man'

sentences express the proposition that the pupil forms a subset of those entities which are sad/alone:

(77) a. L'élève est <u>triste</u>.   b. l'élève <u>triste</u>   c. le <u>triste</u> élève
           the pupil is sad   the pupil sad   the sad pupil
           'The pupil is sad.'   'the sad pupil'   'the poor pupil'

(78) a. L'élève est <u>seul</u>.   b. l'élève <u>seul</u>   c. le <u>seul</u> élève
           the pupil is alone   the pupil alone   the alone pupil
           'The pupil is alone.'   'the solitary pupil'   'the only pupil'

In the DP*s in (77b, c)/(78b, c) *triste/seul* are used attributively. Used post-N, as in (77b)/(78b), they again mean 'sad'/'alone', and the DP*s pick out that entity which is both a pupil and sad/alone. The AP* is thus intersective, providing information which distinguishes the relevant pupil from the other(s). In contrast, used pre-N, as in (77c)/(78c), the AP*s provide no distinguishing information: (77c) doesn't distinguish one pupil from others; it merely conveys the speaker's pity/ sympathy towards him; pre-N *seul* in (78c) is quantificational, indicating that there's just one pupil. The interpretation of the DP*s in (79) follows the same pattern:

(79) a. le triste élève seul   b. le seul élève triste
           the sad pupil alone   the alone pupil sad
           'the poor solitary pupil'   'the only sad pupil'

Third, and relatedly, some attributive AP*s which are post-N when they qualify the *ex*tensionality of the noun are pre-N when they qualify the *in*tensionality of the noun:

(80) a. un fumeur <u>gros</u>   b. un <u>gros</u> fumeur
           a smoker large   a large smoker
           'a fat smoker'   'a heavy smoker'

Fourth, pre-N adjectives can, in addition to being non-intersective, contribute to the definition provided by the head noun itself:

(81) a. petite amie   b. belle mère   c. chauve-souris
           little friend   beautiful mother   bald-mouse
           'girlfriend'   'mother-in-law', 'stepmother'   'bat'

This is also the case with some proper names which incorporate pre-N AP*s (Leeman-Bouix 1994: 102):

(82) a. Haute-Bretagne   b. Extrême-Orient   c. Basse-Normandie
           high-Brittany   extreme-orient   low-Normandy
           'Upper Brittany'   'Far East'   'Lower Normandy'

(iii) Chaplin, le grand petit homme
       C. the big little man
       'C. the great short man'

Fifth, unlike post-N AP*s, pre-N ones can affect DP* determination. In the DP* in (83b), which contains a post-N AP*, the PL indefinite article has the same form as (83a), which contains no AP*; in (83c), in contrast, which contains a pre-N AP*, the form of the PL indefinite article is different (§3.2):[29]

(83) a. <u>des</u> films   b. <u>des</u> films intéressants   c. <u>de</u> bons films
          of.the films   of.the films interesting   of good films
          'films'   'interesting films'   'good films'

Indefinite articles aren't alone in being affected by pre-N AP*s. Superlative AP*s like *les plus intéresssants* 'most interesting' (§2.3.3.3) can affect definite determination, too. In (84) the AP* is used predicatively:

(84) Ses livres sont <u>les plus intéressants</u>.
      his books are the more interesting
      'His books are the most interesting.'

In (85b, c) it's used attributively, first post-N, then pre-N. Used post-N the superlative AP* doesn't affect the form of the definite determination (cf. (85a)); used pre-N the definite article disappears:

(85) a. les livres b. les livres <u>les plus intéressants</u> c. ∅ <u>les plus intéressants</u> livres
          the books   the books the more interesting   the more interesting books
          'the books'   'the most interesting books'   = (85b)

Pre-N AP*s are thus mostly appositive (non-restrictive) (Longobardi 2001: 579), expressing inherent and subjective properties, while post-N AP*s are restrictive. Bouchard (2002: 147ff.) relates a number of facts to this basic distinction. First, typically post-N (restrictive) AP*s can be pre-N if they're interpreted as an inherent property of the noun. In (86a) the wide valley is being distinguished from valleys which aren't wide; in (86b) no such distinction is being made and wideness is seen as an inherent property of valleys:[30]

---

[29] See also the contrast between (iia) and (iib) in footnote 30. Goosse (2000: 121) suggests that this phenomenon is being lost and that forms like (i) are increasingly heard:
(i)   a. des bons résultats   b. des vieux messieurs
           of.the good results   of.the old gentlemen
           '(some) good results'   '(some) old gentlemen'
In the classical language, the article *de* was used even with SG (mass/count) AP*–noun combinations:
(ii)   a. de bonne musique   b. de bel ouvrage
           of good music   of beautiful work
           '(some) good music'   'a good (piece of) work'
           (cf. *une bonne musique*)   (cf. *un bel ouvrage*)
[30] Ricalens-Pourchot (2005: 65) gives the examples in (i)–(ii):
(i)   a. les occasionnelles émeutes   b. les émeutes occasionnelles
           the occasional riots   the riots occasional
           a, b: 'the occasional riots'

(86) a. une vallée large   b. une large vallée
          a valley wide   a wide valley

Second, AP*s appear pre-N more readily in definite than in indefinite DP*s (and, hence, in subject than in object position) because it's more natural to present the inherent properties of known entities than of unknown entities. Third, complex AP*s are more likely to be post-N than pre-N because the semantic complexity created by modification makes AP*s less likely to express an inherent property. Fourth, participial AP*s are post-N because they're construed as processes and therefore can't be presented as inherent properties. Finally, frequently occurring adjectives are more often pre-N because high frequency of occurrence corresponds with broad semantics and greater likelihood of being presented as an inherent property.

It's sometimes claimed that the heaviness (in terms of syllable count) of either the noun or the adjective can affect AP* placement. To be precise, it's suggested that short adjectives are typically pre-N, longer ones, usually post-N, and that a heavy noun can follow an attributive AP* it would otherwise precede. *Passionnant* 'exciting', usually post-N, as in (87a), can be pre-N with a heavy noun, as in (87b):

(87) a. un film <u>passionnant</u>   b. un <u>passionnant</u> tour de force
          a film exciting   an exciting round of strength
          'an exciting film'   'an exciting feat of strength'

This issue is taken up by Miller *et al.* (1997) as part of a defence of the Principle of Phonology-Free Syntax. The authors maintain that, while lexical, semantic and discourse factors play a role, a syntactic property like attributive-AP* placement can't be sensitive to a phonological feature like the syllable count of either the noun or the AP*. They suggest that counterexamples to the purported 'rules' aren't hard to come across (p. 73):

(88) a. une <u>inimaginable</u> joie   b. de la nitroglycérine <u>pure</u>
          an unimaginable joy   of the nitroglycerine pure
          'an unimaginable joy'   'pure nitroglycerine'

They also cite (1997: 73) statistics from Glatigny (1967) suggesting that in around 10 per cent of A–N and N–A combinations, the first element contains more syllables than the second, contrary to what the 'rule' would predict. And they mention Wilmet's (1980) study which shows that while the six most frequently occurring adjectives (*grand* 'big', *petit* [ptit] 'small', *bon* 'good', *jeune* 'young', *beau* 'pretty' and *vieux* 'old') are monosyllabic and massively pre-N, the seventh, *blanc* 'white', also monosyllabic, is massively post-N. Also, 80.4 per cent of the combined occurrences of the monosyllabic *bas* 'low', *droit* 'straight', *sec* 'dry', *pur* 'pure' and *dur* 'hard' are post-N. Miller *et al.* conclude that it's not so much

(ii) a. de titanesques transformations   b. des transformations titanesques
          of titanesque transformations   of.the transformations titanesque
          a, b: 'transformations of titanic proportions'

grammar per se that's at stake here as questions of style.

In what follows, the issue of pre- and post-N attributive AP*s is seen from the perspective of two broader questions which have been the subject of much recent work: (a) the order of attributive AP*s within multi-AP* sequences (see Scott 2002 for recent detailed discussion); and (b) the position of the noun within a sequence of attributive AP*s.

3.7.1   Attributive-AP* order

Ignoring the issue for the time being of where a noun appears within a sequence of attributive AP*s, a number of linguists have looked at the order in which such AP*s occur within DP*s, and have claimed that their unmarked order is universal, along the lines of (89), for example:

(89)   Attributive-AP* ordering:
   a. Event nominals: possessor>cardinal>ordinal>speaker-oriented>subject-oriented>manner (appositive)>manner (restrictive)>thematic[31]
   b. Object nominals: possessor>cardinal>ordinal>quality>quantity[32]>shape>colour>origin>material   (adapted from Scott 2002: 102)

It's suggested that this is possible because: (a) in addition to comprising FPs encoding nominal φ features, DP* comprises a set of distinct FPs, each of which corresponds to a unique semantic class of attributive AP*;[33] (b) the hierarchy of these adjectival FPs is universally fixed by UG; and (c) each attributive adjective is merged as the specifier of the relevant FP (Cinque 1994; Longobardi 2001).[34] Thus, fixed unmarked DP*-internal attributive-AP* linear order falls out from a UG-determined adjectival-FP hierarchy, just as fixed underlying linear NP*-internal thematic-dependant order falls out from a UG-determined thematic hierarchy (§2.1.3).

Scott's (2002) account of attributive-AP* order based on semantic *class* is attractive because it explains why the 'same' adjective can be ordered in more than

---

[31] For a similar model for attributive-AP* order in event nominals, see Longobardi (2001: 580, ex. (50)).
[32] The label 'quantity' subsumes (in order) size (length, height, speed, width and weight), temperature and age.
[33] The existence of a single SpecFP position for each class of adjective explains why, where two adjectives of the same class appear together, co-ordination is required, as in (i), and no grammatically determined ordering constraints apply:
(i)   les écrits [linguistiques et politiques] de Chomsky
       the writings linguistic and political of C.
       'C.'s linguistic and political writings'
[34] This is in line with Cormack's (1995: 93) maxim 'All structure is head mediated' which specifically rules out an adjunction analysis of attributive AP*s, but rather sees them licensed via a phonologically null functional operator head. It's diametrically opposed to the view adopted by Starke (2004).

one way (see the order of *triste* and *seul* in (79a, b) on page 85). This is possible because the 'same' adjective can belong to more than one class and its position is determined by its class. The adjective *triste*, for example, is either a subjective comment, merged as a relatively high adjectival SpecFP, or else it describes the psychological state of the referent of the noun, and occupies a lower adjectival SpecFP.

3.7.2 Noun placement

In the light of the model of UG-determined DP*-internal attributive-AP* order described in §3.7.1, consider the cross-linguistic variation illustrated in (90):

(90) a. [$_{DP*}$ a nice blue German <u>dress</u>] (English)
b. [$_{DP*}$ one bèle bleuve <u>cote</u> alemande] (Walloon)
c. [$_{DP*}$ une belle <u>robe</u> bleue allemande] (French)
a–c: 'a nice blue German dress' (adapted from Longobardi 2001: 573, ex. (43))

Although attributive-AP* order in (90) is constant, as expected, the languages differ with respect to where the (underlined) noun appears. It's standardly assumed that the pattern in (90) is the result of cross-linguistic variation in the extent to which the noun raises out of NP* (Bernstein 1991; 2001: 542; Crisma 1993; Cinque 1990; Valois 1991): in French it raises to F1°; in Walloon, to F2°; in English, as far as F3°, only.

(91)

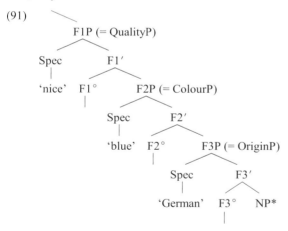

In French object nominals (see (89b)) adjectives in the hierarchy down to quality are pre-N, those from shape downwards are post-N, which some flexibility in respect of quantity. Thus, the assumption that attributive AP*s occupy fixed UG-determined positions, while nouns are subject to cross-linguistically variable degrees of N movement, accounts for the data reviewed so far. (The model in (91) is illustrative of the principle, only. A more elaborate hierarchy would be needed to capture the fact that nouns in Spanish, Italian and especially Sardinian raise even higher than in French. Within Romance, there seems to be a geographical continuum, with robust N movement in the south-east and weaker N movement in the north-west, although even in the north-west, N movement is stronger than it is in English.)

3.7.3   Complications

The approach to attributive-AP* order and N movement in §§3.7.1, 3.7.2 is complicated by comparative data like (92a–c), from Lamarche (1991: 223, ex. (16)), where attributive-AP* order in French is the reverse of that found in English:

(92)   French: English:
   a. une femme canadienne enceinte   a′. a pregnant Canadian woman
   b. une voiture blanche rouillée   b′. a rusty white car
   c. une bière blonde froide   c′. a cold pale beer

The linear-order problem is aggravated by one of scope. The idea that linear attributive-AP* order derives from structural hierarchy predicts that linear precedence matches scope asymmetry. In other words, if A1 precedes A2, then A1 has scope over A2. This prediction is borne out in English, as in (93a), but not in French, as in (93b), which is synonymous with (93a) despite the fact that the order of the adjectives is reversed:

(93)   a. [possible [financial worries]]   b. des [[soucis financiers] éventuels]
                                                        of.the worries financial possible
                                                        = (93a)

This is also true where, in order to encode distinct scopal differences, more than one linear order is possible within an AP* sequence. In (94) both orders are possible for the two pre-N AP*s, with a consequent scope difference:

(94)   a. a [handicapped [elderly person]]   b. an [elderly [handicapped person]]

While both examples in (94) denote a person who is both elderly and handicapped, (94a) implicitly contrasts such a person with one who is elderly but not handicapped, (94b), with one who is handicapped but not elderly. The examples in (95) show that the same flexibility is available with the two *post*-N AP*s in French:

(95)   a. une [[personne handicappée] âgée]   b. une [[personne âgée] handicappée]
           a person handicapped elderly   a person elderly handicapped
           'an elderly handicapped person'   'a handicapped elderly person'

Significantly, though, the pragmatic correspondences don't match up in terms of *absolute* order; rather, they match up in terms of *relative* order: (94a) corresponds to (95b), while (94b) matches (95a).[35]

These aren't the only problems facing the model of attributive-AP* ordering in §3.7.1 and N movement in §3.7.2. Two others might be mentioned. First, in the

---

[35] The data in (94) and (95) are taken from Lamarche (1991: 223, ex. (17)/(18)).

universal-AP*-order-combined-with-variable-N-movement hypothesis, all AP*s, wherever they occur within a multi-AP* sequence, pre- or post-N, occupy the same *kind* of position, namely, a DP*-internal adjectival SpecFP. Thus, we expect the same *kind* of AP* to be compatible with *every* adjectival SpecFP. Yet this flies in the face of much cross-linguistic evidence suggesting that the syntactic properties of pre-N AP*s are more restricted than those of post-N ones, irrespective of how far out of NP* the noun raises. Consider the contrast in (96) and (97):

(96) a. a proud father   b. *a proud of his daughter father

(97) a. un père fier   b. un père fier de sa fille
          a father proud   a father proud of his daughter
          = (96a)   = (96b)

The attributive AP* *proud* is pre-N when bare but not when it co-occurs with a dependant; in French *fier* 'proud' is post-N when bare and occupies the same linear position when it has a dependant. If the difference between (96a) and (97a) is merely the position of N, (96b) and (97b) are expected both to be grammatical, contrary to fact.

Second, the approach to attributive-AP* order and N movement is unable to account straightforwardly for the kind of effects that pre-N (but not post-N) AP*s can have on DP* determination seen in (83) on page 86. With the N-movement approach, pre- and post-N AP*s all appear in an adjectival SpecFP position within the extended NP*. The distinction between pre-N and post-N attributive AP*s is epiphenomenal, a side-effect of N movement. As such, it's not expected to affect nominal determination.

3.7.4   Solving the problem

How might these issues be handled? One approach to the data in (92)–(95) has been proposed by Sproat and Shih (1988; 1991) (see also Dimitrova-Vulcha-nova 2003). For these authors, the robust empirical generalisation isn't universal unmarked left-to-right attributive-AP* ordering, as expressed in (89); rather, it's universal relative distance from the noun. It's not that an attributive AP* of one semantic class occurs further to the left, or further to the right, than the other, but rather that one occurs further away from, or closer to, the head noun than the other. For example, AP*s denoting absolute properties (shape, colour) are closer to the noun than those denoting relative properties (quality, quantity), while subjective AP*s are further from the noun than objective AP*s. Such an approach can handle the data in (92)–(95), but it can't handle the data in (90): in (90a) *German* is closer to the noun than *blue*, while in (90c) *bleue* 'blue' is closer than *allemande* 'German'. On the face of it, therefore, the 'mirror-image' approach is no better than the 'universal-order' approach. Also, the 'mirror-image' approach doesn't answer the question why, in a given language, some AP*s are pre-N while others are post-N.

Observe from examples (94) and (95) that any analysis of attributive-AP*

placement is going to have to allow flexibility. The difference between the a and b examples is one of scope. Further, the analysis needs to cope with the data in (98), where the difference between the unmarked (98a) and the marked (98b) relates to information structure, and exploits a strategy used generally in Romance whereby the right DP* periphery contains a contrastive focus (Bernstein 1999; 2001):

(98) a. une voiture bleue allemande   b. une voiture allemande bleue
          a car blue German   a car German blue
          'a German blue car'   'a blue German car'

One way of making the 'universal-order' more flexible is suggested by data such as (99), from Lamarche (1991: 219, ex. (8a)):

(99) a. un groupe important de femmes   b. un groupe de femmes important
          a group important of women   a group of women important
          'a large group of women'   = (99a)

Assume that the DP*s in (99) both contain the NP* *groupe de femmes* underlyingly, and that the head noun in (99a) undergoes N movement over the AP* *important*. In the synonymous (99b) the AP* is preceded, not by the noun alone, but by the entire string *groupe de femmes*. Consider now the data in (100), from Lamarche (1991: 220, ex. (10b)):

(100) a. *une machine rouge à coudre   b. une machine à coudre rouge
          a machine red to sew   a machine to sew red
                                                   'a red sewing-machine'

The DP* in (100b) is headed by the complex noun *machine à coudre* (§2.1.1). Here, the attributive AP* *necessarily* follows the entire complex, rather than just the head noun, as shown by the ungrammaticality of (100a). What the data in (99b)/ (100b) suggest is that more than mere N movement is needed to capture N–AP* ordering. Phrasal movement is needed as well, optionally in (99b), necessarily in (100b). Significantly for our purposes, such an approach is suggested by Laenzlinger (2000; 2005) to deal with the contrasting order in which attributive AP*s appear in (92). In fact, the data in (92) are something of a simplification. Consider the English example in (101) and the *two* possible French equivalents in (102):

(101) a pretty little blue floral Scottish <u>skirt</u>

(102) a. une jolie petite <u>jupe</u> bleue fleurie écossaise
      b. une jolie petite <u>jupe</u> écossaise fleurie bleue

The order of the pre-N AP*s is the same in both languages. In fact, Laenzlinger claims this is true across all languages. In contrast, the post-N AP*s in French either come in the same order as those in English, or else their order is reversed (as in (92a'–c')). While the 'universal order' in (102a) can be accounted for with simple N movement, the 'mirror-image' order in (102b) can't. Rather than adopting Lamarche's (1991: 227) suggestion (see also Miller *et al.* 1997: 72 and Sadler and Arnold 1994) that pre-N AP*s are heads while post-N AP*s are phrases, Laenzlinger (2005) assumes that pre- and post-N AP*s are all phrases occupying SpecFP positions (as in (91)), but that some are located in SpecFP positions within a higher nominal-internal domain (DP*), while others are located within a lower nominal-internal domain (ClfP*). The strict order of the pre-N AP*s is UG-determined; their pre-N position is due to the fact that in no language does N movement raise the noun to the their left. Conversely, the reason why the French post-N AP*s are post-N is that the noun *does* raise to their left; the reason why they have two possible orderings is that two kinds of movement are available. The first, N movement, has already been seen, and readily accounts for the order in (102a). The second is phrasal movement. Laenzlinger suggests that each adjectival FP (FP$_{Adj}$) is immediately dominated by an agreement FP (FP$_{Agr}$) and that a projection of the noun can raise to SpecFP$_{Agr}$. This is illustrated in (103) and (104). On the basis of the familiar structure in (103) (now augmented with agreement FPs above each adjectival FP), NP* first raises to the specifier of FP$_{Agr}$ above *italienne*, resulting in an intermediate word order of *rouge voiture italienne*, and then the FP$_{Agr}$ dominating *voiture italienne* raises to the specifier of FP$_{Agr}$ above *rouge*, as in (104), resulting in the final word order *voiture italienne rouge*:

(103)

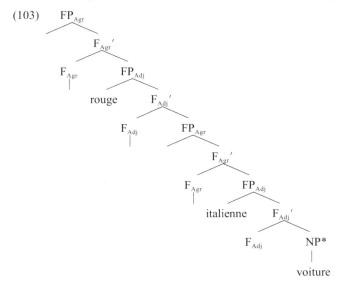

(104)

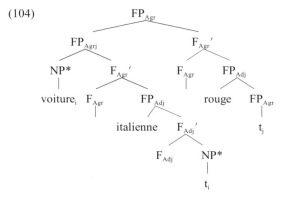

Laenzlinger's approach to nominal structure, AP* order and N/NP* movement provides a perspective on a phenomenon relating to en_2 cliticisation.[36] Compare the two indefinite DP*s in (105):

(105) a. trois articles intéressants   b. trois bons articles
       three articles interesting   three good articles
       'three interesting articles'   'three good articles'

In direct-object position, a subpart of DP* can be pronominalised using en_2. When this happens the behaviour of attributive AP*s is sensitive to the pre-N-versus-post-N distinction: while the pre-N *bons* seems unaffected by en_2-pronominalisation (106b), post-N *intéressants* is preceded by *de* 'of' (107b):

(106) a. Ce livre contient trois <u>bons</u> articles.
      this book contains three good articles
      'This books contains three good articles.'

    b. Ce livre <u>en</u> contient trois <u>bons</u>.
      this book en_2 contains three good
      'This book contains three good ones.'

(107) a. Ce livre contient trois articles <u>intéressants</u>.
      this book contains three articles interesting
      'This book contains three interesting articles.'

    b. Ce livre <u>en</u> contient trois <u>d'interessants</u>.
      this book en_2 contains three of-interesting
      'This book contains three interesting ones.'

We can account for this contrast by taking recourse to the informal notion that *de* is used to license AP*s which would otherwise be 'orphaned', for example, in *quelqu'un <u>d'intéressant</u>* 'someone interesting', where *intéressant* cannot be accommodated within the minimal DP* structure containing *quelqu'un*. The occurrence of *de* with *intéressant* in (107b), but not with *bon* in (106b), suggests that the constituent targeted by pronominalisation with subnominal *en*$_2$ – marked ? in (108) – is lower than the point at which pre-N AP*s are attached but higher than the point at which post-N AP*s are attached:

(108)

      pre-N AP*   ?

      post-N AP*

Given the above discussion, we might assume that the constituent marked ? is ClfP*.

3.8   Grammatical DP*s: non-clitic proforms

In the final section of this chapter I turn to what can be termed grammatical DP*s, that is, non-clitic proforms, or DP*s devoid of lexical content. In fact, some grammaticalised DP*s have already been mentioned, for example, *tout* 'all', *rien* 'nothing', *beaucoup* 'lots'. The non-clitic personal proforms are *moi* 1SG, *toi* 2SG, *lui* 3SG.M, *elle* 3SG.F, *nous* 1PL, *vous* 2PL, *eux* 3PL.M, *elles* 3PL.F.[37] The list can be supplemented with *soi* 3SG, the non-clitic equivalent of the non-specific subject clitic *on* (§4.4.4), used with human referents of either or unknown gender:

(109) Chacun pour soi!
     everyone for self
     'Everyone for him/herself!'

Similarly non-clitic are the reflexive proforms ending in *-même(s)* '-self/-selves': *moi-même* 1SG, *toi-même* 2SG, *lui-même* 3M.SG, *elle-même* 3F.SG, *nous-même(s)*[38] 1PL, *vous-même(s)*[38] 2PL, *eux-mêmes* 3M.PL, *elles-mêmes* 3F.PL, *soi-même* 'oneself'.

Non-clitic proforms are distinguished from clitic proforms (§4.4). Non-clitic (stressed, tonic, strong, disjunctive) proforms (henceforth, non-clitics) are independent forms with (usually) the distribution of DP*s. Clitic (unstressed, atonic, weak, conjunctive) proforms (henceforth, clitics) are phonologically, morphologically and syntactically dependent on a host. Unlike clitics, which appear in a fixed order and position, forming a single prosodic unit with the verb, non-clitics (usually) appear in environments where they can bear stress independently. Thus, they can be contrastive and co-ordinated:

---

[37] In Québécois the PL proforms also exist with suffixed *autres* 'others': *nous/vous/eux/elles autres*. For recent sociolinguistic and stylistic discussion, see Blondeau (2004). Cf. Spanish *nosotros* 'we/us' and *vosotros* 'you'.

[38] As plurals, *nous-même(s)* and *vous-même(s)* typically have final *-s*. However, where *nous* is used as a 'royal we', that is, as a facetious alternative to *moi* 'me', or where *vous* is used as a polite SG, these reflexives lack final *-s*.

(110) a. Je veux lui, pas toi!   b. Il veut voir toi et moi.
         I want him not you   he wants see you and me
         'I want *him*, not *you*!'   'He wants to see you and me'

Their form doesn't vary with their syntactic function:

(111) a. Moi, je m'en vais.   b. Moi, tu m'énerves.
         me I me-of.it go   me you me-annoy
         'I'm leaving' (*moi* = subject)   'You're annoying me' (*moi* = direct object)

      c. Moi, il m'a donné un livre.
         me he me-has given a book
         'He gave me a book' (*moi* = indirect object)

They enjoy considerable syntactic independence appearing as the dependant of a verb or preposition, dislocated (§5.3.1) or as a one-word utterance:

(112) a. J'aime ça.   b. Je suis contre ça.   c. Ça, c'est bon!
         I-like that   I am against that   that, it-is good
         'I like that'   'I'm against that.'   'That's good!'

      d. – Qu'est-ce que tu veux? – Ça!
         what-is-it that you want that
         'What do you want?' 'That!'

    Other non-clitics are:

– the locatives *ici* 'here' and *là* 'there';

– the demonstratives *celui* M.SG, *celle* F.SG, *ceux* M.PL, *celles* F.PL: unlike the demonstrative determiners (§3.2), which only *optionally* co-occur with a restrictor (proximal *-ci*/distal *-là*, a *de*/*à*-marked nominal or a relative clause), the demonstrative proforms *necessarily* co-occur with one:

(113) Des livres? J'aime celui-là et celui de Jean, mais pas celui que tu m'as prêté.
      of.the books I-like this-there and this of J. but not this that you me-have lent
      'Books? I like that one and J.'s, but not the one you lent me.'

– *ceci* 'this' and *cela* (and its informal reduced form *ça*[39]) 'that':

---

[39] Gadet (2003) gives the regional example in (i) in which direct-object *ça* is preverbal like a clitic (§4.4.1), although the relevant underlying grammatical difference here may of course relate to the verb rather than the proform:
(i)   %On peut ça faire.
       one can that do
       'We can do that.'
Even outside these specific regional varieties, the distribution of *ça* doesn't quite match that of *cela*. For example, unlike *cela*, *ça* behaves like a clitic (§4.4.4) in functioning as a resumptive proform in dislocation structures (§5.3):
(ii)   a. Les voisins, ça boit.   b. *Les voisins, cela boit.
          the neighbours that drinks   the neighbours that drinks
          'The neighbours like their drink.'

(114) a. Lisez ceci!   b. Cela peut arriver.
      read this   that can arrive
      'Read this!'   'That can happen.'

These proforms regard their referent as a single, global entity, with no internal structure, divisions or φ features. In (115) *ça* doesn't refer to any individual baby, it refers to the concept of a baby in the house:

(115)   Un bébé dans la maison, ça va être de trop.
        a baby in the house that goes be of too
        'A baby in the house will be too much.'

This semantic subtlety is illustrated by the exchanges in (116a, b):

(116) a.   – Tu aimes les fleurs? – Oui, j'aime ça.
       b.   – Tu aimes les fleurs? – Oui, je <u>les</u> aime.
           you like the flowers yes I them like that
           a: 'Do you like flowers?' 'Yes, I do (like flowers).'
           b: 'Do you like <u>the</u> flowers?' 'Yes, I do (like <u>the</u> flowers).'

In (116a) *ça* denotes the generic notion of flowers, corresponding to a generic interpretation of the DP* *les fleurs* 'the flowers' (Auger 1993; §3.2); in (116b) the clitic *les* refers to a set of individualised flowers, corresponding to a specific interpretation of the DP* (§3.2). The contrast is also illustrated in (117):

(117) a.   Je cherche <u>ma</u>/<u>une</u> femme; est-ce que je vais la trouver?
           I seek my/a woman; Q I go her find
           'I'm looking for my wife/a woman; will I find her?'

       b.   Je cherche une femme qui sache coudre; *est-ce que je vais la trouver?
                                       est-ce que je vais trouver ça?
           I seek a woman who knows sew; Q I go her find that
           'I'm looking for a woman who can sew; *will I find her?'
                                        will I find one?'

The non-individuation in the interpretation of the referent of *ça* is doubtless the reason why it can be felt to be pejorative with specific human referents (especially PL):

(iii)   a. J'aimerais <u>ça</u>, qu'on aie un bébé.   b. *J'aimerais <u>cela</u>, qu'on aie un bébé.
          I-would.like that, that-one has a baby   I-would.like that, that-one has a baby
          'I'd like us to have a baby.'
Nadasdi (1995: 6) labels *ça* in (iia) a non-specific subject clitic.
    Further, Leeman-Bouix (1994: 145) illustrates various uses of *ça* where it *can't* be replaced by *cela*. While *cela* refers both deictically (*Donnez-moi <u>cela</u>!* 'Give me that!') and anaphorically (*Et avec <u>cela</u>?* 'Anything else?' lit. 'And with that?'), *ça* can, in addition, refer more vaguely, to a general situation:
(iv)   a. Ah, <u>ça</u> oui! (cf. *Ah, <u>cela</u> oui!)   b. <u>Ça</u> va? (cf. *<u>Cela</u> va?)
          oh that yes   that goes
          'You bet!'   'Alright?'

(118) a. Tu sais, les voisins, <u>ça</u> boit!
you know, the neighbours, that drinks
'You know, the neighbours, they like their drink!'

   b. <u>Ça</u> criait, <u>ça</u> lançait des postillons, <u>ça</u> frappait du poing sur la table, <u>ça</u> essayait de se convaincre soi-même que <u>ça</u> connaissait quelque chose.
that shouted, that threw of.the saliva, that hit of.the fist on the table, that tried of self convince self that that knew something
'They would shout, they would spit, they would bang their fists on the table, they would try to convince themselves that they knew something.'
(Michel Tremblay *Hotel Bristol New York, N.Y.*, 46–7)

However, such a pejorative attitude isn't unambiguously present, and the generic use of *ça* can convey a note of affection (Jones 1996: 214):

(119) a. A quarante ans, une femme, <u>ça</u> se repose.
at forty years a woman that self rests
'At the age of forty, a woman should be resting.'

   b. Un bon étudiant, <u>ça</u> prend toujours des notes.
a good student that takes always of.the notes
'A good student always takes notes.'

– the interrogatives (*qui, quoi, (le)quel* M.SG, *(la)quelle* F.SG, *(les)quels* M.PL, *(les)quelles* F.PL): with [–HUMAN] referents *quoi* is used (§5.8.3); *qui* is used with [+HUMAN] referents:[40]

(120) a. Tu as vu quoi?   b. Tu as vu qui?
you have seen what   you have seen who
'What did you see?'   'Who did you see?'

The remaining four (long) interrogative proforms are transparent combinations of definite article and interrogative determiner (§3.2):

(121) Tu veux lequel/laquelle/lesquels/lesquelles?
you want the.which.M.SG/F.SG/M.PL/F.PL
'Which one(s) do you want?'

Unlike *qui/quoi*, these proforms presuppose a closed set of possible answers. Compare (122a, b):

(122) a. Tu as beaucoup d'amis. <u>Qui</u> veux-tu inviter?
   b. Tu as beaucoup d'amis. <u>Lequel</u> veux-tu inviter?
you have lot of-friends who/which want-you invite
'You have many friends. Who/Which one do you want to invite?'

In (122b) – but not (122a) – the speaker presupposes that one of the addressee's friends, rather than some other person, will be invited (on the broader issues of interrogation see §5.6). The short forms are interrogative determiners used

---

[40] On the [–HUMAN] use of interrogative *qui* see Rottet (2004).

pronominally, and appear in one syntactic environment only, namely, as the inverted dependant of *être* 'to be' (§5.7); Comorovski (2004) suggests it's a clitic;

– the relatives (*qui*, *lequel* M.SG, *laquelle* F.SG, *lesquels* M.PL, *lesquelles* F.PL, *quoi*, *dont*, *où*): *qui* and the *lequel* sequence are superficially parallel to the interrogatives: *qui* is used with [+HUMAN] antecedents,[41] irrespective of whether there's an overt head noun, as in (123a), an indefinite expression, as in (123b), or a zero antecedent, as in (123c):

(123) a.   les étudiants [avec qui j'ai cours]
       the students with who I-have lesson
       'the students I have a class with'

    b.   quelqu'un [pour qui j'ai beaucoup de respect]
       someone for who I-have lot of respect
       'someone for whom I have a great deal of respect'

    c.   ∅ [pour qui sonne le glas]
       for who rings the bell
       'for whom the bell tolls'

Lequel, etc., are insensitive to the [±HUMAN] distinction,[42] but require an overt head noun:

(124) a.   la chaise [sur laquelle j'étais assis]
       the chair on which I-was seated
       'the chair on which I was sitting'

    b.   les personnes [sur lesquelles je comptais]
       the people on which I counted
       'the people on whom I was counting'

Where no head noun is available, *qui* or *quoi* is used:

(125)   Il me faut quelquechose/quelqu'un [sur quoi/qui me reposer].
       it me needs something/someone on what/who me rest
       'I need something/someone on which/whom to rest.'

Dont and *où* are traditionally described as prepositional relative proforms because they stand for a *de/à*-marked DP*:

---

[41] Goosse (2000: 113) gives the example in (i) of [–HUMAN] use of relative *qui*:
(i)   les objets familiers, à qui l'ouverture des volets donne leur douche de lumière
       the objects familiar to who the-opening of.the shutters gives their shower of light
       'the familiar objects who are bathed in light when the shutters are opened'
He suggests that such usage 'appears to indicate a search for elegance'.
[42] Goosse (2000: 122) suggests that relative *lequel*, etc., is losing its sensitivity to number/gender, too, with *lequel* used with SG and PL, and M and F antecedents. See Massot (2004).

(126) a. l'homme [dont je dépends]   (dont = de l'homme)
       the-man of.which I depend
       'the man on whom I depend'

    b. l'université [où j'ai étudié]   (où = à l'université)
       the university at.which I-have studied
       'the university at which I studied'

However, given the analysis of *de*/*à* in §3.3 as inherent-case markers, such a label is inappropriate; rather, *dont* and *où* are inherent-case-marked-DP* relative proforms. (On the broader issues of relativisation, in particular subject and object relatives see §§5.6.1, 5.8.1.)

– *oui* 'yes' and *non* 'no', which replace finite assertive clauses; thus, in addition to functioning as one-word responses to yes–no questions, as in (127a), *oui*/*non* also appear in subordinate contexts, introduced by finite complementiser *que*/*si*, as in (127b, c):

(127) a. – Tu viens? – Oui/Non.
       you come yes/no
       'Are you coming?' 'Yes/No.'

    b. [$_{CP*}$ Si oui], dis-le-moi.   c. Elle dit [$_{CP*}$ que non].
       if yes say-it-me   she says that no
       'If so, tell me.'   'She says not.'

Further, while *oui*/*non* can't follow a subject DP* in canonical subject position, as shown in (128a), they can follow a dislocated (§5.3.1) – that is, clause-external – subject DP*, as in (128b):

(128) a. *Jean oui.   b. Marc ne veut pas venir, mais Jean, oui.
       J. yes   M. NEG wants not come but J. yes
                                   'M. doesn't want to come, but J. does.'

If dislocated topics are clause external, then *oui*/*non* arguably replaces the entire clause here, as shown clearly in (129):

(129) Marc ne veut pas venir, mais Jean, il veut venir.[43]
      M. neg wants not come but J. he wants come
      'M. doesn't want to come, but J. does want to come.'

The notion that *oui*/*non* specifically replace an *assertive* clause is supported by the contrast between (130a, b):[44]

---

[43] These data also provide further evidence that left-dislocated phrases are merged in their surface left-peripheral position, rather than moved there. See §5.3.1.

[44] Judgements aren't categorical here. Nevertheless, a Google search on 20 April 2004 found approximately 1,730 and 4,386 webpages containing the strings <espère que oui> and <espère que non>, respectively (ignoring webpages containing the irrelevant string <espère que non seulement>), but just 19 and 68 containing <souhaite que oui> and <souhaite que non>, respectively (and, again, ignoring webpages containing the irrelevant string <souhaite

(130) a. J'espère que <u>oui</u>/<u>non</u>.   b. *Je souhaite que <u>oui</u>/<u>non</u>.
           I-hope that yes/no   I wish that yes/no
           'I hope so/not.'

See §5.1.2.

que non seulement>). Given that there were approximately 477,000 and 538,000 webpages containing <espère> and <souhaite>, respectively, the small number of <souhaite que oui/non> hits is unexpected if the sequence is grammatical.

4

The extended verb phrase: IP*

Having looked at the morphosyntax of verbs in §2.2.1, and lexically and pragmatically determined VP* structure in §§2.2.2, 2.2.3, I turn now to the extended VP*, that is, the clausal structure above the lexical VP*, encoding such inflectional features as tense, mood and aspect. The aim of the chapter is to explore how the interplay between verbs and other clausal constituents sheds light on the structure of the clause. As we shall see, even independently of the pragmatic properties of the left periphery (§5), much evidence suggests that the clause is a much more richly articulated structure than the traditional analysis in terms of a single IP projection suggests. Following the practice developed thus far, this domain of clause structure is therefore labelled IP*. We'll see that the IP*-internal hierarchy of FPs parallels the ClfP*-internal hierarchy of FPs seen in §3. For example, just as the mass–count distinction is an aspectual property of nominals encoded within ClfP*, so the perfective–imperfective distinction is an aspectual property of clauses encoded within IP*. This parallel between nominal and clausal structure is welcome in view of the various phonological, morphological, syntactic and semantic similarities found across nominal and clausal structures in a number of languages (Bernstein 2001).

4.1 Inflectional heads and adverbial positions: Cinque (1999)

The discussion throughout the chapter relies heavily on the approach to clause structure set out in Cinque (1999).[1] Cinque's starting point is the three-part cross-linguistic observation in (1):

(1) a. Where more than one affix or adverbial marking an inflectional feature (essentially, subcategories of tense, mood and aspect) co-occur in the same simple clause, they follow a strict universal order.
     b. No more than one member of a given affixal class can co-occur in the same simple clause.
     c. No more than one member of a given adverbial class can co-occur in the same simple clause (unless they are syntactically co-ordinated).

Cinque argues that the most satisfying way to account for these observations is to

---

[1] See also Cinque (2004b).

reject the traditional adjunction analysis of adverbials (which was incapable of handling the affixes, anyway), and to conclude, rather:

(2) a. that VP* (§2.2) is augmented, not by a single IP, and not even by an IP split in two (Pollock 1989), but rather by an IP*, that is, a hierarchical array of inflectional FPs;

  b. that the head of each inflectional FP within IP* is the locus of a unique inflectional feature (a subcategory of tense, mood and aspect) with a marked/restrictive and an unmarked/default/general/ambiguous value;

  c. that the order in which these inflectional heads is merged is fixed by UG (contra Ouhalla 1991);

  d. that each FP makes available a single medial $F°$ and a single left-branching SpecFP position (Kayne 1994);

  e. that each $F°$ can check a single inflectional affix of the verb, in strict cyclic order;[2] and,

  f. that each SpecFP position can host a single (possibly co-ordinated) adverbial.[3]

Cinque's hierarchy of IP*-internal inflectional FPs is very extensive, and will doubtless be revised over time (see footnote 5). It's partially reproduced in (3), and augmented with some unlabelled FPs not included in Cinque's list, together with some example adverbials merged in the specifier of each FP:

(3) Inflectional heads and their specifiers (based on Cinque 1999):[4]

$Mood_{Speech\ act}$	franchement
$Mood_{Evaluative}$	heureusement
$Mood_{Evidential}$	évidemment
$Mood_{Epistemic}$	probablement, sans doute
T_{Past}	maintenant
$Mood_{Irrealis}$	peut-être
FP	intelligemment
$Asp_{Habitual}$	généralement, normalement, d'habitude, ordinairement
FP	pas
$T_{Anterior}$	déjà, encore
FP	soudain, tout à coup, brusquement, peu à peu[5]
$Asp_{Terminative}$	plus, encore
$Asp_{Continuative}$	toujours, jamais
FP	guère

---

[2] See Baker (1985; 1988) and Speas (1991a, b).
[3] The nature of the relationship between $F°$ and SpecFP is subject to cross-linguistic variation and cyclic diachronic development. See Rowlett (Forthcoming).
[4] For extensive discussion of categories of adverb in French see Bonami et al. (2004).
[5] This class of adverbial is added to Cinque's hierarchy by Lahousse (2003c: 182).

Asp$_{Retrospective/Proximative}$	tout à l'heure[6]
Asp$_{PlCompletive}$	complètement, partiellement, entièrement, en partie
FP	tout,[7] rien
Voice	bien, mal

Where adverbial orders are found which don't respect (3), Cinque (1999: 3) argues that this is due to one of a number of possible factors, none of which is problematic for (2). The first possibility is that the 'offending' adverbial isn't an independent IP* adverbial at all, but rather a direct modifier of another IP* adverbial, as in (4b), where *encore* precedes *pas*, and as in (5b), where *jamais* precedes *plus*:[8]

(4) a. Il n'est pas encore là. b. Il n'est [encore pas] là. (Cinque 1999: 171)
   he NEG-is not still there   he NEG-is still not there
   'He isn't (t)here yet.'   'He isn't (t)here again.'

---

[6] Cinque (1999: 96) hesitates between proposing distinct Asp$_{Retrospective}$ and Asp$_{Proximative}$ FPs and conflating them into a single projection. The fact that, in French, one and the same adverbial, *tout à l'heure*, can refer to *either* a near past *or* a near future suggests that we're dealing with a single projection denoting proximity, in either direction, to speech time:

(i) a. Je l'ai vu <u>tout à l'heure</u>. b. Je le vois <u>tout à l'heure</u>.
   I him-have seen ADV   I him see ADV
   'I've just seen him.'   'I'll be seeing him soon.'

[7] This is the position occupied by left-floated direct-object *tout* (Cinque 1999: 119). On floating *tout* see §4.3.1.

[8] Direct adverbial-on-adverbial modification is possible even with adverbials whose relative order respects (3). Consider the word order of lexical infinitives and the adverbials *plus* 'no longer' and *jamais* 'never', as set out in (i):

(i) a. décider de ne plus fumer b. ?*décider de ne fumer plus
   decide of NEG no.more smoke decide of NEG smoke no.more
   'to decide not to smoke any more'
  c. décider de ne jamais fumer d. décider de ne fumer jamais
   decided of NEG never smoke   decide of NEG smoke never
   'to decide never to smoke'   ≈ (ic)

While all speakers allow a lexical infinitive to raise above *jamais*, as in (id), not all speakers allow one to raise above *plus*, as in (ib) (Cinque 1999: 173 fn. 29). However, when *plus* and *jamais* co-occur, all three word orders in (ii) are grammatical for all speakers:

(ii) a. décider de ne plus jamais fumer
  b. décider de ne plus fumer jamais
  c. décider de ne fumer plus jamais
   decide of NEG (smoke) no.more (smoke) never (smoke)
   'to decide never to smoke again'

The grammaticality of (iia, b) is expected, given the pattern in (i); that of (iic) is surprising, given (ib), since (for the relevant speakers) lexical infinitives don't raise over *plus*. However, if, in (iic), *plus* modifies *jamais* directly, rather than occupying the specifier of its own inflectional FP, the lexical infinitive doesn't need to 'raise above [plus]' in order to precede *plus*. Since *plus* is 'part of' [plus jamais], the infinitive needs only to 'raise above [jamais]'. Presumably, such an adverbial-on-adverbial-modification configuration is also available in (iia) (but not (iib)).

(5) a. Je ne fume plus jamais.   b. Je ne fume [jamais plus]. (Cinque 1999: 9)
         I NEG smoke no longer never   I NEG smoke never no longer
         'I'm not smoking ever again.'   ≈ (5a)

The second reason why adverbials might be ordered contra (3) is that the part of the clause immediately below a focal adverbial has been fronted via a manoeuvre akin to scrambling, as in (6b) (Cinque 1999: 22):

(6) a. Certains quartiers sont toujours [complètement sous les eaux].
         some neighbourhoods are still completely under the waters
         'Some neighbourhoods are still completely under water.'

     b. Certains quartiers sont [complètement sous les eaux]$_i$ toujours t$_i$.
         some neighbourhoods are completely under the waters still
         'Some neighbourhoods are completely under water still.'

Third, the 'offending' adverbial might have been right dislocated (§5.3.2), as in (7b):

(7) a. Jean ne voyage ordinairement pas en train.
         J. NEG travels ordinarily not on train
         'J. doesn't ordinarily travel by train.'

     b. Jean ne voyage pas en train, ordinairement.
         J. NEG travels not on train ordinarily
         'J. doesn't travel by train, ordinarily.'

Where none of these factors is relevant, and a given adverbial really does occupy a base position other than the one indicated in (3), then, Cinque (1999: 19) suggests, it must be being used with a different function, and its different base position reflects this.[9] None of these factors, Cinque argues, undermines (2).

Where cross-linguistic variation *is* found relates to how far underlyingly VP*-internal material (the verb and its dependants) raises into IP*, and the details with respect to French are investigated in the rest of this chapter. A lexical verb is universally merged in V° and raises through the θ heads within VP* (§2.2.2). Beyond VP* the verb moves successive cyclically through a sequence of inflectional heads on a journey which is longer or shorter depending on the inflectional properties of the verb and on the language-specific strengths of the inflectional heads.[10] The patterns found with various inflectional categories of French verb are considered in §4.2. Similarly, while the thematic dependants of V° are universally merged in VP*-internal θ positions (§2.2.2), if their interpretation precludes them being marked with inherent – that is, θ-role-associated – case, they'll need to move to a VP*-external SpecFP position for case-checking purposes, and may raise even

---

[9] The same phenomenon is found in the context of attributive AP*s in §3.7.
[10] For example, while active past participles in both Italian and French raise out of their base V° position (to check some strong feature against an inflectional head), Italian past participles raise further than French ones, and can precede certain classes of adverbial which French past participles can't.

further for other pragmatic reasons. Such patterns of movement in French are discussed in §4.3. In §4.4 I consider the IP* syntax of clitics. In §4.5 I discuss sentential negation.

4.2   The IP* syntax of verbs

In §4.1 we saw that adverbials are strictly ordered underlyingly. Cinque's (1999) account of this ordering was based on a hierarchical array of IP*-internal inflectional FPs above VP*. In contrast to the strict ordering found with adverbials, the situation with verbs is more variable: verbs aren't strictly ordered with respect to any given class of adverbial. On the one hand, there's cross-linguistic variation in that, for example, finite verbs in French precede certain classes of adverbial which finite verbs in English follow. On the other hand, there's language-internal variation in that, for example, within French finite verbs precede certain classes of adverbial which infinitives follow.

Since Emonds (1978) and Pollock (1989), it's been assumed that this cross-linguistic and language-internal variation is due to the fact that, unlike adverbials, verbs undergo movement. To be precise, they undergo V movement,[11] not only through VP*-internal θ° positions, but also out of VP* and through IP*-internal inflectional F° positions, the very F° positions whose specifiers are the adverbials discussed by Cinque (1999) (§4.1). Variation in verb–adverbial ordering then relates to which adverbial(s) the verb moves past on its journey through successive F° positions. In the following sections, I look at the various inflectional subcategories of verb (§§4.2.1–4.2.2), and use Cinque's (1999) model of clause structure in (§4.1) to illuminate the V-movement patterns of each. The IP* syntax of imperatives is discussed in the context of non-subject clitics in §4.4.1.

4.2.1   Finite verbs

Evidence from patterns of adverbial placement, amassed since Emonds (1978: 163–8), suggests that a French finite verb occupies a high position within IP*.[12] This is illustrated in (8), where a finite verb co-occurs with *franchement* 'frankly', which occupies the highest adverbial-related IP*-internal inflectional specifier position in (3):

(8)   a.   Jean a franchement – besoin de se laver.
       b.   *Jean franchement a besoin de se laver.
             J. (has) frankly (has) need of self wash
             'J. frankly needs a wash.'

The position of the finite verb to the left of *franchement* suggests it occupies the

---

[11] For broader discussion of V movement see the contributions in Hornstein and Lightfoot (eds.) (1994) as well as Roberts (2001).
[12] But see Williams (1994: 189).

topmost head position within IP* (§4.3).

In contrast, the data in (9) suggest that the finite verb in English raises only as far as one of the lower IP*-internal inflectional F° positions:

(9)   a. *John calls never/always.   a'. John never/always calls.   (SpecAsp$_{Continuative}$P)
          b. John disagrees completely.   b'. John completely disagrees. (SpecAsp$_{PlCompletive}$P)
          c. John sings well/badly.   c'. *John well/badly sings.   (SpecVoiceP)

The examples suggest the English finite verb leaves VP* and raises above SpecVoiceP, but doesn't raise above SpecAsp$_{Continuative}$P. Cartographic details aside, the comparative data in (8) and (9) show that finite verbs raise higher in French than in English.

The contrast between (8) and (9) can be analysed as follows: in French and English alike, a fully inflected finite verb is merged under V° and, in both languages, the verb's inflectional features force it to raise out of VP* into the (low) IP* domain. In French the strength of the inflectional features of the finite verb requires it to raise to the highest IP*-internal F° position; the French finite verb's uninterpretable agreement features are strong and need to be checked early. In English, in contrast, finite verbs don't bear strong uninterpretable agreement features, so overt raising isn't required, and, on the grounds that covert raising is in some relevant sense 'cheaper' than overt movement, the finite verb stays in the low IP* domain in overt syntax, raising only covertly.[13]

This approach to finite-verb syntax allows a number of fundamental insights to be captured. First, the position occupied by a finite lexical verb is higher in French than in English. Second, the contrasting extent of V movement in French and English is ultimately due to the nature of verbal inflectional morphology, more specifically, subject–verb agreement. In French, a finite verb's uninterpretable agreement features are strong (and therefore need to be checked in overt syntax by raising the verb to an appropriate functional head) because subject–verb agreement is morphologically rich (§2.2.1.2).[14] In English, in contrast, subject–verb agreement is morphologically impoverished, which means that finite verbs don't bear strong uninterpretable features, and overt verb raising is therefore neither required nor (for reasons of economy) possible.[15]

---

[13] Such an approach to finite-verb syntax in English is superior to earlier accounts of inflectional morphology which 'built' words out of morphemes in the syntax, rather than drawing fully formed words directly from the lexicon. While the earlier account wasn't significantly different for verb-raising languages like French, it required 'affix hopping' (whereby the inflection moves down onto the verb) in non-verb-raising languages like English. The checking approach is preferable since it avoids the need to posit lowering.

[14] For Pollock (1997: 151), what's relevant is that SG/PL are distinguished, as are 1PL/2PL.

[15] There are a number of possible variations on a theme here, all of which have been proposed in the literature. Version 1: impoverished inflectional morphology means that the uninterpretable agreement features of English finite lexical verbs are weak: verb raising to inflection can therefore be covert. Version 2: impoverished inflectional morphology means that English finite lexical verbs bear no uninterpretable agreement features at all: verb raising

4.2.2   Non-finite verbs

While finite verbs in French move to I*°, the same can't be said of non-finite verbs, as shown in (10), for example, where the infinitive follows the IP*-internal negative marker *pas* 'not' (§4.5), rather than preceding it:

(10) a. ... pour ne <u>pas fumer</u>.   b. *... pour ne <u>fumer pas</u>.
        for NEG not smoke.INF   for NEG smoke.INF not
        '... in order not to smoke.'

The flexibility illustrated in (11) suggests that French lexical infinitives have the freedom of movement enjoyed by English finite lexical verbs, seen in (9b):

(11) a. Il me demande de <u>sortir souvent</u>.   b. Il me demande de <u>souvent sortir</u>.
        he me asks of go.out often   he me asks of often go.out
        a, b: 'He asks me to go out often.'

Cinque (1999: 143–4) delimits the IP* domain within which infinitival lexical V movement is possible in French. Lexical infinitives raise minimally to the left of *tôt* 'early', and typically raise to the left of *bien* 'well', *beaucoup* 'lots', *guère* 'barely', *jamais* '(n)ever' and *toujours* 'always'. Infinitival V movement to the left of *plus* 'no more' is only marginally possible, and impossible to the left of *pas* 'not':

(12) a. *tôt partir/partir tôt 'to leave early'
      b. bien parler/parler bien 'to speak well'
      c. beaucoup fumer/fumer beaucoup 'to smoke lots'
      d. ne guère fumer/ne fumer guère 'hardly ever to smoke'
      e. ne jamais fumer/ne fumer jamais 'never to smoke'
      f. toujours sourire/sourire toujours 'to always smile'
      g. ne plus fumer/?*ne fumer plus 'no longer to smoke'
      h. ne pas fumer/*ne fumer pas 'not to smoke'[16]

Cinque (1999: 226 fn. 1) doesn't comment on where *tôt* might be located, or indeed whether it occupies an IP*-internal specifier position at all; it might plausibly be a VP*-internal circumstantial, in which case the pattern in (12a) indicates only that infinitives raise out of VP*. Support for the idea that infinitives minimally leave

to inflection can therefore be covert. Version 3: impoverished inflectional morphology means that the uninterpretable agreement features of English finite lexical verbs are weak: these *features* can therefore raise to inflection in overt syntax, while leaving the phonetic form of the verb behind. See Collins (2001: 56).

[16] Lexical infinitives can precede *pas* in deliberately archaic styles (examples from Pollock 1997: 153 fn. 1):

(i) a. Les Français ont assez souffert pour <u>n'admettre pas</u> qu'on les flatte.
       the French have enough suffered for NEG-admit not that-one them flatter
       'The French have suffered enough <u>not to accept</u> being flattered.'
    b. La liberté, c'est ... , de pouvoir <u>n'agir pas</u> selon ce qu'on est.
       the freedom it-is of be.able NEG-act not according.to this that-one is
       'Freedom is being ... , able <u>not to act</u> on the basis of what one is.'

VP* comes from the syntax and semantics of the adverbial *bien*. Of relevance is the ambiguity of *bien* and the correlation, as expected, between its interpretation and its position. *Bien* is either a manner adverbial meaning 'well' or a sentence modifier meaning 'indeed':[17]

(13)   a.   J'ai fait <u>bien</u> mes devoirs.   b.   J'ai <u>bien</u> fait mes devoirs.
          I-have done well my homework   I-have well done my homework
          'I did my homework well.'   'I indeed did my homework.'

With infinitives, 'well' *bien* most naturally follows, while 'indeed' *bien* typically precedes:

(14)   a.   Il a décidé de chanter <u>bien</u>.   b.   Il a décidé de <u>bien</u> chanter.
          he has decided of sing well   he has decided of well sing
          'He decided he would sing well.'   'He decided he would indeed sing.'

If 'well' *bien* occupies SpecVoiceP, as in (3), this suggests that the infinitive raises out of VP* and above VoiceP.[18]

    Infinitival verb placement is sensitive to lexical factors (Roberts 2001: 121). Consider the data in (15) and (16):

(15)   a.   n'être pas   b.   ?ne pouvoir pas   c.   *ne fumer pas
          NEG-be not   NEG-be.able not   NEG smoke not
          'not to be'   'not to be able'   'not to smoke'

(16)   a.   n'être plus   b.   ne pouvoir plus   c.   ?*ne fumer plus
          NEG-be no.more   NEG-be.able no.more   NEG smoke no.more
          'no longer to be'   'no longer to be able'   'no longer to smoke'

---

[17] Cinque (1999: 118) calls 'indeed' *bien* concessive. The notion that the two versions of *bien* are distinct is supported by the fact that emphatic *bien* is compatible with predicates which don't allow manner *bien*, for example, *aller* 'to go':
(i)   a.   *Je suis allé <u>bien</u>.   b.   Je suis <u>bien</u> allé.
          I am gone *bien*   I am *bien* gone
                                     'I did indeed go.'
A stronger version of concessive *bien* is *bel et bien* 'well and truly'. The two versions of *bien* can co-occur:
(ii)   J'ai (bel et) bien fait bien mes devoirs.
      I-have *bel et bien* done *bien* my homeworks
      'I well and truly did do my homework well.'
Independently of infinitival V movement, the syntactic distinction between the two kinds of *bien* is supported by clitic-placement contrasts, as in (iii):
(iii)   a.   . . . pour <u>le bien</u> faire.   b.   . . . pour <u>bien le</u> faire.
          for it *bien* do   for *bien* it do
          ' . . . in order to do it well.'   ' . . . in order to indeed do it.'

[18] As for concessive *bien*, given its pragmatic force, it makes sense to assume that its pre-infinitival position is due, not to shorter V movement, but rather to the fact that the adverbial occupies the specifier of one of the Mood projections in (3). If concessive *bien* is attached higher than *pas*, the attested orders are accounted for.

Infinitival auxiliaries can precede *pas* (15a) (and *plus* (16a)).[19] In contrast, lexical infinitives can't precede *pas* (15c) and can only marginally precede *plus* (16c). Infinitival modals are a halfway house: while they can precede *plus* (16b), the question mark against (15b) indicates marginal acceptability.[20]

In the context of the massively exploded model of IP* in (3), the question arises as to which of Cinque's (1999) inflectional heads are relevant to infinitival V movement. Since infinitives aren't *generally* able to raise above *pas*, we might posit that $T_{Anterior}$ (or the head associated with *pas* itself) is the head against which the feature associated with the infinitival suffix is checked. If furthermore this feature is weak, then V movement to $T_{Anterior}$ is overt or covert, allowing lexical infinitives to raise to any head up to, but no further than, $T_{Anterior}$. The reason why lexical infinitives can't precede *pas* is that such movement would be unmotivated. The reason why pseudo-modals and auxiliaries *can* raise to the left of *pas* would then be related to their lexical (rather than their morphosyntactic) features which might motivate (optional) V movement above $T_{Anterior}$ in order to check (weak) features against one or more of the aspectual or mood heads above $T_{Anterior}$ in (3).[21]

Turning to present participles, the data in (17) suggest that they have the same flexible V-movement patterns as infinitival auxiliaries (cf. (15a) and (16a)):

(17) a. La plupart ne venant pas de l'Union européenne seront refoulés.
          the most NEG coming not from the-union European will.be turned.back
          'Most not from the EU will be turned back.'

      b. Je crois qu'en ne pas craquant, on peut y arriver.
          I believe that-by NEG not cracking one can there arrive
          'I believe that by not cracking we can make it.'

The IP*-internal syntax of imperatives is considered in §4.4.1, and that of past participles, together with past-participle agreement, in §5.8.2.

4.3   Licensing DP*s within IP*

In §4.2 I considered verb syntax, showing that V movement through IP* varies with properties of the verb. I now consider the IP* syntax of the arguments

---

[19] While both *être* 'to be' and *avoir* 'to have' can both precede and follow *pas*, they typically follow *pas*: *pas* is preverbal over 80% of the time. As for the distinction between the auxiliary and copular/lexical uses of these verbs, the auxiliary uses are slightly more likely to precede *pas* than the copular/lexical uses. This difference supports the view that infinitival verb placement is related to θ structure. If θ structure *is* relevant, and if athematic infinitives occur higher than thematic infinitives, epistemic pseudo-modals are expected more readily to precede *pas* than deontic pseudo-modals.

[20] Pollock (1989: 375; 1997) describes the order illustrated in (16c) as 'somewhat marginal' and 'more exceptional', apparently with 'a very literary ring'. In contrast, Hirschbühler and Labelle (1994b) report that speakers reject the order in (16c).

[21] In §5.2.3 I discuss a correlation between the infinitival V-movement patterns of pseudo-modals and the availability of clitic climbing.

of verbs, first DP*s, then clitics (§4.4). Like verbs, dependant DP*s can move out of their VP*-internal θ position into IP*. This can be seen by considering the positions they occupy relative to adverbials, which occupy fixed positions within IP* (§4.1). I start by considering regular subject and indirect-object DP*s. (The IP* syntax of *direct* objects is discussed in the context of past-participle agreement in §5.8.2.) Then, in §§4.3.1, 4.3.2, I look at the complications of quantifier float and remote quantification.

A subject DP* occupies the highest IP*-internal specifier position, even higher than SpecMood$_{Speech\ act}$ in (3) on page 103. I shall call this 'canonical subject position' SpecIP*. The subject raises from within VP* to SpecIP* as part of a derivation. The DP* which raises to SpecIP* doesn't have any inherent 'subject-hood'; rather it's the verb's dependant which bears the θ role which is ranked highest on the thematic hierarchy (§2.2.2.2). It's standardly assumed that raising to SpecIP* allows a DP* to be structurally licensed with nominative case. This is possible because finite I*° licenses nominative case via spec–head agreement, as in (18) (§4.2.1):

(18)   [$_{IP*}$ [$_{Spec}$ subject] [$_{I*'}$ [$_{I*°}$ verb] . . . [$_{VP*}$ t$_{subject}$ t$_{verb}$]]]

This configuration allows nominative case to be checked on the subject DP* and the D/EPP feature to be checked on I*°.

Raising to SpecIP* also has a pragmatic dimension. Consider the data in (19) and (20):

(19)   Qu'ont fait les enfants?
       what-have done the children
       'What did the children do?'

(20)   a.   Les enfants se sont <u>tous</u> acheté une bicyclette.
            the children self are all bought a bicycle
            'The children all bought themselves a bicycle.'

       b.   !<u>Tous les enfants</u> se sont acheté une bicyclette.
            all the children self are bought a bicycle
            'All the children bought themselves a bicycle.'

In response to the wh question in (19), the answer in (20a) is felicitous, while (20b) isn't. In (19) the subject DP* *les enfants* is topical, and the unknown content of the wh phrase is focal. The formal difference between (20a, b) is the position of the predeterminer *tous* 'all' (§3.2.4). In (20a) the predeterminer has become separated from the subject DP* via quantifier float (§4.3.1); in (20b) the quantifier hasn't floated and the entire DP* *tous les enfants* raises to SpecIP*. Significantly, this has a pragmatic consequence. In (20a) *les enfants* is topical, while *tous* is part of the focus; in (20b), in contrast, the entire DP* *tous les enfants* is topical. The pragmatic infelicity of (20b) can therefore be attributed to the mismatch between the pragmatic assumptions of the questioner and those of the respondent. Relevant for our purposes is that SpecIP* is topical.[22]

As for indirect objects, in all but a very small number of cases, these are found only if a subject and direct object are already present (Van Peteghem 2006: 98). Thus, indirect objects are truly 'second' objects. Like subject (and direct-object) DP*s, indirect-object DP*s raise out of their VP*-internal θ position (unlike $à$-initial inherent-case-marked DP*s, which can remain within a lexical XP*). Unlike subject (and direct-object) DP*s, indirect-object DP*s are marked with $à$, as in (36c, d) on page 30 in §2.2.2.1. In §2.2.2.1 I distinguish indirect-object marker $à$ from inherent-case marker $à$. Unlike inherent-case marker $à$, which can case license a DP* dependant (in association with its θ role) in any appropriate lexical XP*, indirect-object marker $à$ is a structural case licenser appearing in clausal structures, only. This suggests that indirect-object $à$ is the realisation of an IP*-internal F°. Kayne (2004)[23] takes indirect-object marker $à$ to be a probe in the sense of Chomsky (2001). Thus, the indirect object and $à$ don't form a constituent underlyingly. The two 'get together' as the indirect object raises out of VP* in order to be case licensed (Kayne 2004: 198–9). First, an Agr(eement)I(ndirect)O(bject) head merges above VP* and attracts the indirect object into its specifier position. Next, the indirect-object marker $à$ merges with AgrIOP, as in (21):

(21) $[_{àP} [_{à°} à] [_{AgrIO} [_{Spec} \text{ indirect object}] [_{AgrIO'} \text{AgrIO}° [_{VP*} \cdots t_{\text{indirect object}} \cdots]]]]$

This has the desired impact on word order: $à$ immediately precedes the indirect object. However, this account is problematic for the analysis of $au(x)$, found with inherent-case-marked DP*s and indirect-object DP*s alike, as in (22):

(22)   a. Je pense au(x) étudiant(s).   b. Je parle au(x) étudiant(s).
            I think to.the student(s)   I speak to.the student(s)
            'I'm thinking about the students.'   'I'm speaking to the student(s).'

In §3.3 $au(x)$ was analysed as a DP*-internal element which allows case and definiteness to be checked on one and the same head. While this works fine with the use of $au(x)$ in (22a), it's hard to see how it can be made compatible with the structure in (21).[24]

4.3.1   Quantifier float

In §3.2.4 we saw *tout* 'all' functioning as a bare DP* and as a predeterminer within a larger definite DP*. In this section, we investigate the syntactic mobility of both bare and predeterminer *tout*, that is, its ability to occupy IP*-internal positions. For example, in the absence of a marked intonation pattern, bare direct-object *tout* appears to the left of an infinitive or past/present participle, as in

---

[22] I return to the issue of the topicality of SpecIP* in the discussion of dislocation in §5.3.
[23] Kayne's discussion is actually about the $à$ found with causatives (§5.2.3). It is, however, clear that the $à$-marked argument in causatives is an indirect object.
[24] I am grateful to Adam Ledgeway for pointing this out to me.

(23), rather than to the right:

(23)   a. J'ai tout vu – .   b. tout voir –   c. en tout lisant –
           I have all seen   all see   in all reading
           'I saw everything.'   'to see everything'   'by reading everything'

Postverbal *tout* is natural with focal stress, only (Cinque 1999: 219 fn. 30), as in (24):

(24)   a. J'ai vu TOUT.   b. voir TOUT   c. en lisant TOUT
           I have seen all   see all   in reading all
           'I saw *everything*.'   'to see *everything*'   'by reading *everything*'

The phenomenon illustrated in (23) is known as (leftward) quantifier float, or QF.[25] With finite verbs, bare direct-object *tout* is postverbal, irrespective of whether or not it bears focal stress, as in (25):

(25)   a. Je vois tout.   b. Je vois TOUT.
           I see all   I see all
           'I can see everything.'   'I can see *everything*.'

Given the model of IP* structure in §4.1, and the conclusions reached in §4.2 about V-movement patterns, these data can be captured by concluding that (unstressed) bare *tout* raises to an IP*-internal SpecFP position above (and therefore to the left

---

[25] In parallel to leftward QF of *tout*, its negative equivalent, *rien* 'nothing' (§3.5), also most naturally precedes infinitives and past participles, as in (i):

(i)   a. J'ai rien vu – .   b. rien voir –   c. en rien faisant
           I-have nothing seen   nothing see   in nothing doing
           'I didn't see anything.'   'to see nothing'   'by doing nothing'
In makes sense, therefore, to assume that the IP* syntax of bare *tout* matches that of *rien*.
    While in the unmarked language, *personne* 'nobody' isn't subject to QF, as in (ii), in some Eastern varieties it appears to be, as in (iii) (Gadet 2003; Wolf 2000: 698):

(ii)   a. J'ai vu personne.   b. Je veux voir personne.
           I-have seen nobody   I want see no nobody
           'I didn't see anyone.'   'I don't want to see anyone.'
(iii) a. %J'ai personne vu.   b. %Je veux personne voir.
           I-have nobody seen   I want nobody see
           = (iia)   = (iib)
However, the pattern illustrated in (iii) may be less a peculiarity of *personne* in these varieties than a property of IP* verb syntax in these varieties generally, which shows independent signs of Germanic influence. Compare the standard examples in (iv) with those in (v):
(iv)   a. J'ai fini le travail.   b. Je le laisse regarder la télé.
           I-have finished the work   I him let watch the tv
           'I've finished the work.'   'I let him watch tv.'
(v)   a. %J'ai le travail fini.   b. %Je le laisse la télé regarder.
           I-have the work finished   I him let the tv watch
           = (iva)   = (ivb)

of) the positions occupied by infinitives and participles but below (and therefore to the right of) the position occupied by finite verbs.[26] The SpecFP position to which bare *tout* raises is located between $Asp_{PlCompletive}$ and Voice in (3).

A more complex QF situation is found when *tout* is non-bare and becomes detached from the rest of PreDetP. When *tout* does this, it's called a floating quantifier (FQ), and was illustrated in (20a, b) on page 111 in §4.3. Consider the examples in (26):

(26)   a.   Toutes les filles ont rigolé.   b.   Les filles ont toutes rigolé.
            all the girls have laughed   the girls have all laughed
            'All the girls laughed.'   'The girls all laughed.'

The underlined subject DP* in (26a) is a PreDetP which has the simplified structure in (27) (§3.2.4) and has raised out of its VP*-internal θ position to SpecIP* (§4.3):

(27)   [$_{PreDetP}$ toutes [$_{DefP}$ les filles]]

The near synonymous (26b) illustrates rightward QF. A number of properties of (26b) are noteworthy. First, the same morphological agreement between the FQ and DefP is found in (26a) and (26b). Second, although the FQ can appear in the two positions illustrated in (26a, b), it can't appear in both positions simultaneously, as shown in (28):[27]

(28)   *Toutes les filles ont toutes rigolé.
        all the girls have all laughed

Third, (26a) and (26b) are nearly synonymous.[28] Taken together, these properties suggest that the derivation of (26a) and that of (26b) have much in common. Rather than assuming some kind of rightward movement implied by the name rightward QF, it's standardly assumed: (a) that the DefP and the FQ form a PreDetP constituent like (27) underlyingly in *both* (26a) *and* (26b); (b) that PreDetP raises from VP* to some SpecFP position between the position occupied by the aspectual auxiliary and that occupied by the past participle; and (c) that DefP is then extracted

---

[26] To account for focally stressed postverbal bare *tout* in (24) and (25b), we might conclude: *either* (a) that stressed bare *tout* remains in VP*; *or* (b) that it raises to a VP*-peripheral SpecFocusP position; *or* (c) it raises to SpecFP like unstressed bare *tout* but that the remnant clause below FP fronts (Cinque 1999).

[27] Examples like (28) aren't actually hard to find, but are usually attributed to performance errors. See also example (32) on page 116.

[28] But see the pragmatic difference discussed in the context of (20a, b). A corollary of this pragmatic difference is mentioned by De Cat (2000) in respect of (ia, b):

(i)   a.   Tous les navires ont chaviré.   b.   Les navires ont tous chaviré.
           all the vessels have sunk   the vessels have all sunk
           'All the vessels sank.'   'The vessels all sank.'

In (ia) a group reading is preferred (the vessels not only all sank but they all sank together); in (ib) a distributive reading is preferred (the vessels all sank but they did so independently of each other).

from PreDetP and raises to SpecIP*, as shown in (29), stranding the FQ in SpecFP:

(29)

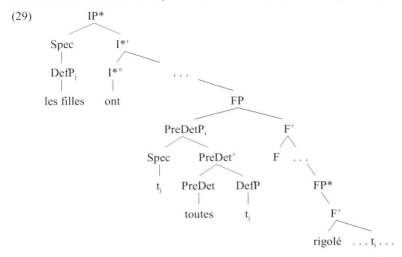

Given that the topmost specifier position is an escape hatch (§3.2.4), DefP first raises to SpecPreDetP, and then out of PreDetP altogether.[29] I return to the nature of FP below.

Consider now the examples in (30):

(30) a. Jean les a tous lus.   b. Jean leur a tous téléphoné.
          J. them has all.M.PL read   J. to.them has all.M.PL called
          'J. read them all.'   'J. phoned them all.'

Here, the FQ has floated off an (in)direct object. Unlike the subject in (26b), the (in)direct objects in (30) have been pronominalised as clitics (§4.4). In fact, QF from an (in)direct object is generally only possible if the object cliticises.[30] This

[29] The discussion in the text of QF supports the analysis in §3.2.4 of predeterminer *tout* as a head (rather than a specifier) with a definite DefP as its complement.

Where the DefP complement of the predeterminer is pronominal, QF is obligatory, as shown in (i):

(i) a. *Toutes <u>elles</u> ont rigolé.   b. <u>Elles</u> ont toutes rigolé.
         all they have laughed   they have all laughed
                                                       'They all laughed.'

A particularly interesting case is represented by the proform *on*. The agreement peculiarities of *on* are discussed in §4.4.4. In the example of QF in (ii), *on* has been separated from *tous*. However, while *tous* is clearly PL, *on* triggers SG agreement on the verb:

(ii)   On va tous mourir.
        one go.SG all.PL die
        'We're all going to die.'

[30] In marked varieties, an FQ can float off a non-pronominalised (in)direct object, as in (i):

constraint can be explained in terms of the analysis of cliticisation in §4.4, whereby a clitic is a functional head which is licensed by a non-overt DP* raising to its specifier position. Assume that the FP hosting the clitic, the FP hosting the FQ and the FP responsible for case licensing a non-pronominalised (in)direct-object DP* are hierarchically structured as in (31):

(31)   ... [$_{IP*}$ ... [$_{CliticP}$ ... [$_{FP}$ ... [$_{Agr(I)OP}$ ...]]]]

If the (in)direct-object DP* fails to pronominalise and remains in Spec(I)OP, it doesn't pass through SpecFP and so doesn't license QF; it's only by pronominalising, and therefore raising to SpecCliticP via SpecFP that QF is licensed. Of course, since the case-checking position of a subject DP* is SpecIP*, which is even higher than SpecCliticP, the configuration required for QF is produced irrespective of whether or not the subject pronominalises.[31]

I turn now to the nature of SpecFP in (29), that is, the position occupied by FQs and bare direct-object *tout*. The non-standard example in (32), in which there are *two* FQs, suggests that FQs aren't associated with a unique position:

(32)   %les empereurs qui sont <u>tous</u> déjà <u>tous</u> en train de faire le spectacle
       the emperors who are all already all in train of do the show
       'the emperors who are all already all doing the show'

Cinque (1999: 119–20) presents empirical evidence suggesting that FQs occupy dedicated positions within IP* depending on whether they are related to the subject, direct or indirect object, and that each of these positions is distinct from that occupied by bare direct-object *tout*. The notion that distinct positions are available for subject- and (in)direct-object-related FQs is based on ordering restrictions found when FQs co-occur, as in the examples in (33), after Cinque (1999: 116):

(33)   a.   Les filles$_S$ leur$_{IO}$ ont toutes$_S$ tous$_{IO}$ parlé hier. (*tous$_{IO}$ toutes$_S$)
            the girls to.them have all.F all.M spoken yesterday
            'All of the girls spoke to all of them yesterday.'

       b.   Les filles les ont toutes$_S$ tous$_{DO}$ lus. (*tous$_{DO}$ toutes$_S$)
            the girls them have all.F all.M read
            'All of the girls read all of them.'

(i)   a.   %J'avais <u>toutes</u> fait <u>les quêtes</u>.   b.   %Elle a pas <u>tout</u> fait <u>le concert</u> en play back.
           I-had all done the collections   she has not all done the concert in play back
           'I had done all the collections.'   'She didn't lipsynch the entire concert.'
       See also De Cat's (2000: 4) examples from Québécois in (ii), where the FQ is pronounced [tut], irrespective of the φ features of the antecedent:
(ii)   a.   Il a [tut] pris les crayons.   b.   Il a [tut] mangé les écrevisses.
           he has all taken the pencils   he has all eaten the crayfish
           'He took all the pencils.'   'He ate all the crayfish.'
[31] The data in (i) and (ii) in footnote 30 are therefore problematic and remain on the research agenda for the time being.

   c. Je les leur ai tous$_{IO}$ toutes$_{DO}$ montrées. (*toutes$_{DO}$ tous$_{IO}$)
       I them to.them have all.M all.F shown
       'I showed all of them to all of them.'

The data show that FQs can co-occur and that, when they do, a subject FQ must precede direct- and indirect-object FQs alike, and that an indirect-object FQ must precede a direct-object FQ.

The notion that the positions occupied by FQs are distinct from the one occupied by bare direct-object *tout* derives from two sources. First, as expected given (33b, c), FQs necessarily precede bare direct-object *tout*:

(34)   a. Je leur ai tous$_{IO}$ tout$_{DO}$ montré. (*tout tous$_{IO}$)
         I to.them have all.M all shown
         'I showed everything to all of them.'

       b. Les filles ont toutes$_S$ tout$_{DO}$ montré. (*tout toutes$_S$)
         the girls have all.F all shown
         'All of the girls showed everything.'

Second, and more significantly, FQs and bare direct-object *tout* have divergent orderings with respect to *complètement* 'completely' and *toujours* 'always': while FQs precede, bare direct-object *tout* follows (Cinque 1999: 119):

(35)   a. Nous l'avons <u>tout complètement</u> mangé. (*complètement tout)
         we it-have all completely eaten
         'We completely ate it all.'

       b. Nous avons <u>complètement tout</u> mangé. (*tout complètement)
         we have completely all eaten
         'We completely ate everything.'

Cinque (1999: 120) suggests that FQs can't intervene between *déjà* and *plus*. However, the example in (36) was found on the Internet:

(36)   Nous ne serions déjà tous plus de ce monde.
      we NEG would.be already all no.more of this world
      'We would already no longer be for this world.'

Cinque also disputes the existence of an FQ position preceding *pas*.[32] However, example (37), found on the Internet, again suggests otherwise:

(37)   Ils n'ont <u>tous pas</u> ces caractères antiques.
      they NEG-have all not these characters antiquated
      'They don't all have these antiquated characters.'

---

[32] Native-speaker informants I have consulted found examples (36) and (37) somewhat odd. It's interesting, and perhaps significant, that the disputed FQ positions both precede negative adverbials. The 'problem' may be not so much that these positions can't host FQs, but rather, as Cinque himself conjectures (1999: 120), that scope properties allow negation naturally to interact with FQs, and that this interaction requires negation to dominate an FQ.

Putting these observations together, we get the partial ordering of clausal specifiers in (38a), where the numbered FQ positions are to be understood as those areas within IP* where the three ordered FQs in (38b) can appear (FQ$_1$ and FQ$_3$ are in brackets because their existence is disputed by Cinque 1999: 120):[33]

(38) a. (FQ$_1$)>pas>FQ$_2$>déjà>(FQ$_3$)>plus>FQ$_4$>toujours>guère>FQ$_5$[34]>complète-ment>tout>bien

b. FQ$_S$>FQ$_{IO}$>FQ$_{DO}$

If we're right to assume that the positions occupied by FQs are those positions through which argument DP*s can transit on their way to SpecCliticP, then (38) paints a rich picture of the IP* syntax of argument DP*s.[35]

4.3.2   Remote quantification

In this section I discuss the IP*-internal movement of the adverbials/quantifiers found as bare pronominals and in complex determiners (§3.6). In (39a) and (40a) the bare quantifiers *beaucoup* 'lots' and *trop* 'too (much)' occupy their expected position following the past participle and infinitive; in (39b) and (40b) they precede:

(39) a. J'ai lu beaucoup.   b. J'ai beaucoup lu.
         I-have read lots   I-have lots read
         a, b: 'I have read lots.'

---

[33] Attributing FQs to their own IP*-internal FPs neatly accounts for De Cat's (2000) observation that FQs can appear in a sentence even when the sentence already contains one example from each possible class of adverbial.

[34] Cinque (1999: 219 fn. 33) claims that FQ$_5$ isn't available in the presence of *(ne) plus*. However, the example in (i) suggests otherwise:

(i)   . . . enseignants . . . qui n'ont plus toujours tous à l'esprit la relation entre X et Y.
        teachers who NEG-have more always all to the-mind the relation between X and Y
        '. . . teachers who no longer all always have in mind the relationship between X and Y.'

[35] The model in (38a, b) is possibly too flexible. De Cat (2000: 13–14) gives the examples in (i), where *toutes* is *not* ambiguous (cf. (ii), where it is), and this suggests that the FQ positions can't all freely be associated with all arguments:

(i)   a. Elles$_i$ vont toutes$_{i/*j}$ gentiment les$_j$ caresser.
            they go all nicely them caress
            'They're all going to caress them nicely.'
        b. Elles$_i$ vont gentiment toutes$_{*i/j}$ les$_j$ caresser.
            they go nicely all them caress
            'They're going to caress them all nicely.'

(ii)   Elles$_i$ vont toutes$_{i/j}$ les$_j$ caresser.
        they go all them caress
        = (ia) or (ib) (modulo *gentiment*)

(40)　a.　Il veut acheter <u>trop</u>.
　　　　 he wants buy too.much
　　　　 a, b: 'He wants to buy too much.'

　　　 b.　Il veut <u>trop</u> acheter.
　　　　 he wants too.much buy

Unlike *tout* (§§3.2.4, 4.3.1), these quantifiers: (a) don't need focal stress in order to remain in situ; and (b) don't need to be 'bare' in order to be separated from the regular postverbal position of direct objects. In (41a) and (42a) they appear within a larger DP*; in (41b) and (42b) the quantifier is detached, with the rest of the DP* in situ, a phenomenon known as remote quantification (Obenauer 1983, 1984; Rizzi 1990):

(41)　a.　J'ai lu [<u>beaucoup</u> de livres].
　　　　 I-have read lots of books
　　　　 a, b: 'I've read lots of books.'

　　　 b.　J'ai <u>beaucoup</u> lu [– de livres].
　　　　 I-have lots read of books

(42)　a.　Il veut acheter [<u>trop</u> de livres].
　　　　 he wants buy too.much of books
　　　　 a, b: 'He wants to buy too many books.'

　　　 b.　Il veut <u>trop</u> acheter [– de livres].
　　　　 he wants too.much buy of books

This flexibility strongly suggests that, unlike *tout*, these quantifiers are specifiers rather than heads.

The alternative word order in (39b)–(42b) is parasitic upon the dual status of these elements as quantifiers and adverbials (§§2.3.2, 3.6). They can function as adverbials (of intensity) independently of a direct object, as in (43):

(43)　Je t'aime <u>beaucoup</u>.
　　　 I you-love lots
　　　 'I love you lots.'

Indeed, (39b), for example, is ambiguous between one interpretation quantifying the activity and another quantifying the material read. (In (39a) only the latter interpretation is possible.) It would make perfect sense to utter the sentence in (44):

(44)　J'ai <u>beaucoup lu</u>, mais je n'ai pas <u>lu beaucoup</u>.
　　　 I-have lots read, but I NEG-have not read lots
　　　 'I did lots of reading, but I didn't read much.'

In the first clause, *lire* 'to read' is intransitive and *beaucoup* 'lots' quantifies the activity; in the second clause, *lire* is transitive and *beaucoup*, its direct object.

In (41a) and (42a) there's no ambiguity. The syntactic form of the direct object (pseudo-partitive) shows that the quantifier is associated with it. Note in particular the ungrammaticality of (45a, b):

(45)　a.　*J'ai lu [– de livres]
　　　　 I-have read of books

　　　 b.　*Il va visiter [– de musées].
　　　　 he goes visit of museums

The availability of remote quantification is sensitive to lexical semantic structure of the transitive verb. Compare (46a, b):

(46) a. Je te vois beaucoup.   b. Je t'aime beaucoup.
          I you see lots   I you-love lots
          'I see you lots (= often).'   'I love you lots (= intensely).'

In (46a) *beaucoup* 'lots' quantifies frequency, in (46b), intensity. Remote quantification is possible with verbs like *voir* 'to see', but not verbs like *aimer* 'to love, like'. The problem with manipulating, say, (47a) to form (47b) is that *beaucoup* 'lots' needs simultaneously to qualify VP* (because of the lexical semantics of *aimer* 'to like') *and* quantify VP* (in order indirectly to quantify the direct object):

(47) a. J'ai aimé [beaucoup de films].   b. *J'ai beaucoup aimé [– de films].
          I-have loved lots of films   I-have lots loved of films
          'I liked several films.'

The negative adverbial/quantifier *pas* 'no' (§2.3.2.1) also undergoes remote quantification, as in (48):[36]

(48) a. Je n'ai pas lu [– de livres].   b. *Je n'ai pas aimé [– de films]).
          I NEG-have not read of books   I NEG-have not loved of films
          'I didn't read any books.'

4.4   Clitics

In this section I discuss how nominal constituents are realised as clitics rather than as the DP*s seen in §3. Clitics are discussed here because they are

---

[36] The interrogative adverbial/quantifier *combien* 'how much/many' behaves in similar, but not identical, fashion to those reviewed in this section. While, like the adverbials/quantifiers discussed in the text, *combien de NP* can be a direct-object DP*, as in (ia), *combien* can't undergo remote quantification of the kind illustrated in (41a) and (42a), as shown in (ib):
(i)   a. Tu as lu [combien de livres]?   b. *Tu as combien lu [– de livres]?
           you have read how.many of books   you have how.many read of books
           'How many books did you read?'
This is because, when used as regular adverbial, *combien* always indicates quality, as shown in (ii):
(ii)   a. *Tu le vois combien?   b. Tu m'aimes combien?
           you him see how.much   you me-love how.much
                                               'How much do you love me?'
However, as a consequence of its status as an interrogative (§3.4), *combien* can undergo wh fronting (§5.6.1), either together with the rest of the DP*, as in (iiia), or, significantly within the context of a discussion of remote quantification, on its own by splitting off from the rest of its containing nominal, as in (iiib):
(iii) a. Combien de livres tu as lus [–]?   b. Combien tu as lu [– de livres]?
           how.much of books you have read.M.PL   how.much you have read of books
           'How many books did you read?'   = (iiia)
Note that the past participle only agrees with the direct object when the entire nominal fronts (§5.8.2).

generally restricted to IP* contexts.[37] I assume, therefore, that they are associated with IP*-internal FPs.

4.4.1   Non-subject clitics

The φ-feature-marked third-person direct-object clitics are homophonous with the definite articles (§3.2): *le* (*l'*) M.SG, *la* (*l'*) F.SG and *les* M/F.PL:

(49) a. Elle <u>le</u> voit.   b. Il <u>la</u> veut.   c. Nous <u>les</u> adorons.
        she him sees   he her wants   we them adore
        'She can see him.'   'He wants her.'   'We adore them.'

Despite the homophony, the definite articles and the direct-object clitics have distinct morphosyntactic properties: the articles appear in DP*s, the clitics, in IP*s. While the articles *le/les* fuse with *de/à* (§2.4.2), the clitics *le/les* don't.

Where the direct object isn't φ-feature marked, the default M.SG *le* (*l'*) is used (§2.1.2.3), similarly in predicative contexts, even with F predicative AP*s/DP*s:

(50) a. Il a téléphoné à 5h du matin; je ne <u>l'</u>ai pas apprécié.
        he has telephoned at 5 of.the morning I NEG it-have not appreciated
        'He called at 5am; I didn't appreciate it.'

     b. Tu es très belle et <u>le</u> seras toujours.
        you are very beautiful.F and it will.be always
        'You're very beautiful and always will be (it).'

     c. Diana n'était pas la reine d'Angleterre et ne <u>le</u> sera jamais.
        D. NEG-was not the.F queen of-England and NEG it will.be ever
        'Diana wasn't the queen of England and never will be (it).'

The default M.SG *le* also appears with the dummy verb *faire* to form a pro-VP*:

(51) Je dois travailler mais je ne veux pas <u>le faire</u>.
     I must work but I NEG want not it do
     'I have to work but I don't want to.'

The third-person *in*direct-object clitics are *lui* SG and *leur* PL; no gender distinction is made:

(52) a. Jean <u>lui</u> parle.   b. Jean <u>leur</u> parle.
        J. IO.3SG speaks   J. IO.3PL speaks
        'J.'s speaking to him/her.'   'J.'s speaking to them.'

---

[37] One non-IP* context in which (non-subject) clitics (as well, indeed, as the negative clitic *ne*; §4.5.1) can appear is with the presentatives *(re)voilà* and *(re)voici* (Rowlett 2002):
(i) a. <u>Le</u> revoilà!   b. <u>En</u>₂ voici un autre!
       him again.see.there   of.it see.here an other
       'There he is again!'   'Here's another one!'
The reason for this is historical: the presentatives derive from the verbal forms *(re)voir ici/là* 'to see (t)here again'.

In addition to corresponding to regular indirect objects of lexical verbs, indirect-object clitics mark the dative of alienable possession, the dative of (dis)interest and the ethic dative, illustrated in (53)–(55)[38] (example (55a) is from Togeby 1982: 401, (55b), from Lamiroy 2003):

(53) a. Je <u>lui</u> ai arraché un cheveu.   b. Il <u>m'</u>a brisé le cœur.
          I him have pulled.out a hair   he me-has broken the heart
          'I pulled one of his hairs out.'   'He broke my heart.'

(54) a. Je <u>lui</u> ai fait un café.   b. On <u>nous</u> a ouvert la porte.
          I him have made a coffee   one us has opened the door
          'I made him a coffee.'   'They opened the door for us.'

(55) a. Il <u>te</u> prend un petit couteau de cuisine et il <u>te</u> le lui plante dans le dos.
          he you takes a little knife of kitchen and he you it him plants in the back
          'I'm telling you, he took a little kitchen knife and planted it in his back!'

      b. Il <u>te</u> lui a donné une de ces gifles!
          he you him has given one of these slaps
          'I'm telling you, he gave him such a slap!'

While in the third person (§4.4.1) direct-object clitics are distinguished from indirect-object clitics – *le/la/les* versus *lui/leur* – no such distinction is made with first- and second-person clitics. The forms *me* (*m'*) 1SG, *te* (*t'*) 2SG, *nous* 1PL and *vous* 2PL are all underspecified for the feature distinguishing direct from indirect objects (Pullum & Zwicky 1986: 75–8), and therefore compatible with both:

(56) a. Jean <u>te/nous</u> voit.   b. Jean <u>te/nous</u> parle.
          J. you/us sees   J. you/us speaks
          'J. can see you/us.' (*te/nous* = DO)   'J.'s speaking to you/us.' (*te/nous* = IO)

Just as the first- and second-person object clitics *me* (*m'*), *te* (*t'*), *nous* and *vous* differ from third-person object proforms *le* (*l'*), *la* (*l'*), *les*, *lui* and *leur* in being compatible with both direct and indirect objects (§4.4.1), so they differ in being potentially coreferential with the subject, that is, reflexive/reciprocal:

(57) a. Je <u>me</u> lave.   b. Tu <u>te</u> salis.
          I me wash   you you dirty
          'I'm washing (myself).'   'You're getting (yourself) dirty.'
          (referent of *je* = referent of *me*)   (referent of *tu* = referent of *te*)

---

[38] The stylistic status of the three isn't the same. The ethic dative is characteristic of low registers and prevalent in some regional varieties, for example, southern France (Charaud 2000: 648). Also, the ethic dative doesn't always follow the clitic-ordering constraints in Table 4.1 on page 127. It's usually only found in matrix positive declaratives, but see (i), where the ethic dative appears in the subordinate infinitival:
(i)   T'aurais dû <u>te</u> voir l'air qu'elle avait.
       you-would.have had.to you see the-air that-she had
       'You should have seen what she looked like.'

c. Nous nous adorons.
we us adore
'We adore ourselves/one another'
(referent of *nous* same)

d. Vous vous parlez.
you you speak
'You talk to yourselves/one another.'
(referent of *vous* same)

In contrast, third-person object clitics can't be coreferential. Where the third-person object is coreferential with the subject, a distinct third-person reflexive/reciprocal clitic *se* (*s'*) is used. *Se* (*s'*) is highly underspecified: it can be F or M, SG or PL, reflexive or reciprocal, DO or IO:

(58) a. Elle s'habille.
she self dresses
'She's dressing herself.'
(*s'* = F.SG.DO)

b. Ils se parlent.
they self speak
'They are talking to themselves/one another.' (*se* = M.PL.IO)

Ambiguity between a reflexive or reciprocal interpretation of PL reflexive/reciprocal clitics can be resolved in favour of the reciprocal using *l'un(e) (à/de) l'autre* or *les un(e)s (à/de) les autres* 'one another', the adverb *mutuellement* 'mutually' or, in some cases, by prefixing *entre-* onto the verb:

(59) a. Les deux filles se sont regardées l'une l'autre.
the two girls self are watched the-one the-other
'The two girls looked at one another.'
NOT 'The two girls looked at themselves.'

b. Vous vous êtes habillés mutuellement.
you you are dressed mutually
'You dressed one another.'
NOT 'You dressed yourselves.'

c. Les Serbes et les Croates se sont entretués.
the Serbs and the Croats self are self.killed
'Serbs and Croats killed one another.'
NOT 'Serbs and Croats killed themselves.'

A number of qualified generalisations can be made about clitics, which contrast with *non*-clitics (§3.8) (See Kayne's 1975 tests for clitichood). Clitics immediately precede an appropriate verb form, as in (60):[39]

(60) a. Je le vois.
I him see
'I can see him.'

b. *Je vois le.
I see him

Phonologically, clitics form a single prosodic unit with the verb and can be neither

---

[39] One marked exception to this generalisation is the appearance of a lower adverbial between a non-subject clitic and an infinitive:
(i) a. Encore faut-il le lui bien faire montrer.
still needs-it them him well do show
'Yet he needs to be shown it.'

b. %une raison pour ne le pas faire
a reason for NEG it not do
' a reason not to do it'

co-ordinated nor independently stressed, as shown in (61):[40]

(61) a. *Je le et la vois.   b. *Je LE vois.
          I him and her see   I *him* see

Neither can they be omitted in co-ordinate structures, as shown in (62):

(62) Je l'ai acheté et (*(l')ai) mangé.
      I it-have bought and it-have eaten
      'I bought it and ate it.'

Clitics are subject to ordering constraints (see Table 4.1 on page 127).[41] Morphologically, clitics are sensitive to grammatical function, for example, *il* 3M.SG.<u>SUBJ</u>, *le* 3M.SG.<u>DO</u>, *lui* 3M.SG.<u>IO</u>. Finally, clitics are said to depend on a verb syntactically to the extent that, if the verb 'inverts' around the subject (§5.7), the non-subject clitic(s) stay(s) with the verb:[42]

(63) a. Vous <u>la lui envoyez</u>.   a'. [<u>La lui envoyez</u>]-vous?
          you it to.him send   it to.him send you
          'You're sending it to him.'   'Are you sending it to him?'

      b. Jean <u>l'aura fait</u>.   b'. Quand [<u>l'aura fait</u>] Jean?
          J. it-will.have done   when it-will.have done J.
          'Jean will have done it.'   'When will Jean have done it?'

Given these phonological, morphological and syntactic properties of clitics, they are regarded as syntactic clitics.

In a recent analysis Shlonsky (2004) follows standard assumptions in treating syntactic clitics as IP*-internal functional heads, licensed in a spec–head configuration by a moved non-overt thematic dependant of the verb, as in (64):

---

[40] The fact that some lower adverbials can intervene between preverbal clitics and verbs (see footnote 39) suggests that such adverbials also form part of a single phonological unit.

[41] With one morphosyntactic category of verb, namely, positive imperatives (§2.2.1.4), the situation is different. First, positive imperatives have enclitics rather than proclitics. Second, enclitic ordering with positive imperatives differs slightly from that of proclitics (see Table 4.2 on page 129). Third, enclitics don't form a single prosodic unit with the verb (but see Yaguello 1994).

[42] The notion of syntactic dependence sometimes assumed to be illustrated by the data in (63) crucially relies on an analysis of 'inversion' in terms of movement of the clitic-plus-verb cluster to the left of the subject. This is, however, not the analysis given in §5.7.

(64)   IP*

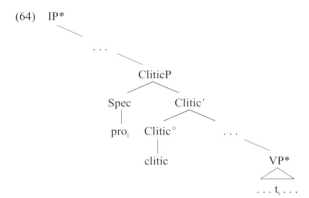

Shlonsky distinguishes proclisis from enclisis. He suggests that enclisis is in a sense preferred in that proclisis is found if and only if the conditions for enclisis aren't satisfied. He sets out the conditions for enclisis as in (65a, b) (2004: 332, his ex. (8)):

(65)   We have enclisis when:
      a.   the verb is inflectionally complete under the cliticization site; and,
      b.   the verb moves at least as far as the cliticization site.

By 'inflectionally complete', Shlonsky means that all the verb's inflectional features have been checked against suitable functional heads, and that the verb therefore has no remaining inflectional features to check. According to Shlonsky (2004) enclisis is left adjunction of the verb – together with any functional heads the verb has already incorporated into – onto the clitic, as in (66):

(66)

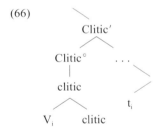

Shlonsky suggests that the configuration of the verb's final landing site in (66) is crucially different from that at intermediate landing sites, and that this is why the verb needs to be inflectionally complete under the cliticisation site for enclisis to be possible. When a verb moves to an intermediate landing site within IP*, its remaining unchecked inflectional features are still accessible for checking via further V movement to higher inflectional heads. Either the verb excorporates from one inflectional head in order to incorporate into the next, or else the entire complex head raises and the inflectional feature of the verb is visible inside the complex head by percolating upwards. In contrast, in the configuration in (66), features of the verb *can't* percolate upwards, and so no further features of the verb can be checked. Therefore, the configuration in (66) – that is, enclisis – is only possible provided all the verb's inflectional features have been checked prior to adjunction to F°, as set out in (65a).

In French, enclisis is found in just one context, namely, 'true' imperatives, as shown in (67a, b) (compare (67c)):

(67)   a.   Fais-<u>le</u>!   b.   *<u>Le</u> fais!   c.   Je <u>le</u> fais.
        do-it   it do   I it do
        'Do it!'   'I'm doing it.'

Adopting Shlonsky's (2004) approach to enclisis means that 'true' imperatives differ from finite verbs, infinitives and present participles in the crucial respect that all their inflectional features are checked by the time they reach CliticP. Specifically, they lack a D/EPP feature to be checked against I*°. Such a conclusion fits well with the observation that imperatives are incompatible with subjects (see Rooryck 1992; 2000c: 117).

Of interest here is the effect of negation on imperatives. Traditional grammars claim that 'true' imperatives can't be negative. Indeed, the examples in (68), containing the bipartite negative markers *ne* and *pas* (§4.5), are ungrammatical:

(68)   a.   *Ne défais-la pas!   b.   *Ne parle-<u>moi</u> pas!   c.   *Ne gênez-<u>vous</u> pas!
        NEG undo-it not   NEG talk-me not   NEG disturb-you not

The ungrammaticality of the examples in (68) can be accounted for by assuming that the IP*-internal inflectional head against which the polarity feature is checked (and which licenses *ne*) is located above (rather than below) CliticP. Since the default value for clausal polarity is positive, a positive 'true' imperative doesn't have a polarity feature and therefore doesn't need to raise above Clitic°. The verb is inflectionally complete under the cliticisation site, resulting in enclisis. In contrast, a negative interpretation depends on a formal negative-polarity feature. If the head against which this feature is checked is above CliticP, a negative imperative isn't inflectionally complete under the cliticisation site, and the conditions for enclisis aren't satisfied, hence the ungrammaticality of the examples in (68). Instead, proclisis is found in what are known as 'surrogate' imperatives, as in (69):[43]

(69)   a.   (Ne) <u>la</u> défais pas!   b.   (Ne) <u>me</u> parle pas!   c.   (Ne) <u>vous</u> gênez pas!
        NEG it undo not   NEG me talk not   NEG you disturb not
        'Don't undo it!'   'Don't talk to me!'   'Don't be embarrassed!'

However, consider the 'true' imperatives in (70) which contain the negative marker *pas*:

---

[43] On the optionality of *ne* see §4.5.1.

(70) a. Défais-<u>la</u> pas!   b. Parle-<u>moi</u> pas!   c. Gênez-<u>vous</u> pas!
          undo-it not   talk-me not   disturb-you not
          a–c: = (69a–c)

Crucially, these imperatives don't contain *ne*. We can tie this observation in with our existing assumptions by concluding that the examples in (70) aren't actually negative imperatives, despite the presence of *pas*. Rather, they are positive imperatives. Enclisis is therefore licensed because the verbs bear no polarity feature, raise no higher than Clitic° and are inflectionally complete under the cliticisation site. The negative adverbial *pas* has narrow scope (constituent negation) and *ne* isn't licensed.[44]

The reason why enclisis isn't licensed in (68) above is the same reason why it isn't licensed in all other verbal contexts: the conditions for enclisis in (65) aren't satisfied. Since finite verbs move to I*°, and CliticP is IP* internal, condition (65b) must be satisfied.[45] And since they nevertheless have proclisis rather than enclisis, the problematic condition must be (65a). In other words, the reason we find proclisis with finite verbs, infinitives and present participles in French is that these verb forms aren't inflectionally complete under CliticP.

Unlike what happens in enclisis, where the verb raises to the clitic, in proclisis the clitic moves to the verb. Thus, the verb first raises over the clitic, to check some inflectional feature, whereupon the clitic attaches to the verb:

(71)

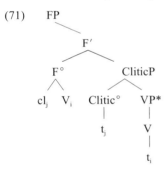

Clustered (pro)clitics are subject to ordering constraints, as in Table 4.1:

---

[44] In contrast to French French, negative true imperatives like (70b, c) are *not* found in Belgian French (Goosse 2000: 118), possibly because of the high level of *ne* retention in these varieties.

[45] Condition (65b) can be thought of as a general condition on cliticisation. The reason why past participles are compatible with neither enclisis nor proclisis is then that they don't raise as high as CliticP.

1	2	3	4	5	6	7
je (j') tu il/elle/on/ce (c') nous vous ils/elles	ne (n')	me (m') te (t') nous vous se (s')	le (l') la (l') les	lui leur	en$_1$ y	en$_2$

Table 4.1. Proclitic ordering.

Column 1 contains the subject proforms (§4.4.4); column 2 contains negative *ne* (*n'*) (§4.5.1); column 3 contains the non-subject clitics which *can* function as reflexives; columns 4 and 5 contain the direct- and indirect-object non-subject clitics, respectively, which *can't* function as reflexives; column 6 contains en$_1$ and *y*, the clitic equivalents of inherent-case-marked nominals; column 7 contains en$_2$, the indefinite subnominal clitic (§4.4.3).[46] The existence of ordering constraints suggests that each clitic is associated with a distinct Clitic head, and that Clitic heads are merged in a strict order.[47]

In addition to ordering constraints, the clitics in Table 4.1 are subject to co-occurrence restrictions: (a) no two items from the same column can co-occur; (b) no item from column 3 can co-occur with one from column 5; and (c) *lui* and *y* are sometimes claimed to be mutually incompatible. Restriction (a) is expected if the elements in each column are associated with a unique IP*-internal head. Restriction (b) remains a mystery. Finally, constraint (c) can possibly be explained on phonetic grounds: *lui y* = [lчii]. However, a number of examples of *lui y* were found on the Internet:

(72)　a.　Une vie sans persécution ne <u>lui y</u> serait plus possible.
　　　　a life without persecution NEG to.him there would.be no more possible
　　　　'A life without persecution would no longer be possible for him there.'

---

[46] The two different 'kinds' of clitic *en* are distinguished here by means of indices. Jones (1996: 254) labels *y* en$_2$ co-occurrence 'literary', and generally untypical of modern usage:
(i)　　Il y en$_2$ a acheté deux.
　　　　he to.it of.it has bought two
　　　　'He bought two of them there.'
The same applies to en$_1$ en$_2$ co-occurrence:
(ii)　　Il a acheté deux <u>livres du libraire</u>.　　→　　Il <u>en$_1$ en$_2$</u> a acheté deux.
　　　　He has bought two books from.the bookseller　he of.it of.it has bought two
　　　　'He bought two books from the bookseller.'　'He bought two of them from him.'
[47] Non-standard varieties have flexible *y* en$_2$ order. See Ayres-Bennett (2004: 209) for discussion of this variation in a historical context. The following examples were found with en$_2$ *y* order:
(i)　　a.　%J'<u>en$_2$ y</u> ajouterais régulièrement.　　b.　%Il <u>en$_2$ y</u> aura bien d'autres
　　　　I-of.it there would.add regularly　　　　　it of.it there will.have well of-others
　　　　'I would add some to it regularly.'　　　　　'There'll be many others.'
The flexibility of en$_1$ en$_2$ order is difficult to test empirically.

b. Les Togolais de la Diaspora ne <u>lui y</u> ont jamais rendu visite.
the Togolese of the diaspora NEG to.him there have never given visit
'The Togolese from the diaspora never visited him there.'

Clusters of enclitics with 'true' imperatives are found to a limited extent, only, for example as in (73a) (compare (73b, c)):

(73)   a. Donne-<u>le-nous</u>!   b. *Donne-<u>nous-le</u>   c. Il <u>nous le</u> donne.
          give-it-us   give-us-it   he us it gives
          'Give it to us'   'He's giving it to us'

Enclitic ordering is set out in Table 4.2:[48]

le (l')		moi		
la (l')	lui	toi	y	
les	leur	nous	en_1	en_2
		vous		

Table 4.2. Enclitic ordering.

4.4.2   Pronominal verbs

Further to their use as a replacement for an (in)direct object which happens to be coreferential with the subject, reflexive/reciprocal clitics form part and parcel of the lexical entry of what are known as inherently pronominal verbs, widespread across Romance. For example, the verb *repentir* doesn't exist independently of a reflexive clitic: *se repentir* 'to repent, regret' (*je me repens, tu te repens*, etc.). With pronominal verbs the clitic behaves like a direct-object clitic,[49] a fact which shows up in past-participle agreement (§5.8.2):

(74)   Elles se sont repenti<u>es</u>.
         they.F self are repented.F.PL
         'They have repented.'

The presence of a direct-object reflexive clitic is a necessary but not sufficient condition for pronominal-verb status. Thus, despite common usage in the tradition of descriptive grammar, and despite the fact that *se* (*s'*) is a direct object here,

---

[48] Enclitic clustering is subject to (register-sensitive) variation, in terms of both order and form:

(i)   a. Donne-<u>le-moi</u>!   b. %Donne-<u>moi-le</u>!
          give-it-me   give-me-it
          'Give it to me!   = (ia)

(ii)   a. %Donnez-<u>en-moi</u>!   b. Donnez-<u>m'en</u>!   c. %Donnez-<u>moi-z-en</u>!
          give-of.it-me   give-me-of.it   give-me-of.it
          'Give me some!'   b, c: = (iia)

Table 4.2 contains no equivalent to *se* in Table 4.1. This is because *se* is necessary third person, and imperatives are incompatible with third-person implicit subjects.

[49] Unlike what's found with regular transitive verbs, the direct-object clitic of inherently pronominal verbs can't be replaced by a DP* direct object.

there's no reason to treat *s'asseoir* 'to sit down', *se coucher* 'to go to bed' or *s'endormir* 'to fall asleep', for example, as pronominal. The relevant fact is that these verbs exist independently of the reflexive, as in (75):

(75) a. Jean asseyait le bébé sur ses genoux.   b. Je couche les enfants à 20h.
          J. sat the baby on his knees   I lay.down the children at 8pm
          'J. sat the baby on his lap.'   'I put the children to bed at 8pm.'

      c. Le médecin endort le patient.
          the doctor puts.to.sleep the patient
          'The doctor puts the patient to sleep.'

The Bescherelle conjugation guide catalogues fourteen pronominal verbs (for example, *se plaire* 'to please', *se nuire* 'to annoy', *se succéder* 'to follow/succeed') with *in*variant, that is, *non*-agreeing past participles:

(76) Elles se sont succédé(*es).
      they.F self are succeeded(.F.PL)
      'They followed on from one another.'

This shows that the reflexive clitic is behaving like a *in*direct object rather than a *direct* object. In each case the verb has a non-pronominal use, too, and in its non-pronominal use does indeed subcategorise for an indirect object:

(77) Les filles ont succédé aux garçons.
      the girls have succeeded to.the boys
      'The girls followed on from the boys.'

The reflexive clitic used with these verbs is therefore a regular reflexive, and the verbs aren't pronominal. Thus, the generalisation that the reflexive/reciprocal clitic found in pronominal verbs behaves like a direct object can be maintained.

4.4.3   Y and en₁ (and cela)

The items *y* 'to, at it' and *en₁* 'of, from it' are clitic equivalents of DP*s marked with inherent case by *à* 'to, at' and *de* 'of, from', respectively (§3.3):

(78) a. Il pense à mon mariage. →   a'. Il y pense.
          he think to my wedding   he *y* think
          'He's thinking about my wedding.'   'He's thinking about it.'

      b. Il dépend de ton soutien.   b'. Il en dépend.
          he depends of your support   he *en₁* depends
          'He depends on your support.'   'He depends on it.'

Y and *en₁* share a number of properties. First, they can pronominalise arguments of predicates other than verbs; in (79a, b) they pronominalise arguments of adjectives:

(79) a. J'y suis prêt.   b. J'en suis content.
          I-*y* am ready   I-*en₁* am happy
          'I'm ready for it.'   'I'm happy about it.'

This is because, unlike the (in)direct-object clitics (§4.4.1), which are associated with structural case, the clitics y and en_1 are associated with inherent case. Since structural-case licensing occurs in IP*, only, (in)direct objects and their clitic equivalents are restricted to verbs. In contrast, inherent-case licensing occurs within lexical projections on the back of a θ role; thus, inherent-case-marked DP*s and the clitic equivalents are available with predicates of any category.

Second, y and en_1 are both clitic equivalents of the non-clitic *cela* 'that' (§3.8):

(80)   a.   y = [à cela] 'to, at that'[50]   b. en_1 = [de cela] 'of, from that'

Because *cela* refers without regard for internal syntactico-semantic structure, y and en_1 aren't used in contexts where non-individuation is inappropriate. In the examples seen so far, this property is unproblematic: it's perfectly appropriate to think of concepts like someone's wedding or support as single, global, undifferentiated notions. But consider the data in (81), where the inherently case-marked dependant of the verb *penser* 'to think' is human.

(81)   a.   Je pense souvent à mes frères.
            I think often to my brothers
            'I often think about my brothers.'

       b.   Mes frères, je pense souvent à eux.
       c.   *Mes frères, je leur pense souvent.
       d.   Mes frères, j'y pense souvent.
            my brothers I y/leur think often to them
            b–d: ≈ (81a)

In (81a) the dependant of *penser* is an inherent-case-marked DP*; in (81b) the DP* has been pronominalised. Given that *penser* isn't an indirect transitive verb (cf. *parler* 'to speak'; §2.2.2.1) and *à mes frères/à eux* in (81a, b) aren't therefore indirect objects, they can't be cliticised as *leur* 'to them' (§4.4.1) (see footnote 50), hence the ungrammaticality of (81c). In fact, there's no equivalent to (81b) in which the non-clitic pronominal DP* *à eux* is replaced with a clitic. Note that the clitic y in (81d) is crucially *not* the equivalent of the DP* *à eux*; rather, it's the equivalent of the DP* *à cela*. Thus, there's a semantic difference between (81b) and (81d): while non-clitic *eux* in (81b) regards the brothers as individuals, clitic y in (81d) regards the set of brothers as a global, undifferentiated entity. Parallel facts are found with en_1, as in (82):

(82)   a.   Je dépends de mes deux filles.
            I depend of my two daughters
            'I depend on my two daughters.'

---

[50] Y is *not* the clitic equivalent of an indirect object (§2.2.2.1). The indirect-object clitic proforms are *lui* and *leur* (§4.4.1).

b. Mes deux filles, je dépends <u>d'elles</u>.
c. Mes deux filles, j'<u>en</u> dépends.
(my two daughters) I (en_1) depend (of them)
b, c: ≈ (82a)

In (82a) the inherent-case-marked DP* refers to a pair of individuated humans. In (82b) the DP* is pronominalised as non-clitic *d'elles*. In (82c) the clitic en_1 isn't the equivalent of *d'elles*, but rather of *de cela*. Thus, to the extent that (82c) is comparable to (82b) at all, it differs in that the two daughters are referred to as an undifferentiated pair, rather than as two separate entities.

4.4.4   Personal pronouns, aka subject proforms

As a non-pro-drop language (§1.3), French finite clauses require an overt subject. In the absence of a DP* subject, a personal proform is used: *je* 1SG, *tu* 2SG, *il* 3M.SG,[51] *elle* 3F.SG, *nous* 1PL,[52] *vous* 2PL,[53] *ils* 3M.PL, *elles* 3F.PL.[54] Given that common nouns have grammatical gender (§2.1.2.1), the third-person proforms can be used with animates and non-animates, alike. The forms *elle(s)*, *nous* and *vous* are cross-categorial, both clitic and non-clitic (§3.8).[55]

Two other subject proforms are:

– *ce* (*c'*) 'this', which only ever co-occurs with copular *être* 'to be':[56]

---

[51] The default status of M gender and SG number (§§2.1.2.1–2.1.2.3) means that *il* is also used non-referentially with impersonal verbs (§2.2.2.4) and various impersonal constructions (§2.2.3.1).

[52] Like *we* in English, the personal proform *nous* 'we' can be used facetiously for 1SG reference. (See also footnote 38 on page 95 in §3.8.) Where the referent is F (as well as SG), this is shown in relevant agreement contexts:
(i)   Nous nous sommes aperçu̱e que . . .
       we us are noticed.F.SG that
       'We noticed that . . . '

[53] The 2PL personal proform *vous* is also a formal alternative to the 2SG proform *tu*:
(i)   a. Jean, tu vas bien?   b. Monsieur, vous allez bien?
          J. you.SG go well   mister, you.PL go well
          'How are you, J.?'   'How are you, Sir?'

[54] Coveney (2004b) discusses the diachronic and dialectical neutralisation of the gender-based *ils–elles* distinction in favour of *ils*.

[55] As such they can 'double' themselves in dislocated structures (§5.3.1):
(i)   Vous, vous êtes fous!
       you you are mad
       'You're mad, you!'
Here, the first *vous* is a non-clitic, the second, a clitic.

[56] If the copula *être* isn't available, *ce* (*c'*) is replaced with *cela/ceci/ça* (§3.8):
(i)   Une pomme, <u>cela/ça coûte</u> cher.
       an apple that costs expensive
       'Apples are expensive.'

(83) a. Une pomme, c'est bon.   b. *Une pomme, ce coûte cher.
      an apple it-is good   an apple it costs dear
      'Apples are good.'

Ce (*c'*) is used: (a) as a ConF alternative to ModF *il* in some impersonal constructions (§2.2.3.1):

(84) a. Il est important d'être à l'heure.   b. C'est important d'être à l'heure.
      it is important of-be at the-hour   it is important of-be at the-hour
      'It's important to be on time.'

(b) in clefts (§5.5):

(85) C'est toi que j'ai vu.
      it-is you that I-have seen
      'It's you that I saw.'

(c) as the subject of a predicate nominal:

(86) C'est mon chef.
      it-is my boss
      'That's/He's/It's my boss.'

or (d) as a resumptive proform for dislocated constituents of various kinds, for
example, verbal predicates, free relatives (§5.6.1) or generic DP*s (§5.3):

(87) a. Manger, c'est bon.   b. Ne crache pas, ce n'est pas poli.
      eat it-is good   NEG spit not it NEG-is not polite
      'Eating is good.'   'Don't spit, it's not polite.'

     c. Ce que tu as dit, c'était bien.   d. Les papillons, c'est dur à attraper.
      this that you have said, it-was good   the butterflies it-is hard to catch
      'What you said was good.'   'Butterflies are hard to catch.'[57]

Used referentially, *ce* refers – like *cela* 'that' and *ceci* 'this' (§3.8) – in an
undifferentiated, global way. Thus, *les papillons* 'the butterflies' in (87d) can only
be interpreted generically.

– *on* 'one', which triggers 3SG agreement on the finite verb, and can only be used
with human referents.[58] *On* is used: (a) as a vague reference to people in general:

---

[57] On agreement with subject *ce* see below.
[58] The form *l'on* is sometimes used in ModF (but not ConF) as an alternative to *on*. The
context where *l'on* is used most frequently is immediately following the complementiser *que*,
where it allows the complementiser and the proform to avoid elision (*que l'on* instead of
qu'on). The form *l'on* is, however, excluded from three contexts, namely: (a) pronominal
and complex inversion (§5.7.1); (b) resuming dislocated *nous*; and (c) followed by an *l*-
initial word. The first of these exclusions is discussed in §5.7.1; the second is due to a
mismatch between ModF *l'on* and ConF dislocation; the third is doubtless a superficial case
of euphony. See Coveney (2004a).

(88)   En France <u>on</u> boit le café sans lait.
in France one drinks the coffee without milk
'In France <u>people</u> drink their coffee black.'

(b) instead of *nous*:

(89)   <u>On</u> part à la mer.
one leaves to the sea
'We're off to the sea.'

In ConF replacement of personal-proform *nous* with *on* is systematic (Haegeman 2003: 36);

(c) as a contextually determined second-person reference (Goosse 2000: 122):

(90)   a. <u>On</u> se calme!   b. <u>On</u> se moque?
one self calms   one self mocks
'Calm down!'   'Are you mocking me?'

or (d) as a reference to an unidentified human Agent in structures alternating with the passive (§2.2.3.1):

(91)   <u>On</u> a cassé la vitre.
one has broken the window.pane
'Someone smashed the window.'/'The window has been broken.'

Unlike other personal proforms, *on* doesn't have a non-clitic equivalent (§3.8). Generally, this isn't a problem since with most uses of *on*, there's no pragmatic need to use stress. The exception is (89). Where a subject is a pragmatic topic, it's dislocated in ConF (§5.3). Where 1PL *on* is dislocated, *nous* 'we' is used, instead:

(92)   a. <u>Nous</u>, on part à la mer.   b. <u>Nous</u>, on est égaux.
we one leaves to the sea   we one is equal.M.PL
≈ (89)   'We're equal.'

This mismatch between the dislocated phrase and the resumptive proform is widely condemned by prescriptivists. Judge and Healey (1983: 268) label (92b) 'colloquial'. However, the frequency of the pattern illustrated in (92) is such that it can't be dismissed as a production error.

Unlike other personal proforms, *on* can't ellipse in co-ordinate structures. Compare (93a, b):

(93)   a. Il arrive et (il) repart.   b. On arrive et *(on) repart.
he arrives and he leaves.again   one arrives and one leaves.again
'He arrives and leaves again.'   'People arrive and leave again.'

Ce and *on* behave interestingly with respect to external agreement.[59] As a generic proform, *ce* bears no inherent gender, number or person features and therefore

---

[59] For general discussion of subject–verb agreement see §2.2.1.1, and for adjective agreement see §2.3.3.1.

generally triggers default agreement. This means 3SG agreement on the finite verb, and M.SG agreement on adjectival predicates (§2.1.2.3). Thus, in (94) since *ce* denotes the abstract notion of apples, rather than any particular apples, both the verb and the AP* are (M.)SG.

(94) Des pommes, c'est bon.
      of.the apples it-is good
      'Apples are good.'

However, when *ce* is followed by a PL predicate DP*, the copula is marked PL:

(95) a. Ce <u>sont</u> mes cousins.   b. Ce <u>sont</u> ces deux-là que je veux voir.
          it are my cousins   it are these two-there that I want see
          'They are my cousins.'   'It's those two that I want to see.'

The contrast between (94) and (95) stems from a difference in the nature of φ-feature marking on DP*s and AP*s. While DP*s bear φ features inherently, AP*s bear them by association, only. Thus, in (94), since neither *ce* nor the predicative AP* bears inherent φ features, default 3M.SG is found throughout. In (95), in contrast, the predicate DP*s do have inherent φ features and these can percolate to *ce*, triggering PL marking on the verb.

In ConF SG verb agreement is found even where *ce* (*c'*) clearly has PL number:

(96) a. C'est mes cousins.   b. C'est ces deux-là que je veux voir.
          it-is my cousins   it-is these two-there that I want see
          = (95a)   = (95b)

This is reminiscent of the *there's/there are* distinction in Standard English, whereby a PL associate can trigger PL marking on *be*:

(97) a. There's a man here.   b. There are three men here.

Here, too, the distinction is absent in non-standard varieties:

(98) %There's three men here.

As for the agreement patterns with *on*, for some speakers/writers, the semantic content of *on* (as an alternative for the PL personal proform *nous*, which can be F) is sufficient to trigger agreement in number and gender on past participles and adjectives (Leeman-Bouix 1994: 72):

(99) a. On est <u>parti(e)(s)</u>.   b. On sera jamais trop <u>prudent(e)(s)</u>.
          one is left.F.PL   one will.be never too prudent.F.PL
          'We've left.'   'We can never be too careful.'

In §4.4.1 we concluded that weak non-subject proforms are syntactic clitics, merged in Clitic°. Personal proforms are like their non-subject counterparts and unlike DP* subjects in a number of respects: (a) they are dependent on the presence of a finite verb:

(100) a. Partir? Paul/Lui? Jamais!   b. *Partir? Il? Jamais!
         leave P./him never   leave he never
         'Leave? Paul/Him? Never!'

(b) they can't be separated from the finite verb by anything other than a clitic:

(101) a. Paul, évidemment, est parti.   b. *Il, évidemment, est parti.[60]
         P. evidently is left   he evidently is left
         'Paul evidently left.'

(c) liaison between a personal proform and a following verb is compulsory:

(102) a. Les filles ont mangé. [lefij(z)ɔ̃mɑ̃ʒe]   b. Ils ont mangé. [il(*z)ɔ̃mɑ̃ʒe]
         the girls have eaten   they have eaten
         'The girls ate.'   'They ate.'

and (d) the proform *je* and (optionally in informal ConF) the proform *tu* have elided forms (*j'* and *t'*) which appear before vowel-initial verbs. All these properties suggest a close clitic-like relationship with the finite verb, so we might wonder whether subject proforms are clitics.[61]

However, there's a difference between the syntax of non-subject clitics and that of personal proforms, and this suggests that personal proforms aren't syntactic clitics, but rather phonological clitics. The difference relates to the ability of personal proforms, but not non-subject clitics, to ellipse in co-ordinate structures: in (103a) the object clitic can't be omitted from the second conjunct; in (103b) the personal proform *can* be omitted from the second conjunct:

(103) a. Le journal, je [l'achète] et [*(le) lis] tous les jours.
         the newspaper, I it buy and it read all the days
         'The newspaper, I buy and read it every day.'

     b. [Je me réveille] et [(je) me lève] de bonne heure.
         I me wake and me rise of good hour
         'I wake up and get up early.'

Thus, instead of extending to subject proforms the analysis in §4.4.1 of non-subject proforms as Clitic° elements, we might assume that subject proforms behave by and large like DP* subjects: they merge in a VP*-internal θ position and raise to SpecIP* to check an EPP/D feature against the finite verb in I*°. Once there, though, they cliticise phonologically onto the adjacent verb. Provided that co-ordination and (optional) ellipsis/gapping take place *before* phonological cliticisation, the flexible pattern in (103b) is explained.

While the above approach to subject proforms works in ModF/ConF, is some

---

[60] The legal formula *Je, (le) soussigné, déclare par la présente . . .* 'I, the undersigned, do hereby declare . . . ', in which the personal proform *je* is separated from the finite verb, is now fossilised.

[61] The discussion here relates to preverbal personal proforms. Apparently inverted (that is, postverbal) forms are discussed in §5.7.1.

varieties it doesn't. The relevant empirical data relate to subject doubling, illustrated in (104a):

(104) a. Mon chat il dort tout le temps. b. Mon chat, il dort tout le temps.
   my cat he sleeps all the time   my cat he sleeps all the time
   'My cat sleeps all the time.'   'My cat, he sleeps all the time.'

In subject doubling a 'strong' subject (here, *mon chat* 'my cat') co-occurs with a 'weak' subject (here, *il* 'he'). The subject-doubling example in (104a) is superficially very similar to subject (clitic) left dislocation (LD), illustrated in (104b) (§5.3.1). However, subject doubling is crucially different from subject LD, and the following differences are identified by Nadasdi (1995) on the basis of his study of subject doubling and subject LD in the French spoken in Ontario, Canada, following Roberge (1990):

> (a) doubled subjects don't have the characteristic 'comma intonation' of LDed subjects;
> (b) doubled subjects are incompatible with contrastive/emphatic stress, unlike LDed subjects;[62]
> (c) doubled subjects allow liaison, while LDed subjects don't; and,
> (d) doubled subjects follow non-selected CP* material, while LDed subjects precede such material.[63]

Auger (2003b) found similar things looking at the same phenomenon in Picard. Furthermore, she found that subjects which were incompatible with subject LD were

---

[62] In Picard, too, it's suggested that subject doubling is so common that it can't be explained away as pragmatically triggered LD. Indeed, it's found in syntactic contexts where the pragmatic analysis simply doesn't work. Coveney's (2003) study shows that subject doubling in Picard takes place 24% of the time and is subject to age and class differentiation, but not sex differentiation. See also Auger (2003a). According to Queffélec (2000a: 790) subject doubling among French speakers in the Maghreb is near systematic.

[63] Nadasdi (1995) also found (Table 1, p. 7) that subject doubling is more likely to occur when the subject is [+SPECIFIC] and [+DEFINITE]. Given that clitics like to match the features of their associated phrase, and given that personal proforms are [+SPECIFIC] by default, such a preference is expected. In fact, Nadasdi found (Table 2, p. 8) that the specificity continuum – 1/2>3>proper>common>indefinite proforms – corresponds to a falling rate of subject doubling.

Nadasdi makes two further findings which won't be pursued here. First, he finds (Table 3, p. 10) that the nature of the superficial subject is relevant to subject doubling: the subject of an unaccusative/passive is less prone to subject doubling than that of an unergative/active. Second, he finds (Table 4, p. 11) that subject doubling correlates with speakers' relative use of French and English: those who speak relatively less French (and relatively more English) display less subject doubling. Of course, English doesn't have subject doubling and the correlation may be due to interference from English. Alternatively it may be due to a general preference among less competent speakers, irrespective of the syntactic properties of the dominant language, for simple or stylistically narrow structures, or free rather than bound morphemes.

nevertheless compatible with subject doubling.[64] Taken together, these differences suggest strongly that subject doubling isn't the same as subject LD.

In §5.3.1 (subject) LD like (104b) is analysed as: (a) IP*-*external* merger of the LDed DP*; and (b) a binding relationship between the dislocated DP* and the IP*-internal subject. Nothing further needs to be said about the internal structure of IP*. Given the differences between subject doubling and subject LD, Roberge (1990) and Auger (1994) argue that, rather than merging *externally* to IP*, the 'strong' subject in subject-doubling contexts like (104a) merges IP* *internally*. They suggest that it *is* the subject and that it behaves accordingly: it merges in VP* and raises to SpecIP*. This means, of course, that the 'weak' subject in subject doubling isn't the 'real' subject and therefore can't be analysed as such. Instead of merging VP* internally, raising to SpecIP* and phonologically cliticising onto the finite verb, it's suggested that, in subject doubling, the 'weak' subject has been reanalysed, first as an affix, then as a mere agreement marker, realised directly on I*°, much as is the case in Northern Italian dialects (see Poletto 2000 and De Cat 2002: 38 for references). The 'strong' and 'weak' subjects in subject doubling therefore occupy the specifier and head positions, respectively, of IP*.

4.5   Sentential negation

In this section I address the syntax of sentential negation. My starting point is the question, How is a clause made negative? I assume that clausal polarity is feature based, that positive is the default value for the feature, that positive clauses therefore lack a formal polarity feature, but that the verb in a negative clause bears a [+NEG] which needs to be checked on a functional head within IP* (Haegeman 1995; Rowlett 1998a). We've already seen negative adverbials (§2.3.2.1) and negative DP*s (§3.5), and we've also seen the relevance of negation to imperative verb forms (pp. 126ff.). As well as functioning as constituent negations, these negative constituents interact with IP* structure in the expression of sentential negation. French marks sentential negation using a particle, one of the four typologically diverse mechanisms for marking sentential negation referred to by Zanuttini (2001: 513). The negative particle marking sentential negation in French is *ne* (*n'*).

---

[64] While the pragmatic constraints on LD rule out (91b, c) in §5.3.1 in ConF, since existential indefinites can't be dislocated, such strings are grammatical in varieties with subject doubling, crucially because topicalisation isn't involved (Auger 1994: 22):
(i)   a. Personne il m'aime.   b. Tout le monde il se baignait là-bas.
          nobody he me-likes   all the world he self bathed there
          'Nobody likes me.'   'Everyone was bathing there.'
       c. Si tous mes soldats ils étaient curés . . .
          if all my soldiers they were priests
          'If all my soldiers were priests . . . '

4.5.1 *The negative head* ne

Negative *ne* behaves much like non-subject proclitics (§4.4.1). Negative *ne* is: (a) restricted to verbal contexts; (b) always preverbal, even in apparent subject–verb inversion contexts (§5.7):

(105) a. Il <u>ne le fait</u> pas.   b. <u>Ne le fait</u>-il pas?
      he NEG it does not   NEG it does-he not
      'He isn't doing it.'   'Isn't he doing it?'

Negative *ne* intervenes between a subject clitic and the (non-subject-clitic-plus-) verb:

(106) Nous <u>ne</u> te le donnons pas.
      we NEG you it give not
      'We're not giving it to you.'

With 'true' imperatives, where non-subject proclitics aren't found, negative *ne* isn't found, either (§§2.2.1.4, 4.4.1):

(107) *Ne fais-le pas!
      NEG do-it not

Finally, like non-subject proclitics, *ne* has a non-clitic counterpart, namely, *non* (§1.3).

In order to capture the parallel between non-subject proclitics and negative *ne*, it's standardly assumed that *ne* is a clitic which heads its own IP*-internal FP, NegP (Pollock 1989), and is endowed with features from an XP which raises to SpecNegP (Rowlett 1993). And in view of the analysis of 'true' and 'surrogate' imperatives in §4.4.1, Neg° must merge above Clitic°, as in (108):[65]

(108) $[_{IP*} \ldots [_{NegP} \ldots Neg° \ldots [_{CliticP} \ldots Clitic° \ldots [_{VP*} \ldots]]]]$

Rowlett (2002) discusses a number of apparently non-clausal contexts in which *ne* can appear.[66] If these contexts really are non-clausal, they pose a problem for an analysis of *ne* as Neg°. The first relates to the complex conjunction *pour que* (lit. 'for that') 'in order that', which selects a positive or negative SUBJ dependent clause (§5.1), as in (109):

(109) a. Elle le fait <u>pour que</u> je tombe.   b. Elle le fait <u>pour que</u> je (ne) tombe pas.
      she it does for that I fall   she it does for that I NEG fall not
      'She does it so that I fall.'   'She does it lest I fall.'

---

[65] The IP*-internal inflectional head on which *ne* merges must be higher than the one whose specifier is occupied by *pas*. If *ne* and *pas* were associated with the same head, no account for the contrast between 'true' and 'surrogate' imperatives containing *pas* could be given.
[66] A further non-clausal use of *ne* is illustrated in (i):
(i)   Ne plus disponible en français.
       NEG no.more available in French
       'No longer available in French.'

However, a cross-linguistically odd alternative to (109b) is available, namely, (110a), in which the negative markers *ne pas* precede the complementiser *que*. Examples (110b, c) show that other negative adverbials like *plus* and *jamais* can also occur here.[67]

(110) a. Elle le fait <u>pour (ne) pas que</u> je tombe.
     she it does for NEG not that I fall
     = (109b)

    b. Je veux t'offrir ma chaleur . . . <u>pour (ne) jamais que</u> tu pleures.
       I want you offer my warmth for NEG never that you cry
       'I want to give you my warmth so that you never cry.'

    c. . . . les rend invisibles <u>pour (ne) plus que</u> vous soyez conscient de . . .
       them makes invisible for NEG no.more that you be aware of
       ' . . . makes them invisible so that you're no longer aware of . . . '

The construction is problematic since there's no apparent IP* domain between the preposition *pour* and the complementiser *que* which might host *ne*: [$_{PP*}$ pour ? [$_{CP*}$ que]]. Hirschbühler and Labelle (1992/93: 34–7, §1.1) discuss the construction and entertain the possibility either that *ne* and *pas* are generated directly between *pour* and *que*, or that they merge within the subordinate clause and raise. Rizzi (1997) proposes a CP*-internal Neg projection which might host *ne* here. However, the problem remains of what *ne* might cliticise onto in such a configuration.

The second apparently non-clausal context where *ne* is found is illustrated in (111):

(111) a. Je t'ordonne de <u>ne plus jamais ne rien</u> faire.
     I you order to *ne plus jamais ne rien* do
     'I order you never again not to do anything.'
     (= 'I order you always to do something in future.')

    b. On faisait souvent un peu plus pour <u>ne jamais ne pas</u> savoir quoi faire.
       we did often a bit more for *ne jamais ne pas* know what do
       'We often did a bit extra in order never not to know what to do.'

    c. <u>Ne jamais ne pas</u> avoir d'argent sur soi, mais très peu, 40 francs max.
       ne jamais ne pas have money on one, but very little, 40 francs max
       'Never have no money on one's person, but only very little, 40 francs max.'

---

[67] Example (110a) is condemned by prescriptive grammarians. For references to socio-linguistic comment see Rowlett (1998a: 21–2). Blanche-Benveniste *et al.* (1991: 101 fn. 61) claim that (ia, b) aren't equivalent:
(i)   a. Il l'a fait <u>pour pas que</u> . . .   b. Il l'a fait <u>pour que</u> . . . ne . . . pas.
       he it-has done for not that   he it-has done for that NEG not
       a, b: 'He did it so that . . . not . . . '
However, they give no indication as to whether the non-equivalence is semantic, pragmatic or merely stylistic. Google searches on 29 March 2004 found approximately 11,400 web-page occurrences of *pour ne pas que*, 507 of *pour ne plus que* and 25 of *pour ne jamais que*.

    d. Une résolution est prise: <u>ne plus jamais ne pas</u> se sentir maître de sa vie.
       a resolution is taken: *ne plus jamais ne pas* feel master of ones' life
       'A decision has been made: never again not to feel in control of one's life.'

What appears to be a single infinitival IP* contains more than one instance of *ne*. The examples are problematic if an IP* contains a single NegP, since a single NegP provides a home for a single *ne*. The double-negation interpretation of the examples in (111) suggests that the examples in fact contain two NegPs, each with full negative force, one cancelling out the other. Hirschbühler and Labelle (1992/93: 40, example (18)) suggest an analysis in terms of IP*-internal NegP recursion. While such an approach could in principle deal with the grammaticality (and interpretation) of the examples in (111), there are issues. First, given that multiple *ne* isn't permitted within a *finite* clause, why is NegP recursion available in infinitival contexts? Second, given that *pas* isn't usually able to co-occur with another negative XP (§4.5.2), why is such co-occurrence possible in (111)?

An alternative to Hirschbühler and Labelle's IP*-internal NegP-recursion analysis assumes full IP* recursion, in other words, that the infinitives in (111) are in fact themselves biclausal: [$_{IP*}$ ne (plus) jamais . . . [$_{IP*}$ ne pas/rien . . .] . . .], whereby each IP* contains its own NegP. The attraction of this proposal is that the availability of double *ne* is expected, as is the double-negation interpretation. The questions it raises, though, relate to the nature of the verbal content of the higher of the two infinitival IP*s and to the nature of the host of *ne* in the higher clause.

In ConF negative *ne* is dropped, as in (112):[68]

(112) a. Je ⌀ viens pas.   b. Je ⌀ veux rien.   c. <u>Aucun</u> étudiant ⌀ est venu.
        I come not   I want nothing   no student is come
        = (114a)   = (114b)   = (114c)

There's an extensive literature on the sociolinguistics of *ne* drop. A number of factors seem to be relevant, both linguistic and extralinguistic. In a recent study Armstrong and Smith (2002) suggest: (a) that *ne* deletion is spreading to increasingly formal registers; (b) that *ne* is retained more with a DP* than with a pronominal subject; (c) that the presence/absence of non-subject clitics doesn't affect *ne* deletion rates; (d) that the choice of negative XP affects levels of *ne* drop: *pas*, *plus*, *rien*, *jamais* are associated with increasing levels of *ne* retention;[69] and, finally, (e) that *ne* is retained more frequently with subjectless verb forms, that is, infinitives, present participles and imperatives.[70] Gadet (1997: §11) suggests further that *ne* drop is favoured when: (a) there are no reinforcing adverbials like *du tout*

---

[68] It has been claimed (e.g., Prince 1976) that *ne* deletion is impossible where the negative XP is in subject position. This is incorrect; in the case of *personne* 'nobody' and *rien* 'nothing' judgements may have been influenced by phonological issues, namely, word-final [n] and liaison.
[69] Interestingly, the order of *pas*, *plus* and *jamais* here corresponds to their order of merger in Rizzi's (1999) exploded IP* in (3) on page 103.
[70] See also Armstrong (2001).

'at all'; (b) the IP* is matrix rather than subordinate; (c) the verb is IND rather than SUBJ; (d) the verb is (semi-)auxiliary rather than lexical. *Ne* drop is also particularly common in fossilised expressions like *c'est pas* 'it isn't' and *(il) faut pas* 'you mustn't'. A number of these factors are linked with stylistic factors and, therefore, the ModF–ConF distinction. For example, complex sentences and SUBJ verbs (where *ne* is more likely to be retained) are, mutatis mutandis, indicative of a higher register than simplex sentences and IND verbs. Furthermore, *ne* retention is favoured when: (a) the discourse is more formal (use of *vous* rather than *tu*); (b) the delivery is slower; (c) the discourse is a monologue rather than a dialogue; (d) the speaker belongs to a higher socio-economic category; and (e) the speaker is older. Finally, *ne* retention is favoured in written rather than spoken discourse.

There are various reasons to believe that, with time, *ne* will be lost altogether as an overt marker of sentential negation. First, this is exactly what has happened in other languages, for example, English and German, which previously had preverbal negative markers equivalent to French *ne*. Second, there are some varieties of French, namely, in Quebec, where the loss of *ne* is apparently already complete (Sankoff and Vincent 1977), although not in written language (Goosse 2000: 118). Third, some of the specific factors which seem to favour *ne* drop are the very ones associated with the linguistically innovative ConF, namely, main clauses, female speakers, young speakers and unguarded or informal spoken discourse. Fourth, Ashby (1981) (using a 1976 sample) notes that *ne* drop is age dependent, and therefore either a change in progress or age graded.[71] Repeating his study some two decades later, Ashby (2001) (using a sample from 1995) finds that *ne* is dropped more and concludes that the phenomenon is a change in progress, as expected given Jespersen's negative cycle.[72]

In most contexts *ne* alone (that is, without a negative XP) is incapable of marking sentential negation, as shown in (113):

(113) Je ne viens *(pas).
       I NEG come not

Typically, *ne* co-occurs with a negative XP, thereby making sentential negation bipartite, as in (114):

(114) a. Je ne viens pas.   b. Je ne veux rien.   c. [Aucun étudiant] n'est venu.
         I NEG come not   I NEG want nothing   no student NEG-is come
         'I'm not coming.'   'I don't want anything.'   'No student came.'

However, with a small subset of verbs which have been termed pseudo-modals, *ne* has retained the ability to mark sentential negation on its own (see Schapansky 2002):

---

[71] See also Ashby (1976).

[72] Interestingly, in francophone West Africa, it's *ne* retention rather than *ne* drop that's favoured (Queffélec 2000b: 828). Similarly, in Belgian French, *ne* is retained more often.

(115) a. Je ne peux venir.   b. Il ne cesse d'appeler.
         I NEG can come   he NEG ceases of-call
         'I can't come.'   'He doesn't stop calling.'

Where *ne* is the only negative marker, it can't be deleted. Semantically, Schapansky suggests that, when expressed by *ne* alone, negation is contrary rather than contradictory.

Finally, in ModF (but not ConF) negative *ne* appears in a number of non-negative contexts:[73]

(116) a. J'ai peur qu'il ne soit en retard.   b. Elle est plus laide que je n'imaginais.
         I-have fear that-he NEG be in late   she is more ugly that I NEG-imagined
         'I fear he might be late.'   'She's uglier than I imagined.'

4.5.2   Negative concord

Various negative XPs can co-occur without leading to double negation, as in (117):

(117) a. Personne n'a rien fait.   b. Je ne t'appelle plus jamais.
         nobody NEG-has nothing done   I NEG you-call no.more never
         'Nobody did anything.'   'I'll not phone you ever again.'

      c. Personne n'aura plus jamais rien à craindre.
         nobody NEG-will.have no.more never nothing to fear
         'Nobody will have anything to fear ever again.'

      d. Personne ne lui avait jamais rien dit au sujet de la sexualité.
         nobody NEG to.him had never nothing said to.the subject of the sexuality
         'Nobody had ever told her anything about sex.'

If these negative XPs are inherently negative, French thus looks like a negative-concord language (Corblin *et al.* 2004). Negative concord is however not available (in the standard language) with *pas* 'not', as shown in (118):[74]

---

[73] As a characteristic of ModF rather than ConF, 'pleonastic' *ne* might be expected to be losing ground. However, according to Goosse (2000: 127–8), it's still used in spontaneous speech. It even appears in some hypercorrection contexts, such as after *sans que* 'without', suggesting that it's a sociolinguistic variable to which speakers are sensitive.

[74] Leeman-Bouix (1994: 22) gives the non-standard examples in (i) of negative concord with *pas*:
(i) a. %Il ne veut pas voir personne.
         he NEG wants not see nobody
         'He doesn't want to see anyone.'
     b. %J'espère qu'ils se rappelleront pas de rien.
         I-hope that-they self will.recall not of nothing
         'I hope they won't remember anything.'

The unavailability of negative concord with *pas* is a relatively recent development. As late as the seventeenth century, *pas* could co-occur with other negative XPs without leading to double negation.

(118) ?Je n'ai <u>pas</u> vu <u>personne</u>.
     I NEG-have not seen nobody
     ≠ 'I didn't see anyone.'

To the extent that (118) is an acceptable sentence at all, it's an example of metalinguistic negation 'It isn't the case that I saw nobody', that is, 'I saw someone'. Other, more authentic examples of true double negation are given in (119):

(119) a. Ce n'est <u>pas</u> pour <u>rien</u> qu'il a de grandes oreilles.
          this NEG-is not for nothing that-he has of large ears
          'It's not for nothing that he's got big ears.'

     b. J'ai <u>pas</u> <u>rien</u> que ça à faire.
          I-have not nothing that that to do
          'I don't just have that to do.'

Negative concord is also possible with the privative preposition *sans* 'without':

(120) a. sans personne   b. sans jamais rien dire
          without nobody   without never nothing say
          'without anyone'   'without ever saying anything'

Once again, this isn't possible with *pas*:

(121) *sans pas vouloir
      without not want

Interestingly, while *sans* can select a bare infinitival IP*, as in (122a), which can contain negative XPs, as in (120b), the infinitive cannot occur with negative *ne*, as shown in (122b):[75]

(122) a. sans payer   b. *sans <u>ne</u> rien faire
          without pay   without NEG nothing do
          'without paying'

This is odd since infinitival IP*s are typically either positive or negative (§5.1), and when they are negative, they are compatible with negative *ne* (§4.5.1).

---

[75] In fact, Google searches on 4 June 2005 turned up several *sans ne* V_{inf} sequences. The ungrammaticality judgement in the text assumes the attested sequences to be hypercorrective performance errors. (On hypercorrective use of *ne* see above.) This conclusion is based on the observation that the relevant sequences occur considerably less frequently than would be expected if they were grammatical. It's known that *ne* drop allows *ne* to be omitted from finite and non-finite contexts. The Google search found 314,000 webpages containing <rien faire> (without *ne*) and 162,000 containing <ne rien faire> (without preceding *sans*). Negative *ne* was therefore retained 34% of the time. If *sans ne* V_{inf} is grammatical, a similar rate of *ne* retention is expected. However, the figures for <sans rien faire> and <sans ne rien faire> were 68,700 and 290, respectively, giving a *ne* retention rate of 0.42%. Similarly stark contrasts were found with other negative infinitives, suggesting that *sans ne* V_{inf} is in fact ungrammatical, and that use of *ne* in this context is due to hypercorrection.

5

The left clause periphery

This final chapter explores the topmost domain within clause structure, the domain traditionally known as CP. As with VP* and IP*, we'll see that CP is actually a hierarchical array of FPs rather than a single phrase; consequently, the notation CP* is used. In §§5.1, 5.2 I address the interaction between matrix and finite/infinitival subordinate contexts. In §§5.3–5.5 I consider some specifically pragmatic functions of CP*, in particular its role in articulating topic–comment and focus–presupposition. In §§5.6, 5.7 I discuss two phenomena associated with interrogation, namely, wh and inversion. Finally, in §5.8 I tie up a number of issues held over from earlier discussion.

5.1   Finite subordinate clauses

Finite declarative subordinate clauses in French are straightforwardly identifiable since they're overtly marked by a simple subordinating conjunction, typically the declarative complementiser *que* (*qu'*),[1] as in (1):[2]

(1) a. Je sais <u>qu'</u>il pleut.   b. [$_{CP*}$ que [$_{IP*}$ . . .]]
         I know that-it rains
         'I know it's raining.'

Distribution and pronominalisability suggest that a finite subordinate clause is either an adjunct or an argument. For example, pronominalisation using the default M.SG direct-object clitic *le*,[3] as in (2a), and alternation with a (structurally case-marked) direct-object DP* of a transitive verb (§2.2.2.1), as in (2b), suggest that these finite subordinate clauses are direct objects:

(2) a. Je <u>le</u> sais.   b. Je sais [$_{DP*}$ son nom].
         I it know   I know his name
         'I know (it).'   'I know his name.'

Other finite declarative subordinate clauses are marked by more complex

---

[1] As a result of contact with English, *que* can optionally delete in Québécois.
[2] Finite interrogative subordinate clauses are introduced by the interrogative complementiser *si* or a fronted wh phrase (§5.6).
[3] On the default use of the M.SG proform see §§2.1.2.3, 4.4.1.

subordinating conjunctions, as in (3):

(3) a. Je me plains de ce que tu sois en retard.
         I self complain of *ce* that you be in late
         'I complain about you being late.'

     b. Elle s'attend à ce que tu partes.
         she self expects at *ce* that you leave
         'She expects you to leave.'

Pronominalisation using *en*$_1$ and *y*, as in (4), and alternation with *de/à*-marked DP*s (§3.3), as in (5), suggest that these subordinate clauses are inherent-case-marked dependants:[4]

(4) a. Je m'en$_1$ plains.   b. Elle s'y attend.
         I me-of.it complain   she self-there waits
         'I complain about it.'   'She expects it.'

(5) a. Je me plains de toi.   b. Elle s'attend à un cadeau.
         I self am complain of you   she self-expects at a present
         'I complain about you.'   'She expects a present.'

Rather than being an argument of a predicate, a finite declarative subordinate clause can be an adjunct, expressing such notions as cause, condition, time frame, purpose, concession. The subordinate nature of the clause is marked by a subordinating conjunction which is again often *que* final:

(6) a. Je dors [$_{CP*}$ parce que [$_{IP*}$ je suis malade]].
         I sleep because I am ill
         'I'm sleeping because I'm ill.'

     b. Je dis oui [$_{CP*}$ si [$_{IP*}$ tu demandes poliment]].
         I say yes if you ask politely
         'I'll say yes if you ask politely.'

---

[4] The purpose of *ce* in the complex subordinating conjunctions in (3) is to nominalise the CP* introduced by *que* in order to make it compatible with overt inherent-case marking. The sequence *à/de ce que* in (3) is often simplified to *que* (§5.1.1). The subordinate clauses in (3) aren't the same as those in (i):
(i) a. Je me plains de ce que tu as dit.
         I me complain of *ce* that you have said
         'I'm complaining about what you said.'
     b. Elle s'attend à ce que tu as à dire.
         she her expects at *ce* that you have to say
         'She's expecting what you have to say.'
The underlined strings in (ia, b) are free relatives (§5.6): *ce* doesn't function as a nominaliser, and *de/à ce que* isn't subject to the simplification as *que*. The subordinate clauses introduced by free-relative *ce que* in (ia, b) contain an IND verb form and have a 'missing' relativised argument (the dependant of *dire* 'to say'). The subordinate clauses in (3) contain a SUBJ verb and have no 'missing' argument. (The SUBJ mood is expected if the *ce* here is interpreted as *le fait* 'the fact'; §5.1.2.)

c. Je te téléphone [$_{CP*}$ <u>dès que</u> [$_{IP*}$ je saurai]].
   I you telephone as soon as I will.know
   'I'll call <u>as soon as</u> I find out.'

d. Je fais des économies [$_{CP*}$ <u>pour que</u> [$_{IP*}$ nous puissions partir en vacances]].
   I do of.the economies for that we can.SUBJ leave to holidays
   'I'm saving up <u>so that</u> we can go on holiday.'

e. [$_{CP*}$ <u>Bien que</u> [$_{IP*}$ je t'aime]], je veux divorcer.
   well that I you-love I want divorce
   'Although I love you, I want a divorce.'

The form of the complex subordinating conjunctions in (6a, c, d) suggests a PP* analysis (Beaulieu and Balcom 2002): a head P selects a CP* or, since finite CP*s are non-nominal, a null-headed DP* which in turn selects a CP*, as in (7):[5]

(7)   [$_{PP*}$ . . . [$_{DP*}$ . . . [$_{CP*}$ . . .]]]

5.1.1   Generalisation of que *as an all-purpose finite complementiser*

The complementiser *que* introduces [+ASS(ERTIVE)] finite subordinate clauses, either as a simple subordinating conjunction, as in (1a), or as part of a complex subordinating conjunction, as in (3) and (6a, c, d). In (3) the *que*-final subordinating conjunctions can simplify as *que*, as in (8):

(8)   a. Je me plains <u>que</u> tu sois en retard.   b. Elle s'attend <u>que</u> tu partes.
          I self complain that you be in late   she self expects that you leave
          = (3a)   = (3b)

The significance of this simplification is unclear. Recall from the discussion of (3) that *ce* serves here to nominalise the finite subordinate clause and to make it compatible with inherent-case marking (see footnote 4). One way of accounting for the simplification in (8) is based on the idea that inherent-case marking is optional. Such an idea is already suggested by the kind of alternation illustrated in (89) on

---

[5] If these adjunct subordinating conjunctions have the structure in (7), with a null-headed DP*, there's an interesting parallel with the syntax of *malgré (le fait) que* 'despite the fact that', illustrated in (i):

(i)   a. Je viens malgré toi.   b. Je viens malgré le fait qu'il pleuve. (ModF)
          I come despite you   I come despite the fact that-it rains
          'I'm coming despite you.'

       c. Je viens malgré qu'il pleuve. (ConF)
          I come despite that-it rains
          b, c: 'I'm coming despite the fact that it's raining.'

Malgré 'despite' is a preposition and can select a DP* dependant, as in (ia). It can also select a clausal dependant which in ModF is embedded within a DP* structure, as in (ib). In the ConF (ic) *malgré* appears to select a CP* directly. However, an alternative analysis is to assume that DP* is present in (ic) but non-overt, as in (ii):

(ii)   [$_{PP*}$ malgré [$_{DP*}$ ∅ [$_{CP*}$ que . . .]]]

page 47 in §2.2.3.1. There, a DP* argument of a verb either remains VP* internal (and bears inherent case) or raises to SpecIP* (and bears structural nominative case). If inherent case is necessarily marked on the back of the θ role, this means that, in the latter case, the DP* bears *both* inherent *and* structural case. If, instead, inherent-case marking is optional (with semantico-pragmatic interpretation depending on the choice made), no double case marking is needed, and the motivation for raising to SpecIP* is clearer: if the option of marking inherent case isn't taken up, the DP* has to raise in order to be case-licensed. Transferring the notion of optional inherent-case marking to the contrast between (3) and (8), we might say that the option is taken up in (3), hence the presence of *de*/*à* and the need for *ce*, while the option isn't taken up in (8), hence the absence of *de*/*à* or the need for *ce*. Unlike DP*s, finite CP*s aren't nominal, and so don't need to be case licensed. Thus, with these CP* dependants, the option of not marking inherent case isn't problematic.

Simplification of (3) as (8) is informal, but quite standard, and characteristic of ConF; less so is simplification of adjunct subordinating conjunctions, as in (9):

(9)   a.   %Viens ici [que je te voie mieux].   (cf. pour que)
           come here that I you see better
           'Come here so that I can see you more clearly.'

      b.   %Elle a téléphoné [que j'étais pas là].   (cf. alors que)
           she has telephoned that I-was not there
           'She phoned when I wasn't here.'

      c.   %Il est pas venu [qu'il est malade].   (cf. parce que)
           he is not come that-he is ill
           'He hasn't come because he's ill.'

      d.   %Il buvait du vin [qu'il se tenait plus debout].   (cf. de sorte que)
           he drank of.the wine that-he self held no.more upright
           'He drank (so much) wine that he couldn't stand up anymore.'

5.1.2   *Mood*

In §2.2.1.2 we saw the morphological IND–SUBJ mood distinction. (See Table 2.1 on page 25 and Table 2.3 on page 26.) IND is the default mood; SUBJ mood needs to be triggered. The fact that, in bare IP*s, IND alone is found, SUBJ being restricted to subordinate contexts, suggests that the trigger is IP* external.[6]

---

[6] Apparently matrix contexts with SUBJ mood either require an overt finite complementiser, as in (ia), or are frozen expressions, such as (ib), where the postverbal subject suggests that we are dealing with a residual V2 phenomenon:

(i)   a.   Que cela soit fait!   b.   Vive la France!
           that that be.SUBJ done   live.SUBJ the France
           'May it be done!'   'Long live France!'

In both cases the CP* domain has been activated.

Rizzi (1997) suggests that a low CP*-internal head, Fin(iteness)°, plays a role in the triggering mechanism:

(10)   [$_{CP*}$ ... Fin° [$_{IP*}$ ...]]

There's a clear semantico-pragmatic dimension to the triggering of SUBJ mood, often discussed in terms of (non-)assertive force:[7] IND mood is assertive; SUBJ mood is non-assertive. First, SUBJ typically correlates with the *un*availability of the pro-assertive-IP* *oui/non* (§3.8): bridge verbs like *penser* 'to think' (used positively) take a dependent clause with IND mood and are compatible with *oui/non*; verbs like *vouloir* 'to want' take SUBJ and aren't:

(11) a. Jean pense qu'il pleut.   b. Jean veut qu'il pleuve.
          J. thinks that-it rain.IND   J. wants that-it rain.SUBJ
          'J. thinks it's raining.'   'J. wants it to rain.'

(12) a. Jean pense que oui.   b. *Jean veut que oui.[8]
          J. thinks that yes   J. wants that yes
          'Jean thinks so.'

Second, SUBJ is triggered by verbs of desire, as in (11b), verbs, adjectives and nouns of emotion, as in (13), all of which are plausibly non-assertive:[9]

---

[7] The notion of assertion needs to be understood in broad terms here, including the presupposition of a prior assertion (Abouda 2002: 10). Finite subordinate interrogatives (§5.6) systematically have IND mood, as in (i), because they presuppose a (prior) assertion:
(i)   a. Je sais qui a appelé.   b. Je ne sais pas si je viens.
          I know who has called   I NEG know not if I come
          'I know who called.'   'I don't know if I'm coming.'
The example in (ia) asserts that *someone* called; the one in (ib) wouldn't be felicitous unless the speaker had reason to believe that the hearer suspected s/he was coming (and therefore presupposes a prior assertion).

[8] One context in which *vouloir* is compatible with *oui/non* is where it means 'to be of the opinion':
(i)   a. La théorie veut que non, mais la pratique?
          the theory wants that no, but the practice
          'The theory says no, but what about practice?'
      b. La croyance populaire veut que oui, mais pas en Angleterre.
          the belief popular wants that yes but not in England
          'Popular belief says yes, but not in England.'
(Note also that *vouloir* 'to want' takes IND subordinate clauses dialectally.)

[9] The nearly synonymous verbs *espérer* 'to hope' and *souhaiter* 'to wish' (as well as their morphologically derived nouns) select finite dependent clauses containing IND and SUBJ mood, respectively. Leeman-Bouix (1994: 65) explains the contrast in terms of different perspectives on the part of the speaker on the likelihood of the event actually being realised. With *souhaiter*, the speaker comes down on neither one side nor the other. The dependant clause is therefore non-assertive, hence the subjunctive. With *espérer*, in contrast, the speaker leans in the direction of the event actually being realised. The dependent clause is therefore assertive, hence the indicative. Note also that Leeman-Bouix's claim that *espérer*

(13) a. Tu regrettes [qu'il <u>parte</u>].   b. Je suis heureux [qu'il <u>parte</u>].
          you regret that-he leave.SUBJ   I am happy that-he leave.SUBJ
          'You're sorry he's leaving.'   'I'm happy he's leaving.'

      c. Je ne nie pas mon souhait [qu'il <u>parte</u>].
          I NEG deny not my wish that-he leave.SUBJ
          'I don't deny my wish that he leave.'

Third, mood can flip backwards and forwards between SUBJ and IND by 'assertion-toggling' operators like negation or interrogation occurring, for example, with verbs of opinion (Abouda 2002), as in (14), and some impersonal structures (§2.2.3.1), as in (15):

(14) a. Tu crois [qu'il <u>part</u>].   b. Tu ne crois pas [qu'il <u>parte</u>].
          you believe that-he leave.IND   you NEG believe not that-he leave.SUBJ
          'You believe he's leaving.'   'You don't believe he's leaving.'

      c. Crois-tu [qu'il <u>parte</u>]?   d. Ne crois-tu pas [qu'il <u>part</u>]?
          believe-you that-he leave.SUBJ   NEG believe-you not that-he leave.IND
          'Do you believe he's leaving?'   'Don't you believe he's leaving?'

(15) a. Il est probable [qu'il <u>part</u>].   b. Il n'est pas probable [qu'il <u>parte</u>].
          it is probable that-he leave.IND   it NEG-is not probably that-he leave.SUBJ
          'It's likely he's leaving.'   'It's unlikely he's leaving.'

      c. Est-il probable [qu'il <u>parte</u>]?   d. N'est-il pas probable [qu'il part]?
          is-it probably that-he leave.SUBJ   NEG-is-it not probably that-he leave.IND
          'Is it likely he's leaving?'   'Isn't it likely he's leaving?'

The predicates *croire* 'to believe' and *être probable* 'to be probable' are assertive and take IND, as in (14a)/(15a). However, in the presence of negation, (14b)/(15b), or in the context of a yes–no interrogative marked by pronominal inversion (§5.7.1) (Huot 1986), (14c)/(15c), mood can flip to SUBJ. Where the two 'assertion-toggling' operators co-occur, as in (14d)/(15d), IND reappears.

The fourth reason to link the IND–SUBJ distinction to assertion is illustrated in sentence frames like (16), where the dash is replaced with adjectives like *certain* 'certain', *probable* 'likely', *possible* 'possible', *peu probable* 'unlikely' and *impossible* 'impossible': IND is found with the first two, SUBJ with the final two, with variation in the middle:[10]

(16) Il est – [$_{CP*}$ que [$_{IP*}$ . . .]].
      it is that
      'It's – that . . . '

is assertive is supported by the existence, alongside *espoir* 'hope', of a further derived noun, namely, *espérance* 'expectation'.

[10] The availability of the pro-assertive-clause *oui/non* patterns with IND mood (§3.8):
(i)   Il est certain/probable/%possible/*peu probable/*impossible que oui.
       it is certain/probably/possible/little probably/impossibly that yes
       'It's certainly/probably/possibly/unlikely/impossibly true.'

Fifth, the conjunctions *de sorte que, de/d'une (telle) façon (à ce) que* 'in such a way that' take either SUBJ or IND depending on whether they express a purpose (non-assertive) or a consequence (assertive), respectively, as in (17), while *il est de règle que . . .* 'as a rule, . . . ' takes IND when it *de*scribes (assertively) what *does* happen as a rule, and SUBJ when it *pre*scribes (non-assertively) what *should* happen as a rule, as in (18):

(17) a. J'étais gentil de façon qu'il <u>veuille</u> me revoir.   (purpose)
          I-was nice of fashion that-he wants.SUBJ me see.again
          'I was nice so that he would want to see me again.'

      b. J'étais gentil de façon qu'il <u>veut</u> me revoir.   (consequence)
          I-was nice of fashion that-he wants.IND me see.again
          'I was nice in such a way that he wants to see me again.'

(18) a. Il est de règle qu'il <u>pleut</u>.   (descriptive)
          it is of rule that-it rains.IND
          'As a rule, it rains.'

      b. Il est de règle que tu <u>fasses</u> tes devoirs avant de regarder la télé.   (prescriptive)
          it is of rule that you do.SUBJ your homework before of watch the tv
          'As a rule, you should do your homework before watching tv.'

The purpose–consequence ambiguity of the conjunctions *de sorte que/d'une (telle) façon (à ce) que* disappears in favour of a SUBJ-taking purpose interpretation when they're dominated by an imperative, as in (19a); as expected the pro-assertive-clause *oui* is then unavailable, as shown in (19b):

(19) a. Fais-le de sorte que je <u>sois</u>/*suis content.   b. *Fais-le de sorte que <u>oui</u>.
          do-it of sort that I be.SUBJ/be.IND happy   do-it of sort that yes
          'Do it to make me happy.'

Finally, SUBJ is triggered in a number of relative-clause contexts (§5.6.1) where the head of the relative implies non-assertion, for example, is negative, as in (20), minimised, as in (21), or qualified by the kind of adjective which picks out a unique reference, for example, a superlative, *premier* 'first', *dernier* 'last', *seul* 'only', as in (22):

(20) <u>Rien</u> [que tu <u>puisses</u> suggérer] ne pourra plus aider.
      nothing that you can.SUBJ suggest NEG can.FUT anymore help
      'Nothing you might suggest can help any more.'

(21) <u>Peu d'enfants</u> [qui <u>aillent</u> à l'école] sont illettrés.
      few of-children who go.SUBJ to the-school are illiterate
      'Few children who go to school are illiterate.'

(22) a. La <u>plus belle</u> femme [que j'<u>aie</u> jamais vue], c'est Marianne.
          the more beautiful woman which I-have.SUBJ ever seen it-is M.
          'The most beautiful women I have ever seen is Marianne.'

b. La <u>seule</u> chose [qui me <u>fasse</u> peur], c'est le noir.
the only thing which me does.SUBJ fear it-is the black
'The only thing I'm afraid of is the dark.'

Non-assertive free relatives headed by the indefinite expressions *qui/quoi/où/quand/ quel(le)(s) que* 'who/what/where/when/whichever' also take the subjunctive:

(23) a. Qui que tu <u>sois</u>, tu ne peux pas rentrer!
who that you be.SUBJ you NEG can not come.in
'Whoever you are, you can't come in!'

b. Quoi que je <u>fasse</u>, cela ne suffit jamais.
what that I do.SUBJ that NEG suffices never
'Whatever I do, it's never enough.'

c. Quand vous voulez, où que vous <u>soyez</u>!
what you want where that you be.SUBJ
'When you want, wherever you are!'

d. Le corse est enseigné à tous les enfants, quelles que <u>soient</u> leurs origines.
the Corsican is taught to all the children which that be.SUBJ their origins
'All children are taught Corsican, whatever their background.'

We might approach SUBJ triggering in the above data in the following way. As a property of finite verbs, mood is determined by a feature on I*°. Abouda (2002) labels the relevant feature [±ASS(ERTION)], with [+ASS] as its default value, resulting in IND mood.[11] Since SUBJ appears in subordinate contexts, only, triggering must depend on a particular configuration between I*° and CP* (minimally Rizzi's Fin°, which selects IP*, as in (10)). Since a bare IP* has no CP*, no such configuration is possible, and SUBJ can't be triggered. Where SUBJ mood *is* triggered, this is most straightforwardly by an inherently [−ASS] Fin° selecting a [−ASS] IP* and, by transitivity, a SUBJ I*°, as in (24):

(24)

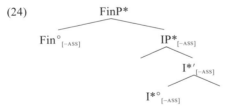

The clearest example of this is the class of SUBJ-triggering conjunctions, illustrated in (17a), as well as concessive *bien que* and *quoique* and purposive *pour que*.

In more complex cases, SUBJ mood isn't triggered directly by an inherently [−ASS] Fin°. Rather, it's triggered indirectly by a long-distance relationship between a higher predicate, CP*, IP* and I*°: the higher predicate, X, selects a non-assertive dependent clause which merges in the specifier of the relevant θ projection; C*° is

---

[11] We see the relevance of [±ASS] again in the context of inversion (§5.7).

marked [−ASS] by percolation; C*° selects a [−ASS] IP*, and, by transitivity, a SUBJ I*°, as in (25):

(25)

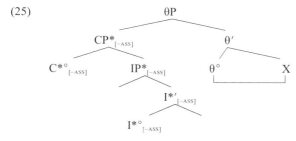

Predicates which can appear as X in (25) include *vouloir* 'to want' and *désir* 'desire'.

In some cases, the triggering mechanism is even more indirect. Consider the (admittedly very formal) example in (26), from Abouda (2002):

(26) Si je pensais qu'il *fût* un bon candidat . . .
      if I thought that-he was.SUBJ a good candidate
      'If I thought he were a good candidate . . . '

The subordinate clause is SUBJ. The matrix clause contains the bridge verb *penser*, which selects IND. (See also (14)/(15).) The trigger for the subjunctive is the hypothetical *si* 'if' in the matrix CP*. Note, though, that *si* doesn't trigger SUBJ in the matrix clause. Rather, its hypothetical semantics turns *penser* into the kind of X predicate in (25) which triggers SUBJ in the subordinate clause. The semantics of the example in (27) is subtly different:

(27) Si je pensais qu'il *était* un bon candidat . . .
      if I thought that-he was.IND a good candidate
      'If I thought he was a good candidate . . . '

Here, there's no subordinate SUBJ. Abouda (2002) distinguishes between strong and weak hypothesis. We can formalise this in terms of an underspecified complementiser *si*. Crucially, in these contexts with mood variation, the perspective of the speaker is what's important.

A different kind of long-distance SUBJ triggering is shown in (28):

(28) a. Je ne voulais pas qu'elle croie que [$_{IP*}$ je sois triste de rester].
          I NEG wanted not that-she believe.SUBJ that I be.SUBJ sad of stay
          'I didn't want here to believe that I was sad to be staying.'

      b. Non pas que je pense que [$_{IP*}$ tu aies tort sur toute la ligne].
          NEG not that I think.SUBJ that you have.SUBJ wrong on all the line
          'Not that I think you're wrong across the board.'

Here, the most deeply embedded IP* is SUBJ, apparently for no reason, given that neither of the immediately dominating predicates, the bridge verbs *croire* 'to believe' and *penser* 'to think', triggers the subjunctive.[12] However, the bridge verbs are themselves SUBJ because of their own CP*s. It looks, therefore, like SUBJ triggering has 'leaked' downwards, presumably on the basis of the same structural mechanism in (25). What all these SUBJ-mood triggering contexts have in common is a configuration involving I*° and Fin°.

Although there are many contexts in ModF where the speaker has no choice of which mood to use, where the grammar dictates one or the other, there are a number in which there's variation and variability. In some cases, this is found within ModF and reflects subtle semantic differences which are dependent on the perspective of the speaker. The subjunctive in (14b, c)/(15b, c), for example, co-exists with the indicative. With (14b)/(15b), Abouda (2002) sees a subtle semantic difference, distinguishing (14b) from (29), for example:

(29) Tu ne crois pas [qu'il part].
      you NEG believe not that-he leave.IND
      ≈ (14b)

The difference relates to the scope of negation. For Abouda, (29) is the result of NEG-raising, while (14b) isn't. NEG-raising transfers negation from one clause to the immediately superior clause. Example (29) is thus derived from a structure like (30), in which the matrix predicate is positive and not expected to trigger SUBJ in the subordinate clause:

(30) Tu crois [qu'il ne part pas].

Thus, (14b), with a SUBJ subordinate clause, tells us what you *don't* think he *has* done, while (29), with an IND subordinate clause, tells us what you *do* think he *hasn't* done.

With (14c)/(15c), Abouda (2002) suggests that yes–no interrogatives with pronominal inversion (PI; §5.7.1) are only *potentially* non-assertive, and that the IND–SUBJ variation relates to whether or not there's a presupposed assertion, whereby IND presupposes assertion, while SUBJ is neutral. In contrast to the pattern in (14c)/(15c), where the subjunctive is possible with interrogative PI, uninverted yes–no questions (with or without *est-ce que*) can't trigger SUBJ, and neither can PI outside the context of yes–no questions, as shown in (31):

(31) a. (Est-ce que) tu crois qu'il part(*e)?
          is-this that you believe that-he leave(.SUBJ)
          'You think he's leaving?'

      b. Peut-être crois-tu qu'il part(*e).
          maybe believe-you that-he leave(.SUBJ)
          'Maybe you think he's leaving.'

Relative-clause minimal pairs like (32a, b) also illustrate a subtle distinction

---

[12] If the negation in (28b) has undergone NEG-raising, then the *penser* clause is expected to trigger SUBJ in the most deeply embedded clause.

related to assertion and expressed using mood:

(32) a. Je cherche un homme [qui <u>sait</u> s'occuper de lui].
         I seek a man which knows.IND self-occupy of him
         'I'm looking for a man who can look after himself.'

      b. Je cherche un homme [qui <u>sache</u> s'occuper de lui].
         I seek a man which knows.SUBJ self-occupy of him
         ≈ (32a)

The indicative in (32a) reflects the speaker's belief that such a man exists (it's just a question of finding one/him[13]); the subjunctive in (32b) indicates no such belief.[14]

The relevance to mood selection of the speaker's perspective, which can subtly vary, is supported by the contrast between (33a) and (33b):

(33) a. Il semble [qu'il <u>parte</u>].   b. Il <u>me</u> semble [qu'il <u>part</u>].
         it seems that-he leaves.SUBJ   it me seems that-he leaves.IND
         'It seems he's leaving.'   'It seems *to me* that he's leaving.'

Mood here is sensitive to the speaker's personal involvement in the assessment of the evidence and his/her readiness to make an assertion on the basis of the evidence, absent from the first example (SUBJ), present and overtly marked in the second (IND).

Finally, some predicates, for example, *supposer* 'to suppose', have underspecified lexical semantics which allow them to select either an IND or a SUBJ subordinate clause, as in (34) (Abouda 2002):

(34) a. Je suppose qu'un moine est toujours charitable.
         I suppose that-a monk be.IND always charitable
         'I suppose that a monk is always charitable.'

      b. Je suppose que les hommes soient eternels sur la terre.
         I suppose that the men be.SUBJ eternal on the earth
         'I suppose that men are immortal on earth.'

What is being explicitly supposed is implicitly assumed to be true in (34a), but taken to be no more than a hypothesis in (34b). The distinction ties in well with the notion of SUBJ triggering being sensitive to the value of the [±ASS] feature.

---

[13] Example (32a) is itself ambiguous. The ambiguity has to do with whether or not the speaker has a *specific* man in mind, or whether *any* man who knows how to look after himself would do. The ambiguity can be lifted by a continuation like (ia) or (ib):
(i) a. . . . mais je ne sais pas si je vais <u>le</u> trouver.
         but I NEG know not if I go him find
         '. . . but I don't know whether I'll find <u>him</u>.' (specific referent)
      b. . . . mais je ne sais pas si je vais <u>en</u> trouver <u>un</u>.
         but I NEG know not if I go of.it find one
         '. . . but I don't know whether I'll find <u>one</u>.' (non-specific referent)
[14] The specific interpretation is unavailable with the SUBJ relative clause. Thus, example (32b) can't be continued with (ia) in footnote 13.

In other cases of mood variability, the semantic motivation is less clear cut. For example, *après que* 'after' selects IND in ModF, but is increasingly often heard with subjunctives, doubtless by analogy with *avant que* 'before' which also selects SUBJ. This 'contamination' is widely believed to have spread after World War I. Leeman-Bouix (1994: 68) observes that *après* and *avant* are unique in being adverbial and prepositional and in introducing an infinitive. Crucially, she suggests, it's the ability to select a ([−REALIS]) infinitive that causes *après que* to take on the subjunctive of *avant que*, rather than the other way round. Conversely, Leeman-Bouix (1994: 69) attributes the non-standard pattern whereby concessive *bien que*, *quoique* and *encore que* select IND instead of SUBJ to the fact that they are *not* compatible with infinitives. (See also the discussion of mood selection diachronically in §1.3.)

In yet other cases, mood variability is restricted to specific regional varieties. The conjunctions *quand* 'when' and *sitôt que* 'once', which take IND in ModF/ConF, take SUBJ regionally. The conjunction *pourvu que* 'provided that' takes SUBJ in standard French, but IND in Belgium. The concessive structure *tout* <AP*> *que . . .* often introduces a SUBJ clause, although standard grammars require an indicative. Conversely, *jusqu'à ce que . . .* 'until . . . ' takes the subjunctive in the standard language, but can appear with the indicative. The verb *s'attendre (à ce) que . . .* usually takes the subjunctive but the indicative is sometimes heard. *Il arrive que . . .* 'It happens that . . . ' increasingly takes the subjunctive. *A condition que . . .* 'provided that . . . ' formerly appeared with a future indicative but now overwhelmingly appears with the present subjunctive. The expression *(il) n'empêche que . . .* 'nevertheless . . . ', which takes the indicative in the standard language, is sometimes heard with a subjunctive, perhaps by analogy with other uses of the lexical verb *empêcher* 'to prevent' (Goosse 2000: 122–3).

5.2   Infinitival clauses

In this section I consider infinitival subordinate clauses. I start with adjunct clauses (§5.2.1). Moving on to selected clauses, the more straightforward cases are those introduced by *de* and *à* (§5.2.2). The complexities posed by bare infinitival dependent clauses are explored in §5.2.3.

5.2.1   *Infinitival adjunct clauses*

In §5.1 we analysed finite adjunct clauses as prepositional structures as in (7). Infinitival adjunct clauses like those in (35) can be analysed in the same way:

(35) a. avant de partir   b. quitte à perdre   c. pour ⌀ te faire plaisir
          before of leave   quits to lose   for you do pleasure
          'before leaving'   'even if it means losing'   'in order to please you'

However, since infinitives (unlike finite clauses) are nominal, there's no need to posit a non-overt DP* structure between the prepositional subordinating conjunction and the infinitive. The parallel analysis is all the more appealing since a number of conjunctions introduce both finite and infinitival clauses:

(36) a. avant de partir   a′. avant qu'il parte
          before of leave   before that-he leave
          'before leaving'   'before he left'

      b. après être parti   b′. après qu'il est parti
          after be left   after that-he is left
          'after leaving'   'after he left'

5.2.2   Infinitival dependants marked with de/à

Infinitival subordinate clauses are typically introduced by *de* or *à*.[15] Where they co-distribute with inherent-case-marked DP*s (and, indeed, inherent-case-marked finite clauses; §5.1), as in (37a–c) and (38a–c), it makes sense to think of *de*/*à* as inherent-case markers (§3.3):

---

[15] There's variation in the syntax of infinitival dependent clauses. While *aimer* 'to like' and *aller* 'to go' are usually followed by a bare infinitive, as in (ia) and (iia), in some regional varieties they take a *de*-marked dependant, as in (ib) and (iib):

(i)   a. Damville n'aimait pas être interrogé.   b. %D. n'aimait pas d'être interrogé.
           D. NEG-liked not be interrogated   D. NEG-like not of.be interrogated
           'D. didn't like being questioned.'   = (ia)   (Goosse 2000: 114)

(ii)   a. Elle va partir.   b. %Elle va de partir.
           she goes leave   she goes of leave
           'She's going to leave.'   = (iia)

The reverse is the case of *se souvenir* 'to remember':

(iii) a. Il se souvient d'avoir appelé.   b. %Il se souvient avoir appelé.
           he self remembers of-have called   he self remember have called
           'He remembers calling.'   = (iiia)

The verb *continuer* 'to continue' selects either a *de*-marked or an *à*-marked infinitival dependant, as in (iv):

(iv)   Il continue de/à chanter.
           he continues *de*/*à* sing
           'He continues to sing.'

Nouns like *capacité* 'ability' and *difficulté* 'difficulty' are subject to variation:

(v)   la capacité/difficulté de/à chanter
           the ability/difficulty of/to sing
           'the ability to sing'/'difficulty singing'

The verb *obliger* 'to oblige' is noteworthy in this context. In an active VP*, it selects a DP* direct object and an *à*-marked infinitival, as in (vi):

(vi)   a. On l'a obligé [à déménager].   b. On l'y a obligé.
           one him-has obliged to move.out   one him-to.it has obliged
           'They forced him to move out.'   'They forced him to.'

In contrast, where *obliger* 'to oblige' appears in a passive VP* (§2.2.3.1), the infinitive is marked with *de*, as in (vii):

(vii) a. Il a été obligé [de déménager].   b. Il en a été obligé.
           he has been obliged to move.out   he of.it has been obliged
           'He was forced to move out.'   'He was forced to (do so).'

The verbs *forcer* 'to force' and *contraindre* 'to oblige' pattern in the same way.

(37) a. Jean m'a convaincu [$_{DP*}$ de son innocence].
          J. me-has convinced of his innocence
          'Jean convinced me of his innocence.'

      b. Jean m'a convaincu [(de ce) qu'il était malade].[16]
          J. me-has convinced of this that-he was ill
          'Jean convinced me that he was ill.'

      c. Jean m'a convaincu [de partir].
          J. me-has convinced of leave
          'Jean persuaded me to leave.'

(38) a. Je m'attends [$_{DP*}$ à des vacances].
          I me-wait to to the holidays
          'I expect holiday.'

      b. Je m'attends [(à ce) que tu sois à l'heure].[16]
          I me-wait to this that you be to the-hour
          'I expect you to be on time.'

      c. Je m'attends [à partir].
          I me-wait to leave
          'I expect to leave.'

The status of the subordinate infinitive as a thematic dependant, and of *de/à* as an inherent-case marker, is supported by three facts. First, the same element, *de/à*, appears in (37a–c)/(38a–c). Second, like the inherent-case-marked DP* and finite clause, the infinitive is pronominalisable using en_1/*y*:

(39) a. Jean m'en_1 a convaincu.   b. Je m'y attends.
          J. me-of.it has convinced   I me-to.it wait
          'J. convinced me of it.'   'I expect it.'

Third, as with co-ordinated inherent-case-marked DP*s (§3.3), *de* needs to appear on all infinitival conjuncts (Abeillé *et al.* 2004):

(40) a. J'ai besoin d'un fromage et *(d')un vin.
          I-have need of-a cheese and of-a wine
          'I need cheese and wine.'

      b. J'ai besoin de manger et *(de) boire.
          I-have need of eat and of drink
          'I need to eat and to drink.'

An infinitival introduced by *de* doesn't always alternate with a *de*-marked DP* or pronominalise with en_1; sometimes it alternates with a structural-case-marked direct-object DP* and alternatives with *le* (Abeillé *et al.* 2004), as in (41):

---

[16] On the simplification of *de/à ce que* to *que* see §5.1.1.

(41)   a. Nous avons choisi <u>une Renault</u>.   b. Nous avons choisi <u>de</u> rester.
            we have chosen a Renault   we have chosen of stay
            'We chose a Renault.'   'We chose to stay.'

        c. Nous <u>l'</u>avons choisi.
            we it-have chosen
            'We chose it.'

Here, the matrix verb *choisir* 'to choose' is direct transitive and selects a direct-
object DP* in (41a) or a *de*-marked infinitive in (41b). The direct-object status of
both is shown by their pronominalisability using *le* in (41c). It makes little sense,
therefore, to think of *de* here as an inherent-case marker; it looks more like a non-
finite complementiser, presumably occupying a head position within CP*. While *de*-
marked infinitives pattern with direct-object DP*s in this way, *à*-marked infinitives
don't, suggesting that, while *de* and *à* are both inherent-case markers, *de* alone
functions as a non-finite complementiser.

5.2.3   *Bare infinitives*

While subordinate infinitives are typically introduced by *de/à*, in some
contexts they're bare. Unlike *de/à*-marked infinitives, which can be dependants of
predicates of various categories, bare infinitives are only ever dependants of verbs.
The empirical complexity explored here points to a variable relationship between
a bare infinitive and the verb on which it depends. I pursue the idea that this
variability boils down to a distinction between monoclausal and biclausal structures,
in other words, that while a bare infinitive sometimes occupies an independent
clause, at other times it undergoes clause union with the verb on which it depends.

In each example in (42) a bare infinitive is a dependant of a pseudo-modal verb
(§2.2.2.5):[17]

(42)   a. Je veux [aller].   b. Il doit [l'aimer].   c. Tu peux [lui parler].
            I want go   he must it-love   you can to.him speak
            'I want to go.'   'He must love it.'   'You can speak to him.'

Unlike what we saw in §5.2.2 the parallel between these bare infinitives and regular
direct-object DP*s isn't clear cut. First, while *vouloir* 'to want to' and *devoir* 'to
have to' readily select a DP* direct object,[18] *pouvoir* 'to be able to' does not:

(43)   Je veux/dois/*peux quelquechose.
        I want/owe/can something

Second, while the bare infinitives in (42) can be pronominalised using *le* (just as the
de/à-marked infinitival dependants of (in)direct transitive verbs can be pronominalised using $en_1/y/le$; §5.2.2), as in (44), they're more typically either ellipsed or

---

[17] Other verbs which can probably be included in this category are *falloir* 'to be necessary',
valoir 'to be worth', *faillir* 'to fail'.
[18] Where *devoir* takes a DP* dependant its meaning is more readily rendered as 'to owe'.

else replaced with the dummy VP *le faire* 'to do it', as in (45):

(44) a. Je <u>le</u> veux.   b. Il <u>le</u> doit.   c. Tu <u>le</u> peux.
      I it want   he it must   you it can
      'I want to (do it).'   'He has to (do it).'   'You're able to (do it).'

(45) a. Je veux <u>(le faire)</u>.   b. Il doit <u>(le faire)</u>.   c. Tu peux <u>(le faire)</u>.
      I want it do   he must it do   you can it do
      = (44a)   = (44b)   = (44c)

Given that these infinitives are bare, the question arises of the nature of the relationship between them and the pseudo-modals on which they depend. Two facts suggest that the infinitives are IP*s (rather than VP*s). First, where a dependant of the infinitive is realised as a clitic, it attaches to the infinitive rather than to the pseudo-modal. Compare (42b, c) with the ungrammatical cases of 'clitic climbing' in (46):[19]

(46) a. *Il <u>le</u> doit aimer.   b. *Tu <u>lui</u> peux téléphoner.
      he it must love   you him can telephone

Second, the infinitive is compatible with sentential negation independently of the pseudo-modal, as in (47):

(47) a. Je veux <u>ne pas</u> aller.   b. Il doit <u>ne pas</u> l'aimer.
      I want NEG not leave   he must NEG not it-love
      'I want not to leave.'   'He must not love it.'

Given the analysis of clitics in §4.4.1 and negation in §4.5, these infinitives must project some IP* structure above VP*. This suggests they're regular clausal dependants of the pseudo-modals, and merged in a SpecθP position above V, as in the schematic underlying configuration in (48):

---

[19] The facts aren't actually as clear cut as the text suggests. Clitic climbing with pseudo-modals is found to a limited extent in the modern language (Cinque 2004a). Goosse (2000: 113) labels the phenomenon, illustrated in (i), *une recherche d'élégance* 'a search for elegance':

(i)   a. Aucun logiciel ne <u>le</u> peut lire.   b. On <u>les</u> doit acheter la veille.
        no software it can read   one them must buy the previous.day
        'No software can read it.'   'You have to buy them the day before.'

Clitic climbing with *y* and *en*, is less stylistically marked:

(ii)   a. les courses que Roger <u>y</u> doit faire   b. les différents usages qu'on <u>en</u>, peut faire
      the errands that R. there must do   the different uses that-we of.it can make
      'the errands R. needs to run there'   'the different uses one can make of it'

(48)    (biclausal)

In fact, there's been an intriguing diachronic development here, one which is arguably unexpected. In previous stages in the development of the language (as indeed in modern Spanish, for example), pseudo-modals readily allowed the kind of clitic climbing seen in footnote 19. Compare (49) with (46):

(49)   L'autre le veut faire choir d'un rocher.   (sixteenth-century poem)
          the-other him wants make fall from-a rock
          'The other one wants to make him fall from a rock.'

If cliticisation is a clausebound phenomenon, the grammaticality of (49) (as well as that of the examples in footnote 19) suggests clause union has taken place: the pseudo-modal and the infinitive aren't independent verbal predicates each merged in its own clause with its own lexical argument structure (cf. (48)); rather, they're merged as a complex predicate within a single clause, the infinitive as the dependant of the pseudo-modal (rather than in SpecθP), projecting a single (composite) lexical argument structure, as in (50):

(50)    (monoclausal)

Since there's a single V, all arguments of the complex predicate are merged within a single VP*, and a pronominalised argument can cliticise onto the pseudo-modal, as in (49). A diachronic shift from the structure in (48) to the one in (50) can be seen as an example of grammaticalisation. If French pseudo-modals have shifted over time from (50) to (48), they would appear to have *de*grammaticalised. Assuming that this characterisation of the diachronic data is along the right lines, I leave the implications for this example of degrammaticalisation on the research agenda.[20]

---

[20] Clitic climbing was criticised in the seventeenth century by language arbiters like Vaugelas (Ayres-Bennett 2004). One possible linguistic motivation for degrammaticalisation relates to the phenomenon illustrated in (47), namely, the independent occurrence of an IP*-related property like negation. Thus, while clitic-climbing structures like (ia) were previously

While in the context of pseudo-modals the monoclausal structure in (50) has receded in favour of the biclausal structure in (48), the two structures are both alive and kicking in a number of other bare-infinitive contexts, namely, perception, movement and causative (PMC) verbs:

(51)   a.   Perception verbs: *apercevoir* 'to notice', *écouter* 'to listen', *entendre* 'to hear', *regarder* 'to watch', *sentir* 'to feel, smell', *voir* 'to see'
       b.   Movement verbs: *(em)mener* 'to lead', *envoyer* 'to send', *porter* 'to carry', *monter* 'to raise', *descendre* 'to lower'
       c.   Causative verbs: *laisser* 'to let', *faire* 'to make'

The empirical base is particularly complex here because, unlike pseudo-modals, PMC verbs are transitive, that is, they license an IP* which can check accusative case, and can therefore license Exceptional Case Marking (ECM).[21] Indeed, this feature further clarifies the contrast between the structures in (48) and (50). The more straightforward (and more ECM-like) case is illustrated in (52a),[22] in which the dyadic PMC verb *voir* has two dependants, a nominal Experiencer, *Jean*, and a clausal Theme, *Marie manger (le gâteau)*:

(52)   a.   Jean voit <u>Marie</u> manger (le gâteau).   b.   Jean voit <u>Marie</u> le manger.
            J. sees M. eat the cake   J. sees M. it eat
            'J. can see M. eating (the cake).'   'J. can see M. eating it.'

       c.   Jean <u>la</u> voit manger (le gâteau).   d.   Jean <u>la</u> voit le manger.
            J. her sees eat the cake   J. her sees it eat
            'J. can see her eating (the cake).'   'J. can see her eating it.'

Since the underlined Agent of the infinitive can't be case-licensed within its IP* (§4.2.2), it needs instead to exploit the transitivity of the PMC verb. Structurally, this means that *Marie* raises out of its containing infinitival IP* and into the IP* headed by *voir* to be licensed like a direct object. This is the classic ECM phenomenon. Support for the notion that *Marie* in (52a) is realised as a direct object of *voir* comes from two sources. First, when pronominalised, it's realised as a direct-object clitic on *voir*, underlined in (52c, d). Second, where the form of *voir* is taken from a compound paradigm (see Table 2.3 on page 26 in §2.2.1.2), and *Marie* precedes (due to cliticisation (§4.4.1) or wh fronting (§5.6.1)), past-participle agreement is triggered (§5.8.2), as in (53):

---

widespread, and are still possible is archaic/formal registers (see footnote 19), the example in (ib) was/is not; in the degrammaticalised, biclausal structure, in contrast, negation can be related to the infinitive independently of the pseudo-modal, as in (ic):
(i)   a.   Je <u>le</u> veux faire.   b.   *Je <u>le</u> veux ne pas faire.   c.   Je veux ne pas <u>le</u> faire.
           I it want do   I it want NEG not do   I want NEG not it do
           'I want to do it.'   'I want not to do it.'

[21] Accusative-case marking and direct-object licensing are discussed in §5.8.2.
[22] The verb *voir* 'to see' is used to exemplify PMC verbs throughout.

(53)   a.   Marie, Jean l'a vue manger (le gâteau).
              M. J. her has seen.F eat the cake
              'J. could see M. eating (the cake).'

        b.   Quelle fille tu as vue manger (le gâteau)?
              which girl you have seen.F eat the cake
              'Which girl could you see eating (the cake)?'

The ECM properties are possible precisely because these constructions are
biclausal, that is, the infinitive is contained within an IP* merged in SpecθP within
the VP* headed by the PMC verb, as in (54) (cf. (48)). Since *manger* occupies an
IP* independently of *voir*, pronominalised internal arguments of *manger* can
cliticise onto it (rather than *voir*), as in (52b, d).

(54) $\theta_{Ex}P = VP*$ (biclausal)

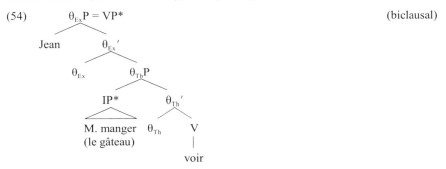

The biclausal structure also allows negation to appear in either clause (or – albeit
less naturally – both) independently, as in (55):

(55)   a.   Jean ne voit pas Marie manger (le gâteau).
              J. NEG sees not M. eat the cake
              'J. can't see M. eating (the cake).'

        b.   Jean voit Marie ne pas manger (le gâteau).
              J. sees M. NEG not eat the cake
              'J. can see M. not eating (the cake).'

        c.   !Jean ne voit pas Marie ne pas manger (le gâteau).
              J. NEG sees not M. NEG not eat the cake
              'J. can't see M. not eating (the cake).'

The oddness of (55c) is pragmatic rather than syntactic; the grammar allows
negation to be associated with either verb, crucially because there are two clauses.
    PMC verbs aren't restricted to the construction illustrated in (52). An alternative
is possible, as in (56a), where the 'subject' of the infinitive is postverbal rather than
preverbal:

(56)   a.   Jean voit manger Marie.   b.   Jean la voit manger.
              J. sees eat M.   J. her sees eat
              'J. can see M. eating.'   'J. can see her eat.'

While (52) has the *bi*clausal structure in (54) underlyingly, much evidence suggests that the (less ECM-like) alternative construction in (56a) has an underlying *mono*-clausal structure along the lines of (50), where the PMC verb combines with the infinitive to form a complex predicate ('to see.eat') with a single argument structure in which *Jean* is Experiencer and *Marie* is Theme. Given the thematic hierarchy, *Marie* is therefore expected to merge below *Jean* within the complex VP*, as in (57) (cf. (50)):

(57) θ_{Ex}P   (monoclausal)

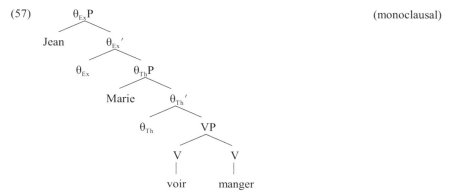

Marie is thus expected to be realised as the direct object, as in (56a).[23] In (56b) the direct object has cliticised onto the PMC verb. The evidence in favour of a mono-clausal analysis of (56) relates to the behaviour of direct transitive and ditransitive infinitives. Compare the data in (58), in which, unlike what we see in (56), the infinitive *manger* is used (mono)transitively, with the parallel set in (52):

(58)   a. Jean voit manger le gâteau à Marie.   b. Jean le voit manger à Marie.
           J. sees eat the cake to M.   J. it sees eat to M.
           'J. can see M. eating the cake.'   'J. can see M. eating it.'

       c. Jean <u>lui</u> voit manger le gâteau.   d. Jean le <u>lui</u> voit manger.
           J. her sees eat the cake   J. it her sees eat
           'J. can see her eating the cake.'   'J. can see her eating it.'

The direct-object status of *le gâteau* is indicated by the way it cliticises in (58b, d). As for *Marie*, the patterns in (58) suggest clearly that it's an *in*direct, that is, *second* object: as a nominal it's realised as an *à*-marked DP*, following the direct object in (58a); as a pronominal it's realised as an indirect-object clitic in (58c, d). In semantic terms, this points to a conceptual structure for the complex predicate in (58a) which differs subtly from the one in (56a). While Marie is the cognitively salient Theme in (56a), it's the cake that's the Theme in (58a). Syntactically, this

---

[23] While superficially identical, example (52b) (without *le gâteau*) and (56b) are structurally distinct. *Marie* is pronominalised as a direct-object clitic in (52b) via ECM, but not in (56b).

distinction points to an underlying structure for (58a) like (59):[24]

(59)

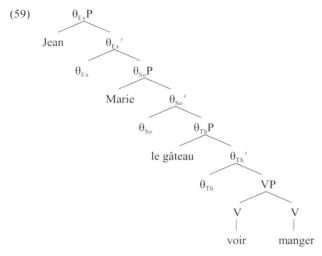

Thus, the notion 'subject' of the infinitive is meaningless here. Since it doesn't bear the most highly ranked θ role, what we might informally think of as the 'subject' of the infinitive is just one of a number arguments of the complex predicate (Guasti 1997).

The clause-union analysis of PMC verbs makes a number of correct predictions. First, triadic infinitives are correctly predicted to be excluded from the monoclausal construction since clause union would produce a four-argument structure, which is ruled out independently, hence the ungrammaticality of (60):[25]

---

[24] I've used the θ role Source for *Marie* here. The exact nature of the θ role isn't important; what matters is that it's located between Experiencer and Theme in the thematic hierarchy.

I leave on the research agenda the issue of whether the subtle semantic difference mentioned in the text is the consequence of some abstract morphological head merged in the syntax.

[25] The situation is actually less straightforward. The example in (i) is just such a sentence.

(i)   On lui a vu donner [une petite pension] [à un homme qui a fui deux lieues].
       one to.him has seen give a little pension to a man who has fled two leagues
       'He was seen giving a small pension to a man who had fled two leagues.'

The PMC verb *vu* 'seen' co-occurs with the ditransitive (= triadic) infinitive *donner* 'to give'. The form of the clitic preceding the PMC verb (the indirect-object *lui* rather than the direct-object *le*) suggests a monoclausal complex predicate has been formed via clause union. If a *bi*clausal structure had underlain the example, the clitic would have been *le (l')*, as in (ii):

(ii)   On l'a vu donner [une petite pension] [à un homme qui a fui deux lieues].
       one him has seen give a little pension to a man who has fled two leagues
       ≈ (i)

The grammaticality of (i) is surprising because its non-pronominal equivalent must be

(60)   *Jean voit donner un cadeau à sa maman à Marie.
        J. sees give a present to her mum to M.

The only way to express the idea that Jean could see Marie giving a present to her mum is to use an underlyingly biclausal structure, as in (61):

(61)   Jean voit Marie donner un cadeau à sa maman.
        J. sees M. give a present to her mum
        'J can see M. giving a present to her mum.'

Second, the kind of narrow-scope negation illustrated in the biclausal construction in (55b) is correctly predicted to be impossible in the monoclausal construction, as shown in (62):

(62)   *Jean voit ne pas manger le gâteau à Marie.
        J. sees NEG not eat the cake to M.

This doesn't mean that material can't intervene between the PMC verb and the infinitive, as in (63):

(63)   a. Je le lui <u>vois distinctement avaler.</u>   b. Je le lui <u>laissais gentiment comprendre.</u>
            I it to.him see distinctly swallow   I it to.him let kindly understand
            'I can distinctly see him eating it.'   'I quietly explained it to him.'

Rather, it means that any intervening material is associated with the IP* of the complex predicate *as a whole*, and that its medial position is due to the fact that the PMC verb undergoes V movement into that IP* domain (§4.2.1), as in (64):

(64)   [$_{IP*}$ ... PMC ... distinctement/gentiment ... [$_{VP*}$ t infinitive]]

Where in the monoclausal structure the 'underlying subject of the infinitive' is agentive, it can, as an alternative to realisation as an indirect object, appear within an adjunct agentive PP*:

(65)   a. Il a fait peindre sa cuisine <u>à Guy.</u>   b. Il a fait peindre sa cuisine <u>par Guy.</u>
            he has made paint his kitchen to G.   he has made paint his kitchen by G.
            'He had G. paint his kitchen.'   'He had his kitchen painted by G.'

In (65a) Guy and the kitchen are both arguments of the complex predicate *faire peindre* (like the direct and indirect objects of a ditransitive verb like *donner* 'to give'). In (65b) the kitchen alone is an argument of the complex predicate, while Guy is a circumstantial contained within an adjoined Agent phrase (as in passive sentences).

The existence of two PMC structures, one biclausal, one monoclausal, raises the

something like (iii), which is ungrammatical:
(iii)   *On a vu donner [une petite pension] [à un homme qui a fui deux lieues] [à lui].
        one has seen give a little pension to a man who has fled two leagues to him
For some unexplained reason, cliticisation saves an otherwise ungrammatical structure.

question of a possible semantic distinction between the two. This issue is taken up by Baschung and Desmets (2000), who look specifically at causative *faire*, the syntactic details of which I turn to below.[26] In terms of the semantics of the two structures with *faire*, Baschung and Desmets point to a subtle difference surrounding whether or not the causer exercises direct causation over the causee. They suggest that the biclausal structure is associated with 'strong control', that is, direct causation, only, while the monoclausal structure is compatible with 'loose control', that is, indirect causation, too. Thus, while the monoclausal structure is available however 'loose' the control, the biclausal structure is only available if direct causation is possible, as in (66a) (it's possible literally to force someone to *eat* spinach), but not in (66b) (it's not possible literally to force someone to *like* spinach):

(66)   a. Je l'/lui ai fait manger des épinards.
          I him/to.him have made eat of.the spinach
          'I made him eat some spinach.'

       b. Je *l'/lui ai fait aimer des épinards.
          I him/to.him have made like of.the spinach
          'I made him like spinach.'

Baschung and Desmets' subtle semantic distinction between biclausal and monoclausal PMC structures containing *faire* can sensibly be extended to all PMC structures. In particular, there's one context where the biclausal PMC structure (associated with 'strong control' according to Baschung and Desmets) is unavailable which is neatly accounted for, namely, where the subject of the infinitive isn't expressed, as in (67a):

(67)   a. Marie a entendu chanter le refrain.
          M. has heard sing the chorus
          'M. heard the chorus being sung.'

       b. Marie l'a entendu chanter.   c. *Marie a entendu le chanter.
          M. it-has heard sing   M. has heard it sing
          'M. heard it being sung.'

Example (67a) looks superficially to be compatible with *either* a biclausal *or* a monoclausal structure: the DP* *le refrain* could be the direct object of the simple predicate *chanter* within a biclausal structure, or else the direct object of the complex predicate *entendu chanter* within a monoclausal structure. However, examples (67b, c), in which *le refrain* pronominalises, suggest that only one of the two structures is actually available: *le refrain* cliticises onto the PMC verb in (67b) in line with a monoclausal structure, and onto the infinitive in (67c) as expected in a biclausal structure. Example (67c) is ungrammatical, suggesting that (67a) *cannot*

---

[26] Baschung and Desmets work in a different theoretical framework to the one assumed here, and use the terms control-*faire* and composition-*faire* for what I'm calling biclausal and monoclausal structures.

have a biclausal structure. This ties in nicely with the distinction between (biclausal) strong control and (monoclausal) weak control: the biclausal structure (with strong control) is arguably expected to be unavailable in the absence of the 'underlying subject of the infinitive' since there's nothing for the PMC verb to have strong control over; the monoclausal structure alone (with weak control) is thus expected to be available.

Particular comment is warranted in respect of causative *faire* which, quite independently of the semantic contrast discussed by Baschung and Desmets (2000), isn't as readily compatible with a biclausal structure as other PMC verbs. Consider (68):

(68)   a.   *Jean fait <u>Marie</u> manger (le biscuit).[27]   b.   Jean fait manger (le biscuit à) <u>Marie</u>.
         J. makes M. eat the biscuit   J. makes eat the biscuit to M.
                                                        'J. makes M. eat (the biscuit).'

The word orders in (68a, b) are those expected in a bi- and monoclausal PMC structure, respectively. The former is ungrammatical. Why might this be so? It can't simply be that causative *faire* necessarily induces clause union. If this were the case, the flexibility illustrated in (66a) would be unaccounted for. Also, consider (69):

(69)   Le professeur <u>les</u> fera <u>le</u> lire/<u>y</u> aller.   (Baschung and Desmets 2000: 210)
       the teacher them will.make it read/there go
       'The teacher will make them read it/go there.'

Here, the position of *le/y* (cliticised onto the infinitive rather than causative *faire*) and the form of *les* (a *d*irect-object clitic rather than an *in*direct-object clitic) both point to a biclausal rather than a monoclausal structure.[28] Note that the examples

---

[27] The counterexample in (i), from the writings of Lacan, is from Goosse (2000: 138):
(i)   . . . qui fait <u>la femme</u> être ce sujet.
       that makes the woman be this subject
       ' . . . which makes the woman be this subject.'
Goosse describes (i) as 'a phenomenon of very literary written language'.
[28] Further data from Baschung and Desmets (2000) suggest that the formal distinction between the bi-/monoclausal structures isn't perfect. The examples in (i) are two expected ways of expressing 'I made him read it':
(i)   a.   Je l'ai fait le lire.   b.   Je le lui ai fait lire.
            I him-have made it read   I it to.him have made read
The example in (ia) has a biclausal structure (the pronominalised subject of the infinitive cliticises as a direct object onto causative *faire*, the direct object of the infinitive cliticises onto the infinitive), while the example in (ib) has a monoclausal structure (the pronominalised 'underlying subject' and direct object of the infinitive cliticise onto causative *faire*, the 'underlying subject' as an indirect object). However, the alternative in (ii) is unexpected:
(ii)   Je lui ai fait le lire.
       I to.him have made it read
Here, the pronominalised direct object of the infinitive cliticises onto the infinitive (suggesting a biclausal structure), while the pronominalised 'underlying subject of the

which suggest that causative *faire* is compatible with a biclausal structure all involve cliticisation of the underlying subject of the infinitive. In the problematic example, (68a), in contrast, the underlying subject of the infinitive is nominal. This observation lends support to the approach to the problem adopted by Bouvier (2000). Bouvier suggests the answer lies in the morphological properties of causative *faire*. He suggests that, unlike other PMC verbs, causative *faire* is morphologically defective in that the IP* structure which merges above VP* is unable to mark accusative case or trigger past-participle agreement (§5.8.2).[29] In other words, unlike other PMC verbs, causative *faire* isn't an ECM verb. The idea that the relevant issue is morphology is supported by the fact that past-participle agreement doesn't take place in (70), even though the structure suggests that it should, and even though the parallel structures with the other PMC verbs *do* have past-participle agreement:[30]

(70)   a.   Quelle fille a-t-il fait(*e) entrer?   b.   Il l'a fait(*e) entrer.
           which girl has-he made enter   he her-has made enter
           'Which girl did he make go in?'   'He made her go in.'

Much less straightforward in the context of PMC constructions is the situation in respect of passivisation. Pollock (1994: 302), cited in Miller and Lowrey (2003: 153), maintains that passivisation is ungrammatical and gives the example in (71):

(71)   *Jean a été vu manger une pomme.
        J. has been seen eat an apple

Veland (1998) notes that such passives are 'in principle' impossible in the modern language (although they were possible previously):

(72)   a.   *Paul a été laissé/vu/entendu/mené sortir.
           P. has been let/seen/heard/led leave

       b.   *Le ministre a été entendu dire que ces mesures seraient rapportées.
           the minister has been heard say that these measures would.be postponed

However, a Google search turned up examples such as those in (73) (see also Miller

infinitive' cliticises as an indirect object onto causative *faire* (suggesting a monoclausal structure). The examples in (iii) are similarly unexpected:
(iii)   Je lui ai fait lui téléphoner / y aller / le lui donner / lui en parler.
         I to.him have done to.him telephone/to.it go/it to.him give/to.him of.it speak
         'I made him telephone him/go there/give it to him/speak to him about it.'
The status of these examples is unclear.
[29] Recall that one of the arguments in support of the biclausal analysis of PMC verbs was the fact that the 'underlying subject of the infinitive' triggers past-participle agreement.
[30] According to Baschung and Desmets (2000: 226) the past participle of causative *faire* does show overt morphological agreement 'in non-standard French', as in (i):
(i)   La secrétaire, le patron l'a faite pleurer.
         the secretary the boss her-has made.F cry
         'The boss made the secretary cry.'

and Lowrey 2003: 154–5):

(73)   a.   Hurley et Grant <u>ont été vus</u> faire des emplettes ensemble.
           H. and G. have been seen do of.the purchases together
           'H. and G. were seen out shopping together.'

       b.   Pierre Nicolas <u>a été vu</u> faire des tours de terrain bien après minuit.
           P. N. has been seen do of.the rounds of field well after midnight
           'P. N. was seen running around the pitch well after midnight.'

Veland (1998) gives the examples in (74):

(74)   a.   . . . <u>ayant été vu</u> tomber de quinze cents mètres.
           having been seen fall of fifteen hundred metres
           ' . . . having been seen to fall fifteen hundred metres.'

       b.   . . . si une banshee venue d'Irlande <u>n'avait pas été entendue</u> pleurer.
           if a Banshee come of-Ireland NEG-had not been heard cry
           ' . . . if a banshee from Ireland hadn't been heard crying.'

There would appear, therefore, to be uncertainty as to whether or not PMC constructions passivise. Why might this be so? I suggest that the answer lies in the fact that PMC verbs are compatible with the two configurations in (54) and (57)/(59). (See also Abeillé *et al.* 1997.) One (the biclausal one in (54)) is compatible with passivisation, while the other (the monoclausal one in (57)/(59)) is not.

   Using (73a) as the basis for discussion, *voir faire* 'to see.do' has either a biclausal or a monoclausal structure. If *voir faire* is *bi*clausal, then, in an active sentence, the DP* Agent of the infinitive *faire* is realised as the direct object of the PMC verb *voir* (by ECM): it intervenes between *voir* and *faire*, as in (75a), but can pronominalise as a direct-object clitic on *voir*, as in (75b) (triggering past-participle agreement; §5.8.2):

(75)   a.   On a vu <u>Hurley et Grant</u> faire des emplettes ensemble.   (biclausal)
           one has seen H. and G. do of.the purchases together
           ≈ (73a)

       b.   On <u>les</u> a vu<u>s</u> faire des emplettes ensemble.
           one them has seen do of.the purchases together
           'They were seen out shopping together.'

If the PMC verb within a biclausal structure passivises, its Experiencer/Agent θ role is suppressed (§2.2.3.1) and won't be realised as subject. Since the Agent of the infinitive can escape from the infinitival IP* (as in ECM), it can be realised as subject instead, as in (73a).

   If, in contrast, *voir faire* is a complex predicate with a *mono*clausal structure (following clause union), the infinitive doesn't have a thematic structure independently of the PMC verb. This makes no difference to the subject and the direct object, which remain Experiencer and Theme, respectively, albeit of a complex predicate now rather than a simple one. It does, however, have an impact on the 'subject' of the infinitive (*Hurley et Grant*) which, rather than being the Agent of the simple predicate *faire*, is now the Source of the complex predicate *voir faire* instead,[31] and is realised, as expected, as an *à*-marked indirect-object DP* following the direct-object DP*, as in (76a), but can pronominalise as an *in*direct-object clitic on *voir*, as in (76b) (*not* triggering past-participle agreement; §5.8.2):

(76) a. On a vu faire des emplettes ensemble <u>à Hurley et à Grant</u>.   (monoclausal)
        one has seen to of.the purchases together to H. and to G.
        ≈ (75a)

     b. On <u>leur</u> a vu faire des emplettes ensemble.
        one to.them has seen do of.the purchases together
        ≈ (75b)

Since *Hurley et Grant* is licensed as an indirect object, passivisation, as in (73a), is *not* expected to be able to cause it to be realised as a subject since indirect objects don't undergo object shift (§2.2.3.2). Thus, native-speaker uncertainty as to the grammaticality of examples like (73a) is due to the existence of the two possible underlying PMC structures, only one of which is compatible with passivisation.[32]

Once again, causative *faire* warrants specific comment. Contrast the grammatical (73b) with the ungrammatical (77):

(77) *Pierre Nicolas <u>a été fait</u> faire des tours de terrain bien après minuit.
      P. N. has been made do of.the rounds of field well after midnight

Example (77) contrasts minimally with (73b) in containing *faire* rather than *voir*, and illustrates a further way in which *faire* differs from other PMC verbs: it doesn't allow passivisation of a biclausal structure. Abeillé and Godard (n.d.) give the example in (78):

(78) *Marie a été fait(e) manger (le biscuit).
      M. has been made eat the biscuit

However, consider the examples in (79):

(79) a. Ce banc <u>avait été fait faire</u> pour nous (par mon père).   (Veland 1998)
        this bench had been done do for us by my father
        'This bench was commissioned for us (by my father).'

     b. Ce reliquaire <u>a été fait faire</u> (par Hervé Gouzien).
        this reliquary has been made do by H. G.
        'This reliquary was commissioned (by H. G.)'

     c. Le château médiéval à Fontainebleau <u>a été fait construire</u> (par Louis).
        the castle medieval at F. has been made build by L.
        'The medieval castle at F. was commissioned (by L.)'.

---

[31] See footnote 24.
[32] Miller and Lowrey (2003: 155) report that informants are sometimes uneasy about accepting these examples, and suggest inserting *en train de* 'in the process of' immediately before the infinitive to improve acceptability. Veland (1998) says that the infinitive is supposed to be replaced by a present participle in the passive structure.

These examples show that causative *faire* isn't incompatible with passivisation per se. A number of observations are in order. First, the 'underlying subject' of the infinitive isn't realised as an argument of the verb. Rather, it appears within an (optional) adjoined Agent phrase. In the light of the data in (67), this leads us to expect causative *faire* and the infinitive in the examples in (79) to appear in a monoclausal rather than a biclausal structure. Second, and as expected, the DP*s which are realised as subject of these passive sentences are the underlying Theme/Patient of the infinitive. Third, the subject of these passive sentences has default M.SG φ features (§2.1.2.3). Where the subject DP* has marked (F.PL φ) features, the passive is ungrammatical, as shown in (80):

(80)   *Des chemises ont été fait(e)(s) faire.[33]
        of.the shirts have been made.F.PL do

The contrast between (79) and (80) suggests a link with Bouvier's (2000) analysis of the morphological defectiveness of causative *faire*. On such a view, the passive examples in (79) are grammatical because the subject DP* has default φ features.

5.3   Dislocation

In this section and in §§5.4, 5.5 I consider how the left clause periphery is used for pragmatic effect. In §2.2.2 we saw how the inherent lexical semantic structure of various subcategories of verb is projected in VP* syntax, and in §2.2.3 we saw how the flexibility of VP* can be exploited to pragmatic ends. In this chapter I consider a number of IP*-*external* devices which achieve similar pragmatic aims by disturbing basic SVO word order. The extent to which the left periphery is used to pragmatic effect is why French is sometimes described, for example by De Cat (2002: 191), as a language which has a highly transparent information structure.

While French is undeniably a configurational SVO language, one study at least – Moreau (1987), using an oral corpus – suggests that only 70% of clauses containing S, V and O actually have SVO order.[34] Quite apart from issues having to do with object clitics (§4.4.1) which characteristically fail to occupy canonical postverbal position, the rigidity of the phonology, in particular the unavailability of prosody to highlight pragmatically salient constituents (Ayres-Bennett and Carruthers 2001: 248ff), has led to the development of various syntactic devices which allow pragmatically determined non-canonical word orders (Harris 1978; 1985). Those illustrated in (81) are the concern of this section and §§5.4, 5.5:

(81)   a.   Le vin, je l'aime bien.   ((clitic) left dislocation, LD; §5.3.1)
              the wine I it-like well

---

[33] Cf. Italian, where causative passivisation is grammatical even with F/PL DP*s.
[34] See Ayres-Bennett and Carruthers (2001: 255, 271 fn. 14).

b. Je l'aime bien, le vin.   ((clitic) right dislocation, RD; §5.3.2)
   I it-like well, the wine
   a, b: 'I like the wine.'

c. Le vin, j'aime bien.   (focus fronting; §5.4)
   the wine, I-like well
   'I like wine.'

d. C'est le vin que j'aime bien.   (clefting; §5.5)
   it-is the wine that I-like well
   'It's (the) wine that I like.'

e. Ce que j'aime bien, c'est le vin.   (pseudo-clefting; §5.5)
   what I-like well, it-is the wine
   'What I like is (the) wine.'

Discussion of the syntactic and pragmatic impact of wh fronting and inversion is postponed until §§5.6, 5.7.

In the discussion of dislocation and focus fronting in (81a–c), I exploit Rizzi's (1997) exploded CP*, as in (82):

(82) $[_{ForceP} \cdots [_{TopicP} \cdots [_{FocusP} \cdots [_{TopicP} \cdots [_{FinP} \cdots [_{IP*} \cdots]]]]]]$

In contrast, given the presence of the finite copula, clefting and pseudo-clefting in (81d, e) are analysed as biclausal structures.

In dislocation, a phrasal constituent (that is, a non-clitic) appears outside IP*, but is 'resumed' by an appropriate IP*-internal clitic, as in (83a, b):

(83)   a. Jean, il m'aime.   b. Il m'aime, moi.
          J. he me-loves   he me-loves me.
          'J. loves me.'   'He loves me.'

Example (83a) illustrates LD:[35] the left-peripheral DP* *Jean* is interpreted as coreferential with the IP*-internal subject proform. Example (83b) illustrates RD: the right-peripheral DP* *moi* is interpreted as coreferential with the IP*-internal direct-object proform. Dislocation can involve a single phrase, as in (83), or multiple phrases, as in (84);[36] LD and RD can even co-occur, as in (84c):

[35] Of interest here is the phenomenon found in unmarked ConF, where subject proforms are thematic DP*s which raise from their VP*-internal θ position to SpecIP*, and then phonologically cliticise onto the finite verb (§4.4.4). Where subject proforms are affixal agreement markers on the finite verb, as in subject-doubling varieties like Québécois and Picard, a superficial word order like that in (83a) wouldn't necessarily constitute LD since the strong subject could occupy SpecIP*.

[36] The York/De Cat corpora include examples containing as many as four dislocated topics:
(i)   Après, Gaetan, il a soufflé, alors, les bougies.
       after G. he has blown then the candles
       'Then, afterwards, G. blew the candles out.'

(84) a. Jean, Marie, il l'aime bien.
      b. Il l'aime bien, Jean, Marie.
      c. Jean, il l'aime bien, Marie.
          (J.) (M.) he her-likes well (J.) (M.)
          a–c: 'J. likes M.'

The same constituent can even simultaneously be LDed and RDed, as in (85):

(85) Jean, il m'énerve, Jean.
      J. he me-annoys J.
      'J. annoys me.'

In addition to argumental topics, dislocated phrases can also be stage topics, that is, clause-level temporal and locative adjuncts or other adverbial constituents of various kinds:

(86) (A) Paris, ils y vont demain.
      to P. they there go tomorrow
      'They're going to P. tomorrow.'

Dislocation is very common in ConF; in the York/De Cat corpora it's found in 18–24% of clauses (De Cat 2002: 79). Dislocation goes back to the eleventh century and the OF period, when it was however rare (Marchello-Nizia 1998a, b).

There's a sociostylistic dimension to LD and RD. Both are: (a) characteristic of spoken, informal or unplanned speech (Campion 1984); (b) the subject of some social stigmatisation within formal schooling among L1 learners; and (c) more prevalent among younger than older speakers, and among speakers from lower socioeconomic categories.[37] Given the distinction made in §1.4 between ModF and ConF, I therefore assume that, whatever triggers dislocation, it's characteristic of (innovative) ConF but not (conservative) ModF. A formal characterisation of the contrast is given below.

Beyond style, dislocation has distinctive prosodic properties. In LD and RD alike, the dislocated phrase is prosodically distinguished from the rest of the clause. For example, LDed subjects are typically distinguishable from non-LDed (and doubled) subjects. However, the prosodies found in LD and RD aren't identical. And to the extent that they're understood at all, they're tendential rather than categorical: in subject-doubling varieties (§4.4.4) there's a grey area where whether or not a clause-initial subject DP* is LDed is unclear. Idealising somewhat, an LDed phrase is perceptually prominent; it has rising intonation, while the rest of the clause has falling intonation.[38] In contrast, rather than having its own characteristic

---

[37] See Ashby (1988).

[38] LD is traditionally thought to involve a pause, described as 'comma intonation', in line with the orthographic representation. However, De Cat (2002: 61) shows that prosodic prominence is crucially due to lengthening of the final syllable of the LDed phrase, rather than a pause, which, as shown by fine-grained acoustic analysis, isn't reliably present. Indeed, the presence of a pause without syllable lengthening isn't perceived as LD.

prosody, an RDed phrase is prosodically dependent on that of the rest of the clause (Rossi 1999); an RDed phrase is destressed (with a lower pitch) after the preceding clause (Lambrecht 1981; Ashby 1994). There's no comma intonation.

Dislocation also has distinctive pragmatic properties: Lambrecht (1981) labels LDed phrases topics and RDed phrases anti-topics. In each case, the dislocated phrase either picks up on a referent already salient in the discourse/context (especially RD) or shifts to a new one (especially LD). De Cat's (2004) experimental evidence (from ConF) shows that dislocation coincides with pragmatic topichood: a phrase is dislocated if and only if it's topical. New (focal) information can't be dislocated; old (topical) information must be dislocated.

The pragmatic nature of dislocation explains why not all phrases are equally susceptible. First, the answer to a wh question can't be dislocated, as shown in (87) and (88), because it's focal by definition (De Cat 2004):

(87)   – Qui a fini son travail?   – Ceux du groupe A (*ils) ont fini leur travail.
       who has finished his work   those of.the group A they have finished their work
       'Who finished their work?'   'Those in group A finished their work.'

(88)   – Qu'est-ce qu'il a senti?   – La chair fraîche il (*l')a senti(e).
       what-is-this that-he has smelt   the flesh fresh il it-has smelt
       'What could he smell?'   'He could smell fresh flesh.'   (De Cat 2002: 50)

Second, a subject can't be dislocated if it's bound by a quantified object since, as shown by Zubizarreta (1998), such a subject is focal:

(89)   [Son]$_i$ jockey (*il) ramènera [chaque cheval]$_i$.   (De Cat 2004, ex. (13))
       his jockey he will.return each horse
       'His jockey will return each horse.'

The subject of a thetic sentence can't be dislocated,[39] as shown in (90), because it's part of a larger focus (De Cat 2004, ex. (14)):

(90)   – Qu'est-ce qui s'est passé?   – Les voisins (*ils) ont mangé mon lapin.
       what-is-it that happened   the neighbours they have eaten my rabbit
       'What happened?'   'The neighbours ate my rabbit.'

We might characterise the relevant contrast between ModF and ConF therefore in terms of the pragmatic status of SpecIP*: *either* topical *or* focal in ModF, *necessarily* focal in ConF. While in ModF a topical DP* subject can occupy SpecIP*, in ConF it can't. Conversely, in ConF focal subjects are incompatible with dislocation because dislocation is triggered by the need for a phrase to be topical.

Third, susceptibility to dislocation is sensitive to grammatical function. For example, subjects are dislocated more often than non-subjects (Jeanjean 1981; Campion 1984; Sankoff 1982). According to Lambrecht (1987), just 3% of

---

[39] A thetic sentence is distinguished from a categorical sentence. In a categorical sentence, the subject is old information (topic) and the predicate is new information (focus). In contrast, in a thetic sentence, both the subject *and* the predicate are new information.

canonical subjects are non-LDed DP*s. In De Cat's (2002) cross-dialectal corpus (n = 679) DP* subjects are LDed 39% of the time and RDed 46% of the time; just 16% of subject DP*s fail to dislocate (Table 3.3, p. 45).[40] Canonical subjects are overwhelmingly pronominal and therefore don't occupy SpecIP*.[41] In contrast, objects much more readily appear clause internally: according to De Cat (2002), 86% of dislocated topics are resumed by a subject clitic, while only 11% are resumed by an object clitic. (The remaining 3% are associated with indirect objects, attributes and temporal adjuncts, which typically aren't resumed at all; see below.) If dislocation is indeed pragmatically motivated, the contrasting behaviour of subjects and non-subjects is expected since subjects, unlike non-subjects, are overwhelmingly pragmatic topics (§1.3).

Fourth, dislocation is sensitive to DP* type: some more readily dislocate than others, and some are incompatible with dislocation altogether. Significantly, the observed patterns can be explained in pragmatic terms: the more likely a DP* is to be topical, the more likely it is to be dislocated. The most readily dislocated DP*s are the most readily topical, that is, definite DP*s, including proper, demonstrative and complex nominals, and strong proforms (De Cat 2002); indefinite DP*s dislocate only if they're non-existential, as shown in (91):

(91) a. Un enfant, il aime pas dire la vérité.   (generic)
          a child he likes not say the truth
          'A child doesn't like telling the truth.'

      b. *Un enfant, il est arrivé ce matin.   (existential)
          a child he is arrived this morning
          'A child arrived this morning.'

      c. *Personne, il m'aime.   (existential)
          nobody he me-likes
          'Nobody loves me.'

Since existential DP*s are inherently *non*-topical, their occurrence in non-topical SpecIP* is unproblematic, and dislocation is neither motivated nor possible. Since generic DP*s, in contrast, *can* be topical, dislocation is possible.

Fifth, susceptibility to dislocation is sensitive to the matrix–subordinate distinction. In De Cat's (2002: 53) study, 74% of preverbal (pro)nominal subjects are LDed in matrix contexts, but in subordinate contexts only 55%. A contrast is expected given that a matrix subject is more (likely to be) topical than a subordinate subject. I consider the notion *relative* topichood in §5.3.1. In the following two sections, I discuss the direction-specific properties of LD and RD. (See Delais-Roussarie *et al.* 2004.)

---

[40] These statistics are the composite of samples from French, Belgian and Québécois speakers. For details of cross-dialectal variation see De Cat (2002: 45).
[41] We might speculate that (?part of) the motivation for the phonological cliticisation of subject proforms onto I*° is to avoid topical material appearing in SpecIP*.

5.3.1 Left dislocation

Rizzi's (1997) left periphery provides a template within which to see LD. TopicP is a 'higher' predication, above IP*: rather than being interpreted on the basis of θ *roles*, checked by a regular lexical–predicative head, the topic and comment in SpecTopicP and CompTopicP in (92) are interpreted on the basis of the *pragmatic roles* they play, encoded as features checked against Topic°. In (83a) the LDed phrase is the subject *Jean*, resumed by the clitic *il*. Given the analysis of subject proforms in §4.4.4, *Jean* can't occupy the canonical subject position because this position is occupied by the subject proform (prior to phonological cliticisation onto I*°). Instead, the LDed phrase occupies a specifier position outside IP*, namely, (Spec)TopicP with the comment in complement position:

(92)

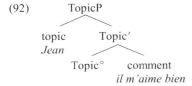

A number of facts suggest that LD is the output of Merge rather than the result of movement of the topic out of the comment (pace De Cat 2002). First, the comment is always syntactically well formed *even without* the LDed topic. This suggests that the comment is a grammatically complete constituent, in a way that constituents containing an antecedentless trace are not. Second, the characteristic prosody of LD isn't found in any clear case of movement. Third, the comment typically contains a resumptive clitic (provided one exists) corresponding to the LDed topic. If LD were the result of Move, this would mean there were two overt realisations of the same underlying constituent within IP* which would be surprising since the relevant varieties of French aren't characterised by clitic doubling. Fourth, the dependency between the LDed phrase and any plausible antecedent within the (relevant) comment isn't subject to the constraints on movement found elsewhere: not only is it unbounded (unlike head movement), it can also cross an island (unlike wh movement). In (93a) the LDed topic is resumed by a clitic in the subordinate clause; in (93b) it's resumed within a relative clause:

(93) a. <u>Moi</u>, [il faut [que <u>j</u>'aille en ville]].
         me it is-necessary that I-go to town
         'I need to go to town.'

      b. <u>Jean</u>, [le jour [où <u>il</u> ne sera pas en retard] sera un jour de fête]!
         J. the day where he NEG will.be not in late will.be a day of celebration
         'The day J. isn't late will be a day of celebration.'

Fifth, the nature of the correspondence between the LDed phrase and the resumptive proform in the comment is flexible. Thus, while in (83) and (84), the match is perfect – LDed subject resumed by subject proform, LDed object resumed by object proform – in (94) it isn't:

(94) a. Jean, je lui ai donné €20.
          J. I to.him have given €20
          'I gave J. €20.'

     b. Tout le monde, le soir de la fête, on était tous fatigués.
         all the world the evening of the party one was all tired
         'On the evening of the party, everyone was tired.'

In (94a) the LDed phrase is resumed by an indirect-object clitic, but isn't itself
marked as an indirect object with *à*; in (94b) the LDed phrase is resumed by *on*
'one'. Further cases of flexibility are illustrated in (95):

(95) a. Ce métier | on se déplace tous les jours.
          this job one self moves all the days
          'In this job you're on the move every day.'

     b. Le même argent | on peut payer un loyer.
         the same money one can pay a rent
         'At that price you can afford to pay rent.'

The vertical line splits these sentences into two halves which are syntactically
independent and only vaguely semantically related. There's no resumptive clitic.
The first half is called a hanging topic,[42] the relationship between the two, 'loose
aboutness'.[43] Intonation rises on the hanging topic, then falls on the rest of the
sentence, as in LD, suggesting a parallel analysis.[44] Given that it's difficult to see
what kind of strictly syntactic relationship the hanging topic might have with the
rest of the clause, an extraction analysis is implausible, suggesting that we have a
base-generated topic–comment articulation. Given the parallel with regular LD, a
non-extraction analysis of LD is suggested, too. I conclude therefore that LD is a
base-generated configuration rather than the result of movement. Zubizarreta (2001:
184) talks about LD involving its own predicate–argument structure: rather than
being merged within the lexical VP* and subsequently raised, the dislocated phrase
is, instead, merged outside the core clause as the 'subject' of the higher predication;
from this position it binds an argument variable within the core clause.
   To account for the fact that LD isn't restricted to a single clause-initial topic,
Rizzi (1997) claims that TopicP can iterate and that, in principle, there's no limit
to the number of topics that can be LDed. In (84a) there are two LDed topics and
each is resumed within IP*. Consider, though, the multiple LD in (96):

---

[42] A hanging topic is a discourse rather than sentence topic.
[43] Ayres-Bennett and Carruthers (2001: 268, following Deulofeu 1977) call these 'binary
constructions'. They're 'very informal' according to Gadet (1997).
[44] Note, though, that, unlike LDed argumental/stage topics, hanging (discourse) topics can't
iterate, must precede argumental/stage topics, and are restricted to pre-matrix-clause
position. Thus, they may well occupy a specifier position in the left clause periphery which
is even higher than (Spec)TopicP.

(96)   Moi, mon frère, sa femme, [elle est malade].   (after Yaguello 2003b: 220)
       me, my brother, his wife, she is ill
       'My brother's wife is ill.'

The multiple LD in (96) differs from (84a) in that the last of the three LDed topics
alone is resumed within the bracketed IP*. However, this difference is only
significant if we assume that resumption is required *within IP**. Note that there's
nothing in the topic–comment articulation in (92) which assigns any particular
status to IP*; the comment is simply whatever occupies CompTopicP, and this
doesn't have to be IP*. Assuming iterability of TopicP, in cases of multiple LD like
(96), the comment in all but the lowest topic–comment articulation is itself a further
topic–comment articulation. Thus, what's relevant is whether or not each successive
topic is resumed within its particular comment. And, as shown in the representation
of (96) in (97), this is indeed the case:

(97)

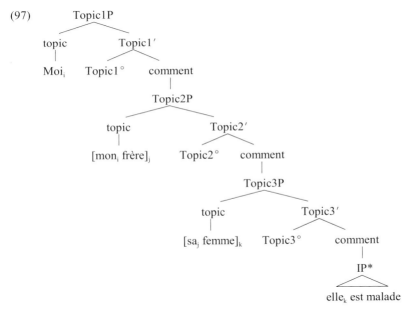

In the highest topic–comment articulation, Topic1P, the topic *moi* 'me' is resumed
by the possessive determiner within *mon frère* 'my brother', contained within the
relevant comment, Topic2P, the complement of Topic1°; in Topic2P, *mon frère* is
resumed by the possessive determiner within *sa femme* 'his wife', contained within
Topic3P; finally, *sa femme* is resumed by *elle* 'she', the subject of the core clause.
Thus, just as in (84a), each LDed topic in (96) is resumed within the relevant
comment (even if this isn't necessarily IP*).
    The order in which topics are resumed within the comment has no impact on the

order in which they are LDed (contra Larsson 1979).[45] However, the inherently hierarchical model of LD in (97) means that the linear order of LDed phrases *does* determine their relative topichood. While *moi, mon frère* and *sa femme* in (96)/(97) are all topics within their own topic–comment articulation, they don't all have the same pragmatic status relative to one another; there's a left-to-right pecking order, which reflects the structural hierarchy of shifting topics: within the context of the entire utterance *moi* is more topical than *sa femme*. Such an approach suggests that the multiple LD in (84a) is similarly hierarchical: that is, rather than being two randomly ordered topics of equal standing, *Jean* is more topical than *Marie*, as a simple consequence of the correspondence between linear order (of LDed topics) and hierarchical pragmatic structure. Similarly, while (98a, b) are truth-conditionally equivalent, (98a) doesn't correspond pragmatically to (98b):

(98) a. Jean, Marie, il la voit demain.   b. Marie, Jean, il la voit demain.
          J. M. he her sees tomorrow   M. J. he her sees tomorrow
          'J.'s seeing M. tomorrow.'   ≈ (98a)

The sentences in (98a, b) are formally identical *apart from* the relative order of the LDed phrases: both are topics, but the topichood of the leftmost LDed phrase is greater than that of the rightmost. Thus, topichood is a relative or scalar notion, rather than a categorical one.

(99) a. $[_{\text{Topic1P}}$ [Jean]$_i$ Topic1° $[_{\text{Topic2P}}$ [Marie]$_j$ Topic2° $[_{\text{IP}}$ il$_i$ la$_j$ voit demain]]]   (98a)
      b. $[_{\text{Topic1P}}$ [Marie]$_j$ Topic1° $[_{\text{Topic2P}}$ [Jean]$_i$ Topic2° $[_{\text{IP}}$ il$_i$ la$_j$ voit demain]]]   (98b)

5.3.2   Right dislocation

Dislocation is also possible to the right:

(100) a. Jean lui a donné les €20, à Marie.
       b. Jean les a donnés à Marie, les €20.
       c. Il a donné les €20 à Marie, Jean.
       d. Il les lui a donnés, Jean, les €20, à Marie.

As with LD, argumental RDed topics are usually resumed with an appropriate clitic, as in (101a), unless it's generic, in which case resumption is optional, as in (101b):

(101) a. Tu les aimes bien, les colliers?   b. Tu aimes bien (ça), les colliers?
           you them like well, the necklaces   you like well that, the necklaces
           'Do you like the necklaces?' (specific)   'Do you like necklaces?' (generic)

RD differs from LD in phonological and syntactic as well as pragmatic terms. In phonological terms, RD doesn't show the characteristic 'comma intonation' of LD. The RDed phrase isn't prosodically prominent, and is actually destressed. Syntactically, an RDed phrase corresponding to an indirect object or an inherent-case-marked DP* typically usually bears overt inherent case marking, as in (102)

---

[45] This observation it a further reason to reject the extraction analysis of LD.

(cf. (94a)):

(102) a. On va <u>les</u> avoir, <u>les Allemands</u>, on va <u>leur</u> montrer, <u>aux Anglais</u>!
one goes them have the Germans one goes to.them show to.the English
'We'll beat the Germans, we'll show the English!'

b. J'<u>en</u> ai acheté, <u>du lait</u>.
I-of.it have bought of.the milk
'I bought some milk.'

More generally, RD is more restricted than LD. According to Lambrecht RD is more presuppositional than LD, LDed constituents are never contrastive/emphatic, RD is compatible with known topics, only. Thus, 'loose aboutness', sufficient for an LDed hanging topic, as in (95), isn't enough in RD.[46] Certainly, the pragmatic function of RD is less clearly delineated than that of LD.

Unlike what we saw with LD (§5.3.1), an analysis of RD can't straightforwardly exploit Rizzi's (1997) CP* for the simple reason that CP* is left peripheral while RD 'happens' on the right. The problem is addressed by Cecchetto (1999) (using data primarily from Italian). Cecchetto rejects (p. 41) the idea (now admittedly largely abandoned, but see De Cat 2002) that LD and RD are configurationally identical, differing only in the direction in which SpecTopicP branches, since such an approach fails to account for a number of empirical differences between RD and LD which aren't predicated to exist assuming configurational identity. He also rejects (pp. 48–55) an (at that time unpublished) reanalysis of RD of Richard Kayne's in terms of repeated LD. On such an approach, in addition to existing in its own right, LD also feeds the derivation of RD via a second instance of LD fronting the remnant IP*.

Instead, Cecchetto (1999) relates RD to LD and the clitic-doubling phenomenon found in several Romance varieties. He suggests (pp. 56–62) that, in the initial stages of the derivation, the three constructions are identical: they all involve raising of an XP from its base position to the specifier of a left-VP*-peripheral projection whose head hosts the clitic.[47] At that point the three constructions diverge: the clitic double moves no further, resulting in regular IP*-internal clitic doubling; the LDed constituent raises to Rizzi's (1997) CP*-internal SpecTopicP position; and, the RDed constituent raises to a left-VP*-peripheral SpecTopicP position (Belletti 2004a).

Ceccheto's (1999) analysis of RD is difficult to reconcile with: (a) the non-movement approach to LD (§5.3.1); and (b) the analysis of non-subject clitics in §4.4.1. What's clear is that RD isn't random right adjunction. Not only would such an approach sit awkwardly alongside the kinds of structures seen elsewhere, it

---

[46] Despite Harris's (1978: 119) claim that RD is grammaticalising (and therefore increasingly pragmatically neutral), Ashby (1982) finds no speaker–variable evidence to indicate a change in progress.

[47] Cecchetto's analysis of clitics differs from the one set out in §4.4.1. However, the differences are irrelevant for our purposes here.

would fail to account for the hierarchical properties of RD (parallelling those of LD; cf. (97)) illustrated in (103) (from De Cat 2002: 16, (1b)):

(103) Elle était vraiment bien, son exposition, à Julia.
it was really good, her exhibition, to J.
'J.'s exhibition was really good.'

5.4   Focus fronting

Focus fronting in English is illustrated in (104):

(104) My dad I called yesterday.

Rizzi's (1997) CP* provides a structural template within which to analyse focus fronting, namely, a focus–presupposition articulation, structurally encoded as a FocusP, whereby the focus raises to SpecFocusP and the presupposition occupies CompFocusP:

(105)

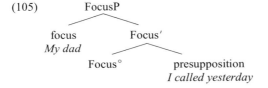

FocusP

focus   Focus′
My dad

Focus°   presupposition
I called yesterday

In contrast to English, French doesn't allow focus fronting:

(106) *Mon papa j'ai appelé hier.
my dad I-have called yesterday

Zubizarreta (2001: 184) accounts for the ungrammaticality of examples like (106) by claiming that, unlike English, French simply lacks FocusP. However, the issue is somewhat more complex, and a number of factors are involved. The first is stylistic. Clear-cut examples of focus fronting, like (107), are grammatical and characteristic of high register ModF rather than low register ConF:

(107) A Jean j'ai donné €20.
to J. I-have given €20
'I gave J. €20.'

Thus, Zubizarreta's conclusion about the absence of FocusP may apply specifically to ConF rather than to ModF. A movement approach to the example in (107) is suggested by a number of factors, all of which contrast with LD: the left-peripheral phrase is necessarily case-marked; there's no 'comma' intonation; no resumptive clitic appears within IP*; the fronted phrase is focal rather than topical. Further, De Cat (2002: 81) notes that, again unlike LD, focus fronting is sensitive to islands and weak crossover effects and existential indefinites can undergo focus fronting.

While focus fronting is characteristic of ModF, something resembling focus fronting is found in ConF, and is more common that is sometimes acknowledged. In fact, there are two separate phenomena to account for. First, there are cases of informational focus, as in (108), from Blanche-Benveniste (2003: 342):

(108) a. 10F, vous auriez?   b. Même de moi, il se méfie.
       10F you would.have   even of me he self mistrusts
       'Would you happen to have <u>10F</u>?' 'He's wary <u>even of me</u>.'

      c. Trente ans, elle avait.   d. Pour un roi, il se prenait.
       thirty years she had   for a king he self took
       'She was <u>thirty</u>.'   'He behaved <u>like he was royalty</u>.'

The 'comma' intonation found here suggests we're dealing with LD, albeit without resumptive proforms. Kroch (2001: 712) discusses the example in (109):

(109) 10F, ce truc m'a coûté.
      10F this thing me-has cost
      'This thing cost me 10F.'

He claims that such structures had a single intonation contour in OF, but 'comma intonation' since MidF. He concludes that these are now instances of LD. Goosse (2000: 134) contrasts (110a) with (110b):

(110) a. Mon erreur, je <u>la</u> reconnais.   b. Mon erreur, je reconnais.
       my mistake I it recognise   my mistake I recognise
       'I recognise my mistake.'   = (110a)

Example (110a) is a regular case of LD, while in (110b) there's no resumptive clitic. Examples like (110b) are often considered characteristic of Belgium or Flanders. However, Goosse suggests that such structures exist in France, too, and indeed are becoming increasingly common, suggesting that focus fronting *à l'anglaise* may be gaining ground.

    Second, there are examples such as those in (111):

(111) a. Les haricots, j'aime pas.   b. Les poireaux, je déteste.
       the beans I-like not   the leeks I detest
       Beans, I don't like.   'Leeks, I hate.'

Again, the intonation patterns point to LD without resumption. Rizzi (1997) notes that LD without resumptive proforms is possible with a restricted class of verb (as well as some prepositions), only, which can select a non-overt referential proform. (See also Zribi-Hertz 1984.) Interestingly, the members of the 'restricted class of verb' which allow structures like those in (111) are the same as those discussed in §5.2.3 which select a bare infinitive which can be ellipsed (rather than pro-nominalised), namely, *adorer* 'to adore', *aimer* 'to like', *désirer* 'to desire', *détester* 'to detest', *préférer* 'to prefer' and *vouloir* 'to want to'. It makes sense, then, to attribute the grammaticality of the examples in (111) to the same abstract feature with allows these verbs to ellipse their bare-infinitival dependant.

    In summary, focus fronting is the result of movement and is found in ModF but not ConF. Superficially similar constructions which are found in ConF are in fact base-generated structures akin to LD.

5.5   Clefting and pseudo-clefting

While true focus fronting is restricted to ModF, and unavailable in ConF (§5.4), there's one focalisation device available in both varieties, namely, (pseudo) clefting, illustrated in (81d, e) on page 173. These structures have been attested since the OF period and have always had marked pragmatics. The examples in (112) illustrate clefts:

(112) a. C'est Luc qui veut te voir.   b. Ce sont mes parents que je vois demain.
          it is L. that want you see   it are my parents that I see tomorrow
          'L. wants to see you.'   'I'm seeing *my parents* tomorrow.'

Clefts take the form *Ce* [*être*] [XP] *que/qui* [IP*], whereby XP is termed the focus, IP*, the coda. A number of comments are in order:

– Only simple forms of *être* are possible (Table 2.1 on page 25 in §2.2.1.2). The most common are present, imperfect and future, as in (113a–c). Compound verb forms (Table 2.3 on page 26) are excluded, as shown in (113a′–g′):

(113) a. C'est L. que/qui . . .   a′. *Ç'a été L. que/qui . . .
      b. C'était L. que/qui . . .   b′. *Ç'avait été L. que/qui . . .
      c. Ce sera L. que/qui . . .   c′. *Ç'aura été L. que/qui . . .
      d. Ce serait L. que/qui . . .   d′. *Ç'aurait été L. que/qui . . .
      e. Ce fut L. que/qui . . .   e′. *Ç'eut été L. que/qui . . .
      f. (Il faut que) ce soit L. que/qui . . .   f′. *(Il faut que) ç'ait été L. que/qui . . .
      g. (Il fallait que) ce fût L. que/qui . . . g′. *(Il fallait que) c'eût été L. que/qui . . .

– In ConF SG *ce* can be replaced with *ça* where the form of *être* prevents elision:

(114) a. %Ça serait trop bien que tu reviennes.   b. %Ça sera lui qui partira.
          that would.be too good that you return   that will.be him who will.leave
          'It'd be great if you came back.'   'He's the one who'll leave'.

– In ModF, where the focus is a PL lexical DP*,[48] *être* is PL, as in (115a–g); in ConF *être* remains SG, as in (115a′–g′):

	ModF	ConF
(115) a.	Ce sont Luc et Anne que/qui . . .	a′. C'est . . .
b.	C'étaient Luc et Anne que/qui . . .	b′. C'était . . .
c.	Ce seront Luc et Anne que/qui . . .	c′. Ce sera . . .
d.	Ce seraient Luc et Anne que/qui . . .	d′. Ce serait . . .
e.	Ce furent Luc et Anne que/qui . . .	e′. Ce fut . . .
f.	(Il faut que) ce soient Luc et Anne que/qui . . .	f′. . . . ce soit . . .
g.	(Il fallait que) ce fûssent Luc et Anne que/qui . . .	g′. . . . ce fût . . .

[48] Or indeed *eux/elles* 'them M/F', but not 1PL *nous* or 2PL *vous*:
(i)   a. Ce sont [$_{DP*}$ eux/elles] qui rient.   b. *Ce sont [$_{DP*}$ nous/vous] qui rions/riez.
           it are them.M/F that laugh   it are us/you that laugh
           '*They* are laughing.'

– The cleft can be either negative or positive, and can contain modifiers like *presque* 'almost' and *vraiment* 'really'; none of these modifications impacts on the presupposed coda:

(116) a. Ce n'est (même) pas Luc que/qui . . .   b. C'est vraiment lui que tu aimes?
            it NEG-is even not L. that   it-is really him that you love
            'It's not (even) L. that . . . '   'Is it really him that you love?'

– Clefting is exhaustively contrastive:

(117) C'est lui et (non) pas elle que j'ai vu.
        it-is him and not not her that I-have seen
        'I saw *him*, not *her*.'

The focus can't therefore be *tout* 'everything', *rien* 'nothing', *quelques uns* 'some'.

– The coda expresses a semantic property, that is, it contains a gap corresponding to the focus.[49] The presence of mas*que*rade suggests that the gap is the result of syntactic movement out of IP* (§5.8.1). Where the gap is the subject, the necessary conditions are met for *que* to convert to *qui*.

– The focus can take one of various syntactic forms. Those in (112a, b) are a direct-object and a subject DP*, respectively; other possibilities are indirect-object DP*, PP and adverbial, as in (118):

[49] In non-standard varieties, the syntactic 'correspondence' between the focus and the gap within the coda isn't always perfect. In (ib) inherent case is marked neither in the coda nor on the underlined focus:
(i)   a. C'est pas de Jean [que je te parle].   b. %C'est pas Jean [que je te parle].
            it-is not of J. that I you speak   it-is not J. that I you speak
            'It's not Jean that I'm talking to you about.'
In (iib) and (iiib), in contrast, inherent case is marked twice, both on the focus and in the coda:
(ii)   a. C'est de ses yeux [que je me souviens].
            this-is of his eyes that I self remember
            'It's his eyes that I remember.'
       b. %C'est de ses yeux [dont je me souviens].
            this-is of his eyes of.which I self remember
(iii) a. C'est à l'amour [que je songe].   b. %C'est à l'amour [auquel je songe].
            it-is to the-love that I dream   it-is to the-love to.which I dream
            'It's love that I'm dreaming about.'
In (ivb) the focus is a strong pronominal DP*, yet reappears as *on* in the finite clause (§4.4.4).
(iv)   a. C'est pas nous [qui parlons comme ça].
            it-is not us who speak like that
            'We don't talk like that.'
       b. %C'est pas nous [qu'on parle comme ça].
            it-is not us that-one speak like that

(118) a. C'est <u>à Jean</u> que j'ai donné le livre.
it-is to J. that I-have given the book
'I gave the book *to J.*'

    b. C'est <u>sur l'étagère</u> que j'ai laissé ton livre.
it-is on the-shelf that I-have left you book
'I left your book *on the shelf.*'

    c. C'est <u>très clairement</u> que Jean a expliqué le problème.
it-is very clearly that J. has explained the problem
'J. explained the problem *very clearly.*'

A number of kinds of clefts are usually recognised. One apparent cleft mentioned in De Cat (2002: 164) can be discarded from the outset. Example (119) is of a simple predicative structure where the subordinate clause is a relative forming part of a larger complex DP* (§5.6):

(119) C'est [$_{DP*}$ une tarte que j'ai fai<u>te</u> ce matin].
this-is a tart that I-have made.F this morning
'It's a tart I made this morning.'

The would-be 'focus' constituent here is necessarily a DP* since relative clauses only ever qualify nominals. It's non-contrastive, non-exhaustive and allows past-participle agreement (§5.8.2). The would-be 'coda' isn't presupposed, can't be recovered from context and so can't be omitted.

There are, however, a number of distinct types of true clefts (see Rialland *et al.* nd and Doetjes *et al.* 2004). They all contrast with relative clauses in not triggering past-participle agreement, a fact which De Cat (2002) attributes to the fact that the fronted non-overt operator, Op, is devoid of φ features:[50]

(120) a. – Quelle voiture tu as conduite?   – C'est [celle de Guy] que j'ai conduit(<u>*e</u>).
         which car you have driven.F   this-is that of G. that I-have driven(.F)
         'Which car did you drive?'   'I drove *G.'s.*'
                                       (non-contrastive focus/post-focus)

    b. – C'est [la voiture de Pierre] que tu as conduit(*e)?
        this-is the car of P. that you have driven(.F)
        'Did you drive P.'s car?'

        – Non, c'est [celle de Guy] (, que j'ai conduit(*e)).
        no, this-is that of G. (that I-have driven(.F))
        'No, it's G.'s (that I drove).'   (contrastive focus/post-focus)

    c. – Qu'est-ce qui se passe?   – C'est [Jean] qui t'appelle.   (all focus)
        what-is-this that self passes   this-is J. that you-calls
        'What's happening?'   'J.'s calling you.'

In the non-contrastive focus/post-focus cleft in (120a) (part of) XP is in exhaustive

---

[50] This in turn suggests that the entity with which Op is construed isn't the focus, but *ce* instead, which, as we saw in §4.4.4, is well known to be devoid of φ features.

focus, and at most only weakly contrastive. The coda is presupposed but can't be omitted. There's a terminal boundary tone at the end of the focus, and this is repeated at the end of the coda. In the contrastive focus/post-focus cleft in (120b) (part of) XP is again in exhaustive focus, but this time it's highly contrastive. The coda is presupposed, has RD prosody if overt, but can also be omitted. According to De Cat (2002: 164) (120a) and (120b) differ in that the coda in (120b) is RDed, unlike that in (120a). In the explicative all-focus cleft in (120c) focus and coda are jointly focal, as in a thetic sentence. (See footnote 39 on page 175.) There's therefore no terminal boundary tone at the end of focus (unless the entire overt sequence XP *qui* IP* is deemed to be the focus and a coda along the lines of *qui se passe* 'that's happening' is assumed to have been ellipsed).

Pseudo-clefts differ from clefts in a number of ways. Compare (121a) with (121b–d):

(121) a. C'est une bêtise que tu racontais.   (cleft)
           this-is a nonsense that you told
           'You were talking nonsense.'

       b. [Ce que tu racontais] est[51] [une bêtise].   (non-dislocated pseudo-cleft)
           this that you told is a nonsense
           'What you were saying is nonsense.'

       c. Ce que tu racontais, c'est une bêtise.   d. C'est une bêtise, ce que tu racontais.
           this that you told this-is a nonsense   this-is a nonsense this that you told
           c, d: = (121b)   (dislocated pseudo-clefts)

Pseudo-clefts are based on simple copular structures whose subject is a free relative (121b). To use the terminology of De Cat (2002: 174), the cleft in (121a) *identifies*, while the pseudo-cleft in (121b) *names*. Examples (121c, d) are the LDed and RDed versions, respectively, of (121b). Pseudo-clefts differ from clefts in that the subordinate clause in a pseudo-cleft has the flexibility of the free relative. In addition to being a direct-object relative, as in (121b–d), the fronted relative proform can be a subject (122a), an inherent-case-marked DP* (122b, c) or a PP* (122d):

(122) a. Ce qui marche, c'est la télé.   b. Ce dont cela dépend, c'est toi.
           this that works, this is the tv   this of.which that depends, this-is you
           'What works is tv.'   'What it depends on is you.'

       c. Ce à quoi il s'attend, c'est moi.   d. Ce sur quoi on compte, c'est toi.
           this to what he self-waits this-is me   this on what one counts this-is you
           'What he expects is me.'   'What we're counting on is you.'

[51] Tense appears in the subordinate clause, and *est* usually retains present tense as default utterance time. However, tense marking in the subordinate can be copied on the copula:
(i)   [Ce que tu racontais] était [une bêtise].
      this that you told was a nonsense
      = (121b)

As with free relatives generally (§5.6.1), where the head is [+HUMAN], the relative in pseudo-clefts isn't usually introduced by *ce* (because of its neuter status), but by a non-neuter proform, instead (§3.8):

(123) a. Celui que je veux, c'est toi.
           that that I want, this-is you
           'The one that I want is you.'

       b. Celle dont cela dépend, c'est Marie.
           that of.which that depends, this-is M.
           'The one it depends on is M.'

And, once again as with relatives generally (§5.6.1), the relative in pseudo-clefts is presuppositional: it's presupposed in (122) that something works, that it depends on something, etc.

One feature of (pseudo-)clefts which often triggers comment is that, within both the matrix and the subordinate clause, canonical SVO word order is maintained. The same is true of a number of other constructions which have similar pragmatic force to (pseudo-)clefts, namely, *Il y a . . .* and *J'ai . . .* , in (124d–f)):

(124) a. Il y a XP que/qui . . .
       b. J'ai XP que/qui . . .
       c. J'ai que XP . . .

       a'. Il y a ma voiture qui est en panne.
       b'. J'ai ma voiture qui est en panne.
       c'. J'ai que ma voiture est en panne.
          'My car's broken down.'

5.6   The syntax of wh

In this section and §5.7, I consider two topics associated with interrogation, namely, wh and inversion. Here, after a brief taxonomy of wh phrases, I consider wh fronting in terms of landing site and trigger. I also discuss the possibility of wh in situ. The syntax of wh in French shares many properties with various other languages: (a) wh phrases contain a characteristic element equivalent to *wh* (often orthographically *qu-* or phonetically [k-] initial); (b) they appear in interrogatives, relatives, exclamatives and clefts (§5.5); and (c) they can undergo unbounded fronting (§5.6.1) (but don't have to; §5.6.2).

The simplest wh phrases are bare non-clitic wh proforms (§3.8):

(125) quand comment combien qui où pourquoi
      when how how.much/many who(m) where why

The complications of the wh proforms *que/quoi* 'what' are discussed in §5.8.3. More complex wh phrases are wh DP*s headed by a wh determiner (§3.4):

(126) a. quel livre
         'which book'

       b. quelles filles
         'which girls'

Finally, the phenomenon of preposition pied piping (§2.4.3.1) suggests that a PP* can also be wh, by inheriting the wh feature of its dependant:

(127) a. sur quelle chaise
         'on which chair'

       b. derrière quoi
         'behind what'

5.6.1   Wh fronting

Wh phrases can front to a left-IP*-peripheral position. Most clearly, fronting affects non-subject wh phrases, for example, in matrix and subordinate interrogatives, as in (128a), (129a) and (130a):[52]

(128) a. [$_{CP*}$ Quel livre [$_{IP*}$ il prend –]]?   b. [$_{IP*}$ Il prend quel livre]?
           which book he takes   he takes which book
           (128a, b)

(129) a. Je sais [$_{CP*}$ quel livre [$_{IP*}$ il prend –]]. b. *Je sais [$_{CP*}$ [$_{IP*}$ il prend quel livre]].
           I know which book he takes   I know he takes which book
           'I know which book he's taking.'

(130) a. Je sais [$_{CP*}$ quel livre [$_{IP*}$ prendre –]]. b. *Je sais [$_{CP*}$ [$_{IP*}$ prendre quel livre]].
           I know which book take   I know take which book
           'I know which book to take.'

In matrix interrogatives wh in situ is possible, too, as in (128b), albeit for some speakers with subtly different pragmatics (§5.6.2). In subordinate interrogatives fronting is compulsory, hence the ungrammaticality of (129b) and (130b).[53]

As for subject wh phrases, long-distance matrix interrogatives show that they, too, undergo fronting:[54]

(131) a. Quel étudiant tu penses [$_{CP*}$ qui [$_{IP*}$ – est parti]]?
           which student you think that is left
           'Which student do you think left?'

       b. Je sais [quel étudiant tu penses [$_{CP*}$ qui [$_{IP*}$ – est parti]].
           I know which student you think that is left
           'I know which student you think left.'

The fact that the canonical subject position is clause initial means that the issue of whether a local wh subject undergoes fronting is unclear:

---

[52] The non-subject matrix wh interrogative in (128a) has wh fronting but no inversion. Goosse (2000: 117) describes it as a device used in literature to indicate popular or children's speech; it's characteristic of ConF, and possibly gaining ground. In ModF fronting a non-subject wh phrase in a matrix interrogative triggers subject–verb inversion (§5.7). For ease of exposition, the examples in this section don't have inversion.

[53] Goosse (2000: 117) gives the example in (i) where subordinate wh in situ is compulsory:
(i)   Je restais aussi sensible que dans mon enfance à l'étrangeté de ma présence sur
       cette terre qui sortait d'où, qui allait où.
       I stayed as sensitive as in my childhood to the-strangeness of my presence on this
       earth that exited from-where that went where
       'I remained just as sensitive as during my childhood to the strangeness of my
       presence on this earth which had come from where, which was going where.'

[54] On the realisation of the complementiser as *qui* see §5.8.1.

(132) a. [$_{?CP*/?IP*}$ Quelle fille a parlé]?   b. Je sais [$_{?CP*/?IP*}$ quelle fille a parlé].
     which girl has spoken   I know which girl has spoken
     'Which girl spoke?'   'I know which girl spoke.'

We'll see data below from non-standard French and ConF suggesting that, despite the indeterminacy of the data in (132), local wh subjects can indeed undergo fronting.

In addition to interrogatives, wh fronting is found in relatives. I deal with PP* relatives first. Example (133a) contains a complex DP* headed by the noun *femme* 'woman' modified by a restrictive PP* relative. The relative is introduced by the fronted wh PP* *avec laquelle* 'with which', containing the wh pro-DP* *laquelle* 'which' (§3.8), coreferential with *femme*. The wh PP* is interpreted as the dependant of the verb *se marier* 'to get married'; as such it would normally appear in the position marked by the dash but has undergone compulsory fronting, hence the ungrammaticality of (133b). The wh proform necessarily pied-pipes the preposition (§2.4.3.1), as shown in (133c):

(133) a. [$_{DP*}$ la femme [$_{CP*}$ avec laquelle [$_{IP*}$ Jean veut se marier –]]]
     the woman with which J. wants self marry
     'the woman J. wants to marry'

   b. *[$_{DP*}$ la femme [$_{CP*}$ [$_{IP*}$ Jean veut se marier avec laquelle]]]
     the woman J. wants self marry with which

   c. *[$_{DP*}$ la femme [$_{CP*}$ laquelle [$_{IP*}$ Jean veut se marier avec –]]
     the woman which J. wants self marry with

The status of *de* 'of, from' and *à* 'to, at' as inherent-case markers (§2.4.2), rather than prepositions, is reflected in the syntax of relativisation. An inanimate PP* relativises transparently as [$_{PP*}$ P [$_{DP*}$ proform$_{wh}$]], only (for example, *avec laquelle* in (133a)). If inanimate *de/à*-marked nominals were PP*s, then they, too, would be expected to relativise in the same transparent way, only. However, inanimate *de/à*-marked nominals relativise in two ways, not just transparently, as in (134a) and (135a), but also as the portmanteau forms *où* 'at/to which, where' and *dont* 'of/from which, whence', respectively, as in (134b) and (135b):[55]

(134) a. [$_{DP*}$ la cave [à laquelle je descendais –]]   b. [$_{DP*}$ la cave [où je descendais –]]
     the cellar to which I descended   the cellar to.which I descended
     a, b: 'the cellar I was going down to'

(135) a. [$_{DP*}$ la cave [de laquelle je remontais]]   b. [$_{DP*}$ la cave [dont je remontais]]
     the cellar of which I remounted   the cellar of.which I remounted
     a, b: 'the cellar I'm was coming back up from'

---

[55] The stipulation in the text that inherent-case-marked DP*s which relativise as *où* and *dont* are necessarily animate stems from the fact that, like the clitics *y* and *en*$_1$ (§4.4.3), *où* and *dont* are interpreted as containing *cela* 'that' which can't readily be used with a human referent (§3.8).

The existence of the portmanteau relative proforms in (134b) and (135b) suggests that *de/à*-marked nominals aren't PP*s, but rather inherent-case-marked DP*s, as suggested in §3.3.

Turning from PP* relatives to direct-object and subject relatives, the situation is more complex. In the (syntactically) simplest case, the wh pro-DP* *lequel/laquelle/ lesquels/lesquelles* (§3.8) fronts to a left-peripheral position along the same lines as the relative pro-PP*s above:

(136) [$_{DP*}$ l'homme [$_{CP*}$ <u>lequel</u> [$_{IP*}$ vous cherchez –]]]
the-man which you seek
'the man you're looking for'

(137) [$_{DP*}$ la dignité [$_{CP*}$ <u>laquelle</u> [$_{IP*}$ – en résulte]]]
the dignity which of.it results
'the dignity which results from this'

Subject and direct-object relatives introduced by the wh pro-DP*s *lequel/ laquelle/lesquels/lesquelles* are actually fairly uncommon, and typical of non-restrictive rather than restrictive relatives. More typical are the structures illustrated in (138) and (139):

(138) [$_{DP*}$ la femme [$_{CP*}$ <u>que</u> [$_{IP*}$ Jean veut épouser –]]]
the woman que J. wants marry
'the woman J. wants to marry'

(139) [$_{DP*}$ la femme [$_{CP*}$ <u>qui</u> [$_{IP*}$ – veut épouser Jean]]]
the woman qui wants marry J.
'the woman who wants to marry J.'

Traditional grammars refer to *que* and *qui* here as the direct-object relative proform and the subject relative proform, respectively. There are a number of reasons to doubt this analysis. First, such an approach would make it difficult to deal with the non-standard patterns of relativisation in (140), (141) and (142).

(140) %[$_{DP*}$ le principe [$_{CP*}$ <u>selon lequel que</u> [$_{IP*}$ la copie privée n'est pas un droit –]]]
the principle according.to which that the copy private NEG-is not a right
'the principle according to which private copying isn't a right'

(141) %[$_{DP*}$ beaucoup de liens [$_{CP*}$ <u>lesquels que</u> [$_{IP*}$ vous pouvez activer – directement]]]
lots of links which that you can activate directly
'lots of links that you can activate directly'

(142) %[$_{DP*}$ la manifestation [$_{CP*}$ <u>laquelle qui</u> [$_{IP*}$ – fut un grand succès]]][56]
the demonstration which that was a big success
'the demonstration which was a great success'

If *que* and *qui* were relative proforms, these examples would contain two such proforms, one after the other. Second, the (true) relative proform *qui* has a

---

[56] On the realisation of the complementiser as *qui* see §5.8.1.

[+HUMAN] antecedent, only (§3.8). In contrast, the *qui* which appears in subject relatives isn't subject to this constraint:

(143) la tarte [$_{CP*}$ qui [$_{IP*}$ – a été faite]]
        the tart that has been made
        'the tart that was made'

Third, if *que* in (138) were a proform, we would expect it to appear in other pronominal environments; yet it does not:

(144) a. *la fille [$_{CP*}$ à que [$_{IP*}$ je parle –]]   b. *la fille [$_{CP*}$ sur que [$_{IP*}$ je compte –]]
        the girl to what I speak'   'the girl on what I count'

Finally, Blanche-Benveniste (1997: 38–9) provides phonological evidence suggesting that *qui* in (139) isn't a relative proform: in the subject relative in (145) the dispreferred sequence of two vowels in *qui est* /kiɛ/ is subject to phonological reduction [kiɛ] → [kjɛ] → [kɛ]:

(145) la femme [$_{CP*}$ qui [$_{IP*}$ – est venue]]
        the woman qui is come
        'the woman who came'

Significantly, where *qui* is indisputably a proform, such reduction doesn't take place, even if non-reduction results in a dispreferred two-vowel sequence. For example, in (146) the sequence *qui on* is pronounced [kiɔ̃] with neither jodisation nor vowel loss:

(146) le prof [$_{CP*}$ avec qui [$_{IP*}$ on a cours]]
        the teacher which whom one has lesson
        'the teacher with whom we have a class'

The fact that reduction *is* found in contexts like (139) suggests that *qui* here is *not* a proform, contra the traditional grammarians' view. An alternative analysis of object and subject relatives is given in §5.8.1, where similarities with other constructions are highlighted.

Relative clauses appear in DP*s of various kinds. In addition to definite DP*s, they can appear in indefinite DP*s and demonstratives, and even alongside clitics:

(147) a. [$_{DP*}$ un homme/quelqu'un/celui [$_{CP*}$ qui [$_{IP*}$ – parle]]]
            a man/someone/the-one that speaks
            'a man/someone/the one who's speaking'

        b. Je le vois [$_{DP*}$ – [$_{CP*}$ qui [$_{IP*}$ – parle]]].
            I him see that speaks
            'I can see him speaking.'

In addition to the non-standard and informal patterns of relativisation illustrated in (140), (141) and (142), other non-standard patterns are illustrated in (148):

(148) a. %[$_{DP*}$ un livre [$_{CP*}$ dont [$_{IP*}$ je n'en ai lu que quelques pages –]]]   (Leeman-
            a book of.which I NEG-of.it have read but some pages   Bouix 1994: 22)
            'a book of which I have read but a few pages'

b. %[$_{DP*}$ la chose [$_{CP*}$ qu' [$_{IP*}$ on a besoin –]]]   (Leeman-Bouix 1994: 101)
the thing that-one has need
'the thing we need'

c. %[$_{DP*}$ la manière [$_{CP*}$ qu' [$_{IP*}$ il est assis –]]]   (De Cat 2002: 202)
the manner that-he is seated
'the way he's sitting'

d. %[$_{DP*}$ le garçon [$_{CP*}$ qu' [$_{IP*}$ il lui ressemble]   (Queffélec 2000a: 789)
the boy that-he to.him resembles
'the boy he looks like'

In (148a) inherent case is marked twice on the genitive dependant of *pages* 'pages', once on *dont* 'of which', once on *en*$_1$ 'of it'. In (148b, c) inherent case isn't marked at all, the inherent-case-marked wh proform *dont* having been dropped in favour of the all-purpose finite complementiser *que* (§5.1.1). In (148d) inherent case is marked within the relative clause rather than on the relative proform, again allowing the all-purpose finite complementiser *que* to appear. The standard counterparts are given in (149):

(149) a. [$_{DP*}$ un livre [$_{CP*}$ dont [$_{IP*}$ je n'ai lu que quelques pages –]]]
a book of.which I-of.it have read but some pages
= (148a)

b. [$_{DP*}$ la chose [$_{CP*}$ dont [$_{IP*}$ on a besoin –]]]
the thing of.which one has need
= (148b)

c. [$_{DP*}$ la manière [$_{CP*}$ dont [$_{IP*}$ il est assis –]]]
the manner of.which he is seated
= (148c)

d. [$_{DP*}$ le garçon [$_{CP*}$ à qui [$_{IP*}$ il ressemble]
the boy to who he resembles
= (148d)

5.6.1.1 Landing site

Despite the linear similarity between (128a) and (129a), there's reason to believe that the landing site for wh fronting isn't the same in matrix and subordinate interrogatives. Specifically, in matrix interrogatives a fronted wh phrase follows an LDed topic, while in subordinate interrogatives it precedes (§5.3.1) (Jones 1996: 474–5). Consider (150), a wh in situ matrix interrogative containing an LDed topic:

(150) Toi, [tu arrives quand]?
you you arrive when
'When do you arrive?'

If the wh phrase fronts,[57] it follows the LDed topic, as in (151a) (cf. (151b)):[58]

(151) a. Toi, quand tu arrives – ?   b. *Quand toi, tu arrives – ?
          you when you arrive   when you you arrive
          ≈ (150)

However, if the interrogative in (150) appears in a subordinate context, a fronted wh phrase precedes an LDed topic, as in (152b) (cf. (152a)):

(152) a. *Dis-moi toi, quand tu arrives – . b. Dis-moi quand toi, tu arrives – .
          tell-me you when you arrive   tell-me when you arrive
                                                 'Tell me when you arrive.'

The null hypothesis is that the matrix/subordinate distinction doesn't affect the position of an LDed topic, which occupies SpecTopicP throughout. The contrast between (151) and (152) therefore suggests that the fronted wh phrase occupies a position lower than SpecTopicP (such as SpecFocusP[59]) in the matrix interrogative in (151a), but a position above SpecTopicP (such as SpecForceP) in the subordinate interrogative in (152b).[60] This contrast is illustrated in (153a, b):

(153) a. Matrix wh fronting:
          [$_{TopicP}$ Topic [$_{FocusP}$ wh phrase Focus° [$_{FinP}$ ... [$_{IP*}$ ...]]]]

      b. Subordinate wh fronting:
          [$_{ForceP}$ wh phrase Force° [$_{TopicP}$ Topic [$_{FinP}$ ... [$_{IP*}$ ...]]]]

As for the landing site for wh fronting in relatives, the linear order of relative PP*s and LDed topics suggests that wh fronting in relatives patterns with that found in subordinate interrogatives:

---

[57] De Cat's (2002: 96) study suggests that, while LD is slightly preferred over RD in declaratives, RD is strongly preferred over LD in wh interrogatives (especially matrix ones, and irrespective of the wh-fronting–wh-in-situ contrast).

[58] A Google search came up with examples like (i) with the wh phrase preceding the LDed topic in an apparent matrix context:

(i)   Comment cela, ça se passe?
       how that that self passes
       'How does that happen?'

I assume that such examples actually involve ellipsis of something like *Je veux savoir* ... 'I want to know ... '. In other words, the example is subordinate, and the wh-phrase–topic word order is expected, as in (152a).

[59] The idea that wh fronting should target SpecFocusP in matrix (but not subordinate) non-subject wh interrogatives ties in well with the fact that focus fronting, which also targets SpecFocusP, is incompatible with wh fronting in matrix (but not subordinate) contexts (§5.4).

[60] As in other languages, the wh phrase *pourquoi* 'why' can occupy a higher position than other wh phrases in matrix wh interrogatives. It can therefore precede LDed phrases in matrix interrogatives rather than follow them. See Rizzi (2001).

(154) a. la femme avec qui Jean, il veut se marier
       the woman with whom J. he wants self marry
       'the woman J. wants to marry'

    b. *la femme Jean, avec qui il veut se marier
       the woman J. with whom he wants self marry

In (154a) the relative PP* precedes the LDed topic. If the topic occupies Spec-TopicP (§5.3.1), then the relative PP* must occupy a higher specifier position, such as SpecForceP:

(155) $[_{ForceP}$ relative XP Force° $[_{TopicP}$ Topic $[_{FinP} \ldots [_{IP*} \ldots]]]]$

Given the judgements in (128b), (129b) and (130b), there's a correlation between optionality and landing site: optional wh fronting (in matrix wh contexts) targets SpecFocusP; compulsory wh fronting (in subordinate wh and relative contexts) targets the specifier of ForceP, the topmost FP within Rizzi's exploded CP. This can be attributed to the phenomenon of selection: unlike matrix interrogatives, subordinate interrogatives and relatives are selected 'from above' (§5.6.1.2).

Finally in this section, the notion that the landing site for wh fronting is a left-IP*-peripheral specifier position, as suggested here, is supported by the non-standard patterns of relativisation illustrated in (140)–(142), where the fronted wh PP*/DP* is followed by an overt complementiser.

5.6.1.2 Trigger

As with all XP movement (§1.5), wh fronting is triggered by the need to create a spec–head configuration within which to check an uninterpretable feature located on a functional head. Let's call this feature [Q]. Given the absence of subject–verb inversion accompanying wh fronting in ConF, assume that [Q] is borne outside IP*.[61] Thus, wh fronting can achieve the required spec–head configuration without impacting on IP*. The null hypothesis is that [Q] is located on the CP* head into whose specifier the wh phrase fronts. In matrix interrogatives, this means that [Q] is located on Focus°:

(156) $[_{FocusP}$ Où Focus°$_{[Q]}$ $[_{IP*}$ il est allé –]]?
    where he is gone
    'Where did he go?'

In subordinate interrogatives and relatives, where wh fronting targets SpecForceP, [Q] is assumed to be located on Force°, as in (157):

(157) Je me demande $[_{ForceP}$ où Force°$_{[Q]}$ $[_{IP*}$ il est allé –]].
    I me ask where he is gone
    'I wonder where he went.'

---

[61] Where wh fronting co-occurs with subject–verb inversion (as in matrix wh interrogatives in ModF) the situation is different (§5.7).

The CP*-internal [Q] head is phonologically null in (156) and (157). However, in ConF it can be overt, as illustrated in (140)–(142) in the case of relatives, and (158) in the case of interrogatives (§5.7.1):

(158) a. %Où qu'il est allé?
     b. %Où est-ce qu'il est allé?
     c. %Où c'est qu'il est allé?
       where $C°_{[Q]}$ he is gone
       = (156)

     a'. %Je me demande où qu'il est allé.
     b'. %Je me demande où est-ce qu'il est allé.
     c'. %Je me demande où c'est qu'il est allé.
       I me ask where $C°_{[Q]}$ he is gone
       = (157)

ConF examples like (159) provide further evidence that local subject wh phrases can undergo fronting:

(159) a. Quelle fille a parlé?
     b. %Quelle fille qui a parlé?
     c. %Quelle fille est-ce qui a parlé?
     d. %Quelle fille c'est qui a parlé?
       which girl $C°_{[Q]}$ has spoken
       = (132a)

     a'. Je sais quelle fille a parlé.
     b'. %Je sais quelle fille qui a parlé.
     c'. %Je sais quelle fille est-ce qui a parlé.
     d'. %Je sais quelle fille c'est qui a parlé.
       I know which girl $C°_{[Q]}$ has spoken
       = (132b)

The position of the local subject wh phrase to the left of the $C°_{[Q]}$ head shows that it's moved out of SpecIP*.

5.6.2   *Wh in situ*

In §5.6.1 we saw wh fronting in various relative and (matrix and subordinate) interrogative contexts. Mostly, wh fronting was compulsory. With relatives and subordinate interrogatives, compulsory wh fronting was attributed to selection. The grammatical instances of wh in situ in (128b) and (163b) are in local matrix wh contexts. In long-distance and subordinate (wh and relative) contexts, wh in situ is ungrammatical (echoic contexts aside[62]):

(160) a. *Marie pense que tu allais où?
       M. thinks that you went where

     b. Où Marie pense que tu allais – ?
       where M. thinks that you went
       'Where does M. think you were going?'

(161) a. *Je demandais tu allais où.
       I asked you went where

     b. Je demandais où tu allais – .
       I asked where you went
       'I asked where you were going.'

(162) a. *l'endroit [tu allais où]
       the-place you went where

     b. l'endroit [où tu allais –]
       the-place where you went
       'the place where you were going'

The ungrammatical status of wh in situ in examples (161a) and (162a) is expected

---

[62] In echo questions, matrix and subordinate wh in situ are both grammatical:
(i)   a. Tu as fait QUOI?!
        you have done what
        'You did WHAT?!'

        b. Il a dit que tu as fait QUOI?!
          he has said that you have done what
          'He said you did WHAT?!'

since subordinate interrogatives and relatives are selected: the superordinate predicate requires a wh dependant, entailing wh fronting within the subordinate clause. Less straightforward is the example in (160a), where the in situ wh phrase occurs in a non-selected context.[63] In matrix interrogatives, uniquely, we saw in (128a, b) that wh fronting isn't compulsory and that wh in situ, as in (163b), was available as an alternative:

(163) a. [$_{CP*}$ Où [$_{IP*}$ tu vas –]]?   b. [$_{IP*}$ Tu vas où]?
           where you go   you go where
           a, b: 'Where are you going?'

Wh in situ is a familiar phenomenon (see Watanabe 2001 for a recent overview). It's found in multiple-wh questions in English, where only one wh phrase fronts in interrogatives, leaving all others in situ:

(164) a. You think [<?someone> believes [we bought <?something> <?somewhere>]]
           ↓
       b. Who do [you think [– believes [we bought what where]]]?

Fronting a single wh phrase is therefore sufficient to check [Q].

Wh in situ is also familiar from languages like Chinese, where regular (non-multiple-)wh questions fail to show wh fronting, neither in matrix (165a), nor in subordinate (165b), nor in island contexts (165c):

(165) a. hufei mai-le shenme ne/∅   b. zhangsan xiang-zhidao [lisi mai-le shenme]
           H. buy-PERF what PRT   Z. wonder L. bought-PERF what
           'What did H. buy?'   'Z. wonders what L. bought.'

       c. hufei xihuan nei-ben shei xie de shu
           H. like that-CL who write de book
           'For which person x does H. like the book that x wrote?'

It's standardly assumed that [Q] is checked here *either* by an interrogative particle (*ne* in (165a)) *or* by a phonologically null 'operator'[64] raising in overt syntax from the overt wh phrase (as in (165b, c)).[65] In neither case, therefore, does the (overt) wh phrase need to front.

Wh in situ in French as illustrated in (163b) differs from both these cases: it's not restricted to multiple-wh interrogatives, and it doesn't happen to the exclusion of wh movement (cf. (163a)). An analysis of wh in situ in French is suggested by the following observation: Although (163a) and (163b) are translated in the same way, there is, for some speakers, a subtle pragmatic difference between the two: (163b)

---

[63] Watanabe (2001: 219) also observes that wh in situ in French is clausebound.

[64] It matters little for present purposes whether this non-overt operator is thought of merely as a formal wh feature or as an XP extracted from some high specifier position within the wh phrase. See Watanabe (2001: 211–2) for discussion.

[65] Watanabe (1992a, b) suggests that the reason why the island in (165c) doesn't result in ungrammaticality is that the phonologically null operator raises from a position attached to, but not within, the island.

is strongly presuppositional in a way that (163a) isn't. The question in (163b) presupposes that you're going somewhere (and asks where), while the one in (163a) doesn't presuppose you're going anywhere at all; rather, it asks whether you're going (somewhere), and where you're going. Thus, an answer of *Nulle part* 'Nowhere' is a felicitous response to the question in (163a), but not to the one in (163b).

Given the approach to (wh) movement adopted in §5.6.1.2 in terms of checking a [Q] feature, and given that feature checking isn't deemed to be optional (§1.5), the reason why there's no wh fronting in (163b) must be that wh fronting is not only not needed, but also impossible. In other words, there's no [Q] feature to be checked. (Indeed, it's arguable whether any structure at all is merged above IP*.[66]) The absence of [Q] immediately accounts for the absence of wh fronting. And given the pragmatic contrast between (163a) and (163b), while both contain a wh phrase, we can further attribute (non-)presuppositionality to the presence/absence of [Q]. The interrogative in (163a) contains [Q] and a wh phrase. It therefore asks two kinds of question: first, a yes–no question (because of [Q]) along the lines of 'Are you going (somewhere)?'; second, a wh question (because of the wh phrase) along the lines of 'Where (are you going)?'. Because of [Q], a genuine yes–no question is being asked; there's no presupposition as to what the answer might be, and the answer *Nulle part* 'Nowhere' is felicitous. And because of [Q], wh fronting is triggered. In contrast, the interrogative in (163b) contains a wh phrase but no [Q]. It therefore asks a wh question, only, but no yes–no question. Given the *absence* of [Q], there *is* a presupposition, and the answer *Nulle part* is *not* felicitous. And no wh fronting is triggered.[67]

5.7   Subject–verb inversion

I turn now to the complexities of subject–verb 'inversion'. The label inversion is inappropriate, as we'll see, but I retain it in line with general practice. Three kinds of inversion are usually distinguished in ModF. They don't share the same distribution (see Table 5.1 on page 200), and aren't uniquely associated with interrogation, but one context in which all three are found is matrix non-subject wh interrogatives, as in (166):

---

[66] Boskovic (1996) suggests that clauses can be bare IP*s. And if structure is only projected to the extent that the presence of (non-default) features warrants it, the absence of [Q] means there's no need to project structure above IP*.

[67] In the variety of French discussed in Butler and Mathieu (2004) wh in situ isn't presuppositional as suggested in the text. Such non-presuppositionality could be dealt with by a proposal by Cheng and Rooryck (2000). Rather than contrasting wh fronting with wh in situ in terms of the presence/absence of [Q], Cheng and Rooryck distinguish the two in terms of distinct numerations: wh in situ sentences contain a null morpheme which checks [Q], and wh fronting is therefore neither required nor permitted; wh fronting sentences contain no such morpheme, and wh fronting is therefore required in order to check [Q].

(166) a. Quand <u>est-elle</u> partie?   (pronominal inversion (PI); §5.7.1)
          when is-she left
          'When did she leave?'

      b. Quand <u>Claire est-elle</u> partie?   (complex inversion (CI); §5.7.1)
          when C. is-she left
          'When did C. leave?'

      c. Quand <u>est partie Claire</u>?   (stylistic inversion (SI); §5.7.2)
          when is left C.
          = (166b)

The inversion in (166a) is called pronominal inversion (PI) because what the finite verb appears to invert around (*elle* 'she') looks like a subject proform (§4.4.4);[68] note that *elle* here can't be replaced by a DP*, as shown in (167):

(167) *Quand est-Claire partie?   (cf. (166a))
        when is-C. left

The inversion illustrated in (166b), called complex inversion (CI), is formally (and distributionally) very similar to PI. The complexity is the presence of two apparent subjects, a preverbal DP* (*Claire*) and the same postverbal element found in PI. Because of the similarities between them, PI and CI are discussed together in §5.7.1. The term stylistic inversion (SI) for the inversion in (166c) is again retained here in line with general practice, although there's nothing specifically stylistic about it. SI is possible with a DP* subject, only, whereby the subject follows the entire verbal group (the finite aspectual auxiliary *and* the past participle in (166c)). SI is discussed in §5.7.2, where we'll see that two *sub*categories of SI need to be distinguished.

Inversion in French is of interest in a number of ways. Pragmatically, it's marked. While a preverbal subject is usually topical (dislocated in ConF, non-dislocated in ModF; §5.3), a postverbal subject is never topical; it's either a unique focus or part of a larger focus (Lahousse 2003a). Syntactically, it's interesting because none of the three kinds of inversion can plausibly be claimed to involve inversion along the lines of English subject–auxiliary inversion for example, that is, movement of a finite verb from I°* to the left of SpecIP*. Stylistically, inversion isn't found robustly in all varieties. It's uncommon in spoken French,[69] and in our discussion of wh fronting (§5.6.1) we suggested ConF lacks inversion entirely. The lack of inversion occurring alongside wh fronting was attributed in §5.6.1.2 to the fact that

---

[68] PI is also known as (subject) clitic inversion.
[69] In De Cat's (2002: 42) study the different kinds of inversion are used to varying extents in different contexts and in different geographical varieties. For example, PI is found in matrix yes–no interrogatives 2% of the time in her Belgian sample, 21% in Quebec, but not at all in the sample from France. In contrast, *est-ce que* is found in matrix wh interrogatives 53% of the time in the Belgian sample, 72% in Quebec and 73% in France. CI is particularly rare in the spoken language and doesn't appear at all in the York/De Cat corpora (De Cat 2002: 42).

[Q] appears external to IP* in ConF, and can therefore be checked (via wh fronting) without further impacting on IP*. The occurrence of inversion in ModF suggests that in this grammar, [Q] appears internal to IP*. Thus, inversion is triggered (in ModF, but not ConF) because of the position of [Q].

In (166) we saw inversion in matrix interrogatives. Inversion isn't uniquely triggered by interrogation, however, and neither is it restricted to matrix contexts. PI/CI are triggered by sentence-initial adverbials like *peut-être* 'maybe' and *sans doute* 'doubtless', as in (168), while SI is licensed in some non-interrogative subordinate contexts, as in (169):

(168) a. Peut-être <u>viendra-t-il</u>.
        Maybe will.come-he
        'Maybe he'll come.'

      b. Sans doute <u>Marie veut-elle</u> venir.
         without doubt M. wants-she come
         'Marie doubtless wants to come.'

(169) a. Il est parti sans que <u>soit fini son travail</u>.
        he is left without that be finished his work
        'He left without his work being finished.'

      b. N'oublie pas ce que <u>t'a dit ton père</u>!
        NEG-forget not this that you-has said your father
        'Don't forget what your father told you!'

Table 5.1 shows which kind of inversion is possible in which context. A number of observations are in order. First, PI and CI have identical distributions, suggesting that they should, at a relevant level of abstraction, be thought of as one and the same phenomenon, thereby reducing from three to two the number of kinds of inversion to be accounted for.[70] Second, given the pattern of yeses and noes, the fifth and sixth lines of Table 5.1 should within the formal analysis be integrated into earlier lines. Taking these observations into account, Table 5.1 is revised as Table 5.2 below.

	PI	CI	SI
Matrix yes–no, *peut-être*, etc.	Yes	Yes	No
Matrix wh	Yes	Yes	Yes
Subordinate yes–no	No	No	No
Subordinate wh	No	No	Yes
V1 conditionals	Yes	Yes	No
Subordinate non-wh	No	No	Yes

Table 5.1. Inversion in ModF in interrogative and non-interrogative contexts (version 1).

[70] In fact, there's one context, namely, *incises*, found in literature and used to interrupt direct quotation, in which PI is found but not CI:
(i)   "Surtout", (*Jean) <u>dit-il</u>, "ne venez pas avant midi!"
        above.all J. said-he *ne* come *pas* before midday
        "Above all", he said, "don't come before midday!"

	PI/CI	SI
Matrix yes–no, V1 conditionals, *peut-être*, etc.	Yes	No
Matrix wh	Yes	Yes
Subordinate yes–no	No	No
Subordinate wh/non-wh	No	Yes

Table 5.2. Inversion in ModF in interrogative and non-interrogative contexts (version 2).

Third, all four logically possible combinations are attested: PI/CI without SI, both PI/CI and SI, neither PI/CI nor SI, SI without PI/CI. The feature relevant to PI/CI seems to be the matrix/subordinate contrast: PI/CI is dependent upon the presence of the triggering feature on $I*°$ rather than $C*°$ (and found in matrix but not subordinate contexts). The details of PI/CI are explored in §5.7.1. The situation with SI is less clear, and in §5.7.2 I follow recent work by Karen Lahousse in positing two distinct kinds of SI.

5.7.1 Pronominal and complex inversion

We saw in §4.2.1 that French finite verbs undergo V movement to the highest head within IP*, landing to the right of SpecIP*, the canonical subject position:

(170) $[_{IP*}$ subject $[_{I*'}$ verb$_{fin}$ . . . $[_{VP*}$ . . . t_v . . . $]]]$

In view of the standard analysis of English subject–auxiliary inversion we might similarly analyse PI in terms of a further instance of V movement, taking the finite verb over the top of the subject, out of IP* and into CP*:

(171) $[_{CP*}$ . . . verb$_{fin}$ $[_{IP*}$ subject $[_{I*'}$ t_v . . . $[_{VP*}$ . . . t_v . . . $]]]]$

An approach to PI along these lines (that is, in terms of V movement over the subject) is advocated by Rizzi and Roberts (1989) and immediately accounts for the postverbal position of the subject, assuming of course that the postverbal pronominal is indeed the subject. However, a simple V-movement analysis leaves a number of questions unanswered. Perhaps the two most important are:

(172) a. Why is PI restricted to pronominal subjects? If PI really is parallel to English subject–auxiliary inversion, why can't the finite verb invert around a DP* subject?
   b. What position is occupied by the preverbal DP* subject in CI?

Rizzi and Roberts (1989) answer these questions as follows. The finite verb in French can check nominative case in a spec–head configuration, only. This is fine if the verb remains in $I*°$, but not if it raises to a head within CP*. However, the pronominal subject *can* be licensed if it incorporates into the inverted verb. Incorporation is possible with heads, only, not with DP*s. DP* subjects are excluded from PI, therefore, because they can't be checked if they stay in SpecIP*, and can't incorporate into the inverted verb, either. As for the position of the preverbal DP* subject in CI, Rizzi and Roberts suggest that CP* has two specifiers, a higher specifier, occupied by the fronted wh phrase, and a lower one, occupied by the preverbal subject DP*. Rizzi and Roberts' analysis is problematic for a number of reasons. Consider (173), where an adverbial clause intervenes between the wh phrase and the preverbal subject DP* (Jones 1999):

(173) Dans quelle ville, <u>quand le vote a eu lieu</u>, les électeurs sont-ils allés à la pêche?
       in which town when the vote has had place the voters are-they gone to the fishing
       'In which town, when the vote took place, did the voters go fishing?'

If the fronted wh phrase and the preverbal subject DP* occupy the two proposed SpecCP* positions, the intervening adverbial clause would need to be adjoined to a C*′ position, a possibility ruled out by Merge (§1.5), or else would need to occupy an additional intervening specifier position.

   The movement-to-COMP analysis of the finite verb in PI/CI also fails to account for the French–English contrast in (174) (Jones 1999):

(174) a.   *When did Mary dance and did John sing?

       b.   ?Quand neigera-t-il et ferons-nous du ski?
            when snow-it and will.do-we of.the ski
            'When will it snow and when will we go skiing?'

The English example in (174a) is ungrammatical because two intermediate projections (C*′) have been co-ordinated. This follows from the standard analysis of English subject–auxiliary inversion in terms of movement to COMP. The French example in (174b) is marginal but much better than (174a). If French PI is analysed along the same lines as English subject–auxiliary inversion, the contrast is unexpected and unexplained.

   A minor revision to the Rizzi and Roberts (1989) analysis of PI/CI is offered in Cardinaletti and Roberts (2002) and Cardinaletti (2004). (See also Jones 1999.) Instead of resorting to double specifiers, these analyses suggest that, in PI/CI contexts, only, an additional FP is merged at the top of IP*. Written at a time when the topmost projection within IP* was called Agr(eement)P, this approach to PI/CI has become known as the 'Agr recursion' analysis.[71] In this analysis the wh phrase occupies SpecCP*, the (preverbal) DP* subject, the specifier of the higher AgrP, and the (postverbal) pronominal subject, the specifier of the lower AgrP, as in (175):

(175) $[_{CP*}$ XP$_{wh}$ $[_{AgrP}$ subject DP* verb$_{fin}$ $[_{AgrP}$ subject pronominal t$_v$ ... $[_{VP*}$ ... t$_v$ ...]]]]

The attraction of Agr recursion is that it allows: (a) each relevant phrase to occupy a specifier position within its own projection; and (b) the finite verb to raise from the lower Agr head, over the top of the pronominal subject, to the higher Agr head,

---

[71] Cardinaletti and Roberts (2002) originally called the two proposed projections Agr1P and Agr2P. Cardinaletti (2004) renames them AgrSP and Subj(ect)P.

thus locating it between the DP* subject and the pronominal subject.[72] The lower Agr head checks the φ features of the finite verb and the nominative case of the subject, while the higher Agr head checks a predication feature (Cardinaletti 2004: 120–1). Thus, both the inverted verb and the preverbal DP* subject in CI are located within IP*.

Under Agr recursion, the answer to question (172a) therefore remains unchanged. As for question (172b), Agr recursion provides an additional specifier position for the (preverbal) DP* subject to occupy. Since the (postverbal) pronominal subject is licensed by incorporation, the finite verb doesn't need to check the pronominal's case feature, and is therefore able to check the case feature of the DP* in a spec–head configuration. The weakness of Agr recursion is that it's hard to see – not least from the perspective of comparison with Germanic – why the inverted finite verb should be unable to check the case feature of a DP* subject *prior to inverting* and, therefore, why simple inversion is impossible with DP* subjects.

Of course, these issues stem from the assumption – made in Rizzi and Roberts (1989), Cardinaletti and Roberts (2002) and Cardinaletti (2004) – that PI/CI really *do* involve inversion, that is, that they involve V movement across the pronominal subject. In order to avoid these issues, and better answer the questions in (172), it has been suggested (for example, by Barbosa 2001) that PI and CI *don't* involve V movement beyond I*°, and that the finite verb actually occupies I*° in PI/CI and non-PI/CI contexts alike. There are a number of advantages to such an approach, some having to do with its consequences for our understanding of the nature of the postverbal pronominal and the preverbal DP*. Before these are explored, though, I need to explain how the idea that PI/CI doesn't involve further V movement can be aligned with our understanding of wh fronting.

The theoretical attraction of traditional movement-to-COMP analyses of matrix non-subject wh interrogatives is that they straightforwardly allow inversion to be related to wh fronting: both target the pre-IP* domain because this is the minimal domain in which checking allows a feature on the verb to be associated with a feature on the wh phrase. Further, the approach accounts for why inversion *isn't* found in matrix subject wh interrogatives in ModF: neither fronting nor inversion takes place because the required checking configuration can be achieved within IP*.

Given that, in French as in English, wh fronting in matrix non-subject wh interrogatives targets a relatively low position within CP* (lower than SpecTopicP at least; §5.6.1.1), we concluded in §5.6.1.2 that the motivation for the wh fronting was the same as the motivation for the inversion: the need to check the wh feature of the wh phrase against [Q] on I*°. In English the required checking configuration is produced by fronting the wh phrase and inverting the finite auxiliary. In ConF, while the wh phrase fronts, the finite verb doesn't invert because [Q] is located within CP*. In ModF, in contrast, inversion does take place. However, we've just

---

[72] Agr recursion also allows the adverbial clause in (173) either to adjoin to a phrasal projection, or else itself to occupy a specifier projection within its own FP.

concluded that the inversion is only apparent, and that, in reality, the finite verb in PI/CI in ModF occupies the same position as in uninverted sentences. How is this so? How do French and English differ? Cyrille-Thomas (2003) suggests that the crucial difference hinges on the properties of CP*. In English C*° can be targeted by V movement, and the finite verb bearing [Q] can raise from I*°. In French, in contrast, C*° *can't* be targeted by V movement. How, then, can the wh feature of a fronted wh phrase be checked against [Q] on I*°? The answer given by Cyrille-Thomas is that a long-distance checking configuration is created.[73] In the structure in (176) the wh feature of the fronted wh phrase in SpecCP* can be checked against [Q] on the finite verb in I*° because a chain is formed between the finite verb and the empty C*°:

(176) $[_{CP*}$ wh phrase $[_{C*'}$ e $[_{IP*}$ $[_{I*'}$ verb$_{fin}$ . . . $[_{VP*}$ . . . t$_v$ . . .]]]]]

The value of the chain is that, together with the local spec–head configuration between SpecCP* and C*°, the wh phrase in SpecCP* can be linked with the finite verb in I*°. However, formation of a chain between I*° and C*° doesn't come for free: specifically, it comes at the expense of the ability of I*° to check SpecIP*. The biuniqueness condition on checking means that, from a given position, a single head can't check two specifiers, so if I*° checks the wh phrase (long distance via the chain with C*°), as it needs to (given that it doesn't raise out of IP*), it can't simultaneously check the subject in SpecIP*.

In English, where subject–auxiliary inversion involves V movement to COMP, nothing needs to be said about the grammatical subject: it quietly sits in SpecIP* and becomes postverbal as a side effect of V movement across it. If we'd adopted Agr recursion, a similar analysis could have been given for the postverbal pronominal in PI/CI. However, we rejected Agr recursion and concluded instead that PI/CI doesn't involve V movement beyond I*°. Given our analysis in §4.4.4 of weak preverbal subject proforms as phonological clitics, that is, as DP*s which first raise from their VP*-internal SpecθP position to SpecIP*, and then phonologically (pro-)cliticise onto the finite verb, something definitely *does* need to be said about the postverbal pronominal in PI/CI. If the verb hasn't moved, the pronominal can't quietly sit in SpecIP* and wait to become postverbal, and it clearly doesn't phonologically procliticise either. In fact, this outcome is a welcome result. If it *had* been possible to account for PI/CI so straightforwardly, the question would have remained why inversion isn't possible around a DP* subject. By having to explain the postverbal pronominal found in PI/CI, we can address in a non-ad-hoc manner why DP*s are excluded.

A number of facts suggest that the immediately postverbal element found in PI/CI is *not* the same as the preverbal subject proform. First, as we've seen, while preverbal subject proforms co-distribute with preverbal DP* subjects, the postverbal element in PI/CI doesn't:

---

[73] See also Chomsky's (2005) notion of feature inheritance/spreading.

(177) a. Jean/il est parti.   b. Est-il/*Jean parti?
           J./he is left   is-he/J. left
           'J./he left.'   'Did he/J. leave?'

Second, while the postverbal element in PI/CI co-occurs with a preverbal lexical DP* subject (in CI), the preverbal subject proform doesn't (irrelevant LD contexts (§5.3.1) and subject-doubling varieties like Picard and Québécois (§4.4.4) aside):

(178) a. Jean est-il parti?   b. *Jean il est parti.
           J. is-he left   J. he is left
           'Did J. leave?'

Third, while preverbal subject proforms can be omitted in a second conjunct, the postverbal element can't:

(179) a. Il va au bar et (il) commande une bière.
           he goes to.the bar and he orders a beer
           'He goes to the bar and orders a beer.'

       b. Va-t-il au bar et commande*(-t-il) une bière?
           goes-he to.the bar and orders-he a beer
           'Is he going to the bar and ordering a beer?'

Finally, the preverbal subject proforms don't systematically have postverbal counterparts. For example, *ce* and *je* are pronounced [sə] and [ʒə] before consonant-initial verbs, but [s] and [ʒ] before vowel-initial ones due to elision. In postverbal position, they are either impossible, as in (180b) and (181b), or else they're pronounced [s] and [ʒ], as in (182), possibly involving a phonological modification to the verb, as in (183c) and (184c):[74]

(180) a. ce furent   b. *furent-ce
           this was   was-this

(181) a. je prends   b. *prends-je
           I take   take-I

(182) a. était-ce [etɛs]   b. sais-je [sɛʒ]
           was-this   know-I

(183) a. je peux [ʒəpø]   b. *peux-je   c. puis-je [pwiʒ][75]
           I can   can-I   can-I

(184) a. je trouve [tʁuv] b. *trouve-je   c. †trouvé-je [tʁuvɛʒ]
           I find   find-I   find-I

---

[74] As such, there's an interesting parallel with some northern Italian dialects, where non-inverted and inverted subject proforms must be distinguished, not least because they are morphologically different:

(i)   a. El vien.   b. Vien-lo?   (Paduan, Zanuttini 2001: 525 (25))
           he comes   comes-he
           'He's coming.'   'Is he coming?'

[75] The 'uninverted' form, *je puis*, is an archaic/literary alternative to *je peux*.

The postverbal counterparts of the vowel-initial subject proforms appear with epenthetic [t] when the verb is phonologically vowel final, as in (185):

(185) a. il trouva [iltʁuva]   b. *trouva-il [tʁuvail]   c. trouva-t-il [tʁuvat̲il]

In one case, the subject proform *ça* 'that', quite clearly a clitic given its availability as a resumptive proform in dislocation structures like (186), is categorically excluded from postverbal position, as shown in (187):

(186) Les voisins, ça boit.
       the neighbours that drinks
       'The neighbours like their alcohol.'

(187) *Quand (les voisins) va-ça arrêter de boire?
       when the neighbours goes-that stop of drink
       'When are the neighbours/they going to stop drinking?'

The inverted equivalent of *ça* is *il*:

(188) a. Cela, ça te gêne.   b. Cela te gêne-t-il?
         that that you disturbs   that you disturbs-it
         'That disturbs you.'   'Does that disturb you?'

Similarly, *l'on* 'one, we', the high-register alternative to *on*, is excluded from PI:

(189) a. Voit-on loin?   b. *Voit-l'on loin?
         see-one far   see-one far
         'Can you see far?'

These properties suggest that the postverbal element in PI/CI isn't simply an inverted subject proform, but an affix instead (Zwicky and Pullum 1983), and not related to the canonical subject position at all. As for what *kind* of affix it is, a clue comes from the conclusion that the 'inverted' verb actually remains in I*° and that the verb in I*° has a long-distance checking relationship with the fronted wh phrase in SpecCP*, a checking relationship which, due to the biuniqueness condition on checking, prevents I*° from checking a subject in SpecIP*: if (the [Q] feature on) the finite verb in I*° checks (the wh feature on) the fronted wh phrase in SpecCP*, then (the D/EPP feature on) the finite verb in I*° *can't* simultaneously check (the case feature of) the subject in SpecIP*. It's precisely to solve this problem that the immediately postverbal element in PI/CI, now conceived of as an affix, appears: it's an agreement marker (on I*°) and is licensed by the [Q] feature (on I*°) precisely because I*° can't check the subject (in SpecIP*). Crucially, the affixal agreement marker (re-)endows I*° with the ability to check the subject (in SpecIP*).

Analysing the immediately postverbal element in PI/CI as an affixal agreement marker has a number of merits. It explains why a pronominal 'subject' can co-occur with a DP* subject only if the pronominal subject is 'inverted', as in (178a) (cf. (178b)). It's difficult to see how (178b) could be excluded in any principled way under Agr recursion. In the present analysis, (178b) is excluded precisely because only one subject position is available. The two 'subjects' can co-occur only if the pronominal 'subject' is postverbal (and therefore actually an agreement marker),

and the pronominal 'subject' can be postverbal only if the finite verb bears [Q].
This analysis also explains the ungrammaticality of (190a, b):

(190) a. *Il est-il parti?   b. *Jean est-Jean parti?
          he is-he left   J. is-J. left

The Agr-recursion analysis excludes subject clitics from the higher SpecAgrP and
DP* subjects from the lower SpecAgrP in part because of the pragmatic mismatch
between the status of (pro)nominals on the one hand, and the relevant Agr head on
the other. In the present analysis the problems are strictly syntactic. Starting with
(190a), in the absence of a DP* subject, a preverbal subject clitic is necessarily
present because French is a non-pro-drop language. The non-pro-drop status of
French is due to the inability of $I^{*\circ}$ to identify the φ features of the subject. In PI,
however, $I^{*\circ}$ bears an affixal agreement marker, which *is* able to identify the φ
features of the subject. Thus, where the affixal agreement marker is licensed, we
expect pro-drop-like behaviour, that is, the absence of an overt (non-LDed)
preverbal subject and the presence of pro instead. The example in (190a) is
therefore ungrammatical because the presence of the overt subject clitic is
uneconomical. As for (190b), ungrammaticality is due to the fact that there's no
position for the postverbal DP* to occupy.

Interesting support for the explanation for the ungrammaticality of (190a) comes
from comparison between the affixal agreement marker found in PI/CI in ModF on
the one hand, and the *-ti/-tu* elements which mark yes–no interrogatives in some
varieties of French on the other. The element *-tu* is illustrated in the Québécois
examples in (191):[76]

(191) a. Le déjeuner est-tu prêt?   b. Tu l'as-tu battu?
          the dinner is-tu ready   you him-have-tu beaten
          'Is dinner ready?'   'Did you beat him?'

The form of (191) suggests a structural parallel with PI/CI, and that *-ti/-tu* should
be analysed like the affixal agreement marker. However, there are two differences
between *-ti/-tu* and the affixal agreement marker (Taraldsen 2001: 172). First, in
terms of morphology, while the affixal agreement marker agrees with the φ features
of the subject, *-ti/-tu* is invariant, suggesting that it's not endowed with φ features.
Second, in terms of syntax, while the affixal agreement marker co-occurs with either
a lexical DP* subject or pro, *-ti/-tu* co-occurs with either a lexical DP* subject
(191a) or a subject clitic (191b); it does *not* co-occur with pro, as shown in (192)
(cf. (191a)):

---

[76] The example in (i), with *-ti* rather than *-tu*, is from Goosse (2000: 116), who suggests that
the structure is restricted to popular French, and in decline:
(i)   Vous en avez-ti des moins chers?
        you of-that have-ti of.the less expensive
        'Do you have any less expensive ones?'

(192) *pro est-tu prêt?
       is-tu ready
       'Is it ready?'

These two differences can be related. If what allows an affixal agreement marker in ModF to license pro is its morphological richness, then the impoverished morphology of -*ti*/-*tu* is expected not to license pro, and to require an overt subject proform, instead. I propose, therefore, that -*ti*/-*tu* is like the affixal agreement marker found in PI/CI in ModF in that it: (a) is an affix; (b) is licensed by the presence of [Q] on I*°; and (c) endows I*° with the ability to license the subject in SpecIP*. It differs from the affixal agreement marker in that it: (a) is devoid of φ features and morphologically invariant; and (b) is therefore unable to license pro in SpecIP*. While -*ti*/-*tu* appears in certain varieties of French, only, and may be in decline, the present discussion is important because the analysis proposed provides support for the analysis of the affixal agreement marker found in PI/CI in ModF. In particular, the data concerning -*ti*/-*tu* provide further evidence against Agr recursion. Given the formal parallel between -*ti*/-*tu* and the postverbal 'subject' in PI/CI, a parallel analysis seems intuitively appropriate, as pursued above. If we had adopted Agr recursion for the affixal agreement marker, it would have made sense to do so for -*ti*/-*tu*, too. This would have meant merging -*ti*/-*tu* in the lower SpecAgrP position. Such a conclusion is counterintuitive, to say the least. The problem, though, is that such a conclusion then begs the question of why -*ti*/-*tu* can't appear preverbally in the same way that subject proforms can. In the analysis proposed here, in which -*ti*/-*tu* and affixal agreement markers don't have anything to do with subject/specifier positions, the issue simply doesn't arise.

I turn now, finally, to the preverbal DP* found in CI and, more generally, the SpecIP* position in PI/CI. Given our conclusions: (a) about the position of the 'inverted' finite verb in PI/CI (it remains in I*°); (b) about the checking relationship between the fronted wh phrase and the finite verb (it's long distance, via a chain linking I*° and C*°); and, finally, (c) about the nature of the immediately postverbal element (it's an affixal agreement marker on I*°), there seems little alternative to the conclusion that the preverbal DP* in CI is a regular subject which merges in its VP*-internal SpecθP position and raises to SpecIP* (§4.3):[77]

---

[77] The question arises of whether the preverbal DP* subject in CI has to be lexical, or whether a strong proform can appear, too, as in (i):

(i)   ?Comment toi as-tu trouvé un travail?
       how you have-you found a work
       'How did you find a job?'

The status of (i) is unclear, possibly for stylistic reasons. Like all kinds of inversion, CI is restricted to ModF, a high-register variety. In contrast, the use of strong pronominals as canonical subjects is decidedly low register, unless such pronominals can be appropriately focalised, as in (ii):

(193) $[_{CP*} \ldots XP_{wh} \ldots [_{IP*}$ subject DP* $[_{I*}$ verb$_{fin}$+affix $\ldots$]]]

That the preverbal subject DP* in CI is IP* internal is supported by the absence of the 'comma' intonation associated with LD (§5.3.1), and correctly predicts that the preverbal subject DP* in CI follows all CP*-associated material, not only LDed phrases, as in (194), but also fronted wh phrases, as in (195):

(194) a. Ce livre, Jean va-t-il le lire?   b. *Jean ce livre, va-t-il le lire?
          this book J. goes-he it read   J. this book goes-he it read
          'Is J. going to read this book?'

(195) a. Quand Jean va-t-il partir?   b. *Jean quand va-t-il partir?
          when J. goes-he leave   J. when goes-he leave
          'When is J. going to leave?'

As for PI, SpecIP* is clearly not occupied by an overt subject DP*. Instead, and extraordinarily for a normally non-pro-drop language like ModF, SpecIP* in PI is occupied by a null pronominal, pro. The conventional wisdom on pro drop is that pro needs to be licensed and identified by I*°. In non-inversion contexts, I*° doesn't license pro. In PI, in contrast, a feature on I*° licenses the affixal agreement marker, which not only endows I*° with the ability to license SpecIP*, but also turns I*° into a pro licenser (see De Crousaz and Shlonsky 2003). This is actually rather attractive, since one of the core licensing properties of pro is identification: I*° in pro-drop languages is sufficient to identify the φ features of the subject, and the subject can therefore be non-overt, for reasons of economy. Of course, the affixal agreement marker on I*° in PI/CI very clearly identifies the φ features of the subject and would therefore be expected to turn I*° into a pro-licenser.

The sequence *(qu')est-ce que/qui* '(what) is it that', which appears in a number of the contexts we've been considering deserves special attention.[78] I start with *est-ce que/qui* (§5.6.1.2). Diachronically the sequence is clearly the result of PI applying to *c'est que/qui* 'it's that'; in the modern language(s) things aren't so straightforward. The occurrence of *est-ce que* in ModF, characterised by PI, is unsurprising, and an analysis of the sequence in those terms makes sense. However, the fact that *est-ce que* is found in ConF, too, despite the fact that ConF *isn't* characterised by PI, suggests that a different analysis is needed here. I suggest that the sequence *est-ce que* has been grammaticalised as a complementiser in ConF, an atomic element drawn from the lexicon ready made, rather than the output of PI.[79]

(ii)   a. Seul toi/moi as/ai le droit.   b. LUI veut rester.   c. MOI suis le plus beau.
            alone you/me have the right   him wants stay   me am the more beautiful
            'You/I alone have the right.'   'HE wants to stay.'   'I'm the best looking.'

[78] The *que–qui* alternation is discussed in §5.8.1. For recent historical discussion of *(qu')est-ce que* see Rouquier (2003).

[79] The reanalysis/grammaticalisation of *est-ce que/qui* as an atomic complementiser is sometimes talked about in teleological terms as a device for avoiding inversion. We must be careful, though, when talking about purpose in syntactic innovation. However informal the language we might do it in, suggesting that a speech community grammaticalised a

The complexity of *est-ce que/qui*, and the fact that two analyses are needed, stems from variation along two cross-cutting dimensions, one syntactic, one pragmatic. Syntactically, as we've seen, ModF differs from ConF with respect to the position of unselected [Q], $I^{*\circ}$ in ModF, $C^{*\circ}$ in ConF. The presence of [Q] on $I^{*\circ}$ in ModF triggers PI. The presence of [Q] on $C^{*\circ}$ in ConF fails to trigger PI, but does allow $C^{*\circ}_{[Q]}$ to be realised in a number of different ways, namely, ⌀, *que/qui*, *est-ce que/qui* and *c'est que/qui*, as we saw in (158) and (159). Pragmatically, sentences – including interrogatives – are either cleft or non-cleft (§5.5). The interaction between these various dimensions of variation is illustrated in (196) in the context of the question 'Who can you see?':

(196)		ModF ([Q] on $I^{*\circ}$)	ConF ([Q] on $C^{*\circ}$)
	Non-cleft	Qui vois-tu?	Qui [⌀] tu vois? Qui [que] tu vois? *Qui [est-ce que] tu vois?* Qui [c'est que] tu vois?
	Cleft	*Qui est-ce que tu vois?*	Qui [⌀] c'est que tu vois? Qui [que] c'est que tu vois? Qui [est-ce que] c'est que tu vois? Qui [c'est que] c'est que tu vois?

The dual status of, say, *Qui est-ce que tu vois?* 'Who can you see?' stems from the fact that it appears twice in (196) (italicised). Bottom left is from ModF and is derived from the cleft sentence *C'est qui que tu vois?*, to which wh fronting and PI have applied. Top right is from ConF and is derived from the non-cleft sentence *Tu vois qui?*, to which wh fronting has applied and where $C^{*\circ}_{[Q]}$ has been realised as the atomic complementiser *est-ce que* drawn straight from the lexicon. Thus, *Qui est-ce que tu vois?* has a different pragmatic status depending on which grammar produced it: it's a cleft in ModF but not in ConF.

(197)		ModF ([Q] on $I^{*\circ}$)	ConF ([Q] on $C^{*\circ}$)
	Non-cleft	Qui parle?	Qui [⌀] parle? Qui [qui] parle? *Qui [est-ce qui] parle?* Qui [c'est qui] parle?
	Cleft	*Qui est-ce qui parle?*	Qui [⌀] c'est qui parle? Qui [que] c'est qui parle? Qui [est-ce que] c'est qui parle? Qui [c'est que] c'est qui parle?

syntactically complex structure into a lexical item 'in order to avoid' inversion begs all sorts of questions about linguistic motivation which are beyond the scope of this book.

Turning to *est-ce qui* as in *Qui est-ce qui parle?* 'Who's speaking?', for example, it makes sense to say something similar, namely, that there are two 'versions'. In ModF *est-ce qui* is derived from a cleft and characterised by PI; in ConF it's derived from a non-cleft and not characterised by PI. Instead, *est-ce qui* is one of a number of atomic complementisers realising $C^{*\circ}{}_{[Q]}$. The empirical data set for 'Who's speaking?' is given in (197).

The two analyses of *est-ce que/qui*, one for ModF, another for ConF, address a number of issues. Consider first the examples from ConF in (198) and (199), taken from the bottom right-hand corner of (196) and (197):[80]

(198) a. Qui <u>est-ce que</u> c'est que tu vois?
      who is-it that it-is that you saw
      'Who can you see?'

    b. Qui <u>est-ce que</u> c'est qui parle?
      who is-it that it-is that spoke
      'Who's speaking?'

(199) a. Qui <u>c'est que</u> c'est que tu vois?
      who it-is that it-is that you saw
      = (198a)

    b. Qui <u>c'est que</u> c'est qui parle?
      who it-is that it-is that spoke
      (198b)

If *est-ce que* in (198) were always the result of PI, then these examples would be derived from the uninverted underlying structures in (200):

(200) a. C'est qui que c'est que tu vois?   b. C'est qui que c'est qui parle?

The problem with such a derivation is that the purported uninverted underlying structures in (200) each contain two instances of clefting, and it's difficult to see, from a pragmatic perspective, how double clefting could be motivated. The same is clearly true of the examples in (199). If, instead, and as proposed here, *c'est/est-ce que/qui* is an atomic complementiser in ConF drawn from the lexicon, without the pragmatic force associated with clefts, there's no need to derive the examples in (198) from the double cleft structures in (200): the examples in (198) contain a single, pragmatically motivated instance of clefting and a formally complex, but syntactically atomic, complementiser merged on a [Q] functional head within an exploded CP.

The two analyses of *est-ce que/qui* make contrasting predictions with respect to tense marking. In ModF these sequences are clefts which have undergone PI; the form *est* is a regular finite verb. Given that clefts are compatible with tenses other than present, the inverted forms in (201) are predicted to be grammatical:

---

[80] The following non-invented examples were found on the Internet:
(i)   a. Qui <u>c'est que</u> c'est que vous écoutez aussi attentivement.
        who it-is that it-is that you listen.to so attentively
        'Who are you listening to so attentively?'
    b. Mais qui <u>c'est que</u> c'est qui est là?
        but who it-is that it-is that is there
        'But who's there?'

(201) a. Qui était-ce que tu voyais?   a'. Qui était-ce qui parlait?
      b. Qui sera-ce que tu verras?   b'. Qui sera-ce qui parlera?
      c. Qui serait-ce que tu verrais?   c'. Qui serait-ce qui parlerait?
      d. Qui fut-ce que tu vis?   d'. Qui fut-ce qui parla?

Clefts with tenses other than present are actually rare, and were condemned by Vaugelas, but they do exist (§5.5). And the prediction that they allow PI is borne out by the attested examples in (202):

(202) a. Quand <u>sera-ce que</u> nous serons petits?   (ModF)
        when will.be-it that we will.be small
        'When shall we be small?'

      b. Qui <u>était-ce qui</u> avait préparé . . . ?   (ModF)
        who was-it that had prepared
        'Who had prepared . . . ?'

      c. Pourquoi <u>fut-ce que</u> les Romains firent telle chose?   (ModF)
        why was-it that the Romans did such thing
        'Why did the Romans do such a thing?'

In contrast, in ConF the sequence *est-ce que/qui* is an atomic complementiser drawn ready made from the lexicon. It's not therefore expected to have tense-related variant forms. And this expectation is indeed met: the examples in (202) are stylistically highly marked and not characteristic of ConF, where invariant *est-ce que* is found, as in (203):

(203) a. Quand <u>est-ce que</u> nous serons petits?   (ConF)
        when is-it that we will.be small
        = (202a)

      b. Qui <u>est-ce qui</u> avait préparé . . . ?   (ConF)
        who is-it that had prepared
        = (202b)

      c. Pourquoi <u>est-ce que</u> les Romains firent telle chose?   (ConF)
        why is-it that the Romans did such thing
        = (202c)

The dual analysis of *est-ce que/qui* proposed here also explains the mystery of the mismatching grammaticality judgements in (204) (Jones 1999):

(204) a. Je me demande quand <u>est-ce</u> que le train arrivera.
        I me ask when is-it that the train will.arrive
        'I wonder when the train will arrive.'

      b. *Je me demande quand <u>arrivera-t-il</u>.
        I me ask when will.arrive-it

The sequence *est-ce que/qui* is found (in ConF) in the selected context of subordinate interrogatives, as in (204a), while PI isn't (in any variety), as shown in

(204b).[81] If, unlike what is suggested here, *est-ce que/qui* is treated as PI in all varieties, then the divergent judgements are unexplained: why should PI be acceptable in (204a) but not in (204b)? If, as suggested here, *est-ce que/qui* is an atomic complementiser in ConF, rather than the result of PI, then an explanation is possible: PI in (204b) is ungrammatical, even in ModF, because, in selected contexts, [Q] is located within CP* rather than IP*; *est-ce que* in (204a) is grammatical (in ConF) because it isn't the result of PI; rather, it's one of the available lexical realisations of $C*°_{[Q]}$ (alongside ∅, *que* and *c'est que*):

(205) a. Je me demande quand ∅ le train arrivera.
     b. Je me demande quand que le train arrivera.
     c. Je me demande quand c'est que le train arrivera.
       a–c: = (204a)

Finally, the analysis of *est-ce que/qui* as an atomic $C*°_{[Q]}$ in ConF explains two ways in which it behaves like another interrogative complementiser, namely, *si*. First, where ModF requires *si* to introduce an embedded yes–no interrogative, as in (206a), ConF allows *est-ce que*, as in (206b):

(206) a. Il demande s'il pleut.   b. Il demande est-ce qu'il pleut.
      he asks if-it rains (ModF/ConF)   he asks is-it that'it rains (ConF)
      a, b: 'He wants to know whether it's raining.'

Second, in a construction noted by Goosse (2000: 114) which is possibly dying out but still alive in some regions, *est-ce que* parallels *si* in co-ordinated conditions, as in (207):

(207) [Est-ce que vous viendrez] ou [si c'est lui]?
      is-it that you will.come or if it-is him
      'Will you come or will he?'

If the two bracketed constituents are both CP*s with parallel internal structures, *est-ce que* looks like a complementiser, just like *si*.

The analysis of PI/CI above, together with the account of wh fronting, offers a perspective on Gadet's (2003: 101) stylistic ranking of ways of asking *What are you saying?*:

(208) a. Que dis-tu?   (wh fronting, PI:
       what said you   almost exclusively written)

---

[81] The examples in (i) of subordinate wh interrogatives with PI/CI (from Leeman-Bioux 1994: 54) must therefore be attributed to hypercorrective performance errors:
(i)   a. Il y a un débat pour savoir [jusqu'où] doit-il aller.
          it there has a debate for know.far must-he go
          'There's a debate as to how far he must go.'
     b. Reste à savoir [dans quelles conditions] (les choses) vont-elles avancer.
          remains to know in which conditions the things go-they advance
          'It remains to be seen under what conditions things will go forward.'

b. Qu'est-ce que tu dis?   (clefting, wh fronting,
    what is-it that you said   PI: unmarked)

c. Tu dis quoi?   (wh in situ, no PI: familiar)
    you said what

d. C'est quoi que tu dis?   (clefting, wh in situ, no PI:
    it-is what that you said   popular)

The two versions with PI are ranked higher than the two without. In fact, Gadet's use of 'what' questions masks some of the variation found in matrix non-subject wh interrogatives. The full picture is illustrated with the paradigm of 'who' questions in (209), in particular (209d, f):

(209)		Clefting	Wh fronting	PI	Register
a.	Qui vois-tu? who you-see	No	Yes	Yes	Almost exclusively written
b.	Qui est-ce que tu vois? who is-it that you see	Yes	Yes	Yes	Unmarked
c.	Tu vois qui? you see who	No	No	No	Familiar
d.	Qui tu vois?[82] who you see	No	Yes	No	Familiar
e.	C'est qui que tu vois? it-is who that you see	Yes	No	No	Popular
f.	Qui c'est que tu vois? who it-is that you see	Yes	Yes	No	Popular
	a–f: 'Who can you see?'				

The pattern of yeses and noes in (209) is consistent with the fundamental grammatical distinction between high-register ModF ([Q] within IP*, therefore inversion) and low-register ConF ([Q] outside IP*, therefore no inversion): the examples with PI (209a, b) are both ranked higher than those without (209c–f).[83]

Consider now the other differences between the examples in (209). Of the two

---

[82] In the absence of contextualisation, some of my informants rejected this example as being French at all! However, once appropriate contextualisation was provided, the structure was ranked as in (209).

[83] In fact, as we saw from the discussion of *est-ce que* in §5.7.1, example (209b) can actually be generated by *both* ModF *and* ConF, and consequently isn't unambiguously characterised by clefting/inversion. The fact that (209b) can be the output of either grammar underlies its unmarked stylistic status.

with inversion (and wh fronting[84]), the one without clefting (209a) is ranked higher than the one with it (209b), suggesting that in addition to its pragmatic value, clefting is perhaps also a stylistic variable within ModF. Of the four examples (209d–f) without inversion, the picture is less clear since speakers aren't unanimous in their register rankings. Examples (209c, d) are both labelled familiar (like (208c)) since my informants had difficulty distinguishing between them in terms of register; examples (209e, f) are both labelled popular (like (208d)) since my informants disagreed as to how to order them with respect to one another in terms of register. This reinforces the notion of clefting as a stylistic variable (in ConF and ModF alike), while the distinction between wh fronting and wh in situ is not.[85]

Before we leave PI/CI and move on to SI, consider one unexpected context in which CI is optionally found, illustrated in (210a, b):

(210) a. Combien de personnes sont(-elles) venues?
           how.many of people are-they come
           'How many people came?'

       b. Lequel des deux est(-il) parti?   c. Qui a(*-t-il) raté son examen?
           which.one of.the two is-he left   who has-he failed his exam
           'Which of the two left?'   'Who failed his exam?'

Thus far, we've seen CI in the contexts in Table 5.2 on page 201. These include matrix non-subject-wh interrogatives, where the analysis is clear: the wh phrase fronts to SpecCP* and non-locally checks the finite verb in I*°; the biuniqueness condition on checking prevents the verb from additionally licensing SpecIP*; the [Q] feature on I*° licenses the affixal agreement marker which re-endows I*° with the ability to license SpecIP*. The interrogatives in (210a, b) are different: the wh phrase is subject. In the subject wh interrogatives we've seen in ModF so far, given that [Q] is on I*°, the subject wh phrase stays in SpecIP* where it can check both the [Q] and D/EPP features on I*° without violating the biuniqueness condition on checking. Such an approach accounts for the examples in (210a, b) *without* the affixal agreement marker. What, then, of those *with* the agreement marker? What motivates the appearance of the affixal agreement marker?

To answer this question, we can revisit the mobility of certain quantifiers. We saw in §4.3.2 that complex quantifiers can appear outside the direct-object DP* they're associated with, as in (211):

(211) a. J'ai lu [$_{DP*}$ assez de livres].   b. J'ai assez lu [$_{DP*}$ – de livres].
           I have read enough of books   I-have enough read of books
           'I've read enough books.'   ≈ (211a)

While the details aren't identical, a similar mobility is found with the wh quantifier

---

[84] Given that [Q] necessarily triggers fronting of a wh phrase (if present), but triggers inversion only if it's on I*°, PI without wh fronting is correctly predicted not to occur.
[85] This observation is in line with the analysis in §5.6.2 of the wh-fronting-versus-no-wh-fronting in terms of the pragmatic distinction of (non)presupposition, rather than register.

combien 'how much/many', as in (212) (see footnote 36 on page 120 in §4.3.2):

(212) a. [_DP* Combien de livres] as-tu lu<u>s</u> – ?   b. [Combien] as-tu lu [_DP* – de livres]?
how.many of books have-you read   how.many have-you read of books
'How many books have you read?'   ≈ (212a)

Note that the past participle agrees in (212a) (*lus* 'read') but not (212b) (*lu*) (§5.8.2). Relevant is that a past participle agrees in gender and number with a preposed direct object. The agreement in (212a) is straightforward, and indicates that the DP* *combien de livres* inherits the M.PL features of *livres*. The pattern in (212b) indicates *either* that preposed *combien* doesn't 'count' as a direct object (and therefore doesn't trigger agreement), or that *combien* does 'count' as a direct object, but doesn't inherit the M.PL features of *livres*.

Now consider (213):

(213) a. [_DP* Combien de diplômés] sortent par an?
how.many of graduates exit.3PL per year
'How many graduates leave each year?'

    b. Il sort [_DP* combien de diplômés] par an?
it exit.3SG how.many of graduates per year
≈ (213a)

Example (213a) is a regular subject wh interrogative: the PL feature of the subject wh phrase is reflected in the finite verb. Example (213b) is the impersonal equivalent of (213a), and is characterised by two crucial properties: the argument of the verb is assigned inherent case in SpecθP within VP* on the back of its θ role, and so doesn't need to raise to SpecIP* for case reasons; there's no [Q] feature on I*°, so no wh fronting is triggered (§5.6.2). Impersonal *il* merges in SpecIP* instead (§4.4.4), triggering default 3SG agreement on the finite verb. These two properties aren't inextricably linked, and it's possible for wh fronting to be triggered within an impersonal construction and, as in (212), there's flexibility as to what fronts, as shown in (214):

(214) a. [Combien] sort-i<u>l</u> [_DP* – de diplômés] par an?
how.many exit.3SG-it of graduates per year

    b. [_DP* Combien de diplômés] sort-i<u>l</u> – par an?
how.many of graduates exit.3SG-it per year
a, b: ≈(213b)

In (214a) *combien* alone fronts to SpecCP* in order to check [Q] on I*° via a chain between C*° and I*°. Because of the biuniqueness condition on checking, I*° can't then check SpecIP*, so impersonal *il* disappears, to be replaced by the affixal agreement marker on I*° and, presumably, pro in SpecIP*. In (214b) the entire DP* fronts, with identical consequences. Now consider (215), which is formally identical to (214b) apart from the features of I*°:

(215) [$_{DP*}$ Combien de diplômés] sortent-<u>ils</u> par an?
        how.many of graduates exit.3PL-they per year
        ≈(213b)

The example is, of course, parallel to (210a), which is where our discussion started. The example is problematic, given our assumptions so far: PL agreement on the verb suggests that the wh DP* occupies SpecIP*; the presence of the postverbal affixal agreement marker suggests that the wh DP* occupies SpecCP*. In order to have our cake and eat it, as it were, we can appeal to the ability of the quantifier to separate from the rest of the DP*, as in (216):

(216) [$_{TopicP*}$ [Combien] Topic° [$_{IP*}$ [$_{DP*}$ – de films] [$_{I*'}$ sortent-ils . . . [$_{VP*}$ . . . par an]]]]?

Thus, PL agreement on the verb is triggered because of the PL DP* in SpecIP*, while the postverbal affixal agreement marker is present because a wh phrase fronts to SpecCP*.

5.7.2   Stylistic inversion

SI differs from PI/CI on a number of levels. Stylistically, while PI/CI are characteristic of ModF, only, SI is higher register still, predominantly a written, if not literary, phenomenon. Syntactically, while PI/CI are characterised by a post-verbal affixal agreement marker, SI has a postverbal DP* subject, as in (217a) (cf. (217b)):

(217) a. Où est allé <u>le chef</u>?   b. *Où est allé <u>il</u>?
          where is gone the boss   where is gone he
          'Where did the boss go?'

Also syntactically, and as shown by Table 5.2 on page 201, while PI/CI are found in matrix contexts, only, SI is licensed in matrix and subordinate contexts alike. Most significantly, though, while not presenting the complexity of the two apparent subjects found in CI, SI is structurally more complex than PI/CI: the postverbal DP* subject doesn't follow the finite verb; it follows a larger verb group. Of course, where the verb group comprises a finite verb, only, as in (218a), this detail goes unnoticed. However, as soon as the verb group comprises a finite aspectual/modal auxiliary together with a non-finite lexical verb, as in (218b, c), the difference becomes clear:

(218) a. Quand <u>partent</u> les enfants?   b. Quand <u>sont partis</u> les enfants?
          when leave the children   when are left the children
          'When are the children leaving?'   'When did the children leave?'

      c. Quand <u>doivent partir</u> les enfants?
          when must leave the children
          'When do the children have to leave?'

SI potentially gives rise to ambiguity, as in (219):

(219) Je me demande [quelle femme aime Jean]?
I me ask which woman loves J.
Either: 'I wonder which woman J. loves?'
(*Jean* is the subject; the wh DP* *quelle femme* has fronted, triggering SI)
or: 'I wonder which woman loves J.?'
(the wh DP* *quelle femme* is the subject, triggering no inversion; *Jean* is the direct object)

SI has been the subject of much recent work by Karen Lahousse,[86] and the following discussion relies heavily on her work, which suggests that SI is triggered by a combination of factors. Lahousse's major claim, however, is that there are two kinds of SI. Lahousse (2003a, d) argues that SI in non-interrogatives is licensed in one of two ways, in matrix and subordinate contexts alike. Starting from the fundamental observation that postverbal subjects are always non-topical, Lahousse suggests that subjects can be *appropriate* non-topics, and SI thus licensed, in either (or both) of the two ways set out in (220):

(220) Non-interrogative SI is licensed provided:
a. the clause contains a (possibly non-overt) initial stage topic;[87] and/or,
b. the subject has narrow (restrictive/exhaustive) focus.

This captures the essence of the traditional view that SI is licensed either by a preposed phrase (the stage topic in (220a)) or by a heavy subject (on the view that heavy subjects are typically focal). The examples in (221a, b) contrast because (in the absence of any context) (221b) alone contains an initial stage topic licensing SI:

(221) a. *Chantent les enfants.   b. Dans la cour chantent les enfants.
          sing the children   in the playground sing the children
                                      'The children are singing in the playground.'

In (222) the stage topic licensing SI is non-overt, but recoverable from the preceding discourse (Lahousse 2003a: 138):

(222) Elle ouvre la porte. ∅ Apparaît la jeune élève, âgée de 18 ans.
she opens the door appears the young pupil aged of 18 years
'She opens the door. The young 18-year-old female student appears.'

The examples in (223a, b) contrast because the subject in (223b) alone bears restrictive/exhaustive focus, marked by *ne . . . que*, satisfying (220b) (Lahousse

---

[86] Lahousse follows the tradition of Blinkenberg (1928), Le Bidois (1952), Kayne (1972), Kayne and Pollock (1978, 2001), Bonami, Godard and Marandin (1999), Marandin (2001), Korzen (1983) and Bailard (1981). See also Kampers-Manhe *et al.* (2004).

[87] Lahousse (2003a, d) takes the notion stage topic from Erteshik-Shir (1997). A stage topic indicates either 'the spatio-temporal parameters of the utterance' (Erteshik-Shir 1997: 26) or else a vaguer notion of contextual relationship including addition, succession, matching, origin and immediate cause (Lahousse 2003a: 134). Cf. Haegeman's (2000) Sc(ene)P(hrase) proposal. Indirect objects, purposes, modal adverbials, subject-oriented adverbials don't have the status of stage topics and therefore don't license SI (Lahousse 2003a: 135).

2003a: 132):

(223) a. *Sont venus mes élèves. b. Ne sont venus que mes élèves.
          are come my pupils   NEG are come but my pupils
                                        'My pupils alone came.'

In subordinate contexts, non-interrogative SI is similarly licensed, as in (220). If the subordinating conjunction is itself a stage topic, for example, a temporal subordinating conjunction (Lahousse 2003c), SI is licensed, as in (224) (although nothing prevents additional SI-licensing factors co-occurring with a stage-topic subordinating conjunction):

(224) Pierre allait sortir quand sonne le téléphone.
       P. went go.out when rings the telephone
       'P. was about to go out when the telephone rings.'

If the subordinating conjunction isn't a stage topic, for example, a causal subordinating conjunction, then SI is licensed only in the presence of some other licensing factor, that is, another stage topic (independent of the subordinating conjunction), as in (225a), or an exhaustive focus, as in (225b):

(225) a. . . . parce que là renaîtrait le phénix.
          because there would.be.reborn the phoenix
          '. . . because the phoenix would be reborn there.'

      b. . . . pas parce que l'amour a disparu, mais parce qu'est apparue une différence.
          not because the-love has disappeared but because is appeared a difference
          '. . . not because love disappeared, but because a difference appeared.'

Lahousse (Forthcoming) suggests that the two SI-licensing mechanisms in (220) produce two structurally distinct types of SI, 'genuine' SI, illustrated in (226a), which is triggered by an initial stage topic, and 'focus' SI, illustrated in (226b), which is not:[88]

(226) a. Quand partira ton ami?
          when will.leave your friend
          'When will your friend leave?'

---

[88] Lahousse rejects the idea that her 'genuine' SI needs to be subdivided into stylistic SI (licensed by an initial phrase which has been extracted) and unaccusative SI (licensed by an initial phrase which has *not* been extracted). Claims for the need for such a subdivision have been made, for example, by Bonami *et al.* (1999) on the basis of a purported sensitivity of unaccusative SI, but not stylistic SI, to the category of the head verb, and on the basis of a purported availability in unaccusative SI, but not stylistic SI, of en_1 pronominalisation out of the postverbal subject. Lahousse presents empirical data suggesting that such distinctions are actually unfounded, and that stylistic and unaccusative SI should be conflated into a single category, which she labels genuine SI.

b. Rendront un devoir <u>les élèves qui ont raté l'examen de chimie</u>.
   will.submit an assignment the pupils who have failed the-exam of chemistry
   'Those students who failed the chemistry exam will submit an assignment.'

The distinctive properties of the two types of SI are explored below.

Lahousse (Forthcoming) argues that the postverbal subject in genuine SI is a new-information focus which fails to raise out of its base position in VP* (à la Déprez 1988; 1990). The D/EPP feature on I*° is then satisfied, not by SpecIP*, but long distance by the SI-triggering phrase in SpecCP*. The position of the subject following the verb group is a consequence of the fact that the finite and non-finite verbs are VP* external. This is illustrated in (227):

(227)   Genuine SI (after Lahousse Forthcoming):
   a. [$_{VP*}$ subject [$_{V*°}$ verb] YP]
      (verb raising to I*°)
   b. [$_{IP*}$ [$_{I*°}$ verb] [$_{VP*}$ subject [$_{V*°}$ t$_{verb}$] YP]]

Thus, in genuine SI, the verb group occupies its 'regular' positions within IP*. As Lahousse (2003d: 191) points out, this explains why the adverbial *souvent* 'often' appears in the same position with respect to the verb group in both canonical subject–verb word order, as in (228b), and genuine SI, as in (229b):

(228) a. *Ici, des lapins <u>souvent</u> se cachent.   b. Ici, des lapins se cachent <u>souvent</u>.
           here some rabbits often self hide   here some rabbits self hide often
                                                          'Rabbits often hide here.'

(229) a. *Ici <u>souvent</u> se cachent des lapins.   b. Ici se cachent <u>souvent</u> des lapins.
           here often self hide some rabbits   here self hide often some rabbits
                                                          ≈ (228b)

What distinguishes genuine SI from canonical subject–verb word order is the position of the subject. For Lahousse, the position of the postverbal subject in genuine SI is its VP*-internal SpecθP position (Taraldsen 2001). For Cecchetto (1999) and Belletti (2001b) the postverbal subject actually undergoes very short movement, to the specifier of a low FocusP immediately above VP*. On either account, thinking of genuine SI as inversion misses the point entirely: the verb doesn't invert around the subject. Rather, the subject fails to raise to the left of the verb. In fact, SpecIP* arguably doesn't exist, for the simple reason that I*° doesn't license it. And I*° doesn't license it because the D/EPP feature of I*° is checked against a higher specifier via non-local checking.

Evidence to support this 'non-inversion' approach to genuine SI comes from a correlation noted by Kayne and Pollock (1978), namely, between the availability of SI on the one hand, and the possibility of omitting impersonal *il* (§4.4.4) on the other: the two are possible in almost identical contexts, including some identified by Lahousse (2003b) not identified by Kayne and Pollock, for example, those in (230)–(233):

(230)   Temporal adverbial clauses:
a. Quand seront partis les enfants, . . .
when will.be left the children
'When the children have left, . . . '

b. Quand (il) aura été procédé au réexamen de cette loi, . . .
when it will.have been proceeded to.the re-examination of this law
'When (someone) will have proceeded to re-examine this law, . . . '

(231)   *Peut-être*, etc., clauses:
a. Peut-être sont partis les enfants.
maybe are left the children
'Maybe the children left.'

b. Peut-être sera(-t-il) procédé au réexamen de cette loi.
maybe will.be-it proceeded to.the re-examination of this law
'Maybe (someone) will proceed to re-examine this law.'

(232)   Clause initial PP*s:
a. Dans quelques jours seront partis les enfants.
in some days will.be left the children
'In a few days the children will have left.'

b. Dans quelques jours (il) sera procédé au réexamen de cette loi.
in some days it will.be proceeded to.the re-examination of this law
'In a few days (someone) will have proceeded to re-examine this law.'

(233)   Absolute inversion contexts:
a. Partirent alors les enfants.
left then the children
'Then the children left.'

b. (Il) sera procédé alors au réexamen de cette loi.
it will.be proceeded then to.the re-examination of this law
'Then (someone) will have proceeded to re-examine this law.'

This correlation suggests the two phenomena should be related. Lahousse's analysis of genuine SI does just that, in terms of non-realisation of SpecIP*. Given the unavailability of pro in a non-pro-drop language like French (PI aside), impersonal *il* merges, in uninverted contexts, directly in SpecIP* to check D/EPP and then phonologically cliticises onto I*°. Those contexts where impersonal *il* can be omitted must therefore be contexts where, exceptionally, either: (a) D/EPP is checked by pro in SpecIP* (Kayne and Pollock 1978); (b) D/EPP is checked by something other than pro, so SpecIP* isn't needed; or (c) there's no D/EPP feature to check. Lahousse's analysis of genuine SI suggests that (b) is the right answer: D/EPP is checked by the SI-triggering phrase in SpecCP*, and SpecIP* isn't therefore licensed. The absence of SpecIP* means that in the (a) examples above, the DP* subject fails to raise to SpecIP*, while in the (b) examples, impersonal *il* isn't required.[89]

Lahousse (Forthcoming) contrasts genuine SI (§5.7.2) with focus SI in respect of the pragmatic status of the inverted subject: while the subject in genuine SI is a new-information focus, the subject in focus SI is an exhaustive focus. This pragmatic contrast has a knock-on effect for the syntax (Kayne and Pollock 2001): while the subject in genuine SI stays low (remaining in SpecθP within VP* or else raising only as far as the left-VP*-peripheral SpecFocusP position) and doesn't reach SpecIP*, the subject in focus SI occupies a high position, raising first to SpecIP* (to check D/EPP), and then to the specifier of Rizzi's (1997) CP*-internal FocusP (§5.4). The reason why the subject looks like it's been inverted is that the remnant IP* – the aboutness topic of the clause – subsequently raises to the specifier of Rizzi's TopicP. This is illustrated in (234):

(234)   Focus SI (after Lahousse Forthcoming):
         (verb raising to I*°; subject raising to SpecIP*)
    a.   ... [$_{IP*}$ [exhaustive-focus subject] [$_{I*°}$ verb] ...]
         (movement of exhaustive-focus subject to SpecFocusP)
    b.   ... [$_{FocP}$ [exhaustive-focus subject] Foc° [$_{IP*}$ t$_{subject}$ [$_{I*°}$ verb] ...]]
         (movement of remnant IP* to SpecTopicP)
    c.   ... [$_{TopP}$ [$_{IP*}$ t$_{sub}$ [$_{I*°}$ verb] ...] Top° [$_{FocP}$ [exhaustive-focus subject] Foc° t$_{IP*}$]]

Lahousse's (Forthcoming) distinction between genuine SI and focus SI explains a number of empirical contrasts, two of which I mention here. First, while the subject DP* in focus SI must be clause final, as shown in (235), in genuine SI it can be followed by verbal dependants, as in (236):

(235) a. *Seuls passeront Jean et Pierre <u>sous la fenêtre</u>.   (focus SI)
          alone will.walk J. and P. under the window

      b. Seuls passeront <u>sous la fenêtre</u> Jean et Pierre.
          alone will.walk under the window J. and P.
          'J. and P. alone will walk under the window.'

(236) a. Quand passeront Jean et Pierre <u>sous la fenêtre</u>?   (genuine SI)
          when will.walk J. and P. under the window
          'When will J. and P. walk under the window?'

      b. *Quand passeront <u>sous la fenêtre</u> Jean et Pierre?
          when will.walk under the window J. and P.

This follows from the analysis of the two kinds of SI: since in genuine SI in (236a)

---

[89] Where there *are* licensing differences between genuine SI and impersonal-*il* omission (additional constraints on the former which don't apply to the latter; Lahousse 2003b: chs. 5–7), these can be attributed to a morphosyntactic property of SI proper which is absent from impersonal-*il* omission, namely, that subject–verb agreement is conditioned by raising (the φ features of) the postverbal DP* subject.

the verb alone leaves VP*, VP*-internal dependants follow the subject;[90] since focus SI in (235b) involves remnant-IP* fronting following subject raising to CP*-internal SpecFocusP, all clause-internal constituents precede the subject.

Second, quantifier float (QF; §4.3.1) is possible in focus SI but not in genuine SI, as shown in (237):

(237) a. Ont <u>tous</u> réussi ceux qui ont assez travaillé.   (focus SI)
           have all succeeded those who have enough worked
           'Those who did enough work were successful.'

      b. *Quand ont <u>tous</u> fini les enfants?   (genuine SI)
           when have all finished the children

This follows from: (a) the analysis of QF in §4.3.1 whereby floated *tout* needs to bind the trace of a raised subject; and (b) the subject-movement–subject-non-movement contrast in the analysis of the two kinds of SI. The subject in focus SI in (237a) raises through IP* to the left IP* periphery, satisfying the licensing requirements of QF; the subject in genuine SI in (237b) raises only as far as the VP* periphery (if indeed it raises at all), thus failing to satisfy the licensing requirements of QF.

5.7.3   Subject–verb inversion: summary

Summarising the discussion of inversion in ModF, the following observations can be made. PI has (almost) the same distribution as CI; the two kinds of inversion are identical in terms of trigger and structure. They differ with respect to the phonology of SpecIP*, overt in CI, covert (pro) in PI, as in (238):

        PI/CI
(238) Op
       Quand   les enfants   vont-ils partir
       Peut-être   pro
       Op/when/maybe the children/pro go-they leave
       '(When) will the children/they leave?'/'Maybe the children/they will leave.'

PI/CI are triggered by a [Q] feature on I*° and its need to be checked by a phrase in SpecCP*, which can be a non-overt yes–no operator Op, an overt wh phrase or

---

[90] In fact, there is a hierarchy determining which, if any, dependants may follow the subject in genuine SI. The hierarchy essentially reduces to 'closeness to the verb' (a notion as yet admittedly only inadequately defined): a dependant of the verb may follow the subject in genuine SI if and only if it's 'less close' to the verb than the CP*-internal SI-triggering phrase. Thus, (ia) is grammatical, while (ib) is ungrammatical, because the indirect object is less close to the verb than the direct object (data from Korzen 1983: 80, cited in Lahousse Forthcoming):

(i)   a. [DO Que] dira [SUB P.] [IO à M.]?   b. *[IO A qui] dira [SUB P.] [DO la vérité]?
           what will.say P. to M.   to whom will.say P. the truth
           'What will P. say to M.?'

a member of the *peut-être* class of adverbial. In English subject–auxiliary inversion [Q] raises to C*° and can be checked within a local spec–head configuration; in Romance [Q] and the finite verb remain in I*° and [Q] is checked long distance. Given the biuniqueness condition on checking, long-distance checking between I*° and SpecCP* prevents I*° from licensing SpecIP*. However, the [Q] feature licenses an affixal agreement marker on I*° (the apparently inverted subject proform), thereby re-endowing I*° with the ability to license SpecIP*. SpecIP* can thus host a lexical DP* subject, giving CI. The φ-feature content of the affixal agreement marker can identify the φ features of SpecIP* and SpecIP* can therefore host pro, instead, giving PI. As for SI, we followed Lahousse in distinguishing between genuine SI and focus SI. Only the former is related to PI/CI in being licensed by the need to check a feature against a fronted phrase.

One context where inversion isn't found is subordinate yes–no interrogatives, as shown in (239):

(239) a. *Je sais (Jean) est-il venu.   b. *Je sais est venu Jean.
         I know J. is he come   I know is come J.

This is expected: subordinate yes–no interrogatives contain neither a fronted left-peripheral phrase nor [Q] on I*°. Rather, they are characterised by [Q] on C*° which, in ModF, is realised as *si* and checked by a non-overt yes–no operator merged directly in SpecCP*, as in (240):

(240) Je sais [$_{CP*}$ Op si [$_{IP*}$ Jean est venu]].
       I know if J. is come
       'I know whether J. came.'

In our discussion of wh fronting (§5.6.1) we saw that ConF isn't characterised by inversion and that those contexts which trigger/license inversion in ModF are uninverted in ConF. PI/CI in ModF is triggered by [Q] on I*°. The absence of PI/CI in ConF suggests that [Q] doesn't appear on I*° in ConF, but on C*° instead (the feature is deemed still to be present since it triggers wh fronting). The reason why we never find inversion without wh fronting is thus that, for it to possible, [Q] would simultaneously have to be present on I*° *and* absent altogether, which is logically impossible.

(241)

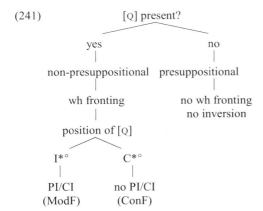

5.8   Residual questions

In this final section I return to a number of issues held over from earlier discussion, namely, *que–qui* alternation (§5.8.1), past-participle agreement (§5.8.2) and the syntax of *que* and *quoi* (§5.8.3).

5.8.1   Que–qui *alternation: masquerade*

Consider the contrast between (242a, b):

(242) a. [$_{IP*}$ Tu dis [$_{CP*}$ que [$_{IP*}$ Jean part]]]
            you say *que* J. leaves
            'You say that J. is leaving.'

       b. [$_{CP*}$ Quel gars [$_{IP*}$ tu dis [$_{CP*}$ qui [$_{IP*}$ – part]]]]?
            which boy you say *qui* leaves
            'Which boy do you say is leaving?'

In (242a) the subject of the subordinate clause remains in SpecIP*; in (242b) it fronts to CP*. In (242a) the subordinate clause is introduced by the complementiser *que*, in (242b), by *qui*. Second, consider the subject and object relatives in (243a, b) as well as the free relatives in (244a, b):

(243) a. la femme [$_{CP*}$ Op que [$_{IP*}$ Jean veut épouser –]]
            the woman *que* J. wants marry
            'the woman J. wants to marry'

       b. la femme [$_{CP*}$ Op qui [$_{IP*}$ – veut épouser Jean]]
            the woman *qui* wants marry J.
            'the woman who wants to marry J.'

(244) a. ce [$_{CP*}$ Op que [$_{IP*}$ je veux faire –]]   b. ce [$_{CP*}$ Op qui [$_{IP*}$ – me fait peur]]
            that *que* I want do   that *qui* me makes fear
            'what I want to do'   'what scares me'

Here, too, there's a correlation between objects and *que*, and subjects and *qui*, suggesting that masque*rade* has taken place in (243b)/(244b): a non-overt wh relative proform (Op) necessarily fronts from SpecIP* to SpecCP*. Thus, instead of treating *que* and *qui* here as relative proforms (the analysis rejected in §5.6.1), they're actually complementisers, and the relative proforms are non-overt. Third, consider the subject and object clefts in (245) (§5.5):

(245) a. C'est Luc [$_{CP*}$ Op <u>que</u> [$_{IP*}$ j'ai vu –]]   b. C'est Luc [$_{CP*}$ Op <u>qui</u> [$_{IP*}$ – vient]]
　　　 that-is L. that I-have seen   　　　 that-is L. that comes
　　　 'It's L. that I saw.'   　　　 'It's L. who's coming.'

Once again, the object patterns with *que*, the subject, with *qui*.

The standard analysis within generative syntax (Rizzi 1990; Pesetsky 1982) is that *qui* is an allomorph of the complementiser *que*, and that the *qui* allomorph is triggered by wh fronting of the subject from a following SpecIP* position:[91]

(246) a. 　　　 ... [$_{C*'}$ que [$_{IP*}$ subject ...
　　　 b. [$_{CP*}$ wh-XP$_i$ [$_{C*'}$ qui$_i$ [$_{IP*}$ t$_i$ ...

It's suggested that wh fronting of the subject from SpecIP* to SpecCP* creates a spec–head agreement configuration between the wh phrase and the complementiser and that *qui* is therefore *que* + agreement.

Taraldsen (2001: 164) questions the validity of this analysis by observing that, for an apparently agreeing form, *qui* doesn't have much in the way of agreement morphology (in comparison, say, with agreeing complementisers in West Flemish). On the basis of comparison with parallel data in Vallader (Rhaeto-Romance) and some Germanic varieties, Taraldsen concludes that *qui* is in fact a portmanteau of *que* followed by an expletive *i* element in subject position,[92] rather than a complementiser following by the trace of a fronted wh phrase. On such an approach the fronted wh subject has moved from a lower position; (246b) is thus modified as (246b'):

(246) b'. [$_{CP*}$ wh-XP$_i$ [$_{C*'}$ que [$_{IP*}$ i ... t$_i$ ...

5.8.2   *Past-participle agreement*

Compound verb paradigms comprise a perfective auxiliary (*avoir* 'to have', *être* 'to be'; §2.2.2.6) and a following past participle (see Table 2.3 on page 26 in §2.2.1.2). Ordinarily, the past participle of *avoir*-taking verbs is invariant:

(247) a. Jeanne a <u>ri</u>.   b. Jeanne a <u>écrit</u> les lettres.
　　　 J. has laughed   　　　 J. has written the letters
　　　 'J. laughed.'   　　　 'J. wrote the letters.'

---

[91] See also the *that*–trace filter in English: *that* – → ∅:
(i)　 a. *Who do you think that – will leave?   b. Who do you think ∅ – will leave?
[92] A potential problem with Taraldsen's (2001) analysis is that, as *que* + *i*, *qui* isn't actually a constituent! See Rooryck (2000b) for a similar suggestion.

However, in a number of contexts, past participles show agreement, namely, *être*-taking intransitives (248a) (§2.2.2.6), passives (248b) (§2.2.3.1), cliticised direct objects (248c) (§4.4.1), wh-fronted direct objects (248d, e) (§5.6.1):

(248) a. Les femmes sont mort<u>es</u>.
the women are dead
'The women died.'

b. Les maisons ont été repeint<u>es</u>.
the houses have been repainted
'The houses were repainted.

c. Les maisons, je les ai repeint<u>es</u>.
the houses I them have repainted
'I repainted the houses.'

d. Quelles maisons avez-vous repeint<u>es</u>?
which houses have-you repainted
'Which houses did you repaint?'

e. les maisons que vous avez repeint<u>es</u>
the house that you have repainted
'the houses you repainted'

On the basis of (248) past-participle agreement (henceforth, PPA) appears to be triggered by direct objects, more specifically, preposed direct objects: in (248c) the non-overt direct object fronts to SpecCliticP, licensing *les*; in (248d) the direct object undergoes wh fronting; in (248e) the non-overt relative proform, Op, also undergoes wh fronting. The traditional generative approach (Kayne 1989) to PPA has been to assume that it's triggered by the overt movement of the direct object to some preverbal position via the specifier of a dedicated IP*-internal FP hosting PPA morphology, say, Agr(eement)P(a)stP(a)rt(iciple)P(hrase). Such an approach is clearly motivated in (248c–e).

Less straightforward are (248a, b) where the PPA-triggering DP*s are subjects. However, the subject in the passive sentence in (248b) would be a direct object in the corresponding active sentence. It makes sense to link PPA in (248a) to auxiliary selection, discussed in §2.2.2.6, where it's suggested that *être* selection is semantically triggered: *être* is selected if the subject is a Theme. Thus, PPA is actually PPA *with a Theme*.

The significance to PPA of overt movement of the direct object through SpecAgrPstPrtP (rather than fronting per se) is that it accounts for contrasts like the one in (249a, b):

(249) a. les voitures [$_{CP*}$ Op qu' [$_{IP*}$ il a – conduit<u>es</u> –]]
the cars that-he has driven.F.PL
'the cars he drove'

b. les voitures [$_{CP1*}$ Op qu' [$_{IP1*}$ il a dit(*<u>es</u>) [$_{CP2*}$ – qu' [$_{IP2*}$ il a – conduit<u>es</u> –]]]]
the cars that-he has said(.F.PL) that-he has driven.F.PL
'the cars he said he drove'

In (249a) the non-overt direct-object relative proform (Op) passes through SpecAgrPstPrtP on its way to SpecCP*, and therefore triggers PPA. In (249b) while the same thing happens within CP2*, triggering PPA on *conduites*, the unbounded nature of the wh fronting involved in relativisation means that Op raises directly from SpecCP2* to SpecCP1*, bypassing SpecAgrPstPrtP in IP1*, and failing to trigger PPA on *dit*.

The importance of the notion that the *entire* direct object undergoes fronting is illustrated in (250):

(250) J'en$_2$ ai bu.
I-of-it have drunk
'I drank some.'

Here, the direct object apparently surfaces as the clitic *en$_2$*, crucially without triggering PPA, even if *en$_2$* is interpreted as a pronominalised form of, say, the PL DP* *des verres* 'glasses'. Recall that *en$_2$* pronominalises a *sub*part of an indefinite DP*, rather than an entire DP*, as in (251):

(251) J'en$_2$ ai bu [$_{DP*}$ trois –].
I-of-it have drunk three
'I drank three (of them).'

Transferring the structure in (251) to (250), therefore, the *entire* direct object in (250) has arguably *not* undergone fronting; only a subpart of it has, the subpart which is pronominalised as *en$_2$*:

(252) J'en$_2$ ai bu [$_{DP*}$ ⊘ –].   (= (250))

Crucially, it's because the entire direct object hasn't fronted that PPA doesn't take place.[93]

PPA is also found in the context of (some) PMC verbs discussed in §5.2.3, as in (253):

(253) a. La femme, Jean l'a emmenée/vue/laissée faire ses courses.
the woman J. her-has led/seen/let do her shopping
'J. led/saw/let the woman (to) do her shopping.'

b. Quelle femme a-t-il emmenée/vue/laissée faire ses courses?
which woman has-he led/seen/let do her shopping
'Which woman did he lead/see/let (to) do her shopping.'

The existence of PPA with these PMC verbs is in line with the biclausal ECM analysis proposed in §5.2.3.

In comparison with subject–finite-verb agreement (§2.2.1.1), PPA is very unstable. It arose during the EModF period due to influence from Italian, where it's marked with rich morphology. In French, for the largest inflectional category of verb, those like *regarder* 'to watch' with infinitives ending in *-er*, PPA is an exclusively orthographic phenomenon, unmarked phonologically: *regardé(e)(s)* [ʁəgaʁde] 'watched(.F)(.PL)'.[94] PPA surfaces orally with a small set of irregular verbs, only, for example *dire* 'to say', and even here it's gender, and not number, agreement that's marked: *dit(s)* [di] ~ *dite(s)* [dit] 'said'. However, even in the

---

[93] A recent orthographic 'tolerance' does now allow *en$_2$* to trigger PPA.
[94] Note, though, that in some Eastern varieties, M past participles are phonetically distinguished from F past participles in terms of final-syllable length.

context of those irregular verbs whose past participles potentially show PPA in gender orally, the standard pattern of PPA is poorly respected in speech and writing (Goosse 2000: 126), with speakers/writers often failing to mark PPA where the standard language requires it. Belletti (2001c) suggests that optional PPA may point to movement through SpecPstPrtP being optional. An alternative approach would be to distinguish between ModF (with PPA) and ConF (without PPA) on the basis of the featural make-up of definite DP*s or the PstPrt head. Such an approach won't account for the obverse of PPA not happening where it 'should', namely, PPA happening where it 'shouldn't', illustrated in (254), where the standard language doesn't require PPA because the reflexive clitic *se* is an *indirect* object rather than a direct object:

(254) a. $le chapeau que Lucienne s'est faite   b. $Ils se sont succédés.
      le hat that L. self-is made.F.SG   they.M.PL self are succeeded
      'the hat L. made for herself'   'They succeeded one another.'

Such cases could be treated as hypercorrection.

5.8.3   *The syntax of* que *and* quoi

Finally, I return to an issue held over from §§3.4, 4.4.1 and 5.6, namely, the specifics of the syntax of 'what' (and how it contrasts with that of 'who'). There's just one word for 'who': *qui*, which behaves like a regular wh phrase, as shown in column 1 in (255); it can undergo wh fronting or remain in situ; it can function as a direct object (255a–i), within an inherent-case-marked DP* (255j–r), and as a subject (255s–y). In contrast, there are two words for 'what': *quoi* and *que*, as shown in columns 2 and 3 in (255):

(255)	1. QUI	2. QUOI	3. QUE/QU'
a.	Jean voit qui?	Jean voit quoi?	*Jean voit que?
	J. sees who	J. sees what	J. sees what
b.	Qui il voit?	*Quoi il voit?	*Qu'il voit?
	who he sees	what he sees	what-he sees
c.	Qui voit-il?	*Quoi voit-il?	Que voit-il?
	who sees-he	what sees-he	what sees he
d.	Qui Jean voit-il?	*Quoi Jean voit-il?	*Que Jean voit-il?
	who J. sees-he	what J. sees-he	what J. sees-he
e.	Qui voit Jean?	*Quoi voit Jean?	Que voit Jean?
	who sees J.	what sees J.	what sees J.
f.	Je sais qui Jean voit.	*Je sais quoi Jean voit.	*Je sais que Jean voit.
	I know who J. sees	I know what J. sees	I know what J. sees
g.	Je sais qui voit Jean.	*Je sais quoi voit Jean.	*Je sais que voit Jean.
	I know who sees J.	I know what sees J.	I know what sees J.
h.	Voir qui?	Voir quoi?	*Voir que?
	see who	see what	see what

i. Qui voir?   Quoi voir?   Que voir?
    who see   what see   what see

j. Jean parle de qui?   Jean parle de quoi?   *Jean parle de que?
    J. speaks of who   J. speaks of what   J. speaks of what

k. De qui il parle?   De quoi il parle?   *De qu'il parle?
    of who he speaks   of what he speaks   of what-he speaks

l. De qui parle-t-il?   De quoi parle-t-il?   *De que parle-t-il?
    of who speaks-he   of what speaks-he   of what speaks-he

m. De qui Jean parle-t-il?   De quoi Jean parle-t-il?   *De que Jean parle-t-il?
    of who J. speaks-he   of what J. speaks-he   of what J. speaks-he

n. De qui parle Jean?   De quoi parle Jean?   *De que parle Jean?
    of who speaks J.   of what speaks J.   of what speaks J.

o. Je sais de qui Jean parle. Je sais de quoi Jean parle. *Je sais de que Jean parle.
    I know of who J. speaks   I know of what J. speaks   I knos of what J. speaks

p. Je sais de qui parle Jean. Je sais de quoi parle Jean. *Je sais de que parle Jean.
    I know of who speaks J.   I know of what speaks J.   I know of what speaks J.

q. Parler de qui?   Parler de quoi?   *Parler de que?
    speak of who   speak of what   speak of what

r. De qui parler?   De quoi parler?   *De que parler?
    of who speak   of what speak   of what speak

s. Qui pue?   *Quoi pue?   *Que pue?
    who stinks   what stinks   what stinks

t. Je sais qui pue.   *Je sais quoi pue.   *Je sais que pue.
    I know who stinks   I know what stinks   I know what stinks

u. Jean dit que qui pue?   *Jean dit que quoi pue?   *Jean dit que que pue?
    J. says that who stinks   J. says that what stinks   J. says that what stinks

v. Qui il dit qui pue?   *Quoi il dit qui pue?   *Qu'il dit qui pue?
    who he says that stinks   what he says that stinks   what-he says that stinks

w. Qui dit-il qui pue?   *Quoi dit-il qui pue?   Que dit-il qui pue?
    who says-he that stinks   what says-he that stinks   what says-he that stinks

x. Qui Jean dit-il qui pue?   *Quoi Jean dit-il qui pue?   *Que Jean dit-il qui pue?
    who J. says-he that   what J. says-he that stinks what J. says-he that stinks
    stinks

y. Je sais qui il dit qui pue. *Je sais quoi il dit qui pue. *Je sais qu'il dit qui pue.
    I know who he says that   I know what he says that   I know what-he says that
    stinks   stinks   stinks

Typically, each *who*-context in column 1 containing *qui* has one grammatical *what*-counterpart in column 2 containing *quoi* or column 3 containing *que* (but see footnote 95). Realisation of direct-object 'what' is sensitive to two factors: wh fronting and position with respect to the verb. Direct-object 'what' is realised as *quoi* if it stays in situ (255a, h) (§5.6.2); bare *quoi* is incompatible with wh fronting (§5.6.1).[95] Instead, fronted direct-object 'what' is realised as *que*, but only provided

---

[95] In fact, there is one exception to this, namely (255i), where direct-object *quoi* precedes the infinitive. Given the otherwise robust nature of the generalisation it's tempting to conclude

it immediately precedes the verb, as in (255c, e), where PI and SI have taken place, and in the infinitival in (255i). If fronted direct-object 'what' *doesn't* immediately precede the verb, as in (255b, d), where CI has taken place, or there's no inversion at all, 'what' isn't realised as *que*.[96] The realisation conditions of direct-object 'what' are such that some of the contexts in column 1 in (255) containing direct-object *qui* have no grammatical counterpart in columns 2/3 containing *quoi/que*. These are (255b, d, f, g), italicised in columns 2/3. Inherent-case-marked 'what' is realised as *quoi* throughout; *que* is systematically excluded, as in (255j–r), irrespective of whether wh fronting or inversion has taken place.

Before we turn to subject 'what', note that the above pattern can be understood by assuming that *quoi/que* share syntactic – as well as obvious morphological – properties with *moi/me*, *toi/te*, *soi/se*, which are pairs of corresponding non-clitic– clitic proforms (§§3.8, 4.4.1): *moi/toi/soi* are non-clitics; *me/te/se* are clitics. Non-clitics are compatible with independent stress and overt inherent-case marking; clitics are not. The distribution of *quoi/que*[97] suggests that they are non-clitic and clitic, respectively: *quoi* appears within an inherent-case-marked DP* or as a non-fronted direct object (that is, in a position where it can bear stress); *que* is a fronted direct object, necessarily cliticising onto a verb (that is, in a position where it can't bear stress).

Note further that neither *moi* nor *me*, etc., is compatible with the canonical subject position, as shown in (256b, c):

that the pre-infinitival position of *quoi* is due, not to full wh fronting, but to the fact that the verb, as an infinitive, doesn't need to raise as high as a finite verb.

[96] Note that *que* is ungrammatical in both subordinate contexts in (255f, g). Ungrammaticality is expected in (255f), since *que* doesn't immediately precede the verb, but not (255g), where it does, thanks to SI. Indeed, (255g) contrasts minimally with (255e). Of course, the interrogative is matrix in (255e) but subordinate in (255g). Recall from §5.6.1.1 that matrix and subordinate non-subject wh interrogatives differ with respect to the landing site of wh movement: SpecFocusP in matrix contexts, like (255e), SpecForceP in subordinate contexts, like (255g). It makes sense to explain the contrast between (255e, g) on this basis: although fronted *que* in (255e, g) is indeed immediately preverbal in terms of linear order, its position in SpecFocusP in (255e) means that it's close enough to the verb, while its position in SpecForceP in (255g) means that it's too far away from the finite verb. I return to this below.

In column 3 of (255d), the subject DP* *Jean* intervenes between fronted *que* and the verb, hence the ungrammaticality. Strangely, where the intervening subject DP* is *ceci* 'this' or *cela* 'that', the problem disappears (Plunkett 2000: 513), as in (i):

(i)   Que cela/ceci veut-il dire?
       what that/this wants-it say
       'What does that/this mean?'

[97] Note that, like pronominal clitics, *que* cannot be co-ordinated: **que ou qui* 'who or what'; cf. *qui ou quoi* (Plunkett 2000: 513).

(256) a. Je suis fatigué.   b. *Me suis fatigué.   c. *Moi suis fatigué.
       I am tired   me is tired   me is tired
       'I'm tired.'

Instead, a member of a distinct set of subject proforms is used (§4.4.4), as in (256a). The relevance of the parallel between *quoi/que* and *moi/me*, etc., is that, if the former share relevant properties with the latter, then we expect them, too, to be incompatible with the canonical subject position (unlike *qui*). And this is indeed what we find, as shown in (255s–y).[98] With *moi/me*, etc., inability to occupy the canonical subject position isn't problematical because a set of subject proforms is available, as in (256a). In contrast, *quoi/que* have no corresponding subject form,[99] and an alternative structure altogether is needed to ask, for example, 'What stinks?'. Further, the alternative strategy used to ask such questions is exactly what we might expect. Here's a thought experiment: Imagine that French subject proforms didn't exist. How might a French speaker say 'I'm tired'? *Je suis fatigué*, as in (256a), isn't a possibility because the proform doesn't exist. As we saw in (256b, c), neither are *Moi suis fatigué* and *Me suis fatigué* (the proforms are incompatible with SpecIP*). In the absence of a subject proform, the only way to say 'I'm tired' is to use a structure which allows *me* or *moi* to appear in a position other than the canonical subject position. Such a structure is a cleft (§5.5):

(257) C'est moi [qui – suis fatigué].
      it-is me that is tired
      'I'm the one who's tired.'/'I'm tired.'

Here, the 1SG focus, underlined in (257), is the dependant of the copula *être*, and therefore realised as non-clitic *moi*. Exactly this clefting strategy provides a way of asking 'What stinks?'. One grammatical alternative to the ungrammatical *Quoi/Que pue?* is the cleft in (258a), while a second, in (258b), is derived from (258a) via wh fronting (§5.6.1) and PI (§5.7):

(258) a. C'est quoi [Op qui – pue]?   b. Qu'est-ce – [Op qui – pue]?
         it-is what that stinks   what-is-it that stinks
         'What stinks?'   = (258a)

---

[98] The syntax of *que diable* 'what the hell' warrants special comment. It's unlike regular *que* in at least two respects. First, unlike simple *que*, *que diable* is compatible with CI:
(i) a. *Que Pierre a-t-il fait?   b. Que diable Pierre a-t-il fait?
        what P. has-he done   what devil P. has-he done
        'What did P. do?'   'What the hell did P. do?'
Second, unlike simple *que*, *que diable* can appear in subject position:
(ii) a. *Qu'a pu le motiver?   b. Que diable a pu le motiver?
        what-has been-able him motivate   what devil has been-able him motivate
        'What could have motivated him?'   'What the hell could have motivated him?'
[99] This begs the question, of course, of why no such proform exists. I leave this issue on the research agenda.

The pattern illustrated in (258a, b) with subject 'what' has been generalised to subject 'who' and direct-obect 'who'/'what', giving the full paradigm in (259a–d):

(259) a. C'est quoi qui pue? → Qu'est-ce qui pue?   (subject 'what')
          it-is what that stinks   what-is-it that stinks

      b. C'est qui qui pue? →   Qui est-ce qui pue?   (subject 'who')
          it-is who that stinks   who is-it that stinks

      c. C'est quoi qu'il voit? → Qu'est-ce qu'il voit?   (direct-object 'what')
          it-is what that-he sees   what-is-it that-he sees

      d. C'est qui qu'il voit? → Qui est-ce qu'il voit?   (direct-object 'who')
          it-is who that-he sees   who is-it that-he sees

While (259a) gives the only ways of expressing a matrix subject 'what' interrogative (cf. columns 2 and 3 in (255s)), those clefts in (259b–d) are alternatives to non-cleft forms in column 1 in (255s), as well as (255c).

As for subordinate direct-object and subject 'what' interrogatives, we again find that neither *quoi* nor *que* can be used, as in (255f, g, t). With subject 'what' this is expected: *quoi/que* are non-subject forms. With object 'what' *quoi* is ruled out because *quoi* is incompatible with wh fronting, and *que* is ruled out since, although it can undergo wh fronting, the unavailability of PI or SI in subordinate interrogatives (see Table 5.2 on page 201) means that it doesn't have a verb to cliticise onto. Instead, what is found in subordinate subject/direct-object 'what' interrogatives is a free relative (§5.6.1):

(260) a. Je sais [ce que Jean voit].   b. Je sais [ce qui pue].
          I know that that J. sees   I know that that stinks
          'I know what J. can see.'   'I know what stinks.'

References

Abeillé, Anne and Danièle Godard. n.d. 'Les prédicats complexes dans les langues romanes.' Ms. Paris 7 and CNRS.

Abeillé, Anne, Danièle Godard and Philip Miller. 1997. 'Les causatives en français: un cas de compétition syntaxique' *Langue française* 115: 62–74.

Abeillé, Anne, Olivier Bonami, Danièle Godard and Jesse Tseng. 2004. 'The syntax of French *à* and *de*: an HPSG analysis' in Saint-Dizier (ed.), 133–44.

Abney, Steven. 1987. *The English noun phrase in its sentential aspect*. Doctoral dissertation. MIT.

Abouda, Lotfi. 2002. 'Négation, interrogation et alternance indicatif–subjonctif' *Journal of French Language Studies* 12, 1–22.

Alexiadou, Artemis and Chris Wilder (eds.). 1998. *Possessors, predicates and movement in the determiner phrase*. Amsterdam: Benjamins.

Alexiadou, Artemis, Martin Everaert and Elena Anagnostopoulou (eds.). 2004. *The unaccusativity puzzle*. Oxford University Press.

Antoine, Gérald and Bernard Cerquiglini (eds.). 2000. *Histoire de la langue française 1945–2000*. Paris: CNRS.

Armstrong, Nigel. 2001. *Social and stylistic variation in spoken French: a comparative approach*. Amsterdam: Benjamins.

Armstrong, Nigel and Alan Smith. 2002. 'The influence of linguistic and social factors on the recent decline of French *ne*' *Journal of French Language Studies* 12, 23–41.

Ashby, William. 1976. 'The loss of the negative morpheme *ne* in Parisian French' *Lingua* 39, 119–37.

1981. 'The loss of the negative particle *ne* in French: a syntactic change in progress' *Language* 57, 674–87.

1982. 'The drift of French syntax' *Lingua* 57, 29–46.

1988. 'The syntax, pragmatics and sociolinguistics of left- and right-dislocations in French' *Lingua* 75, 203–29.

1991. 'When does linguistic change indicate change in progress?' *Journal of French Language Studies* 1, 1–19.

1994. 'An acoustic profile of right-dislocation in French' *Journal of French Language Studies* 4, 127–45.

2001. 'Un nouveau regard sur la chute du *ne* en français parlé tourangeau: s'agit-il d'un changement en cours?' *Journal of French Language Studies* 11, 1–22.

Attal, Pierre (ed.). 1992. *La négation*. Actes du colloque de Paris X–Nanterre, 12–14 novembre 1992, numéro spécial de LINX 29.

Auger, Julie. 1993. 'Syntax, semantics and *ça*: on genericity in colloquial French' *Penn Review of Linguistics* 17, 1–12.

1994. *Pronominal clitics in Québec colloquial French: a morphological analysis*. Doctoral dissertation. University of Pennsylvania.

234

2003a. 'Les pronoms clitiques sujets en picard: une analyse au confluent de la phonologie, de la morphologie et de la syntaxe' *Journal of French Language Studies* 13, 1–22.

2003b. 'Le redoublement des sujets en picard' *Journal of French Language Studies* 13, 381–404.

Ayres-Bennett, Wendy. 2004. *Sociolinguistic variation in seventeenth-century French: methodology and case studies*. Cambridge University Press.

Ayres-Bennett, Wendy and Janice Carruthers, with Rosalind Temple. 2001. *Problems and perspectives: studies in the modern French language*. London: Longman.

Bach, Emmon and Robert Harms (eds.). 1968. *Universals in linguistic theory*. New York: Holt, Rinehart & Winston.

Bailard, Joëlle. 1981. 'A functional approach to subject inversion' *Studies in Language* 5, 1–29.

Baker, Mark. 1985. 'The mirror principle and morphosyntactic explanation' *Linguistic Inquiry* 16, 373–415.

1988. *Incorporation: a theory of grammatical function changing*. University of Chicago Press.

2003. *Lexical categories: verbs, nouns and adjectives*. Cambridge University Press.

Baker, Mark, Kyle Johnson and Ian Roberts. 1989. 'Passive arguments raised' *Linguistic Inquiry* 20, 219–51.

Baltin, Mark and Chris Collins (eds.). 2001. *The handbook of contemporary syntactic theory*. Oxford: Blackwell.

Barbosa, Pilar. 2001. 'On inversion in wh questions in Romance' in Hulk and Pollock (eds.), 20–59.

Baschung, Karine and Marianne Desmets. 2000. 'On the phrasal vs. clausal syntactic status of French infinitives: causative constructions and subject inversion' *Journal of French Language Studies* 10, 205–28.

Batllori, Montse, Maria-Lluïsa Hernanz, Carme Picallo and Francesc Roca (eds.). 2005. *Grammaticalization and parametric variation*. Oxford University Press.

Battye, Adrian, Marie-Anne Hintze and Paul Rowlett. 2000. *The French language today: a linguistic introduction*, 2nd edn. London: Routledge.

Bauche, Henri. 1926. *Le langage populaire*. Paris: Payot.

Beaulieu, Louise and Patricia Balcom. 2002. 'La structure des propositions adverbiales du français: arguments sociolinguistiques' *Journal of French Language Studies* 12, 241–62.

Belletti, Adriana. 1988. 'The case of unaccusatives' *Linguistic Inquiry* 19: 1–34.

2001a. 'Agreement projections' in Baltin and Collins (eds.), 483–510.

2001b. '"Inversion" as focalization' in Hulk and Pollock (eds.), 60–90.

2001c. '(Past-)participle agreement'. Ms. Università di Siena.

2004a. 'Aspects of the low IP area' in Rizzi (ed.), 16–51.

(ed.). 2004b. *Structures and beyond: the cartography of syntactic structures*, vol. 3. Oxford University Press.

Belletti, Adriana and Luigi Rizzi (eds.). 1996. *Parameters and functional heads: essays in comparative syntax*. Oxford University Press.

Benincà, Paola (ed.). 1989. *Dialect variation and the theory of grammar*. Dordrecht: Reidel.

Benincà, Paola and Giampaolo Salvi (eds.). 1998. *Romance syntax: a reader*. Budapest: L. Eötvös University.

Bernstein, Judy. 1991. 'DPs in French and Walloon: evidence for parametric variation in nominal head movement' *Probus* 3, 101–26.

1997. 'Demonstratives and reinforcers in Romance and Germanic languages' *Lingua* 102, 87–113.

2001. 'The DP hypothesis: identifying clausal properties in the nominal domain' in Baltin and Collins (eds.), 536–61.

Bilger, Mireille, Karel van den Eynde and Françoise Gadet (eds.). *Analyse linguistique et approches à l'oral: Recueil d'études offert en hommage à Claire Blanche-Benveniste*. Louvain: Peeters.

Blanche-Benveniste, Claire. 1997. *Approches de la langue parlée française*. Paris: Ophrys.

2003. 'La langue parlée' in Yaguello (ed.), 317–44.

Blanche-Benveniste, Claire, Mireille Bilger, Christine Rouget and Karel van den Eynde, with Piet Mertens. 1991. *Le français parlé: études grammaticales*. Paris: CNRS.

Blinkenberg, Andreas. 1928. *L'Ordre des mots en français moderne*. Copenhagen: Munksgaard.

Blondeau, Hélène. 2004. 'La spécialisation sociolinguistique d'un trait variable du français montréalais: les pronoms toniques du pluriel' in Coveney *et al.* (eds.), 191–213.

Bok-Bennema, Reineke, Bart Hollebrandse, Brigitte Kampers-Manhe and Petra Sleeman (eds.). 2004. *Romance languages and linguistic theory 2002*. Selected papers from Going Romance 2002. Amsterdam: Benjamins.

Bonami, Olivier, Danièle Godard and Jean-Marie Marandin. 1999. 'Constituency and word order in French subject inversion' in Bouma *et al.* (eds.), 21–40.

Bonami, Olivier, Danièle Godard and Brigitte Kampers-Manhe. 2004. 'Adverb classification' in Corblin and de Swart (eds.), 143–84.

Borer, Hagit (ed.). 1986. *The syntax of pronominal clitics*. New York: Academic Press.

2005a. *In name only: structuring sense*, vol. 1. Oxford University Press.

2005b. *The normal course of events: structuring sense*, vol. 2. Oxford University Press.

Boscovic, Zeljko. 1996. 'Selection and the categorial status of infinitival complements' *Natural Language and Linguistic Theory* 14, 269–304.

Bouchard, Denis. 2002. *Adjectives, number and interfaces: why languages vary*. Amsterdam: Elsevier.

2003. 'Les SN sans déterminant en français et en anglais' in Miller and Zribi-Hertz (eds.), 55–95.

Boucher, Paul. n.d. 'Perfect adjective positions in French: a diachronic perspective.' Ms. ALPL Université de Nantes.

2003. 'Determiner phrases in Old and Modern French' in Coene and D'Hulst (eds.), vol. 1, 47–69.

2005. 'Definite reference in Old and Modern French: the rise and fall of DP' in Batllori *et al.* (eds.), 95–108.

Bouma, Gosse, Erhard Hinrichs, Geert-Jan Kruijff and Richard Oehrle (eds.). 1999. *Constraints and resources in natural language syntax and semantics*. Stanford: CSLI.

Bouvier, Yves-Ferdinand. 2000. 'How to passivize French causatives' *Snippets* 2, 6–7.

Brame, Michael. 1982. 'The head-selector theory of lexical specifications and the non-existence of coarse categories' *Linguistic Analysis* 10, 321–5.

Bresnan, Joan. 2001. 'Explaining morphosyntactic competition' in Baltin and Collins (eds.), 11–44.

Brown, Keith (ed.). 2006. *Encyclopaedia of language and linguistics*, 2nd edn. Oxford: Elsevier.

Brugè, Laura. 2002. 'The positions of demonstratives in the extended nominal projection' in Cinque (ed.), 15–53.

Butler, Alastair and Eric Mathieu. 2004. *The syntax and semantics of split constructions: a comparative study*. Basingstoke: Palgrave Macmillan.

Campion, E. 1984. *Left dislocation in Montreal French*. Doctoral dissertation. University of Pennsylvania.

Cardinaletti, Anna. 2004. 'Towards a cartography of subject positions' in Rizzi (2004b) (ed.), 115–65.

Cardinaletti, Anna and Ian Roberts. 2002. 'Clause structure and X-second' in Cinque (ed.), 123–66.

Carruthers, Janice. 1993. *The* formes surcomposés: *the discourse function and linguistic status of a rare form in contemporary spoken French*. Doctoral dissertation. University of Cambridge.

Casagrande, Jean and Bohdan Saciuk (eds.). 1972. *Generative studies in Romance languages*. Rowley, Mass.: Newbury House.

Cecchetto, Carlo. 1999. 'A comparative analysis of left and right dislocation in Romance' *Studia Linguistica* 53, 40–67.

Charaud, Jacques. 2000. 'Les variétés régionales du français' in Antoine and Cerquiglini (eds.), 643–64.

Cheng, Lisa Lai-Shen and Hamida Demirdache (eds.). 1990. *Papers on wh movement.* (MIT Working Papers in Linguistics 13.) Cambridge, Mass.: MIT Press.

Cheng, Lisa Lai-Shen and Johan Rooryck. 2000. 'Licensing wh in situ' *Syntax* 3, 1–19. (www.let.leidenuniv.nl/ulcl/faculty/rooryck/chengroo.pdf)

Chomsky, Noam. 1981. *Lectures on government and binding*. Dordrecht: Foris.
　1991. 'Some notes on economy of derivation and representation' in Freidin (ed.), 417–54.
　1993. 'A minimalist program for linguistic theory' in Hale and Keyser (eds.), 1–52.
　1995a. 'Bare phrase structure' in Webelhuth (ed.), 383–439.
　1995b. *The minimalist program*. Cambridge, Mass.: MIT Press.
　2000. 'Minimalist inquiries: the framework', in Martin *et al.* (eds.), 89–155.
　2001. 'Derivation by phase' in Kenstowicz (ed.), 1–52.
　2005. 'On phases.' Ms. MIT.

Cinque, Guglielmo. 1990. *Types of A' dependencies*. Cambridge, Mass.: MIT Press.
　1994. 'On the evidence for partial N movement in the Romance DP' in Cinque *et al.* (eds.), 85–110.
　1999. *Adverbs and functional heads: a cross-linguistic perspective*. Oxford University Press.
　(ed.). 2002a. *Functional structure in DP and IP: the cartography of syntactic structures*, vol. 1. Oxford University Press.
　2004a. '"Restructuring" and functional structure', in Belletti (ed.), 132–91.
　2004b. 'Issues in adverbial syntax' *Lingua* 114, 683–710.

Cinque, Guglielmo and Richard Kayne (eds.). 2005. *The Oxford handbook of comparative syntax*. Oxford University Press.

Cinque, Guglielmo, Jan Koster, Jean-Yves Pollock, Luigi Rizzi and Raffaella Zanuttini (eds.). 1994. *Paths towards Universal Grammar: studies in honor of Richard S. Kayne*. Washington, DC: Georgetown University Press.

Coene, Martine and Yves D'Hulst. 2003a. 'Introduction: the syntax and semantics of noun phrases: theoretical background' in Coene and D'Hulst (eds.), vol. 1, 1–33.
2003b. 'Introduction' in Coene and D'Hulst (eds.) (2003c), vol. 2, 1–19.
(eds.). 2003c. *From NP to DP* (vol. 1: *The syntax and semantics of noun phrases*; vol. 2: *The expression of possession in noun phrases*). Amsterdam: John Benjamins.
Collins, Chris. 2001. 'Economy conditions in syntax' in Baltin and Collins (eds.), 45–61.
Combettes, Bernard. 1998. *Les constructions détachées en français*. Paris: Ophrys.
Comorovski, Ileana. 2004. '*Quel*' in Corblin and de Swart (eds.), 131–40.
Corblin, Francis and Henriëtte de Swart (eds.). 2004. *Handbook of French semantics*. Stanford: CSLI.
Corblin, Francis, Viviane Déprez, Henriëtte de Swart and Lucia Tovena. 2004. 'Negative concord' in Corblin and de Swart (eds.), 417–52.
Cormack, Annabel. 1995. 'On the treatment of attributive adjectives as adjuncts' *Studia Linguistica* 49, 93–6.
Cornips, Leonie and Aafke Hulk. 1996. 'Ergative reflexives in Heerlen Dutch and French' *Studia Linguistica* 50, 1–21.
Cornulier, Benoît de. 1972. 'A peeking rule in French' *Linguistic Inquiry* 3, 226–7.
Côté, Marie-Hélène. 1999. 'Issues in the analysis and acquisition of clitics in (spoken) French.' Ms. MIT.
Coveney, Aidan. 2002. *Variability in spoken French: a sociolinguistic study of interrogation and negation*, 2nd edn. Bristol: Elm Bank.
2003. 'Le redoublement du sujet en français parlé: une approche variationniste' in Hansen and Mosegaard Hansen (eds.), 111–43.
2004a. 'The alternation between *l'on* and *on* in spoken French' *Journal of French Language Studies* 14, 91–112.
2004b. 'La variation entre *elles* et *ils* en français parlé' in Coveney *et al.* (eds.), 301–29.
Coveney, Aidan, Marie-Anne Hintze and Carol Sanders (eds.). 2004. *Variation et francophonie: mélanges en hommage à Gertrud Aub-Buscher*. Paris: L'Harmattan.
Crisma, Paola. 1993. 'On adjective placement in Romance and Germanic event nominals' *Rivista di Grammatica Generativa* 18, 61–100.
Crysmann, Berthold. 2003. 'Clitic climbing revisited' in Kim and Wechsler (eds.), 67–89.
Cyrille-Thomas, Odile. 2003. *The syntax of fronting in French and Guadeloupe Creole*. Doctoral dissertation. University of Salford.
Davies, William and Stanley Dubinsky. 2004. *The grammar of raising and control: a course in syntactic argumentation*. Oxford: Blackwell.
De Cat, Cécile. 2000. 'Towards a unified theory of French floating quantifiers' *Journal of French Language Studies* 10, 1–25.
2002. *French dislocation*. Doctoral dissertation. University of York.
2004. 'On the impact of French subject clitics on the information structure of the sentence' in Bok-Bennema *et al.* (eds.), 33–46.
Dean Fodor, Janet. 1995. 'Comprehending sentence structure' in Gleitman and Liberman (eds.), 209–46.
Delais-Roussarie, Elisabeth, Jenny Doetjes and Petra Sleeman. 2004. 'Dislocation' in Corblin and de Swart (eds.), 501–28.
Delaveau, Annie and Françoise Kerleroux. 1985. *Problèmes et exercices de syntaxe française*. Paris: Armand Colin.

Déprez, Viviane. 1988. 'Stylistic inversion and verb movement' in Powers and de Jong (eds.), 71–82.
  1990. 'Two ways of moving the verb in French' in Cheng and Demirdache (eds.), 47–85.
Deulofeu, José. 1977. 'La syntaxe et les constructions binaires' *Recherches sur le français parlé* 1, 30–62.
D'Hulst, Yves, Johan Rooryck and Jan Schroten (eds.). 2002. *Going Romance 1999: selected papers*. Amsterdam: Benjamins.
Dikken, Marcel den. 1995. 'Copulas.' Ms. Freie Universiteit Amsterdam.
  1998. 'Predicate inversion in DP' in Alexiadou and Wilder (eds.), 177–214.
Dikken, Marcel den and Pornsiri Singhapreecha. 2004. 'Complex noun phrases and linkers' *Syntax* 7, 1–54.
Dimitrova-Vulchanova, Mila. 2003. 'Modification in the Balkan nominal expression' in Coene and D'Hulst (eds.), vol. 1, 91–118.
Dittmar, N. and B. Schlieben-Lange (eds.). 1982. *La sociolinguistique dans les pays de langue romane*. Tübingen: Narr.
Doetjes, Jenny and Johan Rooryck. 2003. 'Generalizing over quantitative and qualitative constructions' in Coene and D'Hulst (eds.), vol. 1, 277–95.
Doetjes, Jenny, Georges Rebuschi and Anne Rialland. 2004. 'Cleft sentences' in Corblin and de Swart (eds.), 529–52.
Emonds, Joseph. 1978. 'The verbal complex V'–V in French' *Linguistic Inquiry* 9, 151–75.
Engel, Dulcie. 1990. *Tense and text: a study of French past tenses*. London: Routledge.
  1994. 'Plus-que-parfait: past anterior or past punctual?' *Lingvisticae Investigationes* 18, 223–42.
  1996. 'Le passé du passé' *Word* 47, 41–62.
Erteshik-Shir, Nomi. 1997. *The dynamics of focus structure*. Cambridge University Press.
Etiemble, René. 1964. *Parlez-vous franglais?* Paris: Gallimard.
Fillmore, Charles. 1968. 'The case for case' in Bach and Harms (eds.), 1–88.
Forget, Danielle, Paul Hirschbühler, France Martineau and María-Luisa Rivero (eds.). 1997. *Negation and polarity: syntax and semantics*. Amsterdam: Benjamins.
Frei, Henri. 1929. *La grammaire des fautes*. Paris: Geuthner.
Freidin, Robert (ed.). 1991. *Principles and parameters in comparative grammar*. Cambridge, Mass.: MIT Press.
Gadet, Françoise. 1997. *Le français ordinaire*, 2nd edn. Paris: Colin.
  2003. 'La variation: le français dans l'espace social, régional et international' in Yaguello (ed.), 91–152.
Gary-Prieur, Marie-Noëlle. 2001. 'GN démonstratifs à référence générique: une généralité discursive' *Journal of French Language Studies* 11, 221–39.
Georgopoulous, Carol and Roberta Ishihara (eds.). 1991. *Interdisciplinary approaches to language: essays in honor of S. Y. Kuroda*. Dordrecht: Kluwer.
Giorgi, Alessandra and Giuseppi Longobardi. 1991. *The syntax of noun phrases: configuration, parameters and empty categories*. Cambridge University Press.
Giusti, Giuliana. 1997. 'The categorical status of determiners' in Haegeman (ed.) (1997a), 95–123.
Giusti, Giuliana. 2002. 'The functional structure of noun phrases' in Cinque (ed.), 54–90.
Glatigny, Michel. 1967. 'La place des adjectifs épithètes dans deux œuvres de Nerval' *Le Français Moderne* 35, 201–20.

Gleitman, Lila and Mark Liberman (eds.). 1995. *An invitation to cognitive science: language*. General editor: Daniel Osherson. 2nd edn. Vol. 1. Cambridge, MA: MIT Press.

Godard, Danièle. 1986. 'Les déterminants possessifs et les compléments de nom' *Langue Française* 58, 23–35.

Goosse, André. 2000. 'Evolution de la syntaxe' in Antoine and Cerquiglini (eds.), 107–45

Grimshaw, Jane. 1993. 'Minimal projection, heads and optimality.' Ms. Rutgers University.

Guasti, Maria Teresa. 1997. 'Romance causatives' in Haegeman (ed.) (1997a), 124–44.

Guéron, Jacqueline. 2003. 'Inalienable possession and the interpretation of determiners' in Coene and D'Hulst (eds.), vol. 2, 189–220.

Haegeman, Liliane. 1995. *The syntax of negation*. Cambridge University Press.

(ed.). 1997a. *The new comparative grammar*. London: Longman.

(ed.). 1997b. *Elements of grammar: a handbook of generative syntax*. Dordrecht: Kluwer.

2000. 'Inversion, non-adjacent inversion and adjuncts in CP' in Rowlett (ed.), 121–60.

2003. 'La distribution du verbe et du nom en français et en anglais' in Miller and Zribi-Hertz (eds.), 15–51.

Hale, Kenneth and Samuel Keyser (eds.). 1993. *The view from building 20: essays in linguistics in honor of Sylvain Bromberger*. Cambridge, Mass.: MIT Press.

Hansen, Anita Berit and Maj-Brit Mosegaard Hansen (eds.). 2003. *Structures linguistiques et interactionnelles dans le français parlé*. Actes du Colloque international, Université de Copenhague du 22 au 23 juin 2001. Copenhagen: Museum Tusculanum Press.

Harris, Martin. 1978. *The evolution of French syntax: a comparative approach*. London: Longman.

1985. 'Word order in contemporary French: a functional view' *Working Papers in Functional Grammar* 1, 1–16.

Haut conseil de la francophonie. 2005. *La francophonie dans le monde 2004–2005*. Paris: Larousse. (Executive summary: www.francophonie.org/presse/dossiers/sup_20mars_2005.pdf).

Hirschbühler, Paul and Marie Labelle. 1992/93. 'Le statut de (*ne*) *pas* en français contemporain' *Recherches Linguistiques de Vincennes* 22, 31–58.

1994b. 'L'évolution des propositions infinitives négatives en français' in Attal (ed.), 59–90.

Hornstein, Norbert and David Lightfoot (eds.). 1994. *Verb movement*. Cambridge University Press.

Hulk, Aafke. 1996. 'L'«autre» *de*: une tête quantificationnelle?' *Langue Française* 109, 44–59.

Hulk, Aafke and Jean-Yves Pollock (eds.). 2001. *Subject inversion in Romance and the theory of Universal Grammar*. Oxford University Press.

Huot, Hélène. 1986. 'Le subjonctif dans les complétives: subjectivité et modalisation' in Ronat and Couquaux (eds.), 211–46.

Jackendoff, Ray. 1977. *X-bar syntax*. Cambridge, Mass.: MIT Press.

Jeanjean, Colette. 1981. 'L'organisation des formes sujets en français de conversation: étude quantitative et grammaticale de deux corpus' *Recherches sur le Français Parlé* 3, 99–134.

Johnson, Kyle and Ian Roberts (eds.). 1999. *Beyond principles and parameters*. Dordrecht: Kluwer.

Jones, Mari. 2000. 'The subjunctive in Guernsey Norman French' *Journal of French Language Studies* 10, 177–203.

Jones, Michael Allan. 1996. *Foundations of French syntax*. Cambridge University Press.

1999. 'Subject–clitic inversion and inflectional hierarchies' *Journal of French Language Studies* 9, 181–209.

Judge, Anne and Frank Healey. 1983. *A reference grammar of modern French*. London: Arnold.

Kampers-Manhe, Brigitte, Jean-Marie Marandin, Frank Drijkoningen, Jenny Doetjes and Aafke Hulk. 2004. 'Subject NP inversion' in Corblin and de Swart (eds.), 553–79.

Kayne, Richard. 1972. 'Subject inversion in French interrogatives' in Casagrande and Saciuk (eds.), 70–126.

1975. *French syntax: the transformational cycle*. Cambridge, Mass.: MIT Press.

1989. 'Facets of Romance past-participle agreement' in Benincà (ed.), 85–103. Also published in Kayne (2000), 25–39.

1991. 'Romance clitics, verb movement and PRO' *Linguistic Inquiry* 22, 647–86.

1994. *The antisymmetry of syntax*. Cambridge, Mass.: MIT Press.

2000. *Parameters and universals*. Oxford University Press.

2004. 'Prepositions as probes' in Belletti (ed.), 192–212.

Kayne, Richard and Jean-Yves Pollock. 1978. 'Stylistic inversion, successive cyclicity and Move NP in French' *Linguistic Inquiry* 9, 595–622.

2001. 'New thoughts on stylistic inversion' in Hulk and Pollock (eds.), 107–62.

Keenan, Edward and Bernard Comrie. 1977. 'Noun phrase accessibility and universal grammar' *Linguistic Inquiry* 8, 63–99.

Kemenade, Ans van and Nigel Vincent (eds.). 1997. *Parameters of syntactic change*. Cambridge University Press.

Kenstowicz, Michael (ed.). 2001. *Ken Hale: a life in language*. Cambridge, Mass.: MIT Press.

Kim, Jong-Bok and Stephen Wechsler (eds.). 2003. *The proceedings of the 9th international conference on HPSG*. Stanford University.

Klare, Johannes. 1998. *Französische Sprachgeschichte*. Stuttgart: Klett.

Koopman, Hilda and Dominique Sportiche. 1991. 'The position of subjects' *Lingua* 85, 211–58.

Korzen, Hanne. 1983. 'Réflexions sure l'inversion dans les propositions interrogatives en français' *Revue Romane* 24, 50–85.

Kroch, Anthony. 2001. 'Syntactic change' in Baltin and Collins (eds.), 699–729.

Labelle, Marie. 1990. 'Unaccusatives and pseudo-unaccusatives in French' *NELS* 20, 303–17.

1992. 'Change of state and valency' *Journal of Linguistics* 28, 375–414.

Laenzlinger, Christopher. 2000. 'French adjective ordering: perspectives on DP-internal movement types' *Generative Grammar in Geneva* 1, 55–104.

2005. 'French adjective ordering: perspectives on DP-internal movement types' *Lingua* 115, 645–89.

Lagae, Véronique. 1990. 'Les caractéristiques aspectuelles de la construction réflexive ergative' *Travaux de Linguistique* 20, 23–42.

Lahousse, Karen. 2003a. 'La distribution de l'inversion nominale en français dans les principales non interrogatives et les subordonnées circonstancielles' *Lingvisticæ Investigationes* 26, 123–58.

2003b. *The distribution of postverbal nominal subjects in French: a syntactic, semantic and pragmatic analysis.* Doctoral dissertation. University of Louvain and University of Paris 8.

2003c. 'On the non-unitariness of NP subject inversion: a comparison of French NP subject inversion in interrogative and temporal subordinates' in Quer *et al.* (eds.), 177–92.

2003d. 'NP-subject inversion in French and (preposed) adverbs' in Pérez-Leroux and Roberge (eds.), 181–96.

Forthcoming. 'NP-subject inversion in French: two types, two configurations' *Lingua.*

Lamarche, Jacques. 1991. 'Problems for N° movement to NumP' *Probus* 3, 215–36.

Lambrecht, Knud. 1981. *Topic, antitopic and verb agreement in non-standard French.* Amsterdam: Benjamins.

1987. 'On the status of SVO sentences in French discourse' in Tomlin (ed.), vol. 2, 217–61.

Lamiroy, Béatrice. 2003. 'Grammaticalization and external possessor structures in Romance and Germanic languages' in Coene and D'Hulst (eds.), vol. 2, 257–80.

Larson, Richard. 1988. 'On the double object construction' *Linguistic Inquiry* 19, 335–91.

Larsson, E. 1979. *La dislocation en français: étude de syntaxe générative.* Lund: CZK Gleerup.

Le Bidois, Robert. 1952. *L'inversion du sujet dans la prose contemporaine (1900–1950).* Paris: d'Artrey.

Leeman-Bouix, Danielle. 1994. *Les fautes de français existent-elles?* Paris: Seuil.

Levin, Beth and Malka Rappaport Hovav. 2005. *Argument realization.* Cambridge University Press.

Li, Charles (ed.). 1976. *Subject and topic.* New York: Academic Press.

Li, Charles and Sandra Thompson. 1976. 'Subject and topic: a new theory of language' in Li (ed.), 457–89.

Lightfoot, David and Norbert Hornstein (eds.). 1994. *Verb movement.* Cambridge University Press.

Longobardi, Giuseppe. 2001. 'The structure of DPs: some principles, parameters and problems' in Baltin and Collins (eds.), 562–603.

Luraghi, Silvia. 2003. *On the meaning of prepositions and cases: the expression of semantic roles in Ancient Greek.* Amsterdam: Benjamins.

Lyons, Christopher. 1994. *Movement in "NP" and the DP hypothesis. Working Papers in Language and Linguistics* 8. University of Salford European Studies Research Institute (www.esri.salford.ac.uk/publications).

1999. *Definiteness.* Cambridge University Press.

Marandin, Jean-Marie. 2002. 'Unaccusative inversion in French' in D'Hulst *et al.* (eds), 195–222.

Marchello-Nizia, Christiane. 1998a. 'Dislocations en ancien français: thématisation ou rhématisation?' *Cahiers de Praxématique* 30, 161–78.

1998b. 'Dislocations en diachronie: archéologie d'un phénomène du "français oral"' in Bilger *et al.* (eds.), 327–37.

2003. 'Le français dans l'histoire' in Yaguello (ed.), 11–90.

Martin, Robert, David Michaels and Juan Uriagereka (eds.). 2000. *Step by step: essays in minimalist syntax in honor of Howard Lasnik.* Cambridge, Mass.: MIT Press.

Massot, Benjamin. 2003. *Eléments linguistiques pour une vision diglossique du français contemporain.* DEA dissertation. University of Paris 8.

2004. 'L'état de la disparition du S de pluriel en français' Association of French Language Studies conference, Aston University.

Miller, Philip. 1992. *Clitics and constituents in phrase structure grammar*. New York: Garland.

Miller, Philip and Ivan Sag. 1997. 'French clitic movement without clitics or movement' *Natural Language and Linguistic Theory* 15, 573–639.

Miller, Philip, Geoffrey Pullum and Arnold Zwicky. 1997. 'The Principle of Phonology-Free Syntax: four apparent counterexamples in French' *Journal of Linguistics* 33, 67–90.

Miller, Philip and Anne Zribi-Hertz (eds.). 2003. *Essais sur la grammaire comparée du français et de l'anglais*. Presses Universitaires de Vincennes.

Miller, Philip and Brian Lowrey. 2003. 'La complémentation des verbes de perception en français et en anglais' in Miller and Zribi-Hertz (eds.), 131–88.

Moreau, Marie-Louise. 1987. 'L'ordre des constituents dans la production orale entre familiers' *Travaux de Linguistique* 14/15, 47–65.

Nadasdi, Terry. 1995. 'Subject NP doubling, matching and minority French' *Language Variation and Change* 7, 1–14.

Newmeyer, Frederick. 2002. 'Optimality and functionality: a critique of functionally-based optimality-theoretic syntax' *Natural Language and Linguistic Theory* 20, 43–80.

Obenauer, Hans-Georg. 1983. 'Une quantification non-canonique: la quantification à distance' *Langue française* 58, 66–88.

1984. 'On the identification of empty categories' *Linguistic Review* 4, 143–202.

Ouhalla, Jamal. 1991. *Functional categories and parametric variation*. London: Routledge.

Paesani, Kate. 2001. *The semantics and syntax of the* passé surcomposé *in Modern French*. Doctoral dissertation. Indiana University.

Pérez-Leroux, Ana Teresa and Yves Roberge (eds.). 2003. *Romance linguistics: theory and acquisition*. Amsterdam: Benjamins.

Pesetsky, David. 1982. *Paths and categories*. Doctoral dissertation. MIT.

Pinker, Steven. 1995. 'Why the child holded the baby rabbits: a case study in language acquisition' in Gleitman and Liberman (eds.), 107–33.

Plunkett, Bernadette. 2000. 'What's "what" in French questions?' *Journal of Linguistics* 36, 511–30.

Polletto, Cecilia. 2000. *The higher functional field*. Oxford University Press.

Pollock, Jean-Yves. 1986. 'Sur la syntaxe de *en* et le paramètre du sujet nul' in Ronat and Couquaux (eds.), 211–46.

1989. 'Verb movement, Universal Grammar and the structure of IP' *Linguistic Inquiry* 20, 365–424.

1994. 'Checking theory and bare verbs' in Cinque *et al.* (eds.), 293–310.

1997. *Langage et cognition: introduction au programme minimaliste de la grammaire générative*. Paris: Presses Universitaires de France.

1998. 'On the syntax of subnominal clitics: cliticization and ellipsis' *Syntax* 1, 300–30.

Porquier, Rémy. 2001. '"Il m'a sauté dessus", "je lui ai couru après": un cas de postposition en français' *Journal of French Language Studies* 11, 123–34.

Posner, Rebecca. 1997. *Linguistic change in French*. Oxford University Press.

Powers, Joyce and Kenneth de Jong (eds.). 1988. *Proceedings of the fifth eastern states conference on linguistics*. Columbus: Ohio State University.

Prince, Ellen. 1976. 'The semantics and syntax of Neg-raising, with evidence from French' *Language* 52, 404–26.

Pullum, Geoffrey and Arnold Zwicky. 1986. 'Phonological resolution of syntactic feature conflict' *Language* 62, 751–74.

Queffélec, Ambroise. 2000a. 'Le français au Maghreb' in Antoine and Cerquiglini (eds.), 765–96.

2000b. 'Le français en Afrique noire francophone' in Antoine and Cerquiglini (eds.), 797–837.

Quer, Josep, Jan Schroten, Mauro Scorretti, Petra Sleeman and Els Verheugd (eds.). 2003. *Romance languages and linguistic theory 2001*. Amsterdam: Benjamins.

Rialland, A., Jenny Doetjes and G. Rebuschi. n.d. 'What is focussed in *C'est XP qui/que* cleft sentences in French'. MS.

Ricalens-Pourchot, Nicole. 2005. *Les facéties du français*. Paris: Armand Colin.

Rickard, Peter. 1989. *A history of the French language*, 2nd edn. London: Routledge.

Rizzi, Luigi. 1990. *Relativized minimality*. Cambridge, Mass.: MIT Press.

1997. 'The fine structure of the left periphery' in Haegeman (ed.), 281–337. Reprinted 1998 in Benincà and Salvi (eds.), 112–58.

2001. 'Relativized minimality effects' in Baltin and Collins (eds.), 89–110.

2004a. 'Locality and left periphery' in Belletti (ed.), 223–51.

(ed.). 2004b. *The structure of CP and IP: the cartography of syntactic structures*, vol. 2. Oxford University Press.

Rizzi, Luigi and Ian Roberts. 1989. 'Complex inversion in French' *Probus* 1, 1–30.

Roberge, Yves. 1990. *The syntactic recoverability of null arguments*. Montreal: McGill–Queen's University Press.

Roberts, Ian. 1993. *Verbs and diachronic syntax: a comparative history of English and French*. Dordrecht: Kluwer.

2001. 'Head movement' in Baltin and Collins (eds.), 113–47.

Ronat, Mitsou and Daniel Couquaux (eds.). 1986. *La grammaire modulaire*. Paris: Minuit.

Rooryck, Johan. 1992. 'Romance enclitic ordering and Universal Grammar' *The Linguistic Review* 9, 219–50. (Slightly revised version published as Rooryck 2000c).

2000a. *Configurations of sentential complementation: perspectives from Romance languages*. London: Routledge.

2000b. 'A unified analysis of French interrogative and complementizer *qui/que*' in Rooryck (2000a), 223–46.

2000c. 'Enclitic ordering in imperatives and infinitives' in Rooryck (2000a), 115–43.

Rossi, Mario. 1999. *L'intonation: le système du français: description et modélisation*. Paris: Champion.

Rossillon, Philippe (ed.). 1995. *Atlas de la langue française*. Paris: Bordas.

Rottet, Kevin. 2004. 'Inanimate interrogatives and settlement patterns in Francophone Louisiana', *Journal of French Language Studies* 14, 169–88.

Rouquier, Magali. 2003. 'La séquence *est-ce* dans les interrogatives en *qui/que* en ancien et en moyen français' *Journal of French Language Studies* 13, 339–62.

Rowlett, Paul. 1993. 'On the syntactic derivation of negative sentence adverbials' *Journal of French Language Studies* 3, 39–69.

1997. 'Jespersen, negative concord and A′-binding' in Forget *et al.* (eds.), 323–40.

1998a. *Sentential negation in French*. Oxford University Press.

1998b. 'A non-overt negative operator in French' *Probus* 10, 185–206.

(ed.). 2000. *Papers from the Salford negation conference*. Special number of *Transactions of the Philological Society* 98.

2002. 'French *ne* in non-verbal contexts' in D'Hulst *et al.* (eds.), 335–53.

2006a. 'France' in Brown (ed.).

2006b. 'Franglais' in Brown (ed.).

(ed.). Forthcoming. *The specifier–head relationship*. Special number of *Transactions of the Philological Society* 105.

Sadler, Louise and Doug Arnold. 1994. 'Prenominal adjectives and the phrasal/lexical distinction' *Journal of Linguistics* 30, 187–226.

Saint-Dizier, Patrick (ed.). 2004. *Linguistic dimensions of prepositions*. Dordrecht: Kluwer.

Sankoff, Gillian. 1982. 'Usage linguistique et grammaticalisation: les clitiques sujets en français' in Dittmar and Schlieben-Lange (eds.), 81–5.

Sankoff, Gillian and Diane Vincent. 1977. 'L'emploi productif du *ne* dans le français parlé à Montréal' *Le français moderne* 45, 243–56.

Schapansky, Nathalie. 2002. 'The syntax of negation in French: contrariety versus contradiction' *Lingua* 112: 793–826.

Schøsler, Lene (ed.). 2000. *Le passif*. Copenhagen: Museum Tusculanum Press.

Scott, Gary-John. 2002. 'Stacked adjectival modification and the structure of nominal phrases' in Cinque (ed.), 91–120.

Shlonsky, Ur. 2004. 'Enclisis and proclisis' in Rizzi (ed.), 329–53.

Sleeman, Petra. 2003. 'Subnominal empty categories as subordinate topics' in Coene and D'Hulst (eds.), vol. 1, 119–37.

Smith, John-Charles and Martin Maiden (eds.). 1995. *Linguistic theory and the Romance languages*. Amsterdam: Benjamins.

Sorace, Antonella. 2000. 'Gradients in auxiliary selection with intransitive verbs' *Language* 76, 859–90.

2004. 'Gradience at the lexicon–syntax interface: evidence from auxiliary selection' in Alexiadou *et al.* (eds.), 243–68.

Speas, Margaret. 1991a. 'Functional heads and the mirror principle' *Lingua* 84, 181–214.

1991b. 'Functional heads and inflectional morphemes' *Linguistic Review* 8, 389–417.

Sportiche, Dominique. 1988. 'A theory of floating quantifiers and its corollaries for constituent structure' *Linguistic Inquiry* 19, 425–49.

1999. 'Subject clitics in French and Romance: complex inversion and clitic doubling' in Johnson and Roberts (eds.), 189–221.

Sproat, Richard and Chilin Shih. 1988. 'Prenominal adjectival ordering in English and Mandarin' *NELS* 18, 465–89.

1991. 'The cross-linguistic distribution of adjective ordering restrictions' in Georgopoulous and Ishihara (eds), 565–93.

Starke, Michal. 2004. 'On the inexistence of specifiers and the nature of heads' in Belletti (ed.), 252–68.

Tallerman, Maggie. 2005. *Understanding syntax*, 2nd edn. London: Arnold.

Taraldsen, Knut Tarald. 2001. 'Subject extraction, the distribution of expletives and stylistic inversion' in Hulk and Pollock (eds.), 163–82.

Tellier, Christine. 1997. *Eléments de syntaxe du français: méthodes d'analyse en grammaire générative*. Les Presses de l'Université de Montréal.

Togeby, Knud. 1982. *Grammaire française*, vol. 1: *le nom*. Copenhagen: Akademisk Forlag.

Tomlin, Russell (ed.). 1987. *Coherence and grounding in discourse: typological studies in language*. Amsterdam: Benjamins.

Valois, Daniel. 1991. *The internal syntax of DP*. Doctoral dissertation. UCLA.

Van Peteghem, Marleen. 2006. 'Le datif en français: un cas structurel' *Journal of French Language Studies* 16, 93–110.

Vance, Barbara. 1997. *Syntactic change in Medieval French: verb second and null subjects*. Dordrecht: Kluwer.

Vecchiato, Sara. 2000. 'The *ti/tu* interrogative morpheme in Quebec French' *Generative Grammar in Geneva* 1, 141–64.

Veland, Reidar. 1998. 'Une construction dite ne pas exister en français moderne: le passif suivi d'un infinitif nu' *Journal of French Language Studies* 8, 97–113.

Vendler, Zeno. 1967. *Linguistics in philosophy*. Ithaca: Cornell University Press.

Vergnaud, Jean-Roger and Maria Luisa Zubizarreta. 1992. 'The definite determiner and the inalienable constructions in French and English' *Linguistic Inquiry* 23, 595–652.

Vincent, Nigel. 1997. 'The emergence of the D system in Romance' in van Kemenade and Vincent (eds.), 149–69.

Walter, Henriette. 1998. *Le français d'ici, le là, de là-bas*. Paris: Lattès.

Watanabe, Akira. 1992a. 'Wh in situ, subjacency and chain formation' *MIT Occasional Papers in Linguistics* 2.

1992b. 'Subjacency and s-structure movement of wh in situ' *Journal of East Asian Linguistics* 1, 255–91.

2001. 'Wh in situ languages' in Baltin and Collins (eds.), 203–25.

Webelhuth, Gert (ed.). 1995. *Government and binding theory and the minimalist program*. Oxford: Blackwell.

Williams, Edwin. 1994. 'A reinterpretation of evidence for verb movement in French' in Lightfoot and Hornstein (eds.), 189–205.

Wilmet, Marc. 1980. 'Antéposition et postposition de l'épithète qualificative en français contemporain: matériaux' *Travaux de Linguistique* 7, 179–201.

Wolf, Lothar. 2000. 'Le français en Alsace' in Antoine and Cerquiglini (eds.), 687–700.

Yaguello, Marina. 1994. '*Pas touche!* Sur un paradigme impossible: essai de régularisation de quelques constructions "aberrantes" par la phono-syntaxe' *Journal of French Language Studies* 4, 99–101.

(ed.). 2003a. *Le grand livre de la langue française*. Paris: Seuil.

2003b. 'La grammaire' in Yaguello (ed.), 153–258.

Zanuttini, Raffaella. 2001. 'Sentential negation' in Baltin and Collins (eds.), 511–35.

Zribi-Hertz, Anne. 1984. 'Prépositions orphélines et pronoms nuls' *Recherches Linguistiques* 12, 46–91.

1987. 'La réflexivité ergative en français moderne' *Le Français Moderne* 55, 23–54.

1994. 'The syntax of nominative clitics in standard and advanced French' in Cinque *et al.* (eds.), 453–72.

Zubizarreta, Maria Luisa. 1998. *Prosody, focus and word order*. Cambridge, Mass.: MIT Press.

2001. 'The constraint on preverbal subjects in Romance interrogatives: a minimality effect' in Hulk and Pollock (eds.), 183–204.

Zwicky, Arnold M. and Geoffrey K. Pullum. 1983. 'Cliticization vs. inflection: English *n't*' *Language* 59: 502–13.

Index